Divine Words,

Divine Words, Female Voices

Muslima Explorations
in Comparative Feminist Theology

JERUSHA TANNER LAMPTEY

OXFORD
UNIVERSITY PRESS

OXFORD
UNIVERSITY PRESS

Oxford University Press is a department of the University of Oxford. It furthers
the University's objective of excellence in research, scholarship, and education
by publishing worldwide. Oxford is a registered trade mark of Oxford University
Press in the UK and certain other countries.

Published in the United States of America by Oxford University Press
198 Madison Avenue, New York, NY 10016, United States of America.

© Oxford University Press 2018

First issued as an Oxford University Press paperback, 2022

Library of Congress Cataloging-in-Publication Data
Names: Lamptey, Jerusha Tanner, author.
Title: Divine words, female voices : muslima explorations in comparative feminist theology /
Jerusha Tanner Lamptey.
Description: New York, NY : Oxford University Press, [2018] |
Includes bibliographical references and index.
Identifiers: LCCN 2018016581 (print) | LCCN 2018017905 (ebook) |
ISBN 9780190653385 (updf) | ISBN 9780190653392 (epub) |
ISBN 9780190653408 (online content) | ISBN 9780190653378 (cloth) |
ISBN 9780197652794 (paperback)
Subjects: LCSH: Feminist theology. | Qur'an—Feminist criticism. | Bible—Feminist criticism. |
Women in the Bible. | Women in the Qur'an. | Women in the Hadith.
Classification: LCC BT83.55 (ebook) | LCC BT83.55 .L357 2018 (print) |
DDC 297.2082—dc23
LC record available at https://lccn.loc.gov/2018016581

1 3 5 7 9 8 6 4 2
Paperback printed by Integrated Books International, United States of America

To those who critically love tradition, craft pragmatic presents, and imagine more just futures

Contents

Acknowledgments

I MUST BEGIN by acknowledging my deep gratitude to the scholars, thinkers, and theologians I engage with in this book, some of whom I am privileged to know beyond their contributions. I remain ever astounded and humbled by the depths of their insights, commitments, and concerns. My contributions, moreover, are possible only because of what has come before: the risks taken, the struggles waged and endured, and the voices raised. I must also recognize the support I have received from two specific scholars, amina wadud and Kecia Ali, who model intellectual rigor; avid and open learning; and generous and effective mentorship.

I am also grateful for the Union Theological Seminary community: students in my classes on comparative feminist theology who were open to constructive theological exploration and experimentation; staff that made my work possible and easier; and faculty colleagues who inspired, listened, and offered invaluable feedback. While writing, I could not help but be aware that so many of the scholars I engage in this book were members of this same community, this community of rigorous scholarship, deep commitment, and pursuit of justice. In particular, I recognize the exceptional collegiality and sustaining friendship of Sarah Azaransky, who routinely assisted me in navigating the complexities of this project and provided productive and informed suggestions.

My appreciation is also extended to Cynthia Read and Drew Anderla at Oxford University Press for seeing the potential of this project and guiding it through the publication process; to the reviewers of the manuscript for their detailed and constructive feedback; and to my friends and family who offered support, encouragement, and necessary distraction. I am especially grateful to and for Jalilah, my daughter: for her patience, her encouragement, and her fascinating contributions (including discussions of Prophet Muhammad being "pregnant" with the Qur'an!). In all, my ultimate gratitude rests with God, *alhamdulillah*.

I

Beyond the Poisoned Wells

INTRODUCTION

A POISONED WELL. This is the analogy that lawyer and Islamic legal scholar Azizah al-Hibri uses to describe tensions that permeate discussions of Muslim women, egalitarianism, and Islamic feminism. Al-Hibri argues that many "Western" critiques of Islam are grounded in notions of cultural superiority and, as a result, propagate negative stereotypes of Islam and Muslim women.[1] These critiques give rise to efforts that ostensibly aim to improve the situation (typically singular and homogeneous) of Muslim women but rarely attend to the voices and concerns of diverse Muslim women. The political nature of these critiques makes it more complicated for Muslim women to reclaim and reassert rights that are granted in Islamic texts, practices, and traditions. The critiques portray the "well" of Islam as devoid of egalitarian possibilities, and therefore dismiss efforts by Muslim women to search for and reclaim these possibilities. Moreover, the fact that these critiques are often "thinly disguised" as feminist results in Muslim women feeling alienated from "Western" feminisms.[2]

Al-Hibri's analogy of the poisoned well captures the importance that the Islamic tradition retains in the lives, spirituality, and quests for justice of many Muslim women. The tradition is understood as a well, a source of life-giving and egalitarian possibilities. Her analogy also underscores the fact that this well has been negatively affected—"poisoned"—by critiques based on claims of inherent superiority and negative stereotypes. The critiques have tainted the well, even if only superficially and rhetorically. Yet the tradition remains a well, and for many Muslim women the primary well. Muslim women are thus left with the difficult task of articulating strategies for "drinking" from a well that has been depicted by others as a source of harm rather than hope.

While al-Hibri does not do so explicitly, the analogy of the poisoned well can be extended to highlight two additional aspects of many discussions of women,

Islam, and feminism. The first is that the well of the Islamic tradition has also been poisoned by the existence of patriarchy and androcentrism—that is, male dominance and male normativity—within the Islamic tradition. This has resulted in texts and practices that enshrine, normalize, and operationalize hierarchical views of humanity. It has also resulted in fervent attacks on interpretations of the Islamic tradition that promote egalitarianism, equality, and women's rights.[3] In other words, "poisons" that emerge from within also contaminate the well of the Islamic tradition from which many Muslim women seek to draw spiritual and ethical sustenance.

The analogy of the poisoned well also exposes the detrimental impact that discourses based on negative stereotypes, claims to inherent superiority, and male dominance have on interreligious feminist engagement. These discourses often stifle—if not prevent—deep conversations and informed solidarity among women across religious traditions. They pit women and various formulations of feminism against each other, and they also convince many women that such conversations are of abundant risk and little benefit. While al-Hibri hints at the manner in which feminism has been invoked in hegemonic critiques and thus is viewed with ambivalence and suspicion, she does not go as far as to describe this as another manifestation of "well poisoning." Something has been poisoned perhaps, but she does not describe feminism or interreligious feminist engagement as an invaluable and necessary resource.

Such a description, though, is in fact appropriate. Interreligious feminist engagement is a well; it is a theologically legitimate and practically advantageous resource for Muslim women concerned with egalitarianism and women's rights. However, like the Islamic tradition, this well has been tainted by negative stereotypes, claims to superiority, and male dominance. This well is also brimming with historical, comparative, and epistemological challenges that arise out of debates over Islam and feminism, common interpretive strategies, and unproductive experiences in interreligious engagement. Nonetheless, interreligious feminist engagement can be a rich source of insights in the ongoing development of Islamic feminist theology if these challenges are identified, confronted, and skillfully navigated.

Power, Stereotyping, Dominance

While there are many Muslim scholars who passionately promote women's equality and rights, there is also widespread ambivalence toward the general norms, terminology, and approaches of feminism and feminist theology. This ambivalence in part arises from the concern that dominant forms of feminism and feminist theology are not expressive of—and are potentially oppressive to—the experiences, challenges, and liberative strategies of Muslim women. In this way, ambivalence is connected to an assertion of identity, autonomy, and voice that highlights diversity among women and among religious traditions. Ambivalence is not, however, simply an assertion of identity, autonomy, and voice. It is also a position adopted in reaction to various discourses that emerge from outside of and within the Islamic tradition. These discourses append specific—and frequently oppositional—definitions to Islam and feminism, and thereby seek to define what counts as a legitimate or authentic expression of Islam. In doing so, they fuel the ambivalence of female Muslim scholars toward feminism in general, and they also obscure invaluable possibilities related to interreligious feminist engagement.

In the United States, discussions of Islam, gender, and Muslim women are part of a larger and extremely charged discourse in which Islam is depicted as other, different, and foreign. This depiction is not one of mere distinction but is also frequently entangled with evaluation and juxtaposition.[4] Thus, Islam as the "other" is different and also less valuable or in fundamental opposition to generally accepted norms and customs. One of the most common ways of illustrating Islam's "otherness" is through references to the plight of Muslim women. This is clear, for example, in the rhetoric of "saving Muslim women" that is routinely deployed to justify colonial, missionary, imperial, and military engagements in Muslim contexts and with Muslim people. As Lila Abu Lughod illustrates, images of and references to Muslim women are provocative capital in debates on topics ranging from military incursions in Afghanistan and Iraq to European immigration policies to legislation on the wearing of religious symbols to surveillance of US Muslim communities to the broader War on Terror.[5] Although it is difficult to argue that the only—or primary—motivation is concern for the humanity of Muslim women, the rhetoric of salvation proves effective in fostering support for policies and interventions.[6]

The rhetoric of salvation is notable for two additional reasons. First, it is based on, in the words of Gayatri Chakravorty Spivak, the idea of "saving brown women from brown men."[7] Muslim women are to be saved *from* the oppression caused by Islam as a tradition and enforced by Muslim men. Therefore, the act of saving Muslim women is imagined as freeing women from inevitable imprisonment by Muslim men. Although neither is portrayed positively, Muslim women and Muslim men are described as fixed and inverse caricatures. Muslim women are oppressed, passive, and in need of rescue; Muslim men are oppressive, violent, and opposed to egalitarianism.[8] The rhetoric of salvation is fueled by negative stereotypes of Islam and Muslims, as well as by ingrained notions of male dominance and authority. The latter is present in the depiction of Muslim men as having ultimate and complete power over

Muslim women, and equally in the depiction of non-Muslims as the saviors of "helpless" Muslim women.

The rhetoric of salvation also co-opts and deploys aspects of feminism and feminist theology.[9] While it raises legitimate feminist concerns, it does so based on universalized and essentialized assumptions about women and their goals that do not emerge from substantial engagement with the diverse perspectives of Muslim women. More insidiously, when the perspectives of Muslim women are solicited—that is, when Muslim women are asked about their specific struggles, needs, concerns, and goals—some perspectives are labeled as brainwashing or false consciousness.[10] These labels delegitimize perspectives that do not conform to the predetermined assumptions of dominant formulations of feminism.

The pairing of the rhetoric of salvation with a one-size-fits-all feminism contributes to the ambivalence or wholesale rejection many Muslim women feel toward feminism and feminist theology. Real issues that some Muslim women face are highlighted, but the rhetoric simultaneously perpetuates negative stereotypes of Islam and undercuts the autonomy and voice of Muslim women. This places Muslim women in a double bind. They may appreciate attention being drawn to their actual concerns but are far from comfortable with the foundational assumptions of this rhetoric, especially the paternalistic assumption that Muslim women do not (and even could not) really know what they want or need.[11]

Aspects of the Islamic tradition and specific discourses that emerge from within Muslim communities also influence Muslim women's perspectives on feminism and interreligious feminist engagement. Specifically, legacies of patriarchy and androcentrism impact sources, interpretations, and interpretative methods as well as ideas about authority and legitimacy. These legacies stretch back to the original context of the revelation to Prophet Muhammad, seventh-century AD in the Arabian Peninsula. Aspects of this context are preserved in central Islamic sources: the Qur'an and the ahadith (written reports about the sayings, actions, and tacit approval of Prophet Muhammad). The Qur'an—when defined as the verbatim and unchanged Word of God—occupies a central place in Muslim consciousness and acts as a primary criterion of authority. The hadith corpus documents the example, or Sunna, of Prophet Muhammad and provides guidance and stipulations for ritual, social, and familial practice. The relevance of these sources extends beyond their original temporal, geographical, and cultural contexts. Therefore, ongoing debates exist over the manner in which details from the time of Prophet Muhammad should be implemented in new contexts. This is the ubiquitous question of continuity and change. And it is a question amplified within the Islamic tradition because of the status of the Qur'an and the emphasis placed on emulation of Prophet Muhammad.

Opinions on the boundaries of emulation and re-enactment of contextual specifics span a spectrum of possibilities. On one end is the attempt to re-enact every aspect of Prophet Muhammad's lifestyle, including dress, food, and marital customs. This approach assigns the highest degree of righteousness to the earliest generations of Muslims, and advocates for widespread re-enactment of their specific practices. On the other end of the spectrum is the attempt to distill general ethical principles from Prophet Muhammad's life, and then apply those principles in new forms to new contexts. This approach is widely associated with Fazlur Rahman's interpretative theory of double-movement, in which he argues for understanding rituals, laws, and social practices in terms of their function and objectives in their original context.[12] In this approach, contextual details become less important than the pursuit of overarching ethical objectives. In diverse contexts, the objectives will *only* be achieved through forms of practice tailored to those contexts.

Frequently, and unsurprisingly, practices related to women and gender have tended toward the re-enactment end of the spectrum. This is especially obvious in exegetical and juridical texts, and in the relative interpretative silence (or deliberate silencing) of women throughout Islamic history.[13] Ayesha Chaudhry provides an illustration of this in her book *Domestic Violence and the Islamic Tradition*, which traces diverse perspectives on Qur'an 4:34.[14] She uncovers a long-standing and little contested trend of juridical permissions for physical (even if only "symbolic") discipline of women by men, particularly wives by their husbands. Such trends in interpretation, including the lack of women's voices and perspectives, are significant because the Islamic tradition tends to privilege precedent as a measure of authority and legitimacy. This is connected to emulation of Prophet Muhammad and is evident in the way classical scholars justify their own interpretations with extensive references to earlier jurists and interpreters.[15] Even the method of Rahman, which destabilizes direct re-enactment, nevertheless still upholds the idea of the core ethical objectives being discernible in reference to the earliest context. Appeals to precedent consequently become important in legitimating egalitarian claims. Such appeals, though, are hindered by patriarchal and androcentric aspects of the original context of revelation, as well as by the dominance of male perspectives and exclusion—or at least marginalization—of women's perspectives throughout the history of Islamic interpretation.[16]

In contemporary discourse, moreover, precedent as a preeminent Islamic standard of authority is often confined to Islamic sources, rulings, and scholars. While the use of *Isra'iliyyat* (narratives originating in Jewish and Christian traditions) was more common before the fourteenth century, legitimate precedent today is rarely found outside of the Islamic tradition.[17] This reveals a privileging of the tradition, which is not uncommon to many religious traditions. Notably, though, this is another manifestation of negative stereotyping, one that automatically elevates Islamic values, sources, and teachings above the non-Islamic, non-Muslim other. Similar to the negative stereotyping *of* Islam, negative stereotyping *by* Islam deals in oppositions, binaries, and fictional constructions of clear-cut boundaries between Islam and all else. It shapes egalitarian interpretations and perspectives on feminism by demanding references to earlier Islamic history and sources, while simultaneously shunning and devaluing insights that may emerge—or be accused of emerging—from non-Islamic sources.[18]

The varied and tangled discourses of power, negative stereotyping, and male dominance directly impact Muslim women, both in their lived realities and in their quests to voice diverse interpretations of the Islamic tradition. These discourses color gender roles, views of sexuality, and women's statuses and rights. They also function to delineate the range of possible, legitimate, or authoritative interpretations through their demands for correspondence to set values and conclusions. Accordingly, these discourses seek to dictate who can speak, what can be said, and even what can be "thought" or heard; they unavoidably impact the way scholars and the public talk about, teach about, and research Islam, gender, and Muslim women. The questions that are raised, the books that are published and read, the speakers that are embraced by mainstream media and by Muslim communities, and the topics that are foregrounded by both Muslims and others—all are conspicuously shaped by political, stereotypical, and patriarchal conceptions of Islam and Muslim women.[19] The tensions and limitations produced by these conceptions are especially palpable in recurring arguments over the validity—and even referent—of Islamic feminism.

Islam and/or Feminism?

What is the relationship between Islam and feminism? Are Islam and feminism compatible or are they contradictory? Is Islamic feminism an oxymoron? Is feminism a "Western" or foreign imposition on Islam? Does the Islamic tradition offer resources for articulating an egalitarian view of humanity? If so, is such a view accurately referred to as Islamic feminism?

These are just some of the many questions that spur debate and controversy within global Muslim communities themselves and within the communities of scholars that study Muslims, Islam, and women. Other scholars, including Valentine Moghadam, Margot Badran, Haideh Moghissi, miriam cooke, Aysha Hidayatullah, and Fatima Seedat, have extensively chronicled these debates.[20] Therefore, I will only briefly touch on three prominent perspectives, with the goal of providing a foundation on which to better understand the interpretative strategies adopted by Muslim women scholars in the United States.

The first perspective refers to Islamic feminism as a misnomer and dismisses the search within the Islamic tradition for resources to support egalitarianism and women's rights. Proponents of this perspective believe that the core ideas of feminism and the basic principles of Islam are diametrically opposed.[21] Moghissi, as an early example of this view, states that feminism's core idea is that biological difference between men and women should not lead to differences or privileges in legal status. However, according to her, the basic principles of Islam as outlined in the Qur'an do not support equal rights in the family or in society. While she does acknowledge the possibility of multiple interpretations of the Qur'an, she ultimately asserts that "no amount of twisting and bending" can reconcile Qur'anic notions of women's rights and obligations with feminist understandings of gender equality.[22] Being a believing Muslim means, in her view, that one accepts the Qur'an, its nonegalitarian principles, and the resultant enshrinement of sexual hierarchy in law. Consequently, she argues that no believer could simultaneously affirm feminist and Islamic notions of equality. Moghissi attempts to bolster her position by arguing that "Islamic feminism" is actually an outside imposition on Islam from "feminist academics and researchers of muslim background living and working in the West."[23] Intriguingly, this is a contention echoed by scholars who elevate the Islamic tradition and its perspective on women above feminism.

Another variation of this first perspective recognizes some value in Islamic feminism but ultimately maintains that secular feminism is less risky and more effective. Moghadam argues that, at best, the Islamic feminist strategy of reinterpreting the Qur'an is partial and, at worst, perpetuates male dominance and dismisses secular feminism: "So long as Islamic feminists remain focused on theological arguments rather than socioeconomic and political questions, and so long as their point of reference is the Qur'an rather than universal standards, their impact will be limited at best. At worst, their strategy could reinforce the legitimacy of the Islamic system, help to reproduce it, and undermine secular alternatives."[24] While Moghadam is slightly more sympathetic to efforts to re-interpret the Qur'an, she nevertheless still views any improvements to women's status arrived at through Islamic feminism as restricted in comparison with the improvements possible through secular feminism and secular institutions. In both forms of this first perspective, the language and tropes of supremacy and stereotyping ring loud and clear; Islam, feminism, and secularism are defined in opposition, and ultimate value is ascribed to secularism and secular feminism.

The second perspective on Islam and feminism is in many ways the opposite of the first. Premised on depictions of feminism as a foreign, un-Islamic, and therefore illegitimate transplantation into the Islamic tradition, this perspective emphasizes the superiority, perfection, and comprehensive nature of Islam. Proponents of this view—referred to by Badran as "Islamist"—claim that the

Islamic tradition does not need augmentation from other sources as it already contains every necessary component for egalitarianism and women's rights.[25] Thus in response to the question "Does Islam need feminism or feminist theology?," the UK-based scholar Zara Faris, for example, offers a resounding "no" and contends that Islam is liberative and has already addressed all gender issues.[26] If there are gender-related concerns in society, the solution is not feminism or any other foreign transplantation, but better and more extensive implementation of Islam in social practice and institutions.[27] This perspective is not just a form of Islamic aggrandizement. It also displays an anxiety about boundaries, identity, and corruption. The rejection of feminism herein is an attempt to set up walls to protect against the perceived corrosive and polluting effects of external and non-Islamic worldviews.

This stance is a common reaction to domination, colonialism, and imperialism, but it is also an intriguing negotiation of power, negative stereotyping, and male dominance.[28] Muslim women scholars who adopt this perspective make gender egalitarian claims, while still playing by the rules of (male) Islamic classical discourse. They do so not through calls for change or augmentation to the tradition but through calls for reform and purification, which rest on the claim that *true* Islam is inherently egalitarian.[29] This is a concrete example of how the debate over Islam and feminism is shaped by external stereotyping of Islam *and* by internal stereotyping aimed at the non-Muslim other. Ironically, this position works to reinscribe the assumptions and limits of negative stereotyping and male dominance. It does create a small opportunity for making egalitarian claims by leveraging notions of Islamic superiority and perfection. At the same time, though, it requires acceptance of the oppositional and hierarchical depiction of Islam and non-Islam; reiteration of the myth of a comprehensive and monolithic Islam; and avoidance of critical engagement with other perspectives, worldviews, and traditions.

The third perspective on Islam and feminism affirms the validity of searching within the Islamic tradition for egalitarian resources, while simultaneously encompassing various opinions on the label "Islamic feminism" itself.[30] Proponents of this perspective do agree that Islamic sources, especially the Qur'an, contain liberative messages, but they voice diverse and strategic opinions on the use of the term "feminism" to describe their work.

Distinguishing between secular and Islamic feminisms, Badran defines the former as a feminism that is constituted by multiple discourses, including secular nationalist, modernist, human rights, and democratic discourses.[31] She defines Islamic feminism as "a feminist discourse and practice articulated within an Islamic paradigm . . . which derives its understanding and mandate from the Qur'an, seeks rights and justice for women, and for men, in the totality of their existence."[32] Even though Badran distinguishes between these two forms of feminism, she does not view them as being wholly separate; secular and Islamic feminism are interwoven. She argues that Islamic feminism eradicates divisions between religious and secular by drawing on Islamic thought, Islamic classical methodologies, and methodologies and insights from other sources.[33] For Badran, Islamic feminism exists, is transformative, and is open to engaging other discourses and crossing boundaries.

While Badran asserts that Islamic feminism obscures divisions between secular and religious discourses, she acknowledges that the historical usage of these terms has fostered a problematic and restricted depiction of both. Historically, "the term secular came to be associated with modernity, and often with the West, while 'religious' came to be thought of by proponents of secularism as 'traditional' and 'backward,' ultimately to the detriment of both."[34] Moreover, amid fierce identity politics arising in response to colonialism and other political realities, secular was further defined as un-Islamic, anti-Islamic, and non-Islamic, and then used as a tool of delegitimization by some Islamic groups.

Riffat Hassan unpacks the implications of the association of secular with Western and un-Islamic. In examining the relationship between Muslim societies and modernity, she distinguishes between two aspects of modernity: modernization and Westernization. Though many Muslim societies were positively inclined toward modernization—defined as "science, technology and material progress"—she argues they were opposed to Westernization, "which was associated with promiscuity and all kinds of social problems."[35] "Emancipated" women—those women that blurred the traditional gender boundaries between public and private space—were not seen as products of modernization but as icons of Westernization. Thus, every discourse—including feminism—that encouraged emancipation and egalitarianism was likewise associated with secularism and Westernization, the purported opposites of Islam and religion. Discourses aimed at egalitarianism and women's rights were thereby cast as secular, Western transplantations into Islam, and challenged on that basis.

The attempts—emanating from within the Islamic tradition as well as from without—to depict Islam as the opposite of secularism and Westernization contribute to the ambivalence surrounding the label "Islamic feminism." Therefore, while Badran promotes the label and refers to the work of other scholars and activists in this manner, she recognizes that the label is not accepted by all of those to whom she refers, including pioneers in the field and authors of influential texts.[36] She opines that discomfort with the label is primarily related to the "inability to move beyond the notion that feminism is Western and a colonial imposition,"[37] a notion she rejects by underscoring the multiplicity of feminisms and the fact that feminisms can and do originate in Muslim contexts.

However, discomfort with the label is more complex than Badran describes. Ambivalence with the label "Islamic feminism" is not just the outcome of the characterization of feminism as Western or imposed. Ambivalence also results from Muslim women scholars' attempts to simultaneously negotiate multiple objectives, including affirming women's rights and equality; rejecting stereotypical depictions of Islam as inferior, backward, and devoid of egalitarian possibilities; and challenging nonegalitarian interpretations of the Islamic tradition while retaining connection to and asserting authority within that same tradition.

Asma Barlas' perspective on the label Islamic feminism provides a vivid example of the complexity associated with strategically and simultaneously navigating these multiple objectives. Barlas states that she initially and intentionally referred to herself as a "believing woman," and was therefore angered by the application of the label Islamic feminism to her work. Moving beyond anger, she attempted to explain the rationale behind her intentional distinction, highlighting the fact that most feminists believe that "Islam is, by definition, patriarchal, misogynistic, violent and fundamentalist."[38] This assessment was in direct contradiction to her own view of the Qur'an as egalitarian and antipatriarchal; her approach to and understanding of the Qur'an vastly diverged from the understanding held by most feminists. When she encountered the person and work of Badran—who "rather than locating the Qur'an within feminist discourses . . . re-located feminism in the Qur'an"[39]—Barlas gained a new appreciation for the label Islamic feminism as a discourse on gender equality that derived its mandate from the Qur'an and sought human rights and justice in public and private spheres. Ultimately, though, Barlas has again moved away from the label and reasserted that her views are not feminist but rather Qur'anic or Islamic. She also questions the value of feminism if it erases fundamental differences, is based on imperialistic and reductive inclusivism, and silences her personal experience and voice.[40]

Barlas' reflections on Islamic feminism reveal a multifaceted negotiation of power, identity, and authority. She recognizes the power of naming, but she aims to assert her own agency in that process to resist all forms of feminism that automatically associate Islam with oppression and the "West" with liberation.[41] She also asserts her own agency to make a direct—and challenging—claim to authority within the Islamic tradition by referring to her own approach as simply Qur'anic or Islamic. Finally, and in line with other recent reflections on Islamic feminism, she questions the power dynamics and objectives of feminisms that overlook or downplay differences. Seedat echoes a similar view, when she acknowledges the possibility of Islamic feminism but argues against the necessary convergence of Islam and feminism.[42] Her argument arises in resistance to presentations of Islamic feminism as monolithic; to false projections of equivalency among all feminisms; and to Muslim complicity in a project of sameness in which differences are domesticated and thus become invisible, or transparent. Seedat also explicitly situates her resistance to a necessary convergence of Islam and feminism as a form of "anticolonial politics and a refusal to be circumscribed within hegemonic Western constructs."[43] As an alternative, she advocates for perspectives that would ensure the value of real differences and create a space for these differences to be engaged and retained.

Often characterized by polemics, polarization, and dogmatic assertions on all sides, debates over Islamic feminism nevertheless reveal intense struggles for authority, agency, and self-identification. These struggles play out in a crucible of tensions produced by discourses of power, negative stereotyping, and male dominance, all of which aim to corral conclusions on Muslim women and gender into their distinct, yet equally rigid repertoires.

Navigating Tensions: Strategies and Critiques

How do Muslim women scholars in the United States, including Riffat Hassan, amina wadud, and Asma Barlas, navigate this complex tangle of discourses and tensions, assert authority, and promote egalitarianism?[44] What interpretative strategies do they adopt, and what are some of the primary critiques of those strategies?

One widely employed strategy is to focus primarily—sometimes exclusively— on the Qur'an. Referring to the Qur'an as the "inimitable, inviolate, inerrant, and incontrovertible" Word of God, Barlas, wadud, and Hassan all assert that its content is unified, intentional, and purposeful.[45] The Qur'an is not simply a compilation of various verses revealed throughout the course of twenty-three years to Prophet Muhammad; it is a unified whole that expresses a divinely intended worldview and coherent moral ethos.[46] By privileging the Qur'an in this way, these scholars tap into the preeminent status the Qur'an holds within the tradition. They assert power by aligning with a preexisting intra-Islamic notion of Qur'anic authority. Although they tap into this authority, they offer distinctive interpretations, arguing that the Qur'an is fundamentally egalitarian; that it depicts an undifferentiated human creation; that divine sovereignty rules out intrahuman domination; and that the Qur'an is silent on original sin, a "Fall," women's secondary status in creation, or women's extraordinary culpability.[47]

When US Muslim women scholars, such as Hassan, do directly engage ahadith, they adopt a basic hermeneutic of suspicion or "skepticism."[48] They accept content from these sources when it corresponds to their interpretation of the Qur'an and dismiss it when it diverges. This approach again affirms the centrality and authority of the Qur'an, while attempting to grapple with the existence of clearly patriarchal and androcentric traditions within the hadith corpus.[49] Ahadith are thus deemed to be of varying degrees of authority. Some are authentic; others are not. Assessment of the authenticity of ahadith is not new within the Islamic tradition; the field of ahadith sciences (*usul al-hadith*) is devoted to screening and evaluating the hadith corpus. Yet, Muslim women scholars dismiss some ahadith that have been labeled "sound" (*sahih*), authentic, by this classical process. Assessment appears to follow new or more specific criteria. Muslim women scholars, though, have not yet articulated a robust methodology for ahadith assessment.[50]

In advocating that the Qur'an and authentic prophetic teachings (as recorded in the ahadith) are inherently egalitarian, Muslim women scholars are left to explain apparent discrepancies; they are left to explain how seemingly misogynistic, patriarchal, and androcentric interpretations and sources entered the tradition. With the Qur'an, elements of the text that appear to address men only or to correspond to patriarchal norms of male dominance and power are, drawing on Rahman, commonly explained through the distinctions of universal and particular, or prescriptive and descriptive aspects of the scripture.[51] The former asserts that some parts of the Qur'an are for all times and places (universal), and others are specific to the time of Prophet Muhammad (particular). The latter argues that the egalitarian guidance of the Qur'an is present as a prompt to action (prescriptive), while patriarchal aspects are simply accounts of what was present in the original context that are not intended to be emulated (descriptive). Notably, it is the authority and integrity accorded to the Qur'an as the inerrant, unified Word of God that prevents Hassan, wadud, and Barlas from explaining discrepancies through claims of authorship by men in a patriarchal context, or claims of textual or editorial changes. Limitations and discrepancies are attributed to context, language, and interpretations, and "never to the Qur'an itself."[52]

The hadith corpus, in contrast, is not described as the Word of God but as *human* recollections of the actions, sayings, and tacit approval of Prophet Muhammad.[53] One strategy is to co-opt classical ahadith assessment methods and reauthenticate the content and chain of narrators. Hassan does this with several ahadith that negatively portray women, and thereby argues that these ahadith are weak (*da'if*) or fabricated.[54] Another common strategy is to account for discrepancies through notions of corruption and foreign transplantation, including from other religious traditions. Hassan adopts this strategy when she tackles widely held theological assumptions about the created superiority of men.[55] She asserts, for instance, that the Qur'anic creation account of undifferentiated humanity must take precedence over ahadith that align with the Genesis 2 account of Eve's creation from the rib of Adam. Patriarchal ahadith are attributed to other traditions and texts. Aysha Hidayatullah describes Hassan's approach as a Qur'anic "rib-ectomy" in which the Islamic tradition is purified and depicted as superior in relation to corrupting outside forces.[56] This approach is particularly provocative because the authenticity of nonegalitarian hadith reports is undercut by tapping into negative stereotypes of external texts and traditions, and relying on constructs of authority that treat "non-Islamic" as a synonym for "illegitimate." As noted in reference to the second perspective on Islamic feminism, this strategy can help Muslim women scholars to appeal to the dominant discourses within Islam. Yet, the attribution of negative accretions to other religious traditions is a form of horizontal violence that has adverse—perhaps unconsciously adverse— effects on interreligious engagement and comparative theological exploration.

Finally, in relation to Islamic jurisprudence, Muslim women scholars adopt various strategies, while all acknowledging that the existing tradition does contain some laws that appear to privilege men and restrict women. One common approach, found for example in the writings of al-Hibri, is to argue that true and Qur'anically derived Islamic laws are inherently egalitarian and provide numerous rights to women (such as the rights to own property, seek divorce, and maintain personal wealth) that other systems deny or have only recently asserted.[57] In this approach, the presence of nonegalitarian laws is explained through corruption of core Islamic teachings. This implies that the Islamic system is a perfect system, that it is sufficient for ensuring egalitarianism and justice. Therefore, the necessary action is not one of contradicting original laws but of removing cultural accretions and "distorted" understandings of the Qur'an that arise from those accretions, and then upholding Islamic laws and rights.[58]

These strategies profoundly impact discussions of Muslim women and the lives of actual Muslim women. Nevertheless, other Muslim women scholars raise substantial critiques. These critiques revolve around several themes, including the sufficiency and limits of Qur'an-focused reinterpretation; the need to engage more deeply with other Islamic sources; the need to reevaluate underlying assumptions; and the need for new and constructive approaches.

With the first, scholars raise provocative questions about the extent to which the Qur'an can actually be interpreted in an egalitarian fashion. Hidayatullah, as perhaps the most explicit example, questions the success of the overall project of demonstrating that the Qur'an supports gender equality.[59] In surveying and critiquing the contributions of Hassan, wadud, and Barlas, she asserts that the Qur'an may not in fact be reconcilable to our contemporary notions of equality and justice. This is a challenging and challenged assertion. Hidayatullah does not propose this to delegitimize contemporary notions of equality and justice or to reify patriarchy. She does, however, argue that Islamic feminist positions will have to be based on more than the Qur'anic text itself, and that scholars should admit that their perspectives are "guided by conceptions of justice not definitively traceable to the Qur'anic text."[60] Taking a different stance on the same concern, wadud, in more recent writings and lectures, grapples with the fact that there are aspects of the Qur'anic text (for example, Qur'an 4:34) that cannot be understood as egalitarian nor embraced in any action.[61] She charts the development of various approaches to this verse in classical scholarship and in her own thinking, and arrives at the point of saying "no" to the literal meaning and application of this text. Expanding on Khaled Abou Fadl, she calls for a conscientious pause, which reflects her unwillingness to disengage from the tradition, as well as recognition that the revelation of God cannot be confined or limited to the Qur'an. wadud consequently does not focus solely on exegesis of the Qur'an but also on ethical and theological paradigms that shape—and potentially reshape—views on women, gender, and equality.[62]

Critiques of Qur'an-focused interpretation also emphasize the need for in-depth and critical analysis of other sources within the tradition, particularly ahadith and law. Chaudhry, for instance, draws attention to the fact that Muslim feminist scholars have not systematically "tackled" the Sunna (example of Prophet Muhammad) and ahadith.[63] While she acknowledges many legitimate and methodological reasons for a primary focus on the Qur'an, she also identifies specific challenges the Sunna presents to feminist scholars. These challenges include the less delimited nature of the texts and the fact that the Sunna necessitates engagement with Prophet Muhammad's context. The latter involves the challenge of reconciling the view of Prophet Muhammad as an "egalitarian man" with extensive descriptions of him as a man of his time, as a "patriarchal man."[64] Chaudhry's approach focuses on Prophet Muhammad's "small acts" of resistance and emphasizes the flexibility of the texts.

Kecia Ali contends that the Qur'an-centered approach avoids the messy business of women's everyday lives, which are largely shaped by prophetic practices and the legal tradition.[65] As a result, Muslim women scholars must directly and comprehensively engage these sources as well. She acknowledges that some scholars, including al-Hibri, do focus on laws and rights but describes these efforts as "feminist apologetics."[66] In response to Western hegemonic critiques, feminist apologetics emphasizes pro-women laws that do indeed exist in the tradition and depicts them as liberating. However, Ali argues that these scholars fail to problematize the underlying patriarchal infrastructure of Islamic law, which assigns differing value and agency to men and women. As a result, they end up inadvertently reinforcing male normativity and male dominance. Ali thus calls for reevaluation of the latent assumptions and methodologies of the entire legal system, not just legal conclusions.

The concern for revealing and reconstructing entire systems is also evident in the work of Sa'diyya Shaikh, who echoes Ali's concern about the assumptions of the Islamic legal system and connects this to wadud's interest in theological paradigms. Stressing the role of theology and theological method in pursuing egalitarianism and reform in law, she argues that traditional Islamic law is constrained by particular theological understandings of human nature and the God–human relationship.[67] Drawing on Sufi conceptions of gender and religious anthropology, she endeavors to demonstrate that alternate theological maps could provide the basis for creating an emerging feminist *fiqh* (law).[68] She is notably careful to state that her goal in exploring the views of Ibn Arabi is not to locate egalitarian precedent alone; the example of Ibn Arabi is valuable in that it endorses a methodological approach designed to reveal, critique, and reformulate the theological "nature of religious personhood underpinning particular rulings."[69] She argues that such work will help to address structural issues in Islamic law and other areas as well.

There is one final theme in existing critiques: calls for new and constructive approaches. Many of the mentioned critiques are coupled with appeals for innovative approaches, methodologies, and alternatives.[70] There is ample discussion of the fact that something new needs to be done. Strikingly, though, detailed articulation and implementation of actual new approaches and methodologies is rare. As Hibba Abugideiri observes, the "deconstructionist approach" remains the dominant method of Islamic feminists.[71] Part of the reason for the prominence of deconstruction is limitations of the academic disciplines in which many Muslim women scholars in the United States are situated. This positioning promotes the deconstructive approach but is not always amenable to scholar-activists or scholar-theologians who move to imagine or advocate constructive possibilities related to Islam, women, and gender.[72] Deconstructive challenges to patriarchy, androcentrism, and hegemony are invaluable, yet constructive rethinking is also required for egalitarian interpretations of the Islamic tradition to become increasingly transformational. In line with more recent contributions from wadud, Chaudhry, and Shaikh, new, constructive approaches must be imagined *and* implemented, not only to contend with power, negative stereotyping, and male dominance but also to articulate new ways of asserting authority both within and outside of the Muslim community.

Interreligious Feminist Engagement: Impasse or Opportunity?

In this book, I argue that interreligious feminist engagement is a vital resource for developing one such new approach. While I discuss comparative feminist theology in the following chapter, it is crucial at this point to acknowledge that interreligious feminist engagement is not new. More pertinently, it has not always been a productive endeavor for a variety of reasons, including the obstacles presented by certain interpretative strategies; failure to grapple with latent, and sometimes explicit, power and privilege; and a general lack of knowledge about religious traditions other than one's own.

While many Muslim women scholars engage in interreligious dialogue, Hidayatullah has written most extensively on the particular challenges and possibilities of interreligious feminist engagement.[73] She draws attention to the manner in which some Muslim women scholars aim to purify the Islamic tradition and articulate egalitarian interpretations by attributing the origins of negative and nonegalitarian interpretations to biblical traditions.[74] As discussed, it is in this context that she writes about the "rib-ectomy" of the Qur'anic text, and the resultant reinforcement of binary and oversimplified notions of a pure and ascendant Islam versus corrupting outside forces. This approach not only fails to address the reasons why nonegalitarian views persist within the Islamic tradition but also repeats the rhetoric of nonegalitarian Muslim interpreters who similarly argue for a pure and singular Islam. Hidayatullah notes that the result of this approach in interfaith feminist engagement is impasse rather than partnership, since feminist theologians in other traditions see this rhetoric as a reinscription or projection of patriarchy.[75]

Claims of corruption and negative accretions are not just claims about negative aspects of Islamic texts; they are also and always claims about the value and nature of other traditions. Even if this is not the primary objective—which I believe it is not—the claim that patriarchal understandings derive from the inclusion of biblical texts is a claim about the nature of biblical texts themselves. In addition to this somewhat implied comparative jab, there are explicit manifestations of horizontal violence found in arguments that depict Islam as intrinsically superior to other traditions, especially in granting rights to women. Again, the primary intent of such arguments may not be to assess the value of other traditions but to foster greater buy-in and commitment to egalitarian formulations within Islam. Nonetheless, these arguments present a challenge to interreligious feminist engagement. They also shape Muslim motivation for participating in interreligious feminist engagement. If other traditions cause corruption by introducing ideas and practices that are not favorable to women, or if Islam already has all the solutions, then what would be the value of exchange and conversation across the boundaries of religious traditions?

Comparative jabs and horizontal violence are not only present in Islamic discourse. They, especially in the forms of negative stereotyping and assumptions of parity among traditions, are also evident in other feminist theological discourses. It is common, for example, to hear calls for Muslim women scholars to interpret and envision the Qur'anic text in a manner similar to feminist scholars of Christian scriptures. Such demands are often heard by Muslim scholars as evolutionary, universalistic, and grounded in false assumptions of parity. Moreover, they are filtered through the framework of historical and ongoing power dynamics and concerns about domination, stereotyping, and imperialism.

Accordingly, Hidayatullah observes that while many assume that interreligious feminist engagement is fundamentally beneficial to all parties, it can in fact be replete with power and structural issues that make it a site of harm and jeopardy for Muslim women.[76] Some of these issues include a framing of rivalry (the Sarah–Hagar paradigm), language and metaphors drawn primarily from white, Christian experience, and a persistent lack of knowledge about the basic features of the Islamic tradition. Hidayatullah is also upfront about the ambiguous relationship Muslim scholarship has with feminism, and the need for Muslim women scholars to remain vigilant against Islamophobia, tokenism, and complicity in settings of interreligious engagement.[77] In light of these concerns, Hidayatullah distinguishes between *inter*faith and *multi*faith discussions.[78] She describes the former as readily and critically confronting power and disparity, and the latter as unengaged and simply adding Muslim women into cross-religious conversations. She advocates for models of interfaith feminist engagement that go beyond mere inclusion and shallow understandings and seek to acknowledge power and structural concerns.

Zayn Kassam similarly identifies persistent myths that detrimentally impact much interreligious feminist dialogue. These myths include the notion that "we" are at war to eradicate terrorism and liberate Muslim women; that capitalism will improve the lives of women globally; and that Islam is misogynistic. Kassam argues that these myths need to be "identified, examined and overcome" for interreligious feminist engagement to be productive and attentive to the real challenges and concerns of diverse women.[79] While she does not outline concrete strategies or approaches for doing so, she states that if these myths can be overcome, then the groundwork could be set for "very rich interreligious dialogue."[80]

Challenges or impasses in interreligious feminist engagement also arise from a general lack of knowledge about religious traditions other than one's own. Hidayatullah and Kassam underscore this in relation to the Islamic tradition; interreligious feminist interlocutors that they have encountered tend to have extremely limited knowledge of even the basics of Islamic thought and practice. But the inverse is also true and evinced in the portrayals of other traditions by some Muslim women scholars. These portrayals, at times, display only a superficial awareness of the texts, beliefs, and practices of other traditions. Moreover, and more significantly, they display little familiarity with or attentiveness to the feminist concerns, struggles, and strategies in those traditions. Egalitarian interpretations of the Islamic tradition and texts are frequently juxtaposed to nonegalitarian interpretations of other traditions, rather than being placed into

dialogue with feminist interpretations. Comparative references to the Genesis
2 account of creation, for example, cite the text but do not engage with the extensive and diverse Christian egalitarian interpretations of this account. Deep
and informed awareness will need to be cultivated on all sides for interreligious
feminist engagement to be attentive to power and privilege, to transcend negative stereotyping, and to be a productive and effective resource for feminist
theologians, Muslims included.

While these obstacles must be addressed, Hidayatullah's reflections on her
own experience provide a glimpse into the possibilities of interreligious feminist
engagement. She—in discussing her experience in conversations on scriptural
interpretation—acknowledges a layer of similarities, her own limited knowledge
of other traditions, and aspects of other perspectives that have some—yet not
complete—resonance with her own perspective. She concludes that comparative feminist conversations, when effective, are potentially capable of "bringing
certain interpretative nuances and problems into sharper focus, raising new
questions for us in our own work, and broadening the scope of our view for how
we might apply feminist textual strategies in our respective specialty traditions."[81]
In other words, comparative engagement, if attentive to the stated obstacles, can
assist Muslim feminist scholars to clarify their own positions, reflect on new
questions, and consider new strategies and approaches.

Beyond the Poisoned Wells: Overview

The challenge thus becomes identifying a model or approach that goes beyond the
ambivalence of the poisoned wells to reveal the rich possibilities of interreligious
feminist engagement. To do this, an alternate model must, first, attend to the stated
obstacles of interpretative strategies, power and privilege, and lack of knowledge.
Second, it must be equipped to grapple directly yet innovatively with the tangle of
tensions that arises from power, negative stereotyping, and male dominance. And
finally, it must be responsive to the critiques of existing Islamic feminist discourse
and related assertions of the need for new, constructive approaches that reimagine
underlying theological and ethical infrastructures; that negotiate the existence
of patriarchal elements without avoidance, superficial treatment, or resorting to
notions of corruption and horizontal violence; and that move beyond overreliance
on common methods and criteria, such as precedent.

In *Divine Words, Female Voices*, I argue that the approach of comparative feminist theology provides a means to skillfully navigate these challenges, and reveal
novel, constructive trajectories in Muslima interpretation of the Islamic tradition. I use this method to identify a meaningful and unique point of entry into
comparative theological analysis of Islamic and Christian feminist theologies.

This is the reorientation of the comparative endeavor to focus on the two "Divine Words," that is, to compare Jesus and the Qur'an, rather than Jesus and Muhammad, or the Bible and the Qur'an. Throughout the book, I use this theologically sound and comparatively substantial analogy to explore intersections, discontinuities, and insights that arise in relation to the topics of divine revelation, textual hermeneutics, feminist exemplars, theological anthropology, and ritual, tradition, and change.

Chapter 2 focuses on Muslima theology and outlines its unique combination of constructive, theological, and comparative lenses. It situates Muslima theology within the larger method of comparative theology, and argues for the suitability of this method due to its requirement of deep knowledge of other traditions, its capacity to foster identification of more precise and meaningful points of comparison, and its relegation of assumptions of parity. It then outlines the unique specifics of this project as a form of comparative feminist theology, including its Islam-to-Christianity orientation and its focus on feminist theological methods and concerns. The chapter concludes by introducing the new starting analogy of the two Divine Words and resultant reorientation of the comparative project and methodological form.

Using the analogy of the two Divine Words, chapter 3 begins by exploring pressing debates in contemporary Islamic feminist and Muslima theological engagement with the Qur'an, debates that arise out of the underlying problematic of the Word in the world. The chapter then engages diverse Christian perspectives on Jesus Christ from Rosemary Radford Ruether, Jacquelyn Grant, Kwok Pui-lan, and Ada María Isasi-Díaz. These theologians explore topics ranging from the language and symbols invoked to describe Jesus to the value assigned to particular human markings of Jesus (inclusive of but not limited to Jesus' maleness) to the affiliations of Jesus with power and marginal groups. The chapter concludes by returning to Muslima theology and constructively proposing an approach to the Qur'an that embraces hybridity, human experience, and a preference for the marginalized.

Chapter 4 focuses on dominant trends in Islamic feminist engagement with ahadith, including the primary issues presented by the hadith corpus, central interpretative approaches, and critical calls for more extensive and systematic engagement. Extending the analogical starting point of the Qur'an and Jesus Christ, it engages Christian feminist biblical exegetical approaches articulated by Elizabeth Schüssler Fiorenza, Musa Dube, and Phyllis Trible. These exegetes raise similar questions about androcentrism and misogyny, authority and communal function of the texts, and interpretative strategies. The chapter concludes by proposing ways in which Muslima theology can extend beyond both classical Islamic methods of hadith assessment (*usul al-hadith*) and a basic hermeneutic of suspicion to reclaim

hadith literature through additional hermeneutic strategies, revisiting the relegation of extra-Islamic or non-Islamic materials, and collective reading.

Chapter 5 examines extant theological views of Prophet Muhammad as an exemplar, noting tensions between humanization and idealization and introducing
Islamic feminist interventions related to exemplariness, prophethood, and emulation. It then engages Christian feminist perspectives on Mary and Mariology
from Elisabeth Schüssler Fiorenza, Elina Vuola, and Marcella Althaus-Reid.
These theologians explore the way gender, ideal representations, and power are
present in Mariology and Marian dogmas and practices. The chapter returns to
Muslima theology and outlines ways to re-envision the "beautiful example" of
Prophet Muhammad in light of discussions of gender, power, and a hierarchical
status quo.

Chapter 6 focuses on theological anthropology and considers the extent and
reality of human freedom, especially in light of structural and systemic constraint.
It begins by exploring existing formulations of egalitarian anthropology that
foreground *tawhid, fitra, khilafah*, and *taqwa*. It then engages Christian womanist and feminist perspectives on theological anthropology, embodiment, constraint, and survival articulated by M. Shawn Copeland, Jeannine Hill Fletcher,
and Delores S. Williams. These perspectives prompt important considerations
about individual autonomy, systemic injustice, and possible responses to such injustice. The chapter concludes by articulating a Muslima theological expansion of
taqwa—transformative *taqwa*—that centers Hajar and stresses systemic transformation through visibilization, conscientization, and, again, prioritization of the
marginalized.

The final chapter contextualizes woman-led prayer within broader discussions
of authority, tradition, and change. It first analyzes Islamic feminist discourse on
woman-led prayer, female leadership, and androcentric ritual norms, emphasizing
theological and social assumptions. It then engages with Christian feminist
approaches from Delores S. Williams, Elizabeth A. Johnson, Rosemary Radford
Ruether, and Traci C. West that grapple with notions of community, male imagery of God, tradition, and ritual. The chapter concludes with Muslima theology and argues for the necessity of embodied egalitarian ritual, a dynamic view
of tradition, and reassertion of the transformative space between ideal and real
community (*umma*).

2

Muslima Theology as Comparative Feminist Theology

IN THIS BOOK, I articulate Muslima reflections on central theological topics. "Muslima theology" is a label I use to describe my work as a Muslim scholar, theologian, and activist. This label arises in conversation with—not rejection of—diverse formulations of feminism. While I consider my work to be feminist, I am also interested in asserting particular characteristics of my location, approach, and concerns. Therefore, I use the term "Muslima" (meaning, in Arabic, a female who submits to God, a female Muslim) to highlight my personal positioning as a female, as a Muslim, and as an individual committed to critical reappraisal and interpretation of the Islamic tradition in pursuit of egalitarianism and justice. I also use the label to highlight my theoretical positioning as a scholar who draws on gender theory and feminist discourses to interrogate the value assigned to various forms of human difference, including—but not limited to—gender and biological sex.

I do not, throughout this book, apply this label to other scholarship but recognize similar strands of work and the possibility that others may employ this label to describe their own contributions.[1] I instead use the language of "Muslim women scholars" and "Islamic feminists" to collectively refer to scholars and theologians who critically analyze androcentrism and patriarchy within the tradition and sources, and who propose egalitarian alternatives. The language of Islamic feminism is increasingly common within the field, albeit with the continued acknowledgment that not all scholars and theologians self-identify in this manner.

In this chapter, I further discuss Muslima theology, particularly its combination of constructive, theological, and comparative lenses. I expand on and situate the comparative lens of Muslima theology within the field of comparative theology and nascent enterprise of comparative feminist theology. I argue that comparative feminist theology provides a potent method for navigating many challenges of interreligious feminist engagement, *and* for responding to calls for novel, constructive trajectories in egalitarian interpretation of the Islamic tradition. I then outline the specific features of this project as a form of comparative feminist theology, and conclude by identifying a unique point of entry into comparative engagement with Islamic and Christian feminist theologies: the two Divine Words.

Muslima Theology: Constructive, Theological, and Comparative

The approach of Muslima theology is simultaneously constructive, theological, and comparative. The first two characteristics—constructive and theological—are already evident in some existing work of Muslim women scholars. Their value is recognized, as is the need for further expansion and integration of these areas. The third characteristic—comparative—is novel. However, as I argue in this chapter, it is not wholly new and is likely invaluable.

To begin, Muslima theology is constructive. It is not solely focused on retrieval or purification of what already exists in the tradition and sources; it aims to go beyond exegetical work and historical *ressourcement*. As a result, it is rooted in—but not limited to—reinterpretation of the central sources and historical figures. This characteristic responds directly to a number of critiques, including those of Ali and Hidayatullah, that call for structural revision of the entire legal system and consideration of the egalitarian limits of the Qur'an. This characteristic also responds to Abugideiri's critique of the dominance of deconstructive analysis. It aims to foster constructive rethinking of the tradition, methods, and approaches.

An example from a recent essay by Celene Ayat Lizzio clarifies the distinction between deconstructive and constructive articulation. Lizzio evaluates laws of ritual purity and preclusion, noting the unique manner in which they bar female participation in central Islamic rites. She also draws attention to the fact that "centuries of patriarchal intellectual productivity attest to the malleable nature of normative prescriptions" in a variety of areas.[2] Notably, in regard to purity norms for women, the customs and precedent of early generations of Muslims are largely and uncritically embraced, irrespective of their androcentric assumptions. Lizzio notes that more investigation of the notion of purity is required, but she states it is not her intention to argue that women should be compelled to perform rituals during menstrual or postpartum periods. Lizzio provides a brief, insightful, and provocative deconstructive critique. Yet, as her conclusion indicates, she does not venture into the constructive realm. This certainly is not a requirement; her contribution is valuable as it stands. But it is an illustration of the precise area of intellectual engagement that Muslima theology seeks to foster. What would be the constructive side of this deconstructive argument? If this is the critique, then what comes next? What, if anything, should change? There is more than one answer to these questions, but someone will have to risk answering them in order for egalitarian change to occur in the lives of real people. "Undoing" is different from "doing." Change requires both.

The articulation of constructive claims does subject Muslima theologians (and others) to scrutiny, to accusations of deviating innovation (*bid'a*), and to delegitimization. Moreover, constructive claims are contextual, and hence may later—or elsewhere—prove to be partial or insufficient. At the same time, constructive claims disclose new, legitimate, justice-oriented possibilities. They assert faithful, critical, and conscientious interpretations that resonate with the tradition, individual experience, and diverse communal contexts. The constructive characteristic of Muslima theology is also a way for Muslim women to assert authority and transcend a stance that is primarily reactive to power, negative stereotypes, and male dominance within and outside of the tradition. Constructive contributions are not primarily occupied with refuting negative characterizations of the tradition, not premised on androcentric methodology, and not restricted to the limited possibilities of precedent alone.

Muslima theology is also theology. My usage here of "theology" does not align holistically with the field of *kalam* (speculative Islamic theology), which focuses on questions related to divine attributes, free will and predeterminism, sin, and authority. I use the term "theology" to indicate the project of articulating integrated interpretations about God and God's relation to creation, including humanity. The goal is to contextualize discussions of women and gender within a broader theological exploration of the nature of the Divine, the types of interactions between the Divine and humanity (including topics such as creation, revelation, prophethood, morality, and ethics), and the nature and purpose of humanity itself (theological anthropology). Theological exploration serves to problematize and destabilize assumptions that have gained traction in the tradition. The Muslima approach uses theological concepts and the integration of these concepts to assess existing practices, laws, and interpretations and to suggest new practices, laws, and interpretations.

Elements of the theological enterprise already exist in the writings of wadud and Barlas, who invoke principles, including *tawhid* (unicity of God), divine sovereignty, and *shirk* (associating partners with God), as the basis for arguing against male dominance and male normativity.[3] Theological claims are also present in Hassan's discussion of the Fall being absent in Qur'anic depictions of creation and human nature,[4] and in Shaikh's argument that traditional Islamic law is premised on and constrained by particular theological understandings of human nature and the God–human relationship.[5] Even more such intentional, extensive, and—to borrow Shaikh's term—"creative" theological reflection is needed to uncover and evaluate the implicit theological assumptions of existing interpretations and methods. In keeping with the constructive characteristic of Muslima theology, these reflections serve as a basis for reformulating practice, law, and ethics.

Theological reflection, for example, can offer new insights on topics such as the marriage of Muslims to non-Muslims. In reference to this topic, reflection raises questions about the implicit theological assumptions that lie behind the legal permission for men alone to engage in "interfaith" marriages. Ali highlights weaknesses in various legal arguments and conceptual hierarchies related to such marriages.[6] Asma Lamrabet argues for reconsideration on the basis of Qur'anic silence, context, and the ethical objectives of the Qur'an.[7] Theological reflection expands the discussion to focus on assumptions of intratradition homogeneity, universalized notions of Muslim men's capacity for respect and tolerance, depictions of women as collectively impressionable, and depictions of God as automatically favoring one religious community over others.[8] The question then becomes whether we (as communities and individuals) accept these assumptions and their collateral implications with respect to theological anthropology and views of God. If the theological assumptions are found to be distortions of humanity, distortions of God, or distortions of the relationships between humanity and God, then legal, ethical, and contextual practices related to interfaith marriage should be reconsidered.

The theological focus also expands the relevance of this approach beyond the topics of women's rights and statuses. Theological assertions involve the Divine, humanity, and the relationship between them. Therefore, they are relevant to other discourses, especially those related to human diversity. These discourses include examinations of gender more broadly, of sexuality, of race, of ethnicity, of ability, and of religious diversity.[9] All of which share a primary concern with the way human diversity is identified, constructed, and evaluated. In sum, the theological focus provides a way to critically and constructively engage the Islamic tradition, simultaneously stirring new possibilities and retaining deep (and thus provocative) connections.

Finally, Muslima theology is comparative. It is carried out in critical conversation with other discourses on religion, women, and gender, particularly those articulated by women in other faith traditions. Explicit engagement with other traditions is a unique feature of my formulation of Muslima theology; it is not something that is assumed or embraced by all Muslim women scholars, activists, or theologians. In my view, however, comparative engagement is practically advantageous and theologically legitimate.

While the deliberate centering of comparative feminist engagement is novel, interreligious feminist engagement is not actually new. It is already occurring. Sometimes implicit, sometimes unnamed, and sometimes premised on unproductive caricatures, discussions of Muslim women, Islam, and feminism are embedded in an inherently comparative setting. This is evident in the frictions arising in discourses of power, negative stereotyping, and male dominance, as well as in the debates over Islamic feminism. It is also apparent in the comparative jabs employed by Muslim women scholars in an effort to cleanse the tradition of nonegalitarian texts, interpretations, and laws. Even reactionary rejections of all things "un-Islamic" are comparative; they find their ground in identification of something "other" and juxtaposition with that supposed "other." This strategy may appear to provide a way out of comparative engagement and a way into isolated, intratradition autonomy, but it actually results in a decontextualized and mythological construction of Islam and Muslims. Moreover, this myth detracts from effective grappling with tensive—and pervasive—comparative discourses.

Since comparative engagement is ongoing, new strategies for explicit, strategic, and conscientious comparative engagement are necessary. The question is not *whether* to engage comparatively but *how* to engage comparatively. It is a question of approach and method, as well as of objectives. The approach of Muslima theology is grounded in an unequivocal acknowledgement of the historical complexities of the relationship between Islam and feminism, especially hesitancy to holistically adopt the general norms of feminism and feminist theology. Muslima theology, though, seeks to go beyond oversimplified binaries. This begins with recognition that hesitancy about feminism and feminist theology is not exclusive to Muslim women scholars. It is expressed by many scholars and theologians, resulting in the articulation of multiple genres of theology, including the womanist theology of Delores Williams, the mujerista theology of Ada María Isasi-Díaz, the Asian women's theology of Chung Hyun Kyung, and the African woman's theology of Mercy Amba Oduyoye.[10] As with these genres of theology, Muslima theology arises in explicit critique of universal and hegemonic feminisms that portray women's experiences, concerns, and goals in a single fashion. It foregrounds the existence of meaningful diversity, a desire for agency, and recognition of the importance of self-definition. Though not wholly congruent, the overlapping areas of concern among these theologies indicate that there is much to be learned on all sides through direct comparative theological engagement.[11] Comparative feminist engagement can be productive, rather than destructive, distracting, or disfranchising. Admittedly, it has not always been a productive endeavor for a variety of reasons. These realities do not negate the validity of the endeavor; they demand better methods of engagement. Better methods will never circumvent all of the risk entailed in comparative feminist engagement, but the potential payoffs outweigh those risks.

There is another question though. This is the question of legitimacy, specifically theological legitimacy. Is comparative feminist engagement a theologically legitimate approach, or is it only of practical necessity and utility? While these are reasons enough, there are also strong theological justifications for this endeavor. And, since this book is an exercise in constructive Muslima theology, I am interested not only in the theological assumptions of conclusions and claims but also in the theological assumptions of methods.

What are the theological justifications for comparative feminist engagement? As I write about in *Never Wholly Other*, the Qur'anic discourse on religious diversity is extensive, nuanced, and at times ambivalent.[12] The Qur'an discusses various religious communities, as well as the general phenomenon of religious diversity itself. Throughout this discourse, other religious communities are sometimes critiqued and sometimes praised and promised rewards from God. As the result of a comprehensive survey of these references, I contend that critiques of religious communities are always partial and based on individual manifestation of God-consciousness (*taqwa*), rather than based on affiliation with a particular religious community. This is a crucial argument, as many other interpreters have prioritized negative critiques of other communities in order to preserve the paramount status of the community of Prophet Muhammad. Unqualified negative portrayal of other communities, though, is challenged by another central Qur'anic teaching. This is the repeated assertion that communal religious diversity is divinely intended; it is not the result of corruption, human innovation, or deviation. Religious diversity, diverse revelations, and the diverse practices (*manasik*) of various religious communities are willed by God (e.g., Q 22:67). This assertion demands recognition of the value of religious communities outside of the Muslim community.

Recognition of value and even of direct, uncorrupted connection to the Divine does not necessarily require engagement. But the Qur'anic discussion of religious diversity does not end here. Diverse religious communities are also described as all racing after the good (*khayrat*), defined in terms of God-consciousness (*taqwa*): "Each community has its own direction to which it turns. Race to do good deeds (*khayrat*) and wherever you are, God will bring you together. God has power to do everything" (Q 2:148). The differences in religious communities are acknowledged, and a shared pursuit is emphasized. Notably, no communities are automatically disqualified from this pursuit of *taqwa*; members of every community are able to and urged to pursue this ultimate goal. Building on the notion of a shared and accessible pursuit, human diversity more broadly is defined as a sign (*aya*) of God: "One of God's signs is that God created you from dust and—lo and behold!—you became human and scattered far and wide.... There are truly signs in this for those who reflect. Another of God's signs is the creation of the heavens and earth, and the diversity of your languages and colors. There are truly signs in this for those who know" (Q 30:20–22). This seemingly subtle reference has profound theological and comparative implications. A sign of God is a particular reference to the ways God reveals God's self in the creation. For example, each verse of the Qur'an is an *aya*, and various facets of the natural world are also signs. These signs—in the Qur'anic revelation, the natural worlds, and in intentional human diversity—are ways that God teaches and guides human beings. How are humans expected to respond to these signs? Recognition of divine intention or value is one part of the response. However, the desired response extends beyond this. Humans are called to reflect on, to consider, and to study these signs in order to gain a fuller appreciation of the Divine and of Divine–human relationships.

The Qur'an further clarifies the appropriate response to diversity, calling on humans to acknowledge difference and struggle to get to know each another in all of our particularities: "People, we created you all from a single man and single woman, and made you into races and tribes so that you should know (recognize) one another. In God's eyes, the most honored of you are the ones most conscious of God (with the most *taqwa*). God is all knowing, all aware" (Q 49:13). This verse is clearly a call for engagement of a particular kind, engagement aimed at knowledge. Coupled with the earlier references to diversity as a sign of God, this verse underscores the pivotal role diversity plays in revealing insights about God and about ourselves. Moreover, while the verse attends to difference and describes learning about and knowing each other as the appropriate response to difference, it again returns to God-consciousness (*taqwa*) in order to highlight the illuminating balance of commonalities and particularities among diverse human communities.

These theological justifications and motivations for comparative engagement exist—and are well known—but they largely have not informed writings by Muslim women scholars and Islamic feminists. In other words, their implications have not been deeply considered when Muslim women scholars articulate their interpretations related to women, gender, and egalitarianism. This would be un-remarkable if not for the presence of comparative allusions and explicit com-parative claims in some interpretations. Avoidance of comparative engagement is overlooking one legitimate theological resource. Comparative jabs and hor-izontal violence go beyond inattention and are disconnected from Qur'anic messages on religious diversity. It is also striking that, in writings that focus on religious diversity and religious pluralism, some Muslim women scholars invoke these very same Qur'anic descriptions and express a positive view of religious diversity.[13] Using the notions of divine unicity (*tawhid*) and God-conscious-ness (*taqwa*), Barlas and Hassan, for example, argue that God's concern is for all people and that religious diversity is an intentional form of human difference that should not be eradicated. Barlas and wadud, moreover, draw attention to the similarities between domination and oppression based on gender and bi-ological sex, and domination and oppression based on religious difference.[14] These scholars are aware of the intentionality of religious diversity. They are also aware of the ways oppression intersects with multiple forms of human difference. Neither of these insights, however, results in (re)consideration of comparative feminist engagement.

A Muslima approach to comparative feminist engagement must do this. It must combine theological validations of religious diversity, Qur'anic calls for engagement, and attentiveness to intersections among oppressions. Moreover, it must follow through on the theological and practical implications of these insights to affirm comparative engagement, commit to deep learning about other traditions, and be ever vigilant to the ways in which power, negative stereotyping, and male dominance continue to impact and limit feminist the-ological solidarity.

Comparative Theology to Comparative Feminist Theology

The specific approach I adopt to do this is comparative theology. As defined by Francis X. Clooney, S.J., comparative theology is simultaneously compara-tive and theological. It describes "acts of faith seeking understanding which are rooted in a particular faith tradition but which venture into learning from one or more other faith traditions . . . for the sake of fresh theological insights that are indebted to the newly encountered tradition/s as well as the home tradition."[15] Comparative theology is the double process of venturing out of one's tradition(s) to learn deeply about and from other traditions, and then returning to one's own tradition(s) with new insights, questions, and perspectives. This journey grows out of commitment to a particular tradition(s)—not lack of commitment—and is impelled by the idea that there is something profound to be learned about, from, and with other traditions.

A. Bagus Laksana aptly describes comparative theology through the meta-phor of pilgrimage.[16] The pilgrim is compelled to venture out on the basis of her connection with her own tradition(s). She travels forth into an unfamiliar, and perhaps disconcerting, territory because she believes there is something valuable to be learned in the process. The pilgrim does not stay in the new territory, in the realm of the other; a pilgrim by definition is one who returns home. However, the pilgrim does not return home unchanged. She returns with new insights, new experiences, and a new depth of understanding of her *own* commitments and *own* tradition(s). Notably, she does not return "converted"; she does not return having become something else but something more.

These descriptions highlight important facets of the motivation for, process of, and objectives of comparative theology. To begin, the motivation is theological. It is an "act of faith" that is concerned with learning about and reflecting on theological perspectives in other traditions and in one's own. Hence, comparative theology is not simply comparison but comparison in conversation with normative, even confessional perspectives.[17] This self-consciously normative characteristic of comparative theology does not mean that normative or confessional claims are forced on the "other" or uncritically embraced. It means that the starting points, hermeneutical methods, and goals of each individual exploration in comparative theology arise out of the particular tradition(s) and contextual interests of the comparative theologian. There is no general form of comparative theology; there are only specific, theologically rooted explorations. Many early pioneers in comparative theology, including Clooney and James Fredericks, distinguish comparative theology from theology of religions. The latter is the theological endeavor to formulate a perspective on the value of other traditions through the teachings, texts, and practices of one's own tradition(s) alone. While they argue that comparative theology does not engage in—nor require—a priori evaluations of other traditions, they nonetheless assert that something within one's own theological beliefs fosters the need to engage with and learn about religious others.[18]

The process of comparative theology initially consists of deep learning about other traditions. Such learning requires openness, humility, and development of competency in another tradition. Learning about and from the other is described as learning about them on their "own terms," that is, as listening to and taking seriously what people in the other tradition say about themselves and their tradition.[19] This type of learning is not superficial, and requires time and thorough study. Comparative theologians thus frequently specialize in one tradition, primarily Hindu and Buddhist traditions. The method of comparative theology and its high demands for knowledge of other traditions necessitate such specialization.[20] The process is one of depth, not of breadth. Competency is also vitally important because it is a way to maintain respect and responsibility. By learning deeply about another tradition, the comparative theologian develops and expresses respect for its integrity, its theological infrastructure, and its internal concerns. Comparative theologians strive for a dual accountability in this regard; they strive to present their own and the other tradition in a way that is recognizable and meaningful to members of the respective communities.[21] This implies that competency in one's own tradition(s) is also a requirement of the process. Collapsing of particularities or presenting all traditions as "pretty much the same" do not add to the process. In fact, they render the process ineffectual and even harmful.[22]

On the basis of competency, the next step in the process is to place the knowledge of the other tradition in conversation with one's own tradition(s) through limited acts of comparison. This frequently involves side-by-side reading of authoritative texts from the two traditions. However, the focus of comparative explorations is beginning to broaden to include oral theologies, aesthetic and emotive representations, and embodied ritual.[23] The process cultivates a refined sensitivity to both similarities and differences between the traditions; it identifies substantial but provocatively incomplete instances of resonance.[24] Crucially, identification of similarities and difference is not a polemical exercise; the other tradition is not a negative foil for or simple proof of the beauty and abundance of one's own tradition(s). In comparative theology, the overlaps and the ruptures—as well as every nuance in between—are significant because they produce a creative tension capable of prompting new theological considerations.[25] As Fredericks explains, the other "comes to us with stories that we have never heard before, with questions we have not asked, ways of responding to life that we have not imagined. New stories, new questions, and new customs, by expanding our horizons, allow us to see ourselves and our own religious tradition in new ways."[26]

This is the central objective of comparative theology: to produce new theological insights, questions, and approaches. And this objective is risky and destabilizing. Particular beliefs are not always confirmed, and there is always the possibility of seeing something in the other that is beautiful and theologically meaningful. This same destabilization, however, is the precise payoff of comparative theology; we understand ourselves in new ways in the "light" of the other.[27] It is important to emphasize that this does not mean the objective is appropriation, direct cooptation, or abandonment of one's own tradition(s).[28] It is an assertion that we see new facets of ourselves, our traditions, our sources, and our practices when they are illuminated by comparative engagement. We ask new questions of our traditions and "discover patterns hidden beneath the grooves of well-worn narratives."[29] We see new possibilities. Of vital importance to comparative feminist theology, we are prompted to imagine new legitimate and rooted options beyond the dominant forms of theology and interpretation within our traditions.[30] The comparative lens assists in penetrating the "unthought" and the "unthinkable," that is, those aspects of and possibilities within our *own* traditions that are obscured or rendered invisible by prevailing formulations of orthodoxy and interpretations of texts and practices.[31] The goals of comparative theology, therefore, are transformation, imaginative theological reconstruction, and even transgression within and in conversation with the tradition(s) of the comparative theologian.[32]

In this book, I extend and modify the general approach of comparative theology in a few specific ways. The first is that this project has an Islam-to-Christianity orientation. Comparative theology has been and remains dominated by Christian, specifically Catholic, theologians. Moreover, as indicated, the primary traditions of engagement are Hinduism and Buddhism. I am altering the comparative process in both tradition of origin *and* tradition of engagement. By choosing Christianity as my tradition of engagement, I am also modifying the standard approach by engaging a tradition that for me—theologically and contextually—is not "maximally other" but the "near" or proximate religious other.[33] Furthermore, in the US context, Christianity is a dominant and sometimes dominating tradition, and thus the risk of engaging with this tradition in a comparative fashion is subject to all of the tangles and tensions outlined in the Introduction. This reorientation demands vigilance in respect to power and dominant discourses. At the same time, though, the reorientation to Christianity within the approach of comparative theology provides a new strategy for engaging that power from a marginal position. The new orientation also impacts this project in that the questions, topics, and concepts arise originally out of the Islamic tradition. There is overlap, but in keeping with the constructive, theological, and explicitly normative thrust of comparative theology, a shift toward Islamic terminology, methods, and preoccupations is evident.

The Islam-to-Christianity orientation also raises questions about the distinction between comparative theology and theology of religions. As briefly noted, early comparative theologians drew a clear-cut distinction between the field of comparative theology and other related disciplines. In particular, Clooney and Fredericks distinguish comparative theology from theologies of religions, arguing that the latter requires grand and self-centered narratives about the value of other traditions. Comparative theology, in contrast, does not require a preexisting (and nonexperiential) judgment on the value of other religious communities before embarking on interreligious engagement. Fredericks clarifies this distinction by stating that comparative theology is not theological thinking *about* other traditions but theological thinking *with* other traditions.[34] He is correct that theology of religions is largely an intratradition effort to outline perspectives and assessments of other traditions. This does not necessarily require a theologian to learn about or even engage other traditions. In relation to grand narratives or comprehensive theories about religious diversity and other traditions, Fredericks convincingly argues that these theories actually impede engagement because they provide a neat "road map" that constrains listening and learning.[35] More recently, other scholars have questioned the clear-cut distinction between theology of religions and comparative theology, arguing that a latent assessment of other traditions is operative even if that theology is subject to enhancement and revision through the process of comparative engagement.[36]

The debate is relevant to this project because the ability and desire to draw a line between the two fields may in fact be a product of the dominance of Catholic theologians in both fields. The prevailing ethos within Catholic thought and Catholic theology since Vatican II has been a solid inclusivism that acknowledges at least some value in other traditions as "rays of truth."[37] Official Catholic institutions adopted and promote this perspective in theology of religions. There are tensions and contestations around the degree of value present in other traditions and believers, and the manner in which this value is understood in relation to other official teachings, such as the uniqueness of Jesus Christ and the role of mission.[38] Nonetheless, the institutional and widespread embrace of this perspective eliminates some of the urgency and anxiety surrounding religious diversity and interreligious engagement. It has prepared the ground for comparative theology to even be an option. Phrased differently, why devote time and energy to learning deeply about and with other traditions if you do not acknowledge any value in those traditions in and of themselves? What would be the motivation? Even more urgently, why engage with and learn about other traditions that are depicted as surpassed, corrupting, or dominating? When there are political and theological discourses that work against comparative engagement, an alternate motivation—a motivation with theological gravitas—is imperative.

This may be a distinctive concern of non-Catholic, perhaps even non-Christian or marginal, articulations of comparative theology, but a theological justification in Islamic discourse is essential. While not the only theologies in play, there are theological justifications for *not* engaging. There are also practical and strategic justifications. These need to be explicitly confronted and challenged by alternate theological justifications. I do, however, agree with Fredericks that even inclusive and pluralistic theologies of religions are not enough to impel or sustain deep comparative engagement. They legitimate it but do not demand it. Even the positive theological perspectives on other traditions that I have sketched in this chapter do not always lead to theological engagement based on competency and the search for new insights. Practical on the ground engagement, yes, but not theological engagement. The problem in contemporary US-based Islamic discourse, though, is not solely with theology of religions in and of itself. There are pluralistic and inclusive Islamic theologies of religions in circulation. These theologies call for engagement. They call for learning. They praise diversity as divinely intended and revelatory. They describe reflection on diversity as a means to draw closer to God. The problem is lack of enactment of these theologies in terms of actual engaging, learning, and reflecting. Comparative theology is one way to enact these theological perspectives.

Another particular feature of this project is that it is a comparative feminist theology. While some works in comparative theology—including Clooney's own *Divine Mother, Blessed Mother*—deal with female figures and the feminine, the field overall does not focus on feminist discourse, texts, and practices.[39] Michelle Voss Roberts argues for the value of such a focus, contending that it would destabilize generalizations, move beyond texts, and offer new sites of comparison by centering the "outsider within" various traditions.[40] Comparative theology, with its emphases on deep learning about and accurate representation of traditions, has the unfortunate side effect of excluding voices and perspectives that are not part of the authoritative canon of traditions. Women feature prominently in this category. They are often excluded in texts, scriptures, interpretations, and as competent scholars of their own traditions. Comparative theology is typically focused on "insider" to "insider" engagements, but comparative feminist theology seeks to contest the "traditional enough" standard and bring "outsiders within" into the conversation.[41] Voss Roberts argues for the importance of this focus in comparative theology, and she also asserts that the method of comparative theology can have a positive impact on feminist theology. Specifically, comparative theology can enhance feminist theology by drawing attention to ongoing colonial legacies and power dynamics among religious traditions, and by emphasizing competency in other traditions and thus avoiding superficial generalizations and assumptions of parity.[42] It is worth noting that these are primary concerns voiced by Muslim women scholars in relation to interreligious feminist engagement.

As a comparative feminist theology, this project is an engagement with various "outsiders within" Christianity, and it is also undertaken by an "outsider within" Islam. It begins from a Muslima perspective, engages diverse and particular Christian feminist perspectives, and then considers the potential insights, questions, and productive challenges that arise from the engagement. This particular structure impacts the sources and topics that are compared. The writings and perspectives of feminist theologians and scholars in both traditions are the exclusive focus. Moreover, the primary concerns and questions of feminist theologians and scholars dictate the contours of the project. While the topics may be familiar, the sources, perspectives, and methods engaged are distinct. This moves comparative feminist theology beyond a focus on authoritative texts alone. Texts remain important, but they are different texts, texts penned by different hands, seen through different eyes, experienced in different bodies, and invoked for different ends.

This structural shift also leads to revised perspectives on communal resonance and grand narratives.[43] Comparative feminist theology revisits the way in which the "fruits" of comparative theological engagement are received by and resonate with the original tradition(s). A substantial connection to one's own community is a vital component of comparative theology in general.[44] This claim, though, is further specified in comparative feminist theology. Since the outsiders within are centered, the expectation of communal resonance and accountability is unavoidably different. Feminist outsiders within already challenge the structures of authority within their respective communities; they do not desire to uphold the structures as they are. While feminist theologians aim to resonate with their tradition and religious communities in pursuit of change, history demonstrates that reception of their ideas will be a combination of resonance and disregard, if not outright resistance. Therefore, the idea of communal reception must be reconfigured. In comparative feminist theology, the primary community is other feminist theologians, and even liberation theologians more broadly. In a word, theologians who are themselves outsiders within, who are internal critics of the dominant formulations of the tradition. The "fruits" of comparative feminist theology should resonate with these communities within the overall community. Additionally—while not total resonance or acceptance—the insights of comparative feminist theological engagements should prompt critical conversation within the overall community; they should have enough connection with the tradition and enough provocative substance that they stir people to embark on difficult, yet imperative conversations.

Comparative feminist theology also nuances the common assertion that comparative theology avoids grand narratives. Avoidance of grand narratives and theories is clearly laudable in terms of fostering real engagement with and learning about other traditions. It is a valid qualification on the approach of comparative theology, but it is a qualification that needs to be qualified again in light of comparative feminist theology. Comparative theology aims to foster new theological insights and to create "bonds of solidarity."[45] Comparative feminist theology, though, aims to use theological insights and solidarity to create change. It does not only seek out and reflect on ideas that might be interesting or theologically enhancing; the ultimate goals are change, equality, and liberation. This, of course, has implications for the broader field's insistence on avoiding grand claims and determinate endpoints. Complete avoidance presents a dilemma since comparative feminist theology retains the feminist theological commitment to positively impacting the lives of people on the ground and fostering what is often called human flourishing.[46] In this process, some claims, including a desire to effect liberative change and ideas about the form of such change, are expressed. These claims are formulated in advance of actually encountering liberation and in advance of the actual engagement. And while these claims are diverse and reformulated (and better formulated) throughout the comparative engagement, there are claims and goals. The primary goals are liberation and justice.

The coupling of reticence related to grand theories and desire for the "fruits" of comparative theology to resonate with one's own tradition and the engaged tradition do prompt important questions about the extent to which the approach of comparative theology can actually serve these goals and be liberative.[47] The field excludes certain topics and voices, and some argue that it is tinged with hegemony and imperialism.[48] Yet, comparative feminist theology—especially comparative feminist theology arising from a marginal contextual position to engage a dominant tradition—has the ability to negotiate these risks and thereby become a powerful tool of liberation. It offers an alternate way to engage with dominant discourses without surrendering agency, without downplaying concerns or differences, and without the oppressive and dismissive expectation of parity in concerns, methods, and theologies. At the same time, comparative feminist theology provides a way to learn with other traditions, and to gain new and indispensable insights related to egalitarianism. Interrogations of power, attentiveness to on the ground realities, and a thrust toward liberation become empowering aspects of comparative feminist theology.

For Muslima theologians, in particular, comparative feminist theology is a means to conscientiously and critically engage other feminist theologies without glossing important differences or universalizing a particular feminist theological perspective. It also provides a counterpoint to discourses that foster ideas of corruption, contamination, and opposition. Comparative feminist theology—while unpredictable and dynamic—ironically provides a more stable and safe structure for interreligious feminist engagement, which has too often been characterized by power, stereotypical or superficial depictions, and limited knowledge. This is not to downplay critiques of the potential hegemony of comparative theology. Yet, for Muslima theologies that arise in the US context, the double reorientation—from Islam-to-Christianity, and to focus on feminist voices and concerns—of comparative theology creates a process that aims to acknowledge and engage difference; validates tensive, deep grappling with one's own tradition(s); and respects the agency of individuals, marginal groups, and traditions.

Comparative feminist theology enables this by requiring deep knowledge and attentiveness to particularities. It is not premised on—nor capable of being undertaken on the basis of—caricatures or shallow understanding. It necessitates learning about the other tradition on its own terms, learning about the central concerns, various responses to those concerns, and authority structures of the tradition. At the same time, it requires that Muslima theologians have a robust sense of these in respect to their own tradition. This is no doubt a heavy load to bear; it demands a high degree of competency, and also requires time, effort, and resources. One could argue that feminist theologians and scholars in both traditions need to prioritize their efforts and resources by focusing primarily on their own tradition, on their own "fights." This is an understandable stance. However, it is important to reemphasize the inherently comparative nature of the context in which US-based Muslima theology arises. We are not able to wholly disengage from the comparative discourse. If we cannot disengage, then we have to decide whether to engage passively, poorly, or productively. Additionally, new resources, ideas, and approaches are crucial to our own, particular struggles. Instead of a distraction or side project, comparative feminist theology is an invaluable and central resource for our struggles. The intersectionality of injustice and oppression, moreover, means that it is difficult—perhaps impossible—to combat injustice in only one area without concern for injustice in other areas. Solidarity and ally-ship are not secondary concerns; they are primary and indispensable.[49]

Related to the demand for deep knowledge is one of the most significant assets of comparative feminist theology for Muslima theological formulations. This is the lack of assumptions of parity among traditions, and the ensuing lack of a prioritization of similarities. Comparative feminist theology is not premised on, motivated by, justified through, or aimed at commonalities alone. While this is true of comparative theology in general, it is even more pronounced in comparative feminist theology in light of the long-standing feminist contestation of universal norms. This approach does not barter in complete difference either. The dynamic intersections of inexact similarities and incomplete distinctions define it. There is a place from which to start the conversation, but that conversation does not depend on agreement or even end in agreement. The lack of assumptions of parity is of principal importance in Muslima theology because it provides a way to avoid comparative jabs, evolutionary calls for particular methods and conclusions, and horizontal violence.

Comparative feminist theology, in this way, leads to the identification of better points of analogy among traditions. The combination of knowledge, attention to both continuities and discontinuities, and lack of assumptions of parity uniquely cultivates an ability to identify better starting points. The comparative theologian is capable of identifying substantial points of comparison—not congruency—that throw open the door to relevant and thought-provoking engagements. These points of analogy lead both to theological insights and to further investment in the general process of comparative engagement itself.

A New Conversation: Word and Word

The unique point of entry into comparative analysis of Islamic and Christian feminist theologies that I use in this book is the reorientation of the comparative endeavor to focus on the two "Divine Words," that is, to compare the Qur'an and Jesus, instead of Muhammad and Jesus (the central figures) or the Qur'an and the Bible (the scriptures). This is not a new comparative analogy; in the US context, Seyyed Hossein Nasr identified it in the 1960s in his book *Ideals and Realities in Islam*.[50] It is also not an analogy that arises first within feminist theological discourse but is voiced mainly by male Muslim and Catholic scholars. Nevertheless, it is an analogy that is relevant to and fruitful for comparative feminist conversations among Muslim and Christian theologians. Its relevance and potential are evident in the motivations given for the new analogy, the theological knowledge on which it is based, and the observed benefits of reorientation around this analogy.

Theologians and scholars who identify and use this analogy as the basis of comparative and dialogical engagement do so primarily because of their frustration with the limitations and even negative consequences of other points of analogy. Nasr, for example, challenges the typical approach to Muslim/Christian dialogue, which is premised on comparison of "the Prophet to Christ, the Qur'an to the New Testament, Gabriel to the Holy Ghost."[51] Though he acknowledges that such comparisons reveal information about each tradition, he argues that the two Words provide a better and more meaningful comparative entrance point between the traditions. Other scholars maintain that the routine analogies are actually based on weak suppositions and category confusions. Joseph Lumbard asserts that dialogue among Muslims and Christians has largely and mutually operated under false assumptions about the other tradition.[52] From the Muslim side, many explorations of the Christian Jesus are premised on notions and beliefs about the Muslim Jesus. These notions are projected onto Christianity, without endeavoring to understand the place of Jesus in Christian theologies. He argues that it would be better for Muslim theologians to encounter Christian theologies and views on Jesus on their "own terms."[53] At the same time, Christian theologians have largely misunderstood the place of Prophet Muhammad within Islam due to a similar projection and equation of Prophet Muhammad with Jesus. In response to both realities, Lumbard stresses understanding the intricacies and internal logic of the other tradition. He acknowledges that doing so can lead to questioning and uncomfortable conversations about entrenched perspectives— especially related to the shared Jesus—but nonetheless still argues in favor of an approach characterized by these features. Without explicitly invoking the actual field, Lumbard underscores some of the primary assets of the process of comparative theology. Annemarie Schimmel similarly argues against the comparison of Muhammad and Jesus—whom she views as phenomenologically disparate—and in favor of the comparison of the Qur'an and Jesus Christ: "The central position of the Koran . . . stands, phenomenologically, parallel to the position of Christ in Christianity: Christ is the Divine Word Incarnate, the Koran (to use Harry Wolfson's apt term) the Divine Word Inlibrate."[54] Schimmel does not develop this observation, but her perspective underscores its theological validity. Daniel Madigan, who has written most extensively on this topic, also highlights the weaknesses of other analogical schemes. He refers to the common points of comparative—or relational—theological engagement as a "confusion of categories" and describes the consequences as misunderstanding, competition, and tension among traditions.[55] In order to limit these negative outcomes, he emphasizes the importance of taking religious others seriously, of respecting them, and of listening to what they actually say about their tradition and beliefs. This process requires hospitality, study, and an openness to "feeling the weight" of the theological concerns of the other tradition. Madigan, though, states that this should not lead to consensus or identification of theological common denominators. The goal is to gain a *fluency* in the theological methods, languages, and authority structures of another tradition, and then use that fluency to identify meaningful "resonances" between the traditions.[56]

Madigan's promotion of theological fluency highlights another way in which the analogy of the two Words is relevant to comparative feminist theology. The analogy is the product of deep theological knowledge of *both* traditions and attention to their respective theological concerns. Therefore, when Nasr, Lumbard, and Madigan articulate this analogy, they explicitly identify theological justifications emanating from both traditions. Nasr, for example, defines the Qur'an as the "revelation of God and the book in which His [*sic*] message to man [*sic*] is contained,"[57] and then uses this definition to draw a connection to Christian perspectives on Christ as the Word. The theological value of this becomes apparent when Nasr discusses questions that arise when the unlimited Divine Word is limited by human language and the ability of humans to understand that language.[58] He does not draw an explicit comparative reference at this point, but the resonance with Christian theological conversations on the humanity and divinity of Jesus Christ is clear. Drawing on the Gospel of John and Logos Christology, Madigan picks up the thread of revelation and God's communication with and in the world. He draws attention to the fact that the communication of God to people must be in a "human language."[59] This is a shared perspective and common belief in both traditions. Madigan, then, argues that the "language" of God can be Arabic words or "body language" as manifest in incarnation. In both cases, the focus is on recognition of "the presence and expression of the eternal, universal, divine Word in something, that, to someone who does not believe, is merely human—in the case of Christians, in a first-century carpenter from Nazareth; in the case of Muslims, in a seventh-century Arabic text."[60] This focus gives rise to a number of overlapping theological issues related to the relationship between God's self and God's Word, the eternity of the Word, and the relationship between the Divine and historically-conditioned aspects of the Word. These issues and concerns become rich areas of comparative theological engagement. They provide incomplete and provocative overlaps. Conspicuously, Nasr and Madigan use the starting point of the two Divine Words to make another analogical connection between the respective "vehicles" or "bearers" of the Divine Word, Prophet Muhammad and Mary, and to discuss the requirement of purity—as manifest in illiteracy and virginity—of the two vehicles.[61] These analogical connections are based on knowledge of and reflection on the internal concerns and perspectives of each tradition. They are not impositions of external theological systems.

Finally, these theologians and scholars articulate positive benefits connected to use of the new analogy in Muslim–Christian dialogue and comparative theology. One of the primary benefits is better understanding of and respect for the integrity of the other tradition. While Nasr in no way affirms the Christian perspective on Jesus, he does articulate it faithfully and use it as the way to invite Christians into tangible reconsideration of the role of the Qur'an and Prophet Muhammad in Islam. Lumbard and Madigan go beyond understanding and respect of the other. They argue that this analogy and its resultant engagements leads to better understanding of and deeper grappling with one's *own* tradition. Exploring Christology in reference to Qur'anic verses, Lumbard argues that comparative engagement pushes Muslims to revisit other accounts of Jesus in the Qur'an. Madigan similarly highlights a "preparedness to question and to be questioned"[62] that arises within relational engagements based on substantial analogies. This questioning—and even respectful, informed critique—is not a threat but an opportunity to expand, deepen, and more fully articulate one's own theological stance.

The theologically sound and comparatively rich analogy of the two Divine Words has not been used in the context of comparative feminist theology. It is, however, uniquely capable of moving comparative feminist conversations between Muslims and Christians in productive and illuminating directions. There are two important caveats. The first is that Madigan's use of the Gospel of John and Logos Christology to substantiate the analogy can be somewhat problematic in relation to Christian feminist theologies. Logos Christology, when understood as the divine "mind" that rules over society like an emperor, is critiqued and dismissed by many Christian feminist theologians due to the manner in which it supported the institutionalization of male dominance and patriarchy.[63] I retain the term "Word" in this book not to indicate this particular formulation but, in a more general sense, to refer to God's being and communicating in the world. The second caveat also relates to the Gospel of John and the notion of high-descending Christology.

Madigan explicitly promotes high Christology as a better alternative than low Christology in Muslim–Christian dialogue.[64] He premises his argument on a shared affirmation of God's ability and capacity in both traditions. Without dismissing the insight of this suggestion, some Christian feminist theologies move away from the model of high Christology—beginning with a focus on the divinity of Jesus Christ—to prioritize a low Christology—beginning with the focus on the humanity of Jesus.[65] When engaging Christian voices, I defer to their use/nonuse of the denotation Word and also explore their critiques when offered.

My motivation for adopting the analogy of the two Words, of the Qur'an and Jesus Christ, in this study does not stem from the resonance of high Christology with Islamic texts and beliefs. I do not negate this, but I take up the analogy from another perspective: in response to the internal concerns, questions, and tensions that Christian and Islamic feminist theologians identify in their respective traditions. What are their concerns? What are their primary sites of struggle? What questions disturb them? The diverse responses to these questions reveal something striking. They point back to the analogy of the Words. Even when the terminology and concept of "Word" is challenged, feminist concerns in both traditions swirl around the Word, or the Divine, being in the world in all its contextual messiness and the way value has been and is assigned to various markers of that "messiness." More concretely, similar questions and concerns are raised in relation to the Qur'an and Jesus Christ. It is based on this organic overlap in concerns and questions that the analogy is an invaluable place to start a new conversation.

In the remainder of this book, I use the new starting point to reorient the entire comparative project and explore central theological concerns. I begin by placing approaches to the Qur'an in conversation with Christology, and then extend the analogy to explore the hadith corpus in conversation with Biblical exegesis, and Prophet Muhammad in relation to Mary as feminist exemplars. I also use the analogy to examine the topics of theological anthropology and ritual change, topics that are common sites of comparative jabs, hegemonic assertions, and horizontal violence in interreligious feminist engagements. None of the following chapters are comprehensive surveys but rather critical explorations of intriguing areas of resonance and dissonance. In each, I engage in a comparative theological exploration that begins with Islamic feminist discourse, then explores select Christian feminist, mujerista, and womanist voices, and concludes with my own constructive Muslima theological reflections.

Each chapter consists of three distinct sections and three distinct modes of analysis and writing. These sections are intended to mimic the process of comparative theology in content and form. The first section in each chapter provides a critical analysis of the major themes, assertions, and debates within Islamic feminist theology on the chapter topic. Some of these chapters (such as the one on the Qur'an and Jesus Christ) focus on areas with extensive Islamic feminist scholarship. Others (such as the chapter on Prophet Muhammad and Mary) propose new extensions to existing Islamic feminist scholarship. The first section of each chapter concludes with a constructive question that arises directly from the state of scholarship in the field.

The second section of each chapter engages with a few, specific Christian theologians and particular, limited moments in their work. I do not attempt to provide a comprehensive overview of their contributions, nor of the general topic (e.g., Christology or biblical hermeneutics). I choose specific theologians because their work prompts a new question, clarifies a distinction, or presents a challenge to me in my own theological reflection. The selected perspectives are thus based on my own position, but they are also central Christian voices and directly linked to conversations within Islamic feminist theology.[66] In this second section, the mode of writing is also distinct. Modeling the approach of comparative theology, I endeavor to accurately present their perspectives, on their own terms, in their own words, and without insertion of critical or comparative analysis. This section is the act of learning, listening, and accurately representing. The style evinces this. I also intentionally adopt this approach so that readers can have a clear understanding of the theologians' perspectives distinct from my comparative theological engagement.

The third section of each chapter turns to constructive Muslima theological reflection. Again, the form here is important to clarify. My goal in this third section is not comparative analysis but comparative theological reflection as defined throughout this chapter. Therefore, while I do offer a very brief survey of some interesting points of overlap and disconnect among Islamic and Christian perspectives, this is not the goal of the book. It would of course be a worthy project, but it is not this project. This project is focused on constructive theological insights that arise from the interreligious feminist encounter. In this, I sometimes directly cite Christian theologians and concepts, and at other times allow the contributions of Christian theologians to reverberate more implicitly in the background. The third section of each chapter takes on this distinctive task, attempting to offer at least some small insights into new trajectories, considerations, interpretative approaches, and pragmatic strategies in Muslima theology.

Throughout the following chapters, I engage with diverse scholars and theologians from contexts and racial and ethnic backgrounds other than my own. As a white Muslim woman of European descent living and working in New York City at an academic institution, I acknowledge the complexity and privilege of many of my own identities. I endeavor herein to be respectful and attentive to all the theologians I engage, and to humbly attempt to learn from their perspectives, histories, experiences, and realities that may not be my own but in which I am often complicit and embroiled.

What follows is a project of learning from and thinking with. To that end, this is not a neat project. I do not have every answer, and I cannot tie up every loose end. My intention is to raise questions, push boundaries, try on possibilities, acknowledge limits, and start new conversations.

3

Words in the World

THE QUR'AN AND JESUS CHRIST IN CONTEXT

ISLAMIC FEMINIST AND MUSLIMA interpreters widely describe the Qur'an as the Word of God. The Qur'an is both a revelation *from* God and—in its intimate connection with the Divine, as *kalam Allah* (the speech of God)—a revelation *of* God. Due to its resultant authoritative status, the Qur'an occupies a central place in much feminist and egalitarian interpretation of Islamic tradition. Though many scholars and exegetes assert that the Qur'an is related, in some way, to God, they simultaneously acknowledge that it is marked by the particularities and limits of a specific—and *patriarchal*—historical context, that of seventh-century Arabia. The Qur'an as Word of God, thus, has universal significance *and* contextual, worldly specificity in both form and content. It speaks both beyond *and* to its original context.

Islamic feminist and Muslima interpreters strive to illuminate the implications of this dual reality in relation to women, women's rights, and egalitarianism. They raise questions about and engage in debates over the nature and content of the Qur'an, the effectiveness of various exegetical approaches, and the relationship of the Qur'an to other sources of knowledge. Perspectives range from asserting that the Qur'an is inherently egalitarian to advocating deeper engagement with other traditional texts (including ahadith and law) to questioning whether the Qur'an can (or should) actually align with contemporary notions of equality and justice to probing the manner in which human experience factors into interpretation. Notably, all of these perspectives share a single prompting cause: they arise from the underlying and ubiquitous challenge of interpreting the Qur'an as the Word of God *in the world*, the challenge of interpreting the Qur'an as divine, as revealed in a limited, worldly form and context, *and* as continuously relevant to temporally, culturally, and geographically diverse contexts.

In this chapter, I begin by briefly exploring dominant approaches, persistent tensions, and contemporary debates in Islamic feminist and Muslima interpretation of the Qur'an to further emphasize the underlying problematic of the Word in the world. I do not herein focus on exegetical conclusions. Ample analyses of these contributions exist, and I examine some of these conclusions later in this book in relation to theological anthropology.[1] Here, I focus on theological understandings of and debates surrounding the Qur'an as Word of God. Notably, the problematic of the "Word in the world" is not unique to Islamic and Muslima discussions of the Qur'an. It is also evident in Christian feminist, womanist, and mujerista grapplings with Jesus Christ as both divine and human, specifically male. Therefore, in the second section of this chapter, I engage diverse Christian perspectives on Jesus Christ and Christology—from Rosemary Radford Ruether, Jacquelyn Grant, Kwok Pui-lan, and Ada María Isasi-Díaz—with the initial objective of understanding their views accurately, deeply, and on their own terms. This involves reconstruction of their concerns, approaches, and interpretations. I then conclude this chapter by returning to the Qur'an and Muslima theology in light of my engagement with Christian voices. The goal in this return is not comparison but to identify illuminating resonances and dissonances, to entertain new concerns and questions, and to constructively propose an approach to the Qur'an that embraces hybridity, human experience, and a preference for the marginalized.

The Qur'an in the World

In early Islamic egalitarian interpretations of the Qur'an, such as those articulated by Riffat Hassan, amina wadud, and Asma Barlas, the Qur'an is often depicted as the egalitarian foundation on which liberative and just interpretations can be constructed.[2] The essential core of the Qur'an is assessed to be egalitarian and even "antipatriarchal."[3] Nonegalitarian interpretations, practices, and laws are therefore illegitimate divergences from or corruptions of this authoritative and divine core. As noted in the first chapter, this stance is a deployment of the authority of the Qur'an and an expression of particular theological assertions.

Foremost among these theological assertions is the idea that the Qur'an as the Word of God necessarily aligns with or manifests some of the ontological traits of the Divine. Barlas, for instance, explicitly states that her hermeneutical approach arises out of the ontological connection between God and the Qur'an: if God is just, then the Qur'an itself as the Word of God must also be just, meaning egalitarian and antipatriarchal.[4] Barlas' description of Qur'anic content as unified, intentional, and purposeful is also a reference to divine ontology, that is, to the unicity of God (*tawhid*), omniscience of God, and intentionality of God.[5] As a result of these theological assertions, she argues that interpretative conflicts and tensions cannot and should not be attributed to the Qur'an, to God, or to the revelatory act; interpretative conflicts and tensions, for Barlas, are due to the limits and particularities of human interpretative methods.[6]

Some limits and particularities, however, do reside in the Qur'anic text. These limits manifest in the somewhat innocuous form of responses to concerns and practices of the original revelatory context. Qur'an 58:2, for example, condemns the pre-Islamic, Arab practice of *zihar*, a practice of ending a marital relationship by equating one's wife with one's mother, literally by saying, "be like the back of my mother." This text is a rejection of behavior, yet at the same time it is a contextually specific facet of Qur'anic content. In its specificity and thus limitation, it introduces questions of how people in later and diverse contexts should relate to this portion of the Word of God. Is this text simply a historical artifact? Is this text generalizable to other and new issues? Is this text relevant in other contexts, and if so, how exactly? Since the Qur'an is theologically imagined as the Word of God in the world, historical analysis alone—while illuminating—is not sufficient to answer these questions and outline the response of the contemporary "hearer" of the Word to this part of divine speech. Moreover, theological views of the Word impel the idea that a hearer should be responsive, and that the Word itself is deeply relevant to both to its original context and to other contexts.

Limits and particularities are not always as innocuous in relation to contemporary egalitarian concerns. While theological assertions about the connection of God and the Qur'an are made, there are some portions of the Qur'an that appear to address men only or to correspond to patriarchal norms of male dominance and power. Even the example of Qur'an 58:2 speaks directly to men to condemn behavior toward women. The more notorious Qur'an 4:34 also speaks to men, advising them on "strategies" for resolving marital conflict. One of the latter strategies is the permission to "hit" a woman: "Men are in authority (*qawwamun*) over women because God has preferred some over others and because they spend of their wealth. Righteous women are obedient and guard in secret what God would have them guard. Concerning those women from whom you fear disobedience/rebellion (*nushuuz*), admonish them, abandon them in bed, and hit them (*dribuhunna*, from *daraba*). If they obey you, do not seek a way against them. God is Most High, Great" (Q 4:34). This text unsurprisingly garners extensive attention from contemporary Islamic feminist and egalitarian interpreters, most recently in a compilation of essays titled *Men in Charge? Rethinking Authority in Muslim Legal Tradition.*[7] Interpretations of this text present arguments for alternate meanings of the Arabic terminology; for restrictions on the parameters of male authority (*qawwamun*) and on the precise conflict provoking behavior (*nushuuz*); for historical contextualization, including the distinction between prescriptive and descriptive parts of the text; and for ethical differentiation between universal and particular aspects of the text. These interpretations—many of which Ayesha Chaudhry provides a thorough overview—are insightful, diverse, and concerned with real-world impact.[8] What is of most pressing relevance to this chapter, though, is that these interpretations arise at the tensive intersection of the Divine and worldly. They are attempts to answer the question of how a "hearer" can continue to hear—continue to respond to and be in relationship with—the Word of God in their contemporary context and in light of egalitarian theological and practical concerns.

Significantly, tensions are more pronounced due to an extensive amount of egalitarian Qur'anic content surrounding seemingly nonegalitarian verses and sometimes assumed male audience. This content includes exhortations to justice (e.g., Q 4:135), calls to care for the marginalized (e.g., Q 2:177), and statements about the equality and value of all people (e.g., Q 4:1, 30:30, 49:13, 95:4), including explicit statements about women (Q 3:195, 4:124, 9:71, 16:97, 33:35, 40:40). It is this content that wadud centers in her groundbreaking interpretation of the Qur'anic creation narrative. Drawing on Qur'an 4:1, she emphasizes the original creation of a single, unsexed, ungendered *nafs* (soul) and the later, nonhierarchical division of that *nafs* into the *zawj* (pair).[9]

While Kecia Ali critiques this Qur'an-centered approach and emphasizes the necessity of engaging other Islamic sources, including the hadith corpus and Islamic law, she herself clarifies that her critique is a reaction to some interpreters' methodological avoidance of challenging Qur'anic content. It is not a declaration that nonegalitarian verses form the "ineluctable core of the Qur'anic message" and thus render the Qur'an irretrievably or holistically patriarchal.[10] She does not completely dismiss a focus on Qur'anic exegesis but expresses frustration at interpretative projects that foreground egalitarian verses and do not engage— or do not critically engage—with more challenging parts of the Qur'anic text. Additionally, Ali argues that the common interpretative methods of historical contextualization and appeal to Qur'anic ethical principles prove to be effective in relation to some topics, such as marriage and divorce, yet do not yield an egalitarian reading on every gender-related topic.[11] Her call is for recognition of this tension and broader and deeper engagement with both egalitarian and other content.

Not all Islamic feminists are convinced that tensions can be resolved or resolved definitively in favor of egalitarianism. In her recent survey and critique of early contributions, Aysha Hidayatullah challenges the effectiveness of Islamic feminist Qur'anic interpretation in yielding egalitarian interpretations *and* in barring nonegalitarian possibilities.[12] She argues that feminist Qur'anic exegesis has reached an impasse; dominant interpretative approaches—including historical contextualization, intratextual analysis, and appeals to Qur'anic, ethical, and theological principles, such as *tawhid* (the unicity of God)—do not sufficiently or successfully demonstrate "privileging" of egalitarian Qur'anic content over hierarchical content.[13] Hidayatullah contends that even the perception of a tension among egalitarian (or mutuality) verses and hierarchy verses—that is, the very impetus for explaining why the egalitarian verses take precedence—may be a contemporary imposition on the Qur'an. Feminist exegetes should, therefore, move away from what she views as normative prescriptiveness and reliance on anachronistic projections and "textual manipulations."[14] Instead, they should take personal responsibility for the interpretations they articulate and "openly admit" that there is a gap between contemporary and Qur'anic notions of equality and justice.[15] More pointedly, Hidayatullah opines that feminist interpreters of the Qur'an should acknowledge that "no amount of interpretation can make the text definitively cohere with our contemporary sense of justice."[16]

Despite this divergence—and perhaps giving rise to the divergence—Islamic feminist interpreters share an essential concern about practical impact and liberation.[17] Barlas confirms this, stating that interpretation of the Qur'an should focus on uncovering ethical possibilities that are relevant to our contexts.[18] Barlas also expresses concern about the way in which hermeneutical choices impact the reception of interpretations by other Muslims.[19] wadud similarly emphasizes practical impact. She argues that egalitarian Qur'anic interpretation has been and remains vital because it contributes to real change and reforms in Muslim societies and communities. She asserts this but also points out that scholarship in and of itself does not result in change; interpretation is not liberation. Critiquing Hidayatullah *and* Barlas, she states that interpretations and analysis of the tradition must have a mapped-out application in order to serve as "direct currency for other women living under Muslim laws."[20] wadud consequently critiques approaches and interpretations that are not attached to practical applications in contemporary contexts. Referencing her involvement in activism, she reflects on how such work pragmatically (re)shaped her interpretative approach; her work for family equality with the organization Musawah made her "willing to pick and choose from among a wide range of strategies to secure reform on the ground."[21]

Like Barlas, wadud also emphasizes that Qur'anic interpretative strategies can only be effective if they are in some way connected to community perceptions, including views on the status and nature of the Qur'an. For her, this connection is about using and transforming common perspectives to advocate for change, not about reinscribing "orthodox" perspectives. One example of this is wadud's continuing use of the concept of *tawhid* (unicity of God) and her elaboration of this into the tawhidic paradigm. Responding to Hidayatullah's critique, wadud explains that this hermeneutical-theological approach does not eradicate all traces of asymmetry in the text but does eradicate the "choice to highlight this asymmetry and to build upon it systematically into juridical codes and cultural practices."[22] wadud thereby deploys *tawhid*, a central concept in much Islamic thought and practice, to justify egalitarianism. She uses a concept that already resonates with the community and tradition as a way to encourage real change.

Hidayatullah is aware of this strategy and acknowledges that pragmatic concerns impact feminist Qur'anic interpretation. Drawing on Ali, she highlights the way interpreters strategically employ ideas of Islamic orthodoxy and legitimacy to push for egalitarian changes on the ground; they depict their interpretations as aligning with foundational Islamic and Qur'anic principles. In other words, interpretations are presented not as innovations but as reformations to the "true" or "original" Islam. While Hidayatullah states that this is an understandable approach, she simultaneously asserts that it relies too heavily on the authority of the text and that it avoids "the more complicated work of confronting the problem of the Qur'an not always neatly aligning with their notions of justice and equality for women."[23] Therefore, she grants the importance of practical realities but asserts that this strategy is ultimately unsuccessful in securing long-term justice and egalitarianism.[24]

Some other scholars of the Qur'an, especially those with a historical *and* nontheological focus, critique the Islamic feminist insistence on a "liberatory approach." Karen Bauer, for example, describes this approach as using the Qur'an as a "locus of activism" and attempting to move beyond the historical meaning toward "a new set of meanings that might be possible" in light of a concern for social consequences.[25] This critique helps to further illuminate intra-Islamic feminist divergences. Hidayatullah may embrace the idea that other Islamic feminist interpreters move beyond historical meaning, but she does not embrace a move away from the liberative. Her search for the liberative continues, even if she assesses the Qur'anic content as insufficiently aligned with that objective in the contemporary world.

Hidayatullah's position has not been embraced by all scholars. wadud defends gender-inclusive interpretation of the Qur'an and critiques Hidayatullah for inappropriately privileging "six or seven sticky passages."[26] Barlas returns to theological questions in responding to Hidayatullah; she is concerned with the theological conceptions of God and the Qur'an that shape interpretative choices and processes.[27] For Barlas, the Qur'an is the Word of God, and she stresses the intimate relationship between the two. Though she acknowledges that the Qur'an cannot be directly or holistically equated with God, she argues that belief in the two are nonetheless inseparable: "[t]o believe in a God who speaks is *necessarily* to believe in God's speech."[28] Her perspective, as already discussed, is grounded in the idea that there can be no conflict between God and God's speech. More specifically, there can be no conflict that prompts questioning of God's justness or of the Qur'an's connection to God, meaning the Qur'an's sacredness. She therefore rejects Hidayatullah's suggestion that there is a conflict and that that conflict must lead to reimagining the Qur'anic revelation.

Hidayatullah proposes reimagining as a response to her own analysis of hierarchy and mutuality verses in the Qur'an and subsequent conclusion that the Qur'an does not fully accord with contemporary equality or justice due to the presence of androcentric, hierarchical, and patriarchal elements. This conviction is the basis of her critique of other interpretations but also her impetus to reconsider the status and revelatory nature of the Qur'an as the Word of God.[29] While others critique her reconsideration as abandonment of the sacrality of the Qur'anic text, Hidayatullah states that it actually gives her "the ability *not* to abandon the Qur'an as a sacred text."[30] She, like Barlas, believes that God is just and that the Qur'an is the revelation of God.[31] The point of distinction is that Hidayatullah does not see the Qur'an as aligning fully or necessarily with contemporary notions of justice. Therefore, she is left to answer challenging theological questions about what this may or may not indicate about God, about the Qur'an, and about ourselves: "The starting point is that God is just, and that the Qur'an is the word of God, so then the Qur'an must also be just. . . . But if, as it turns out, we cannot be sure that the text upholds the justice we seek, then we are left to question whether the Qur'an is really a divine text. If we do not question the divinity of the Qur'an, then we are left to question whether God is just."[32] She does not question the justness of God. She also does not wholly dispense with the sacredness of the Qur'an. Rather, she wants to reassess what "sacredness" means; she wants to think differently about the revelatory nature of the Qur'an. In other words, how exactly is the Qur'an sacred? What does it mean to say the Qur'an is the Word of God? And how does this meaning define our interpretative possibilities within—and beyond—the Qur'an?

Drawing on the work of Nasr Abu Zayd and Raja Rhouni, Hidayatullah answers by advocating that the Qur'an be understood as a "sacred discourse" instead of as a text alone or a repository of fixed norms.[33] Understanding the Qur'an in this way will allow feminist exegetes to assert human authority and to "consider new, unexpected ways of pursuing feminist justice in Islam that were previously unimaginable or impossible."[34] Although Hidayatullah clearly indicates the cause of her theological concern and the reason why she re-evaluates the revelatory nature of the Qur'an, she does not provide specifics on what this new understanding of the Qur'an would look like in practice and method. She hints that it would require going "beyond" the text, meaning "admitting" that ideas of justice cannot be based conclusively or exclusively on the Qur'an, asserting new forms of authority, and imagining justice outside of the Qur'an's specific pronouncements.[35]

Some possible insights into this new understanding are articulated by Fatima Seedat when she elaborates on Hidayatullah's discussions of sacred discourse and of going "beyond" the text. Seedat attempts to articulate what this "beyond" may be and "how . . . the Qur'an may remain central to Muslim meaning making yet open to evolving understandings of justice."[36] Hidayatullah suggests strategies for *how* to move beyond the text—a discursive approach to Abu Zayd and to notions of sexual equality—but Seedat argues that it is not as clear "*where*" this beyond may lie.[37] She reiterates that the Qur'an is not a closed or fixed text from which we draw norms but a discourse that allows us to *imagine* justice in relation to new and diverse worldly contexts. Such imagining takes place at the intersection of text and human experience.[38]

Drawing on Sa'diyya Shaikh's exploration of a "tafsir of praxis" among South African Muslim women who were physically abused by their spouses, Seedat argues that a person's experience can compel her to go beyond the explicit Qur'anic text and refuse any application of a text that contravenes her experience.[39] In these situations, experience compels women to go "beyond" the legal meaning of the text. She then raises a provocative question: "where adherence to the text results in the experience of injustice, may the experience abrogate the text that produces the injustice?"[40] Notably, her use of the concept of abrogation directly invokes the traditional exegetical use of intra-Qur'anic abrogation to make claims about the application of and relationship among various verses. Seedat argues that Muslim women "might highlight" experience as an authoritative source, and that would not constitute an anti-Qur'anic turn.[41] It would be a reimagining that retains the centrality of the Qur'anic text but highlights the generative process of meaning making. Meanings and conceptions of equality are not fixed and found in the text alone; they are generated through continuous interaction of text and experience.[42] This reimaging of the text is one way the "Qur'an may also remain continuously relevant to the reader."[43]

wadud responds to the proposal of reimagining the sacredness of the Qur'an by probing the meaning of the Qur'an as Word of God and ways in which revelation retains relevance in diverse contexts. She emphasizes that there is not and has never been consensus on what it means to say the Qur'an is the Word of God. She then draws attention to the convergence of transcendent and concrete manifestations in revelation, and asserts that lack of consensus over the manner of this convergence is actually an *opportunity* for egalitarian exegesis: "as soon as we acknowledge that none can know fully what Allah meant, then the door is open to both patriarchal and feminist egalitarian readings."[44] For wadud, no human can definitively reconcile the transcendent and concrete aspects of revelation, and thus multiple interpretations are possible and legitimate. She accordingly rejects Hidayatullah's move to reassess the sacredness of the revelation, describing it as doing away with the divinity of the text. Instead, wadud advocates for an embrace of the tension and "sublime ambiguity" of the Qur'an. Characterized by both critical response and faithful reverence, embrace of ambiguity allows interpreters to read and experience the text in relation to its historical context *and* contemporary contexts, and to challenge literal readings of any verse. Significantly, wadud's perspective—about productive and liberatory ambiguity—comes from her own experience grappling with the text. She dismisses the idea that another interpreter could invalidate her experience. Addressing Hidayatullah directly, she states that Hidayatullah "cannot steal away from those Muslim women—like myself (and some Muslim men)—the experience of finding dynamic and liberatory reading through the text."[45] This is especially true for wadud because this experience brought her personal comfort and sustained her in the fight for political and social change. This experience also aligns with her broader theology and articulation of the tawhidic paradigm in which God is both intimate and transcendent.[46]

Hidayatullah actually references wadud's more recent understanding of the Qur'an as a promising step toward reassessing the Qur'anic revelation.[47] She highlights wadud's views that the Qur'an is not the totality of God's revelation or will; that the language of the Qur'an is tied to the historical context; and that God and the Qur'an cannot be equated. Hidayatullah, though, does not embrace another key aspect of wadud's approach: the view of the Qur'anic revelation as a trajectory that points "us to higher moral practices even if not fully articulating these because of the context."[48] The Qur'anic revelation is limited linguistically to its original historical context, but wadud states that it nevertheless simultaneously guides humanity to "moral excellence and ethical propriety."[49] Attending to the Qur'anic trajectory does not result in static forms; it requires adjustments and changes that continue to lead toward and foster excellence and propriety. What Hidayatullah rejects is the idea that the Qur'an points beyond itself in a *particular* ethical direction. This rejection is connected to her opinion that there is no intrinsic reason to privilege egalitarian aspects of the Qur'an over patriarchal and androcentric aspects. wadud's use of Qur'anic trajectory is likewise tied to her understanding of the Qur'an as both historically limited and expressing a universal ethical framework.[50] The Qur'an, for wadud, has the capacity to continuously hint at and open up new meanings. Another description illuminates wadud's position: "the Qur'an is, as it were, a window to look *through*. A doorway with a threshold one must pass *over* toward the infinite possibilities that point humanity toward a continuum of spiritual and social development."[51] This description clarifies her insistence on continuing to critically and faithfully struggle with the "sublime ambiguity" of the Qur'an.

Islamic feminist debates over the nature and status of Qur'an as the Word of God disclose diverse perspectives on hermeneutical methods, theology, and impact. They also demonstrate a persistent concern with how to understand the Qur'an as sacred—as divine—yet also marked by a particular historical context. This concern is further amplified—and even more pressing—in light of contemporary views on gender-related justice and egalitarianism. Some of the historical markings are androcentric and patriarchal. This raises theological, hermeneutical, and strategic questions, questions about the meaning of the expression "Word of God" and also about the relationship of the Qur'an to God, the nature of God, and the manner in which humans should and can engage with God and God's revelation. Can a Qur'an marked with traces of patriarchy and androcentrism lead to egalitarianism or equality? Does the Qur'an have an egalitarian core or an ethical trajectory? How is the Qur'an to be "heard" by diverse—temporally, geographically, culturally, contextually—audiences? Is the Divine held hostage by the contextual traces of the particular worldly form? Can those traces be effectively explained (perhaps rendered impotent) through historical contextualization, textual analysis, and allusions to Qur'anic principles? Can we engage those aspects differently, struggle with them in new ways that do not compromise notions of justice or rely on severing the relationship with the Qur'an or God? Must other sources be engaged as well? If so, which ones? And how can Islamic feminist exegetes advocate for the authority of other sources in relation to the Qur'an?

Notably, from a theological perspective, this quandary—and the resultant questions—is not particular to the Qur'an. It is a quandary that stems from the assertion that the unlimited Divine has revealed something in the world. Revelation is necessarily limited and specified in order for it to be received, understood, and meaningful to a human (and limited) audience. The quandary, though, exists because theological assertions about such revelations typically—as with Qur'an—assign a broader, more universal relevance to the revelation. The importance of the revelation extends beyond the context of revelation. Thus arises the question of how a revelation to a specific context and in a specific form can be applied to, relevant to, and understood in other contexts. Thus also arises the more specific question of how to deal with aspects of the original revelation, or divine self-disclosure, that do not fully align with our contemporary notions of justice and egalitarianism, and that have been repeatedly invoked to marginalize and devalue women.

Jesus Christ in the World

In Christian theology, this quandary and its resultant questions lie at the center of christological debates and formulations. Responding to the biblical question "Who do you say that I am?," Christian theologians generally assert both the divinity and humanity of Jesus Christ, and then aim to explicate the implications of this assertion.[52] Christian feminist, womanist, and mujerista theologians in particular use this question as an entrance into—perhaps more accurately, as an invitation to—discern the meaning of Jesus Christ for themselves, their communities, and their contexts. They also use the question as an invitation to challenge dominant christological formulations that foreground hierarchy, that assign exclusionary significance to Jesus Christ's historical and symbolic maleness, and that have been used to marginalize women in institutions and in redemptive history.

In this section, I explore four Christian feminist, womanist, and mujerista responses to the question "Who do you say that I am?" These responses come from Rosemary Radford Ruether, Kwok Pui-lan, Jacquelyn Grant, and Ada María Isasi-Díaz. Rosemary Radford Ruether is a pioneer in Christian (specifically Catholic) feminist theology, who completed her PhD in Classics and Patristics at Claremont Graduate School in 1965. Since that time, she has written many books—including the pivotal *Sexism and God-talk: Toward a Feminist Theology*—that critique patriarchy within Christian thought and institutions, articulate feminist theological perspectives on christology and ecofeminism, and push for women's ordination and rights.[53] She is currently Carpenter Emerita Professor of Feminist Theology at Pacific School of Religion and the Graduate Theological Union, and the Georgia Harkness Emerita Professor of Applied Theology at Garrett Evangelical Theological Seminary. Kwok Pui-lan, a central voice in Asian women's theology, earned her ThD from Harvard Divinity School in 1989. In addition to *Postcolonial Imagination and Feminist Theology*, she is the author and editor of over twenty other books in English and Chinese.[54] Her work focuses on the theological concerns of Asian feminist theology and postcolonial theology. She was previously the William F. Cole Professor of Christian Theology and Spirituality at Episcopal Divinity School. Jacquelyn Grant is a founder of womanist theology, who completed her PhD in Systematic Theology at Union Theological Seminary in 1985. She is the author of *White Women's Christ and Black Women's Jesus: Feminist Christology and Womanist Response*, and is especially well known for her articulation of womanist christology in critique of other feminist theological views of Jesus Christ.[55] She is currently the founder and director of the Black Women in Church and Society and Womanist Scholars Program, and Callaway Professor of Systematic Theology at the Interdenominational Theological Center in Atlanta. Ada María Isasi-Díaz is the founder of mujerista theology (Hispanic feminist theology), and she earned her PhD in Christian Social Ethics at Union Theological Seminary in 1990. She authored multiple books, including *En la Lucha/In the Struggle: Elaborating a Mujerista Theology*, in which she articulated theological perspectives arising out of and responding to the particular experiences of Hispanic women in the United States.[56] She was also very involved in movements for women's ordination within the Catholic Church. Prior to her death in 2012, she was Professor Emerita of Ethics and Theology at Drew University.

These theologians' responses to the question "Who do you say that I am?" engage topics ranging from the language and symbols invoked to describe Jesus to the value assigned to particular human markings of Jesus (inclusive of but not limited to Jesus maleness) to the affiliations of Jesus with power and marginal groups. These theologians also introduce various strategies for engaging dominant traditions and emphasize the role of human experience—specifically diverse female experience—in articulating relevant and empowering theological perspectives on Jesus Christ.

Rosemary Radford Ruether: Liberator Jesus of the Synoptic Gospels

In her foundational work, *Sexism and God-talk: Toward a Feminist Theology*, Rosemary Radford Ruether explores the possibility of a feminist christology. Through the pithy, yet defining question "Can a male savior save women?," she introduces her critique of how the maleness of Jesus is valued in classical christology as outlined at the Council of Chalcedon.[57] Ruether argues that classical christology attempts to unite two ideas present in ancient Near East and Hebraic thought: divine wisdom and a messianic king. Both of these ideas originally featured female divine actors, but the female symbols were repressed in Judaism and Christianity. Divine wisdom therefore came to be associated with the idea of the *Logos*, or Son of God. This association led to the perspective that there was a "necessary ontological connection between the maleness of Jesus' historical person and the maleness of the *Logos* as the male offspring and disclosure of a male God."[58] Although Jesus offered a messianic proclamation about the Reign of God—"a coming time of peace and justice" under God—Ruether claims that his message did not conform to the model of a Davidic King-Messiah, a male "conquering warrior who liberates the people from their enemies and then reigns over a new kingdom."[59]

Ruether acknowledges that Davidic tradition and genealogy is later ascribed to Jesus but states that Jesus' original notion of the Reign of God was not nationalist or otherworldly. It was focused squarely on the plight and divine receptivity of marginalized, poor, and oppressed people; on the dismantling of structures of oppression; and on social harmony as the product of a divine response to human repentance.[60] Consequently, Jesus does not model kingship but servanthood. Ruether distinguishes this particular form of servanthood from intrahuman servanthood or slavery, defining it as being in special relationship to God. This special relationship results in a liberated person "freed from all bondage to human masters."[61] For Ruether, Jesus as liberator and servant also directly challenges institutionalized religious authority based on past tradition and limited interpretative control. Jesus "declares that God has not just spoken in the past but is speaking *now*."[62] Jesus, in her view, speaks of the "one to come" and does not present himself as the last word or singular disclosure of God. For Ruether, any presentation of Jesus as such goes directly against the "spirit" of Jesus and aligns with the powers and structures he protested.

While this is the crux of Ruether's understanding of Jesus, she also explains how this original view of Jesus (as liberator and servant) was transformed into a patriarchal and imperial christology associated with the notion of Jesus as Savior. She highlights three particular moments in this transformation. The first, she describes as an early attempt to reconcile the "shock of the Crucifixion" with the experience of the Resurrection.[63] This gave rise to an ultimately unstable merging of charismatic and apocalyptic views of Jesus; Jesus becomes the "suffering servant" who dies to atone and who will soon return as the victorious Messiah (Christ). The second key transformation is the development of an institutionalized ministry in the form of bishops. This institutional ministry seeks to limit the "ongoing speaking in the name of Christ" that characterized the early charismatic leadership of prophets and martyrs who Ruether describes as continuing the "spirit" of Jesus' message.[64] To do so, institutionalized ministry compiled and canonized the sayings and teachings of Jesus into written biographical accounts. This process shifted authority from charismatic and prophetic figures to the institutionalized episcopacy, that is, the church governed by the bishops. This move not only curtailed "speaking" in the name Christ, but it also situated access to Christ only by way of official apostolic teaching offices, positions and roles held only by men.

The third transition away from the liberating servant model of Jesus and toward the patriarchal and imperial Jesus occurs in the fourth century when Christianity becomes the religion of the Roman Empire. As an imperial religion, the messiah is again imagined as a ruling king and newly associated with the person of the emperor; "the Christian emperor, with the Christian Patriarch on his right hand, now represents the establishment of Christ's reign upon the earth."[65] Additionally, this form of messianism is coupled with a "hierarchy of being" in which Christ as the *Logos* (understood here as the mind of God) rules over the entire cosmos in a manner similar to how the emperor rules over the political world and men rule over women. In this hierarchy, women are described as the *a-logi*, "mindless ones, who are to be governed and defined by the representative of divine Logos."[66] Women are not able to represent the Divine in a hierarchy premised on male normativity and imperial kingship. Ruether also observes that when medieval scholasticism later merges this hierarchy with Aristotelian biology, women are further depicted as being "defective physically, morally, and mentally."[67]

As a result of these transformational moments, the incarnation of the divine Logos in a male human is deemed to be an ontological necessity instead of a historical accident. Ontological necessity indicates that the incarnation could have been no other way; it could not have occurred except for in the male human form. Historical accident, on the contrary, would mean that the maleness of Jesus was just one characteristic among others; maleness was a characteristic of the historical Jesus but not a characteristic required for incarnation. The assertion of the ontological necessity of the maleness of Jesus has had a clear ripple effect throughout institutions and teachings: "if Christ has to be incarnated in a male, so only can the male represent Christ."[68] Ruether connects this assertion to resistance to female ordination in Catholic, Anglican, and Orthodox communities. The assumed necessity of Christ incarnating in a male reflects the descending hierarchy through priests and laypeople (including—but excluding—women) and also reflects back on the Divine and highlights the underlying theological assumption that God is in fact male. Ruether does not hold back when she states that male genitalia become a prerequisite for representing Christ.

Ruether recognizes that this patriarchal formulation of christology has dominated, but she also explores the benefits and shortcomings of two alternative christologies, which she labels androgynous and spirit christologies.[69] The first—androgynous—is rooted in the Gnostic gospels and depicts redemption as the process of transcending the division of male and female. She critiques this alternative, arguing that it remains androcentric with the male as the normative human. For women, the process of redemption often includes "transcending their identities as sexual persons and mothers."[70] Such women are even described as being made into men in order to participate in the kingdom of heaven. Acknowledging variations on this model that arise in nineteenth-century romanticism and reformist feminism, she nevertheless argues that none of these models create the possibility of a women fully representing the redeemed human. She connects the second alternative, spirit christologies, to early Christian prophetism and the idea of the ongoing revelation of Christ.[71] In these christologies, women are the spokespeople of Christ, exemplars of Christ (*alter Christus*, literally another Christ), and the form in which visions of Christ manifest. Spirit christologies are more radical than androgynous christologies. They do not simply add women back into the equation, but "they dare to dream of a new dispensation of the Divine in which women will represent new, not yet imagined dimensions of human possibility and divine disclosure."[72] As already noted in relation to the rise of patriarchal christology, Ruether argues that the institutionalized church effectively suppressed spirit christologies. Moreover, she opines that contemporary reformist feminists have typically been too theologically conservative to fully adopt this radical dream.

On the basis of her critiques, Ruether claims that patriarchal, androgynous, and spirit christologies are not sufficient for articulating a feminist christology.[73] None of these options sufficiently explains the way in which Jesus is redemptive for women. What is the solution? While Ruether admits the possibility of "emancipating" oneself from the tradition and from Jesus, this is not what she ultimately asserts. She argues that a feminist christology must be based on "reencounter with the Jesus of the synoptic Gospels, not the accumulated doctrine about him in message and praxis."[74] When the ideas of a Messiah and the Logos are removed—"stripped off"—Jesus of the synoptic Gospels aligns well with the basic assertions of feminism. This is a liberator Jesus that rails against religious and social hierarchies and articulates new modes of human–Divine and human–human relationality. Moreover, this is a Jesus who elevates and centers the oppressed and marginalized. Ruether states that women feature largely in this as they are often the "oppressed of the oppressed."[75] She is careful to clarify that this does not mean that women are elevated for being women; oppression and the oppressed are the defining features. This view bleeds over into her depiction of Jesus; Jesus is the liberator, and he is the liberator because he "has renounced this system of domination and seeks to embody in his person the new humanity of service and mutual empowerment."[76] He is not the liberator because he is male. In Ruether's feminist christology and her description of Jesus in the synoptic Gospels, Jesus' maleness is thus a historical accident not an ontological necessity. She allows that his maleness may have social and historical meaning in his patriarchal context but not theological meaning. In fact, she states that Jesus, "the representative of liberated humanity and the liberating Word of God, manifests the *kenosis* of patriarchy," the self-emptying of patriarchy, through the introduction of a new social order.[77] Ruether describes her view of Jesus as dynamic, as continuing, as going beyond—but not disconnecting from—the historical person of Jesus to call us to "yet incompleted dimensions of human liberation."[78]

Kwok Pui-lan: The Hybrid Jesus/Christ

Kwok Pui-lan's perspective on christology responds to, yet diverges from, that of Ruether, seeking to outline a "postcolonial feminist rethinking of Jesus/Christ."[79] Specifically, Kwok is interested in probing what is revealed and suppressed by the question "Can a male savior save women?" Her probing of this question includes examinations of power, of the use of particular images of Christ in colonial enterprises, and of implicit consent to the male gendering of the savior. Drawing on the postcolonial thinker Homi Bhabha, Kwok seeks to "experiment with thinking at the limits of conventional theology" by listening to diverse theologians who invoke cultural idioms and religious imagination to depict Christ.[80] She places her experimentation with these christologies in the frame of postcolonial hybridity. Hybridity is invoked to explore constructions of power, representation, dominant knowledge, and myths of singular or pure traditions. Hybridity in this way is juxtaposed with the search for the historical, "real," or "original" Jesus. Hybridity is also invested in challenging clear-cut binaries and boundaries in favor of exploring the "fruitful ambiguity" of in-between spaces.[81]

Kwok argues that Jesus/Christ is the most hybrid concept in the entire Christian tradition. Jesus/Christ—as evinced in historical and continuing debates over christological formulations—resists easy explanation and categorization. As the "contact zone" between divine and human, Jesus/Christ is dynamic and disquieting. The question "Who do you say that I am?" is not easily or sufficiently answered, especially with a single christology. Kwok claims that the hybrid nature of Jesus/Christ was a threat to the Roman Empire and other imperial formulations of Christianity; authority and control were closely tied to distinguishing between orthodox and heretical formulations.[82] She therefore argues that exploration of Jesus/Christ as hybrid is an effective means to subvert the "theological hegemony of Europe and white America" and to avoid the "manhunt for Jesus."[83] On this basis, she explores diverse, hybrid images of Jesus/Christ, including the Black Christ, Corn Mother, Shakti, Theological Transvestite, and the Bi/Christ.[84] Some of these formulations are feminist and womanist, while others arise from black liberation and contextual theologies.

Without delving into the specifics of each of these hybrid christological formulations, Kwok's identification of common themes in these formulations is significant. To begin, she asserts that it is impossible to identify the "real" or historical Jesus and thereby construct a pure, original understanding of Jesus.[85] This assertion is placed in conversation with Ruether's attempt to argue for a return to origins and rediscovery of the liberator Christ uncorrupted by patriarchal tradition. For Kwok, this is a futile exercise, since Jesus/Christ has always been hybrid. She clarifies that hybridity is not the same as contextual or indigenized views of Jesus/Christ; the latter assume a pure and real core that is "transplanted" into new cultures, contexts, and eras. For Kwok, there is no singular essence but only the reality of hybridity.

Noting the growth of these hybrid formulations of Jesus/Christ in the twentieth century within communities of colonized and oppressed people, Kwok observes that some of the central debates about Jesus/Christ relate to his passion and suffering.[86] Citing black feminist and womanist thinkers in particular, she highlights how the image of Jesus as the "suffering servant" is critiqued in light of the very real and deep suffering of many black women. A central—and esteemed—component of christological formulations is revisited and reevaluated in light of particular and actual human experience. The Jesus/Christ formulation is placed in conversation with "questions of suffering and healing that they see daily in their communities."[87]

Kwok also draws attention to hidden baggage that accompanies certain symbols of Christ. Speaking particularly about anti-Judaism, she cites the work of Susannah Heschel, Judith Plaskow, and Amy-Jill Levine to argue that Judaism is often invoked as a "negative foil, in order to show that Christianity is liberative for women, or that Jesus was a feminist."[88] Anti-Judaism was also used to support expansion of the Christian empire and of colonial Europe. Even "third world" feminists and liberation theologians have invoked anti-Judaism. The general take-away of Kwok's observations about anti-Judaism is that every articulation of hybrid, liberation, feminist, and/or womanist christology can potentially reinscribe oppressive discourses aimed at other groups. These may be other religious groups, other gender groups, or other cultural groups. Kwok here cautions against what I described in the Introduction as horizontal violence and comparative jabs.

Jacquelyn Grant: Black Women's Jesus

Jacquelyn Grant situates her engagement with the question "Who do you say that I am?" in response to early feminist conversations about contextualized christologies.[89] These conversations focused—as with Ruether—on whether a male savior can save women; on how Jesus shapes women's status in the Church and society; on how Jesus is deployed or invoked to inflict harm on women; and on Jesus' relationship to the patriarchy of his time.[90] In exploring these questions, Grant makes a number of significant observations. First, she emphasizes that the image one holds of Jesus Christ is intimately tied to self-perception; it is not simply a theological or theoretical postulate, but it also shapes how a person sees themselves. Beyond—yet connected to—individual perception, this image permeates and shapes social and religious institutions as well. She also highlights the fact that Jesus' historical maleness was situated in a patriarchal context, that is, in a system of human hierarchy. She struggles with how to understand (and evaluate) the fact that God manifests in maleness in a system that privileges maleness.[91] Finally, she poses a provocative and necessary question about the ways in which various christologies have been used to oppress women both within the Church and in society.[92] Describing the male Jesus as a primary tool for oppressing women, she asks whether women can still look to this Jesus for salvation. Grant does not ultimately accept that Jesus is inherently tied to the oppression of women, but she does emphasize that Jesus has been widely invoked for this end. From these observations, Grant articulates two primary tasks for any Christian feminist christology. First, Christian feminist christology must explicitly critique patriarchialism and demonstrate "how traditional male articulated Christologies have been used 'to keep women in their place,' rather than to save women."[93] Second, a feminist christology must offer a constructive articulation of women's liberation by liberating "Jesus from oppressive and distorted interpretations."[94]

In conversation with these two goals, Grant surveys existing feminist christologies, which she classifies as biblical, liberal, and rejectionist.[95] Biblical feminist christologies, according to Grant, generally present Jesus as a nonconformist, as androgynous, or as a feminist. She appreciates that scholars have reclaimed the biblical text—often used to oppress women—and asserted a model of relationships based on mutuality, but simultaneously critiques their sole focus on sexist oppression and their failure to engage broader tradition beyond the biblical text.[96] Grant then explores the liberal christologies of Letty Russell and Rosemary Radford Ruether. She affirms Russell's notion of the "usability of tradition"—that is, selective acceptance of those portions of tradition that are effective for and relevant to feminist liberation—as well as Russell's definition of Jesus as the new human, or new being, that restores equal relationships.[97] With Ruether, Grant acknowledges her attention to the lack of intersectional analysis in both feminist and black theologies, with the former primarily focusing on sexism and the latter primarily focusing on racism. Grant also appreciates Ruether's vision of christology as "anticipatory" and related to experience, and her description of Jesus as the liberator.[98] Generally in liberal christologies, the maleness of Jesus is superseded by the "Christness of Jesus"; servanthood, as opposed to domination, is affirmed; women's experience becomes a primary theological source; and connections between various christologies and "interconnecting modes of oppression" are highlighted.[99] Nevertheless and in particular critique of Ruether's exploration of racism, classism, and sexism, Grant questions whether liberal feminists are capable of understanding "non-white women's experience."[100]

Finally, Grant examines the reformist, and ultimately rejectionist, views of Mary Daly. She critiques Daly for subsuming racism under sexism instead of exploring each independently and acknowledging that even women who experience sexism may perpetrate racism with other women.[101] However, for Grant, Daly also makes a substantial contribution: she compels other feminist theologians to ask difficult questions about the extent to which Jesus Christ, and even Christianity, can ever be freed from patriarchal contexts. Daly "shakes the foundation" of patriarchalism and forces feminist theologians to consider not only if Jesus can redeem women but if women can redeem Jesus.[102] Grant frames Daly's intervention as a theological version of throwing the baby out with the bath water. Grant herself—along with many other feminist theologians—does not wish to throw the baby Jesus out with the bathwater. One strategy for avoiding this is to "overspiritualize" Jesus and remove him from political realities and concerns of his context. Grant, however, presses for another approach that concedes that "feminists do have much explaining to do when it comes to the feminism of Jesus."[103] Such an approach has to engage with the disconcerting reality that the Divine incarnated in Jesus did not overthrow oppression even though Jesus may have departed from some of the norms of a patriarchal context. It has to ask why Jesus played patriarchal games. And it may also have to ask, in light of this, if Jesus was actually divine, and if so, in what way divine.

While Grant places herself in conversation with other prominent feminist voices, her primary concern is to critique of the limitations of white Christian feminist theologies and christologies that arise from the centering and universalizing of the particular experiences of white women. She argues that Black women's experience challenges the assumptions of these approaches by centering the "triple oppressive reality" of racism, sexism, and classism.[104] Since the experience of Black women diverges so dramatically from that of white women, any feminist theological calls for a turn to women's experience must deliberately and self-consciously identify to which experience they refer.[105] Failure to do so negatively impacts the feminist movement, as white feminists claim the right to define all women's experience and to define the rules of feminist theological interpretation.

In response to this failure and the resultant suspicion of feminism among Black women, Grant outlines the foundations of a womanist theology. She builds on black feminism, which she describes as asserting that human liberation can only be achieved through a multidimensional approach to racism, sexism, and classism. Not one of these forms of oppression can be fought in isolation. She then adopts Alice Walker's definition of a "womanist" to foreground the strength, survival strategies, and "active struggle" of black women.[106] Grant explains that as theology womanist "accents . . . our being responsible, in charge, outrageous, courageous, and audacious enough to demand the right to think theologically and to do it independently of both White and Black men and White women."[107]

In womanist theology, the womanist tradition and the experiences of black women in society and in the Church become the starting points for theological reflection in general and christological formulation specifically. Grant, in fact, contends that the intersection of racism, sexism, and classism in the experience of black women makes their experience a more adequate starting point for christology. If Christ is located with the "outkast, the least" then exploration of black women's experience—specifically their experiences in slavery, segregation, and domestic service—is an appropriate and abundant resource for formulating new christologies.[108] This not only means probing the tridimensional experience of racism, sexism, and classism but also means that the daily experiences of poor black women become the measure for assessing any theological claims made by womanist theologians.[109] Grant goes a step further and—building on aspects of womanist tradition and on the Black Christ of James Cone's black liberation theology—argues that Jesus in womanist theology should be identified with the community of black women.[110] If God aims to liberate the oppressed—the least— then poor black women in their tridimensional oppression are often the least of the least. The particular experience of black women, though, has universal relevance because aspects of their identity (including race, class, and sex) are shared by other groups: "To speak of Black women's tri-dimensional reality, therefore, is not to speak of Black women exclusively for there is an implied universality which connects them with others."[111] "Locating" Jesus Christ and resultant christological reflection in the experience of poor Black women effectively underscores his solidarity with the "least." Jesus Christ in womanist theology identifies with the least, affirms the humanity of the least, inspires "active hope" in the struggle for liberation, and, through resurrection, underscores that oppression is not the end in itself.[112] Her perspective is not a glorification of oppression but a particular contextualization of the least, the nature of oppression, and the path to liberation.

Ada María Isasi-Díaz: *Jesucristo*

Like Grant, Ada María Isasi-Díaz seeks to contextualize christology in particular experiences of marginalization. In her articulation of mujerista theology, she centers Hispana/Latina daily experiences of oppression and struggles for what she calls liberation-fullness of life. These experiences and struggles lead her to ask: "Who is God for us who are pushed to the margins? How do we encounter God at the margins? Who is Christ for us, and how do we present Christ from the margins and to the margins?"[113] In response, she outlines some basic assumptions of her mujerista christology. To begin, her christology prioritizes praxis. Praxis, defined by Isasi-Díaz as experience and action, takes precedence over doctrine. She does not negate the role of doctrine or theology but claims that praxis shapes (and should shape) all doctrine and theology. She also stresses that her christology and all christologies arise out of particular contexts and concerns. There is no universal or singular christological formulation.[114] All christologies also emerge out of preexisting ethical perspectives that inform concepts of good and bad, and patterns of thinking and conscience. On this basis, she asserts that questions about Jesus and Jesus' action are not grounded in knowledge of Jesus but rather reveal aspects of our own ethical views. Despite ardent arguments to the contrary, "what we believe about Jesus is a mirror for our own consciences."[115] Finally, Isasi-Díaz's mujerista christology is rooted in the concept of *Jesucristo*, the merging of the two names Jesus and Christ.[116] This merging forgoes the hard distinction between Jesus, the historical person, and Christ, the official church teaching on Jesus. The "fusion" of the two names equally challenges the possibility of recovering the historical person *and* the necessity of making past christological formulations normative in the present. Instead, "the custom of folding into one word the name Jesus and the title Christ—*Jesucristo*—provides mujerista theology with the creative space needed to elaborate a Christology that responds to what Hispanas/Latinas believe about the message of Jesus of Nazareth."[117] This "creative space" facilitates constructive responses to the questions and concerns of contemporary communities. She emphasizes the necessity of constructive—as opposed to deconstructive—articulations: "the precariousness of our communities is such that we feel an urgency to create understandings that are useful in the work of liberation rather than thinking about what was conceptualized in the past."[118]

On the basis of these assumptions, Isasi-Díaz articulates key features of her christology. One feature is critique of the notion of the Kingdom of God and introduction of an alternative "kin-dom" of God founded on redefined, supportive, and deep personal relationships.[119] Isasi-Díaz argues that the Kingdom of God emphasizes a split between this world and the next; is used by the church to legitimize social, economic, and political power; and presents Jesus as a feared monarch with absolute power. This metaphor is no longer relevant to and seemingly foreign in the present mujerista context. Beyond lack of resonance, the metaphor is also dangerous because it "suggests an elitist, hierarchical, patriarchal structure that makes possible and supports all sorts of systemic oppressions."[120] In contrast, the kin-dom of God shifts from the political to the personal, and blends the notion of *shalom*—defined by her as fullness of life—with the idea of *familia*, family. Notably, Isasi-Díaz defines *familia* in a specific fashion: "The sense of familia that we have in mind when we talk about God's family, the kin-dom, is one in which a true sense of home exists, a sense of belonging and being safe to be and become fully oneself."[121] The kin-dom of God thus is characterized by duty, support, interdependence, and fullness of life. In the kin-dom, the response to the question "Who do you say that I am?" is "Jesus, you are *familia*." Jesus is a "faithful companion," a part of the *familia* in which people learn to love difference, to imagine differences as enriching, and to be open and welcoming to all.[122]

According to Isasi-Díaz, every person who commits to this vision of *familia* in action is considered to be a mediator of the kin-dom, someone who belongs to and extends the kin-dom by reconciling people with humanity and teaching people to love.[123] *Jesucristo* is a unique and essential mediator, as is every other person. No one person mediates in the same way, and thus every contribution is required. Referencing the theological anthropology of *imago Dei*, she point-edly describes other members of the kin-dom as "co-redeemers" along with *Jesucristo*.[124] This description is provocative; therefore, she clarifies that media-tion is akin to the role of discipleship.[125] Discipleship in the kin-dom of God is nonobjectifying, inclusive, and particularly concerned with the poor and oppressed. Moreover, discipleship is distinct depending on one's position in the kin-dom. For the oppressed, it entails the struggle to keep hope alive and realistic. For the oppressor, it entails a "radical conversion" that allows true solidarity and worthiness as members of the *familia*. *Jesucristo* works with the *familia* to sustain and give hope to the oppressed and struggles with the *familia* to help oppressors to understand their negative impact on others. *Jesucristo* begs, supports, cajoles, and, also, "in the midst of the ordinariness of life . . . simply walks with us."[126]

Isasi-Díaz adds that discipleship requires belief in the object of faith as well as acts of faith. While part of belief is loyalty to certain shared "values and understandings" that sustain and enhance links within the *familia*, she is keen to differentiate between commitment to values and "the mere transmission of what has been."[127] Connecting this to her description of all christologies as historical, she maintains that even shared values undergo a constant process of definition in light of present context(s). Contextual redefinition of values is the heart of pastoral theology and care, and it must be extended to other areas of theological reflection as well: "The difference is that in Mujerista theology we make concerns of the present operative not only at the level of pastoral care, at the level of im-plementation, but also at the level of understanding who God is and what God is about, that is, at the level of theology."[128]

In the process of making this claim, Isasi-Díaz admits that her contextual and praxis-oriented approach can be depicted as a "free-for-all" or "anything goes."[129] She contends, however, that it is not; it is a "responsible relativity" in which rel-ativity is defined not as lack of commitment but as awareness of the struggle for liberation-fullness of life. Her approach takes daily life and experiences seri-ously. Belief follows. Belief is vital yet always shaped by experience. The idea of responsible relativity is necessary because it undercuts "objective universals about the meaning of Christ that often have undergirded structures of oppression."[130] There is no singular or universal truth; subjectivity is always present in human articulations. Responsible relativity also means that her christology is not premised on a claim to a singular, ahistorical, decontextualized legitimacy. Isasi-Díaz underscores that there is no single answer to the question, "Who do you say that I am?"[131] Mujerista theology aims to ask deeper and deeper questions about christology and the relationship to God. This process of questioning and listening reveals "markers along the way"; it hints at who *Jesucristo* is and where he is present today but does not fix a singular meaning for all.

Drawing on her experiences with Mexican invocations of the Lady of Guadalupe, Isasi-Díaz's christology also emphasizes the necessity of having a personal and immediate connection with God: "It is unthinkable for us Hispanas/Latinas to conceive God in any other way than as a person with whom we have or can have a deep, intimate relationship."[132] This type of relationship is not manifest in conceptions of the Divine as a force of nature, energy, or power. It is only possible and only present in the personal and the person. Moreover, and of great significance, she argues that this personal divine is not only or singularly incarnated in Jesus; it is "incarnated time and again in Jesus, in Mary his mother, in the holy people of past generations that the church has proclaimed saints, in our ancestors, in the people who during their lives have worked for the benefit of that community."[133] It is ever-present and proximate. Citing the example of the prevalence of images and icons in Hispana/Latina daily life, she argues that these images underscore the closeness, ever presence, and personal relationship with the Divine. The images are not God but provide access to the Divine as "*alteri Christi*," other Christs. She juxtaposes this personal mujerista conception of God with the God commonly declared in churches, "an ominous God whose majesty and power confine Him [*sic*] to a pedestal."[134] In mujerista theology, God cannot be far removed, stern, or adored without expectation of response. Jesus as only God in this way is inaccessible; people are unable to relate to Jesus. In order to relate, Hispanas/Latinas seek *Jesucristo* in general and in particular *Jesucristo* on the cross. This *Jesucristo* is accessible and relatable because he is the one "who suffers as we suffer, who is vulnerable as we are vulnerable."[135] The shared experience of suffering allows a real and deep relationship with *Jesucristo*, a relationship that is closer than permitted by much church and theological doctrine.

Hybridity, Experience, Preference: Muslima Theological Reflections

While comparative analysis is not my primary focus, it is helpful to begin this section by explicitly highlighting some areas of resonance among Islamic feminist perspectives on the Qur'an and Christian feminist, womanist, and mujerista perspectives on Jesus Christ. These areas of resonance underscore the appropriateness and utility of the analogical starting point of the Qur'an and Jesus Christ. I have already noted the underlying theological problematic introduced by a particular and limited revelation, or self-disclosure, of the Divine in the world. In Islamic feminism, this problematic leads to questions about the status of the Qur'anic revelation, in particular, its relationship to God, to other revelation, and to particular contexts (inclusive of the patriarchal context of original revelation and contemporary contexts). In Christian discourse, the problematic leads to christological discussions about the divinity and humanity of Jesus Christ, as well as concerns about the maleness of Jesus and the ways in which that maleness has been symbolically and institutionally privileged. The language of divinity and humanity is not organic to Islamic thought, but the concern is analogous. It is a concern over male-centered, patriarchal, and androcentric aspects of divine revelation/self-disclosure.

Another clear area of resonance is that these aspects—the male-centered, patriarchal, and androcentric verses of the Qur'an and the male form of Jesus Christ—are wielded against women in both traditions. They are granted deep theological and institutional significance, and thereby used to relegate women to mediated relationships with God and hierarchical relationships with men. Women in both traditions highlight the extent of this relegation, and its dire impact on women's daily lives and participation in the traditions. This impact leads scholars and theologians to ask challenging questions about the revelation/self-disclosure of God, about God, and about the historical development of Islamic and Christian traditions. It is easy, for example, to discern a similar motivation in Ruether's question about whether a male savior can save women and Hidayatullah's questioning about whether the Qur'an aligns with contemporary ideas of justice and egalitarianism. While scholars differ in the degree to which they press these questions and in the answers they offer, they all engage such questions and demonstrate an awareness that these questions—even the very difficult, faith-challenging ones—must be asked in order to contest male dominance and normativity in both traditions.

Contestation of male dominance and normativity is facilitated by the fact that the Qur'an and Jesus Christ also offer abundant resources related to egalitarianism and justice. Islamic and Christian theologians, therefore, seek to prioritize and reclaim these parts of their traditions. There are resources to be reclaimed. The challenge presented in both traditions is to develop strategies for doing so that are effective, rooted, and responsive to diverse contexts. Strategies must critically deconstruct patriarchal traditions, interpretations, and practices, and also constructively articulate new egalitarian versions thereof. Some scholars do so by claiming corruption and the need for a return to more legitimate understandings of the Qur'an and Jesus (for example, Barlas and Ruether), while others advocate for recognition of the dynamic roles context and experience have played and should play in articulating tradition (for example, wadud, Seedat, Kwok, and Grant).

While these areas of resonance underscore the validity of starting with the Qur'an and Jesus in comparative feminist theology, there are of course areas of dissonance as well. These include distinctions between a revelation in "word" form and a disclosure in human form (incarnation); and between an intimate, yet ontologically disparate God and a personal God. The dissonances also relate to diverse sources and interpretative methods, and the ways in which authority is defined and institutionalized. There is no complete parity. In fact, complete parity would eradicate the shades and highlights that truly enable the comparative theological project. There are meaningful overlaps, and there are meaningful ruptures and disconnects as well. It is precisely the combination that leads to insights, questions, and strategies. It is to this constructive theological exploration that I now turn.

Can the Qur'an lead to a just and egalitarian society? In conversation with Ruether's question "Can a male savior save women?," I pose this question as a pointed reframing and specification of contemporary Islamic feminist and Muslima debates on the status and nature of the Qur'an as Word of God. This question surfaces the theological, contextual, and practical complexity of the Qur'an. It acknowledges that the Qur'an has some verses that can be understood as androcentric, patriarchal, or primarily addressed to men. The Qur'an simultaneously contains a vast number of verses that speak of equality, justice, and human dignity. This question also raises the issue of contextualization, including considerations of the original context of revelation and the relevance of the Qur'an to other contexts. The Qur'an is rooted in and responsive to the original context of revelation, seventh-century Arabia. The Qur'an also has played and continues to play a role in other contexts, including our own. This question also acknowledges that the Qur'an shapes—negatively and positively—the lives of Muslim women. It is at times invoked to limit rights and status, yet at others to emphasize equality before God and to impel the quest for justice. At stake, then, is not whether the Qur'an has any egalitarian content. It has plenty. At stake is how to grapple with nonegalitarian aspects of the Qur'an as Word of God, nonegalitarian aspects whose "mere existence"—not quantity—is theologically and ethically troubling.[136] At stake is how to claim authority for egalitarian interpretations in light of centuries of female exclusion and marginalization in Qur'anic exegesis. At stake is whether the Qur'an alone is sufficient to bar nonegalitarian interpretations and practices.

The complex nature of the Qur'an—in content, context, and impact—triggers the interpretative process and results in the diversity of perspectives discussed earlier in this chapter. Some scholars answer the question "Can the Qur'an lead to a just and egalitarian society?" by asserting that the true egalitarian Qur'an can be reclaimed despite the dominance and corruption of patriarchal interpretations (Barlas). Others highlight the primacy of historical analysis as a way of understanding and limiting androcentric and patriarchal aspects of the text (Bauer). Some scholars differentiate between universal/general egalitarian prescriptions and specific contextual descriptions (wadud). Others prioritize egalitarian

Qur'anic principles as the essential, enduring message. Some view the Qur'anic text as a sufficient and authoritative resource for contemporary egalitarianism. Others advocate for the necessity of engaging additional sources as well.

Conspicuously, these diverse responses are all attempts to explain the complexity of the Qur'an. Every interpretation—including my own—is an attempt to sort, clarify, and even simplify challenges and tensions spawned by inherent Qur'anic complexity. While espousing divergent conclusions, both Barlas and Hidayatullah, for example, engage in this same process. Barlas does so by asserting that the Qur'an is unequivocally egalitarian. Hidayatullah does so by arguing that the Qur'an does not privilege egalitarianism and therefore does not accord with contemporary ideas of equality and justice. Neither one of these perspectives is a simple description of Qur'anic content or impact; they are interpretations, which, in their own ways, skillfully and pragmatically negotiate tensions within the text, between text and contexts, and between texts and the Divine.

My primary intention in making this observation is not critique. Rather, I aim to foreground the fact that while we try diligently and repeatedly to do so, it is not so easy to sort out the Qur'an. The complexity seems inherent. Here, it is helpful to engage with Kwok's notion of the hybridity of Jesus Christ. Kwok introduces this concept in conversation with other feminist approaches that seek to recover an uncorrupted understanding of Jesus. In contrast, she argues that there is no single, core, or original understanding of Jesus that can be recovered. Her argument is not acquiescence to patriarchal christologies but a theological assertion about the continuously provocative nature of incarnation. The incarnation for Kwok can never be completely explained or pinned down. Jesus Christ is never simply human or simply divine. Jesus Christ is always both, always hybrid. Moreover, Jesus as hybrid becomes the contact zone between humans and the Divine, a contact zone characterized by fruitful ambiguity.

The Qur'an is similarly hybrid, in its complexities, in its merging of divine and worldly, and in its function as a relational access point between humans and the Divine. The Qur'an is divine *and* of this world. It is universal *and* revealed in response to a particular context. It is egalitarian *and* marked with androcentrism and patriarchy.[137] It is intimately related to God *and* it is not God or all of God's revelation. The Qur'an is invoked to oppress women *and* it is a sustaining, hope-inspiring relational link between many women and God. The Qur'an is both/and in all these circumstances.

So, what does this mean? What are the implications of Qur'anic hybridity for human engagement with the Qur'an? To begin, Qur'anic hybridity accounts for the ways in which many people, including many Muslim women, relate to the Qur'an. The Qur'an is a primary point of contact and communication with God. This contact is facilitated through engagement with the content of the Qur'an (interpretation), as well as through embodied ritual practices, such as prayer (*salat*) and recitation, which punctuate the lives of many Muslims. The Qur'an is a locus of relationship with God. It is not the only point of relationship, but it is a central and pervasive one. The fact that the Qur'an is a point of relational contact, however, does not mean contact is always tranquil or easy. The hybrid nature of the Qur'an often ensures it will not be easy at all. I, for example, am drawn into the Qur'an by its beauty and appeals to justice, while simultaneously sidelined by historical references and troubled by verses that describe hierarchical violence and exclusivism. I am pulled in, pulled aside, and pulled back. I meet the Qur'an in its both/and-ness, in its complexity and hybridity.

It is tempting to assign any experience of tension or concern in relation to the Qur'an to deficiencies in human interpretation or piety. If we experience part of the Qur'an as problematic, then this is explained by our lack of understanding, commitment, or religiosity. Without completely ruling out these options (surely humans can fail to understand and can have levels of religious commitment), they are not the sole explanations for experiences of tension. Some of the tension is essential and purposeful; tension perpetuates an enduring and dynamic relationship. Too much tension—or only tension—would certainly sever the relationship between God and humans. However, no tension would render the relationship flat and static, if not dead. In the former, there would be no entrance points for human engagement with the Divine; nothing in the Qur'an would entice, attract, or resonate. In the latter, there would be no engagement, just confirmation; nothing would provoke the thought, reflection, and discernment to which the Qur'an repeatedly calls humans (e.g., Q 2:44, 2:164, 2:219, 2:242, 3:65, 5:58, 7:169, 10:16, 10:24, 12:109, 13:3, 16:11, 20:128, 39:42, 40:67, and 59:21, among many others).

Thought, reflection, and discernment triggered by experiences of tension and hybridity sustain and facilitate engagement across contexts and amid diversity. Theologically, this is how the Qur'an continues to "speak" into the world, how it remains relevant, how it remains alive and pulsating in the hearts/minds (*sudur*) of humans. It is for these reasons that Kwok refers to theological hybridity as "fruitful ambiguity." Notably, yet not surprisingly, Kwok's language aligns with wadud's when she describes the "sublime ambiguity" of the Qur'an that is productively and continuously encountered in a combination of critical response and faithful reverence. Ambiguity is the soil in which the human–Divine relationship is planted, tended, and transformed. The Qur'an is thus a dynamic site of engagement, not simply a fixed disclosure or dictation of norms and expectations.[138] It is a site of unending engagement characterized by attraction, tension, curiosity, challenge, clarity, struggle, reconsideration, return, and repetition of this cycle. It is a site of relationship.

What is the impact of this description of the Qur'an and Qur'anic hy-bridity on feminist interpretations of the Qur'an? Theological hybridity is the prompting cause for interpretation. It is that which incites and invites humans to continuously engage and re-engage with the Qur'an. Therefore, interpretation is always necessary *and* never complete. If the Qur'an is a site of unending engage-ment, then reification of any single interpretation or interpretative approach is a problem. Reification seeks to permanently corral Qur'anic hybridity and set parameters on the human–Divine relationship. Reification of nonegalitarian in-terpretation is widely critiqued by contemporary Islamic feminist interpreters.[139] Hybridity, however, also pushes us to be cautious of reification within egalitarian interpretations. Is there only one correct egalitarian interpretation of the Qur'an? Is there only one appropriate or effective interpretative approach? The insights of existing contributions—which are clearly not all the same—demonstrate that this is not the case. I do not have to agree with or adopt every interpretation or method to appreciate the ways in which they are responses to various aspects of Qur'anic hybridity. One may not agree with Hidayatullah's assessment that there is no way to successfully privilege egalitarian content over hierarchical content in the Qur'an. It is easy, though, to appreciate the theological genesis of her concerns and questions about the coexistence of both genres of content in the Qur'an. Her response, moreover, can lead other interpreters to return to the Qur'an and ask new questions in new ways. It can contribute to and foster engagement with the Qur'an. Rather than vying to disclose the singular reality of the Qur'an, diverse egalitarian interpretations can be reframed as dynamic and particular responses to facets of Qur'anic hybridity.

Qur'anic hybridity also creates new freedom and possibilities for egalitarian interpretations. Isasi-Díaz illustrates this with the idea of *Jesucristo*. *Jesucristo* is a refusal to relinquish incarnational hybridity that opens a creative space in which mujerista theologians can think about Jesus Christ in new ways without being confined to historical analysis alone *or* blind replication of tradition. Kwok echoes this position when she claims that the conceptualization of Jesus Christ as hybrid subverts theological hegemonies *and* the "manhunt" for Jesus. Hybridity presents intermediary possibilities. It does this by refusing to privilege historical meaning or accumulated tradition. With the Qur'an, historical meaning and tra-dition are responses to aspects of Qur'anic hybridity, but they are not the *only* possible or legitimate responses.

One concrete way to claim the creative space in which to explore Qur'anic hybridity is through feminist analyses of actual tradition. "Islamic tradition" is often invoked (deployed) with great zeal and little reference to specific con-tent. There is much to be gained by actually studying traditional interpretations of the Qur'an (*tafsir*). One thing gained is awareness of multiplicity; there are multiple, sometimes divergent, interpretations even among scholars that would be considered part of the same mythologically singular Islamic tradition. As Chaudhry aptly demonstrates in her survey of exegesis on Qur'an 4:34, however, multiplicity does not necessarily encompass egalitarian interpretations. Precolonial exegetes produced diverse interpretations, but their interpretations nevertheless adhered to a shared patriarchal cosmology.[140] This type of analysis does not necessarily recover or reclaim egalitarian precedent within the interpretative tradition. It does not recast "tradition" as egalitarian. The value of this type of analysis is it frees us from the illusion of a consistent and singular tradition, and thereby equips us to effectively challenge nondescript appeals to tradition.

Another benefit is this type of analysis reveals the assumptions interpreters bring to the interpretative process. Chaudhry's survey discloses the central fixations of precolonial interpreters in relation to Qur'an 4:34, such as the procedure of disciplining, extent of discipline, and potential male liability in the case of injury or death of a woman.[141] It also reveals glaring areas of interpretative silence; interpreters did not question, for example, the patriarchal family structure nor dwell on the well-being of women. From fixations and silences, we garner a sense of their latent and explicit assumptions. Chaudhry also juxtaposes precolonial and postcolonial exegeses, highlighting the postcolonial egalitarian cosmology. Postcolonial interpretation demonstrates a broader range of diversity in conclusions and methods, and this broader range results from the *tension* between some Qur'anic content and the egalitarian cosmology.[142]

Ali's work on marriage is similarly effective in revealing the underlying assumptions and infrastructure of marital law.[143] By surveying classical legal tradition, she demonstrates that marriage is attached to concepts of ownership and payment for sexual access. Ali's analysis adds an additional dimension. In its highlighting of underlying assumptions, it challenges the appropriateness of emphasizing seemingly women-friendly aspects of traditional law, such as sole financial responsibility of men, in current contexts. "Women-friendly" laws can reinscribe patriarchy, androcentrism, and assumptions about marriage that are—to borrow Isasi-Díaz's terminology—"foreign" to our current contexts. Significantly, this type of analysis maintains the importance of tradition and acknowledges the ongoing impact of tradition. Qur'anic hybridity is not a call to dismiss tradition but to problematize the assumption that tradition is, should be, or can be merely replicated over time.

Reified claims to the only accurate interpretation and invocations of "Islamic tradition" are ways to assert authority. Such deployment of authority occurs in both nonegalitarian and egalitarian interpretations. In the latter, it is often linked with pragmatic concerns about change, equality, and survival. It is assumed that egalitarian change is more likely to occur—and power more likely to be relinquished—if supported by claims to the *only* authoritative interpretation or tradition. Such claims, though, reinscribe a conception of authority that has never privileged and marginally included women. I am deeply concerned with pragmatic realities on the ground and with effective strategies for change. In emphasizing Qur'anic hybridity, though, I am challenging the effectiveness of appeals to a singular interpretation and mythological tradition, whether egalitarian or nonegalitarian. I am also advocating that existing and actual tradition be engaged not solely as a quest for egalitarian precedent.[144] We will find egalitarian precedent along the way, but egalitarian precedent in content does not validate our current agency and authority to engage Qur'anic hybridity. Precedent is a reference to someone else's agency, authority, and engagement. Qur'anic hybridity, therefore, compels me to consider that existing notions of authority must be redefined, reimagined, and broadened in order to attend simultaneously to practical concerns, interpretative diversity, and theological Qur'anic complexity. How might we reimagine authority in this way? And how can a reimagined authority be authoritative?

One approach increasingly apparent among Islamic feminist and Muslima interpreters is foregrounding the role of human experience in shaping interpretation. Foregrounding contextually defined human experience potentially destabilizes the heavy emphasis placed on precedent and transhistorical replication of tradition. If precedent is shown to be significantly shaped by human experience, this has the promise of at least loosening the grip of male-dominated interpretations. Barlas and wadud have long argued that all interpretation is contextual, meaning it arises out of the "prior text" of the interpreter and the interaction of that "prior text" with the actual text of the Qur'an.[145] wadud, moreover, notes the silence and silencing of women's voices in interpretation of the Qur'an. This is one of the motivations for her early exegesis.[146] In her critique of existing egalitarian interpretations, Hidayatullah broaches experience; she argues that interpreters should acknowledge that their contemporary notions of equality and justice—which in her, view do not align with Qur'anic notions of equality and justice—shape their interpretations and interpretative goals. Without agreeing holistically with her juxtaposition of contemporary and Qur'anic notions of equality and justice, she is accurate that experience is invoked. The fact that some interpreters do not explicitly state this in their own work simply underscores the existing and dominant construct of authority. Likely, they are all aware experience is in play; explicitly acknowledging how experience shapes their interpretations, however, may not be deemed authoritative and therefore not effective.

Shaikh's *tafsir* of praxis explores concrete examples of how women's experience substantially shapes their interpretation of the Qur'an.[147] Her research among battered women demonstrates that the actual experience of violence can preclude

acceptance of interpretations permitting any degree of symbolic or physical violence against women. Similarly, in her later reflections on Qur'an 4:34, wadud
arrives at the point of saying "no" to the literal and explicit meaning of the text
on the basis of her knowledge about the impact of physical abuse on women.[148]
In both of these cases, it is not experience alone that leads to rejection and "no."
Experience is coupled with references to a *relationship* with the Divine; together,
the theological and experiential diverge from some content in the Qur'an.[149] This
brings us back to Seedat's provocative question. Describing the Qur'anic text as
"generative" and "in the process of . . . a continuous and discursive becoming,"
she asks if human experience can abrogate the Qur'an.[150] Human experience *is*
a factor in interpretation. Human experience *does* lead to rejection of certain
interpretations of the Qur'an. Seedat, however, is asking something more. She is
asking whether this is legitimate and authoritative.

Ruether, Kwok, Grant, and Isasi-Díaz all engage an analogous problem of
male-centered authority in Christian thought. To this problem, they propose
the same solution; they turn to human experience. They highlight the role of
human experience in the development, codification, and adaptation of religious
traditions; human experience is always in play in the interpretative process, since
interpretation is conducted by human beings. Moreover, as is evident in Ruether's
survey of the development of patriarchal christologies, these theologians contend
that men have been the primary interpreters of tradition, and therefore male experience has shaped the tradition. Women's experience has been marginalized
and excluded from consideration. In addition to exclusion of female experience,
male experience has been presented as universal and generalizable to all humans.
Ruether, Kwok, Grant, and Isasi-Díaz consequently center female experience to
expose masked and universalized male experience. They also center female experience because it is the way traditions, teachings, and practices remain relevant and
responsive to women in diverse contexts. Kwok, Grant, and Isasi-Díaz go one step
further. They argue that experience is the criterion for assessing the theological
validity of any teaching and practice. Kwok, for example, states that teachings
on the passion and suffering of Jesus Christ must be assessed in light of the experience of people who actually suffer. Grant and other womanist theologians
debate the meaning of this suffering and ways it may glorify oppression of Black
women.[151] When Isasi-Díaz rejects the notion of "kingdom" in favor of the "kin-
dom," she is similarly invoking experience as a measure of authority and legitimacy. Isasi-Díaz is explicit about this when she argues that ethical perspectives
and praxis preexist and shape theological doctrine.

Experience plays a role in interpretation. Experience shapes what we see, ask,
and emphasize in the Qur'an. We cannot but bring ourselves to the process; no
interpreter has ever avoided doing so. Experience also leads us to struggle with

particular aspects of the Qur'an. The experience of struggle is not problematic. It is the nature of Qur'an hybridity, the nature of the relationship producing and sustaining revelation. Such revelation is responsive, relevant, and challenging. It is not simply confirmation. It is a fact that we *do* use experience in interpretation. I argue, however, that we *should* use experience because experience is legitimate and authoritative on theological and practical grounds.

The Qur'an itself affirms the theological authority of human experience. As many Muslim exegetes—including Islamic feminist and Muslima interpreters—observe, the Qur'an is God's Word, God's revelation, but it is not the entirety of God's revelation. Two passages of the Qur'an are often cited as clear indication that divine revelation not only extends beyond the Qur'anic text but that it also can never be exhausted. Qur'an 31:27 states: "And if all the trees on earth were pens and the sea, with seven other seas added, the words of God would not be exhausted. Indeed, God is the Mighty, the Wise." With a similar analogy, Qur'an 18:109 states: "Say: If the sea were ink for the words of my Sustainer, the sea would be exhausted before the words of my Sustainer, even if we added another one like the first to help." The revelation of God is abundant, far beyond anything humans can encompass or confine. Interpreters reference the abundance of revelation to emphasize the greatness and incomparability of God and to challenge the view of the Qur'an as fixed and closed. wadud, for example, uses this as the basis for her descriptions of the Qur'an as a window, a process, and an ethical trajectory pointing beyond the closed text.[152] Assertion of the abundance of revelation leads us to ask where we encounter other parts of God's revelation. As discussed in the preceding chapter, one other locus of divine revelation is found in the manifestation of religious diversity, that is, among other communities of revelation.

Another central locus of revelation, which is directly pertinent to the authoritativeness of experience, is the natural world, including humans. The Qur'an ubiquitously—as with the seas and trees in Surah Luqman and Surah al-Kahf—directs us to reflect on the natural world to gain accurate insight and understanding. Central theological assertions of the Qur'an are explained by reference to knowledge we gain from our experiences in the natural world. The Qur'anic verses (*ayat*) point us to the natural signs (*ayat*) in order to clarify understanding and foster conviction. In both cases, the *ayat* are intentional signs of God that, when reflected on and considered, lead to deeper understanding of God, our relationships with God, and our relationships with other aspects of the created world. The assertion that the Qur'an wants us to reflect on the creation and that we can learn from this sort of extra-Qur'anic, yet Qur'anically mandated, reflection is not particularly novel. What is novel is to take it seriously and draw out the theological-hermeneutical implications.

One such implication is we learn from our human experience in the world, and therefore worldly experience is not antithetical to or rendered redundant by the rest of God's revelation. It is a complementary and necessary source of insight. Qur'an 30:20–22 makes this wondrously clear when it invokes humans as signs of God: "One of God's signs (*ayat*) is that God created you from dust and—lo and behold!—you became human and scattered far and wide. Another of God's signs (*ayat*) is that God created spouses from among yourselves for you to live with in tranquility. God ordained love and kindness between you. There truly are signs (*ayat*) in this for those who reflect. Another of God's signs (*ayat*) is the creation of the heavens and earth, and the diversity of your languages and colors. There truly are signs (*ayat*) in this for those who know."

The fact that human experience is a locus of God's signs does not automatically, however, validate every action, belief, or desire of human beings. The Qur'an critiques certain human behaviors, such as forgetfulness, hastiness, and arrogance (e.g., Q 2:44, 11:9, 18:24, 39:8, 17:11, 17:83, 29:39, 40:35, 71:7). While acknowledging these behaviors, the Qur'an does not present them as foundational to human nature. I return to theological anthropology in detail later in this book, but at this juncture it is essential to introduce the intimate interconnection between human nature (*fitra*), true knowledge, and God-consciousness (*taqwa*).

The Qur'an positively values the shared human nature with which all people are created (*fitra*). Qur'an 30:30 instructs humans to align themselves with this *fitra*: "So as one of pure faith, stand firm and true in your devotion to religion (*din*). This is the natural disposition (*fitra*) God instilled in humankind. There is no altering God's creation." The significance of this appeal to *fitra* is amplified when contextualized with the two preceding verses (Q 30:28–29). Qur'an 30:28 invokes human experience—"God gives you an example from your own lives"— and indicates that reflection on experience leads to knowledge and understanding of God's signs (*ayat*).[153] Qur'an 30:29 next references the reality of less than favorable human behaviors, specifically the act of following "desires without knowledge."[154] Then, comes the verse about *fitra*. The Qur'an calls people to their own experience to gain *reliable* knowledge about God's signs (*ayat*), recognizes that not all people have this knowledge and that some stray by following desires, and then redirects people back to their essential human nature in juxtaposition to the mere following of "desires without knowledge." These three Qur'anic *ayat* encapsulate my argument about the value and authority of human experience.

Basic human nature is also linked with God-consciousness (*taqwa*). Humans are described as being created with knowledge of God, and knowledge of the distinction between God-consciousness (*taqwa*) and evil: "By the soul (*nafs*) and how God formed it and inspired it [to know] its own rebellion and God-consciousness (*taqwa*)! The one who causes it to grow in purity succeeds and the one who buries it fails" (Q 91:7–10). This verse is striking because *taqwa* is the central standard of moral evaluation in the Qur'an: "People, We created you all from a single man and a single woman and made you into races and tribes so that you should recognize one another. In God's eyes, the most honored of you are the ones most conscious of God (*atqakum*). God is all knowing, all aware" (Q 49:13). Humans are described as having a God-conscious *nafs* (soul). Notably, Qur'an 91:10 indicates that this God-conscious *nafs* can be buried. Buried is a vivid description. Humans can cover up or obscure their basic human nature, they can engage in behaviors based on whims and desires, but they cannot permanently eradicate this *fitra*. If this type of *fitra* and *nafs* are asserted, then human experience is of utmost relevance to Qur'anic interpretation. It is a source of knowledge, and accurate, reliable knowledge at that. The charge is to differentiate between true, God-conscious knowledge based on and confirmed by human experience and its alignment with *taqwa*, and human desires devoid of such knowledge. To conflate the two—as Qur'an 30:29 indicates—is to do "wrong."

Qur'an 30:28 also relates directly to the practical authority of human experience. The verse exemplifies the Qur'anic appeal to natural signs (*ayat*), specifically in human experience. However, the specific experience to which it appeals is, today, contextually and ethically problematic. The full verse states: "God gives you an example from your own lives. Do you let those whom your right hand possesses be equal partners in the wealth which We have given you? Do you fear them as you fear each other? Thus, do We detail Our signs (*ayat*) for those who reason." The phrase "those whom your right hand possesses" generally refers to slaves, and slavery was a common practice in seventh-century Arabia. The Qur'an did not explicitly condemn or halt the practice, although it is routinely argued that the Qur'an set in motion a progressive eradication of slavery. Today, this experiential reference no longer functions; it no longer produces the same understanding it did in the original context of revelation. I am aware that this verse uses the example of slavery to elucidate the futility of worshipping anything alongside of God. I meet the verse with this historical and discursive awareness. Yet, this is not the only thing with which I encounter this verse. I also encounter it with my contemporary context and experiences that inform me and form me to know the reprehensibility of slavery.

This verse, therefore, accentuates important considerations related to the authority of human experience. It shows that human experience leads to understanding only if the referenced experiences are tangible, recognized, and relevant. References are not made to imagined, idealized, or prescribed experiences but to actual experiences. Moreover, what counts as tangible, recognized, and relevant is closely tied to context. If understanding is the objective, then diverse, changing experiences will need to be considered in order for the revelation to remain meaningful for people in diverse contexts. As Grant and Isasi-Díaz argue, this is the only way in which revelation stays pertinent throughout time. As a theologian, I am inclined to assert value and truth in revelation (including the Qur'an). But, as a practical matter, if revelation—no matter how true or valuable or how directly connected to God—has no bearing on the lived reality of people, if it answers none of their questions, if it responds to none of their fears and worries, if it offers no hope, if it speaks in a form that cannot heard, then that revelation is dead. Did not the first hearers of the Qur'an have to experience it as speaking to them, their context, fears, and hopes? Is this not why the Qur'an bears marks of its direct responsiveness to that historical context? The question is: How does revelatory responsiveness continue in different times and contexts, times and contexts in which some original experiential references can be intellectually understood but no longer "function" in the same way? Connecting interpretation to and grounding it in real and diverse human experience is one way the text can continue to function.

Beyond theological relevance, another reason for the authority of human experience in the process of interpretation is that if we fail to attend to real human experience—not just fabricated, idealized notions of what experience humans *should* have—we will most certainly perpetrate injustice. We can interpret verses related to women, gender, and marriage in a multiplicity of ways, but if we do not involve diverse women in that process, the interpretations at best will be irrelevant and at worse oppressive. When Isasi-Díaz argues that theology and interpretations should be "useful" like pastoral theology, this is what she is proposing. Pastoral theology attends directly to lived experiences, not just doctrine formulated apart from (most) human experience. Grant, in her critiques of even other feminist theologians, pushes this further and underscores the necessity of paying attention to intersectional experience. It is not enough to attend to women's experience; we also must recognize not all women have the same experience. Their experience is shaped by biological sex and gender but also by race and class.

There does exist aversion to deeply considering actual human experience, especially the experiences of women. There are many conversations about what women *should* be doing and feeling, about how they *should* conform themselves to various Qur'anic dictates and interpretations. Failure to conform or lack of comfort in conforming is chalked up to lack of religious commitment. There is not enough consideration of how people are actually impacted, of what they actually experience. How is revelation inscribed onto bodies? Do we care about those bodies? It seems that a deep fear of human-ness encroaching on Qur'anic textual authority ironically stifles expressions of the Qur'an's humaneness. The two sites of revelation—the Qur'an and the human creation—are often pitted against each other. In conversation with Christian feminist, womanist, and mujerista theologians, this leads me to wonder if there something about the form of Qur'anic revelation that—despite ubiquitous redirection to human experience—leads interpreters to prioritize and singularize the closed, textual corpus over the actual *corpus*, the actual body. Does the revelation in "word" form create blind spots that are not as evident in revelation or disclosure in body form, incarnation? I am not making the facile argument that incarnation in Christian theology automatically leads to a greater appreciation of embodied experience. Certainly, women's experience and bodies have not been acknowledged or valued. Ruether, Kwok, Grant, and Isasi-Díaz's arguments testify to this. There does, though, seem to be a greater baseline theological sensitivity to the authority of experience in the flesh. There are reasons to grant authority to embodied experience in Islamic interpretations as well (for example, *fitra, taqwa*, and natural *ayat*), yet these do appear to be subjugated to textual Qur'anic authority. Islamic feminist and Muslima interpreters therefore are faced with a different sort of challenge. We have to convince people that bodies matter. We also have to convince people that female bodies matter. And again, we have to convince people that diverse female bodies matter. These steps are absolutely necessary for pragmatic egalitarian change on the ground. We can articulate egalitarian interpretations of the Qur'an. We should continue to do this. But this is not the only thing that needs to happen. We need to foster theological-ethical investment in the authority of experience and concern for actual bodies. One of the ways to do this is by *explicitly* stating that it is what we are doing and couching that move in theological and practical rationales. We will have to claim this authority. It will not just be granted. However, once we claim it, its authoritativeness will become clear because it will lead to interpretations that are pointedly relevant, responsive, and aligned with and productive of God-consciousness (*taqwa*).

When we claim the authority of human embodied experience, though, the issue of relativism does arise. If experience matters, and every individual has experience, then are all experiences equally authoritative? When we open up the authority of experience, it will most certainly become an avenue by which some try to assert that their experience is definitive and more important. Those with power will seek to prioritize and universalize their own experiences. How can we avoid this becoming another tool of oppression and injustice, never mind relativism? Isasi-Díaz addresses this concern, acknowledging that the turn to contextual experience can be depicted as a "free for all." She responds that experiential contextualization is not relativism but a "responsible relativity" that prioritizes the struggle for liberation-fullness of life, and simultaneously challenges singular, supposedly universal christologies invoked in the service of oppression.[155] I am intrigued by her notion of "responsible relativity," and I am also inclined to further define it. Yes, experience does challenge singular, ahistorical depictions of tradition. And, yes, it is vital to foreground liberation as a criterion of assessment. But, are there experiences that should carry more authority in the quest for justice, liberation, and equality? This leads directly to Grant's discussion of privileging or centering some experiences when articulating interpretations of Jesus Christ. She concurs with Isasi-Díaz, and she goes further to argue for prioritizing the experiences of the "outkast" or "the least," those who are most vulnerable and oppressed in a society.[156] In womanist theology, she equates the outkast and the least with poor Black women, who experience tridimensional oppression based on sex, race, and class. Notably, she argues that this is not an arbitrary privileging; the tridimensional experience of poor black women intersects with aspects of other people's experiences of oppression and thus is germane beyond poor black women alone.

The language of "the least" is somewhat particular to Christian discourse. Nevertheless, is it possible to identify such a preference that should direct egalitarian Qur'anic interpretation? It is possible and essential. Qur'anic preference is of two irrelated varieties. The first is that interpretation should give authoritative preference to the experiences of the people impacted by interpretations of the Qur'an. For example, if the Qur'an discusses women, then the experiences of actual and diverse women should be referenced and placed in conversation with the Qur'anic text. Those experiences should play a role in shaping interpretation to avoid irrelevance and injustice. This should be the case in Qur'anic references to more neutral biological female experiences, such as menstruation and pregnancy. It should certainly be the case when women are on the receiving end of ethically troubling actions, such as found in Qur'an 4:34.

The second way in which some experience is given authoritative preference is that, if we view God as just and concerned with all of humanity, then we should pay particular attention to the experiences of groups of people who are often dehumanized and marginalized, those who are vulnerable. The Qur'an, as is well known, routinely refers to a variety of such groups of people, including women, orphans, travelers, the poor, the hungry, and slaves.[157] Of great significance is the fact that the Qur'an does not just reference these populations but also defines God-consciousness (*taqwa*)—that is, the central standard of moral evaluation—in terms of the treatment of people from among these populations. Qur'an 2:177 describes true goodness and God-consciousness as manifest in the giving of wealth to "orphans, the needy, travelers and beggars, and to liberate those in bondage."[158] If *taqwa* is assessed in light of the way a person treats these vulnerable and marginalized populations, then should not our interpretations also be held to a similar standard? Our interpretations should align with *taqwa* and produce *taqwa* in society. If they do not, if they further marginalize the marginalized—those whom the South African Muslim liberation theologian Farid Esack refers to as the *mustad'af*, the disempowered—then we must question their authority.[159] Significantly, the groups identified as marginalized may change over time and place. Many of the Qur'anic groupings still hold true in our contemporary context, although some have been redefined or expanded. "Travelers", for instance, today should be read as inclusive of refugees. Slavery continues in a variety of forms, including indentured servitude, sex trafficking, and even the bondage of debt.

While I am arguing for this authoritative preference in experience, I acknowledge that the Qur'an does at times talk directly to an audience of the socially powerful, including men. wadud argues that the Qur'an addresses the powerful directly to ensure justice by compelling them to modify their behavior.[160] I am inclined to agree with wadud's analysis. However, I am not entirely at ease with or willing to equate "talking about" with "talking to," especially when it comes to experience. In this vein, I remain captivated and challenged by Grant's question of why the divine revelation had to play patriarchal games. Even with this concern, though, I do not feel the Qur'an reinscribes a static and necessary system of patriarchy. It does respond to that system. It does, at times, even use that system to communicate tangibly. But, there is simply too much egalitarian content to argue that the Qur'an intended to simplistically reinscribe and confirm the status quo of power relations, even a benevolent patriarchy or model of just rule.

In closing this chapter, I want to return to Qur'an 30:28, the verse that authoritatively elevates human experience as a sign of God while simultaneously using the example of slavery. I already acknowledged that I encounter this verse as ethically problematic, even though I am intellectually aware of its original meaning. What I want to draw attention to at this point is that understandings of the specific experiences referenced in the Qur'an can ethically shift over time and context. Interpreters must decide how to engage parts of the Qur'an that are no longer (not?) ethically neutral. Such verses can be historicized and contextualized. But, when coupled with contemporary lived, human experience, they can also be used—can "function"—in another crucial way. To further explore this, I turn to a more central example, Qur'an 4:34, and its reference to "hitting."[161]

Qur'an 4:34 is the focus of extensive interpretative efforts among Islamic feminist and Muslima scholars. As Chaudhry outlines, contemporary strategies for grappling with this verse include historical contextualization; identifying the verse as descriptive, not prescriptive; contrasting this verse with Prophet Muhammad's statements and behaviors; limiting the meaning of the verb *daraba* (literally, to hit) to symbolic, nonharmful action in highly specific situations; and linguistic reinterpretation of the verb *daraba* to move away from the literal meaning "to hit."[162] In her more recent revisiting of Qur'an 4:34, wadud eloquently traces developments in the interpretation of this verse through the phrasing of "Yes," "Yes, but," "Perhaps not," and "No."[163] "Yes" refers to the context of revelation and the simple embrace the idea of men being authorized to hit women. "Yes, but" refers to juridical interpretations that state that *daraba* means to hit but then limit the situations in which this is permitted and the form of the hitting. "Perhaps not" refers to modern interpretations that move away from the literal meaning of the word, defining *daraba* in new ways. "No" is wadud's conscientious pause and rejection of the implementation of the verse in any shape or form. She does not reject this verse as part of the Qur'anic revelation but insists its literal meaning and implementation run contrary to the spirit of the Qur'an.

Like wadud, I am compelled to say "no" to this verse. I am firmly "no." No to any form, any degree, any rationale. I refuse is implementation, and I refuse to coddle it. Being familiar with the impact of physical violence, especially intimate and domestic violence, leads me to *know* that such violence does not manifest or produce *taqwa*. Surely, it can produce behavioral conformity, but it will never foster equal or liberating social relationships or resilient connections with the Divine.

Building on the arguments I have made about Qur'anic hybridity, the authority of human experience, and an interpretative preference for the marginalized, I want to propose one additional option: the option of "No, and." By "No, and," I refuse the literal meaning and implementation of this verse, but I also assert that there is still a value to this verse, there is still something to learn from this Qur'anic sign (*aya*) of God. I do not want to just shelve Qur'an 4:34, describing it only as a historical artifact. I do not only want to tame its content by reinterpreting and specifying the meanings of various words. I also refuse to surrender it to people who happily or pseudo-apologetically invoke and implement it. Instead, I want to roll it out, struggle with it head-on, and use it to gain knowledge. I want us to discuss it and use it as a means to prioritize practical and theological reflection on the impact of violence and androcentrism. I want us to listen to the voices of women—and any person—who have been beaten or manipulated through threats of violence. I want us to hear their pain, fear, guilt, shame, see their visible and invisible trauma. And, I want us to consider if this trauma could ever be described as the will of a just God. This verse, and others like it, should never be invoked without reference to such experience and deep reflection on the authority of such experience.

Qur'an 4:34 can be an artifact, a weapon, *or* a locus of the relationship with God in all of its beautiful and challenging messiness. With "No, and," I opt for the latter. This verse is still a sign (*aya*) of God, but its ethical, theological, and practical function has changed—as it must to remain relevant and responsive— in our context. My position is a theological perspective on the way Qur'anic hybridity and human experience foster sustained, sometimes tensive relationality. However, I also introduce "No, and" for pragmatic reasons. Is this not what we are doing already with ethically and experientially challenging verses? Are we not grappling with the text and asking new and vital questions because we experience tension? Are we not, because of this verse, struggling to understand the role of experience, to consider what is "beyond the text"? Are we not admitting new voices and sources as authoritative? Are we not expanding the boundaries of concern, garnering a better appreciation of what it means to have God-consciousness (*taqwa*) and manifest it in the world? We are reflecting, considering, and struggling. We are being provoked. We are being challenged. The sign (*aya*) is functioning to sustain and foster relationships among humans and between God and humans. And, this is precisely how the Qur'an can lead to a just and egalitarian society today.

4

Claiming Texts

HERMENEUTICAL APPROACHES
TO AHADITH AND THE BIBLE

*Narrated by Abu Hurayrah: "God's Messenger said: 'And
I command you to take care of the women in a good manner
for they are created from a rib and the most crooked portion
of the rib is its upper part. If you try to straighten it, you
will break it, and if you leave it, it will remain crooked, so
I command you to take care of the women in a good manner."*[1]

THIS HADITH (PL. AHADITH) appears in Sahih Bukhari, one of the most
important and authoritative Sunni compilations of ahadith, written accounts of
sayings, actions, and tacit approval of Prophet Muhammad. It is narrated by Abu
Hurayrah, a close Companion (*sahabi*) of Prophet Muhammad. Abu Hurayrah,
in general, narrated vast numbers of ahadith and is infamous for narrating many
ahadith that negatively depict women.[2] In content, this hadith speaks to men
about women; it has an androcentric frame, yet simultaneously invokes concern
for women. It addresses men and encourages them to take care of women, to avoid
breaking them by attempting to straighten that which is bent. The hadith thus
depicts women as "crooked" or "bent." These terms certainly carry pointed evaluative connotations today. Their connotation in the original context of Prophet
Muhammad's life may have diverged from our contemporary perspectives. It is,
though, notable that the Arabic verb for straighten (*tuqeemu*) comes from the
same root used to describe the ideal path of those who worship God, that is, the
straight path (*sirat ul-mustaqeem*).[3] Women, in this hadith, are not straight and
not straighten-able. The hadith also states that women are created from a rib,
which evokes allusions to the biblical account in Genesis 2–3 of Eve being created
from the rib of Adam, an account that is not found in Qur'anic depictions of
human creation. Finally, this hadith, along with many others, has been and
continues to be deployed to justify a secondary or restricted status of women in
social, legal, and ritual contexts.

For Islamic feminist interpreters, the "rib hadith" raises a host of inter-connected questions related to the stature of authentic hadith collections and narrators, to androcentric framing of ahadith, and to negative or derivative depictions of women. Questions also arise about the proper relationship between Qur'anic content, hadith content, and scriptural accounts from other traditions, as well as about the pervasive way ahadith shape Muslim consciousness and prac-tice. In short, this one hadith—of tens of thousands—foregrounds the com-plexity involved in engaging with a collection of written texts that is held to be authoritative, thoroughly integrated into Muslim life, necessary for concretizing Qur'anic general guidelines, and riddled with androcentrism and patriarchy.

In this chapter, I begin by exploring dominant trends in Islamic feminist en-gagement with ahadith, including the primary issues presented by the hadith corpus, central interpretative approaches, and critical calls for more extensive and systematic engagement. This examination foregrounds concerns about androcen-tric framing and the resultant marginalization of women, misogynistic content, and authoritative stature. Extending the analogical starting point of the Qur'an and Jesus Christ, I then engage Christian feminist biblical exegetical approaches articulated by Elizabeth Schüssler Fiorenza, Musa Dube, and Phyllis Trible. These exegetes raise similar questions about androcentrism and misogyny, authority and communal function of the texts, and interpretative strategies. I focus prima-rily on feminist concerns provoked by biblical form and content, and interpreta-tive strategies. However, in engaging Phyllis Trible, I shift to examine the content of her rereading of Genesis 2–3. This is the biblical account with which the rib hadith is linked in interpretation and in delegitimization by some Islamic femi-nist exegetes. There are certainly many other opportunities for rich comparative engagement on content alone, yet my main goal herein is to articulate new herme-neutical strategies in relation to ahadith. After briefly highlighting intersections and discontinuities among Christian and Muslim approaches, I conclude the chapter by proposing ways Muslima theology can extend beyond both classical Islamic methods of hadith assessment (*usul al-hadith*) and a basic hermeneu-tics of suspicion to "reclaim" hadith literature through additional hermeneutic strategies, revisiting the relegation of extra-Islamic or non-Islamic materials, and collective reading.

Hadith Engagement: Authentication and Beyond

As with the rib hadith, the broader hadith corpus presents unique challenges to Islamic feminist interpreters. Perhaps the most immediately evident challenge is that it contains some written reports—attributed to Prophet Muhammad—that negatively depict women, assign negative characteristics to women and female nature, and juxtapose women with an ideal or normative male human.[4] Hidayet Tuksal sorts these "misogynistic reports" into five general categories: ahadith that describe women as being created from Adam's rib; that describe women as the majority of the inhabitants of Hell; that depict women as deficient in reason and religion, yet capable of leading men astray; that describe women as inauspicious; and that group women with donkeys and dogs (that is, with animals that are negatively depicted in other ahadith).[5] Notably, these misogynistic reports are found in the most respected collections of ahadith, those that are considered "sound," or *sahih*. These ahadith thus raise a formidable content concern but also impel conversations about the methods and standards of authentication used in the compilation of *sahih* ahadith collections. The labeling as "*sahih*" in and of itself indicates that the collections are widely held to be authentic, verified, and traceable back to Prophet Muhammad. Reconsideration of these assumptions is a tensive and fraught enterprise; it is a proposal that often elicits a strong negative reaction from many Muslims.

Another related issue is that many ahadith are androcentric; they center male experience, depicting it as normative. In some reports, this is entangled with misogynist and explicitly negative characterizations of women. Yet, in others, the androcentric framing is a byproduct of the fact that ahadith record the sayings, actions, and tacit approval of Prophet Muhammad, who among many other things, was a man. Moreover, ahadith were primarily narrated, taught, and compiled by men. There were important female narrators, such as Aisha, and there were major female hadith scholars at various points in Islamic history.[6] However, it remains the case that much of the preserved content is focused on men and male concerns. I am not arguing that Prophet Muhammad was solely concerned with men. I am arguing that a combination of a male example with male compliers leads to androcentric framing and to marginalization of women and female concerns. Women are often talked about, as in the rib hadith, and their concerns are preserved frequently only on the edges of narrations. These concerns receive less direct attention overall. One intriguing example of this is found in Sahih Bukhari in The Book of Dress. Contrary to contemporary fixations on Muslim women's clothing, the ahadith in this book focus much more on men's dress and attire.[7]

Not every concern that Islamic feminists face with ahadith is directly related to gender or the presentation (nonpresentation) of women. There are some more general challenges widely acknowledged among diverse interpreters. These include the fact that the hadith corpus is vast and not as clearly delimited as other textual sources, including the Qur'an.[8] Even the six canonical Sunni *sahih* collections contain tens of thousands of narrations.[9] These narrations include different versions of a single hadith, and ahadith that seemingly contradict one another. Another general challenge is that ahadith document diverse categories of Prophet Muhammad's sayings, actions, and tacit approval. They include stipulations that are for all people, stipulations that relate only to Prophet Muhammad, and stipulations that relate to Prophet Muhammad's historical context, cultural context, and personal preferences.[10] As such, even among *sahih* ahadith, there are some that are applicable to all people and times, and others that are restricted to or relevant to Prophet Muhammad alone. There are aspects of Prophet Muhammad's example (Sunna) as preserved in ahadith that are *exemplary* and aspects that are *exceptional*.[11] Conspicuously, there is no stable consensus on which ahadith are of what variety. Arguing for these distinctions is the activity of exegetical, legal, and ethical interpretation; the distinctions are mostly not explicit in ahadith collections themselves. This raises an additional challenge. Interpreting the hadith corpus requires extensive exposure to the vast content and specialized skills and knowledge related to compilation, narrator biographies, genres of ahadith, and the processes of hadith assessment.

The final challenge is somewhat obvious but nonetheless important to explicitly acknowledge. The hadith corpus is not a comprehensive picture of all aspects and details of Prophet Muhammad's life, nor of life in general. The hadith corpus is notable for the breadth of topics it broaches, even seemingly mundane issues, but it is not all-inclusive. It also does not outline an organized or chronological depiction of Prophet Muhammad's life. Weaving together ahadith and other content occurs in biographies of Prophet Muhammad (*sira*). The noncomprehensive and nonchronological nature of ahadith highlights the distinction between the more conceptual idea of the Prophet's Sunna (example) and the actual existing written reports (ahadith) that record snapshots of that example. There is space in between the Sunna and ahadith, space that at minimum arises from the noncomprehensive nature of reports, the historical context of ahadith, and the androcentric framing of reports.[12]

Many prominent Islamic feminist interpreters focus their efforts on the Qur'an, in part due to its preeminent authority but also due to the challenges associated with engaging the hadith corpus.[13] Overall, there has been significantly less systematic and critical engagement with ahadith. While some ignore ahadith all together, the dominant trend is to approach ahadith with a basic hermeneutic of suspicion or "skepticism."[14] This approach is founded on juxtaposition of the Qur'an and the ahadith. Interpreters, such as Barlas, depict the Qur'an as inherently egalitarian and the ahadith as the primary source of misogynistic and patriarchal ideas within Islamic thought.[15] The Qur'an is granted ultimate authority as the Word of God, and all content in the hadith corpus—the potentially fallible human recollections and collections of Prophetic example—that diverges from or contradicts Qur'anic content is delegitimized.[16]

Divergent content is delegitimized through a variety of strategies. One strategy is to borrow the classical screening and evaluation techniques of the field of hadith sciences (*usul al-hadith*). These techniques primarily focus on evaluating the chain of narrators (*isnad*) of a hadith by scrutinizing individual narrators as well as the connections among those narrators. Compilers of the canonical *sahih* ahadith collections used these same methods. Notably, Islamic feminist interpreters who invoke these techniques are using them to contest ahadith included in *sahih* collections; they argue that some ahadith in canonical collections were erroneously classified. Hassan does this with reports that negatively portray women, and claims that these ahadith are in fact weak (*da'if*) or fabricated.[17] Fatima Mernissi also reexamines the status, capacity, and personal and political motivations of specific ahadith narrators in order to challenge the authority of *sahih* ahadith.[18]

In her critical engagement with the rib hadith in relation to Qur'anic narratives of human creation, Hatice Arpaguş similarly begins by reassessing the *isnad*.[19] But she concludes that the *isnad* of the rib hadith is actually *sahih*. Her initial turn to the classical method is nonetheless significant as it underscores the dominant focus on authentication. Her conclusion, however, compels her to deploy other strategies to explain the divergences between the egalitarian Qur'anic account of creation and the rib hadith. To do so, she shifts focus to the content (*matn*) of the hadith and aims to explain the genesis of this content. Her explanation pursues two trajectories: comparison of various versions of the rib hadith, and attribution of the content of the hadith to biblical sources.[20] With the former, she argues that the more misogynistic variation (quoted at the beginning of this chapter) becomes increasingly dominant over time and that this version may even be a later attribution to Prophet Muhammad. In the latter trajectory, Arpaguş argues that the rib hadith is the result of "non-Islamic information" being used to explain "Islamic" textual silences; it results from "a general tendency on the part of Muslim scholars to fill the blanks with biblical and Talmudic sources."[21] She does not contend that Islam is totally uninfluenced by other traditions or sources, but she does claim that the Qur'an should be the ultimate standard of evaluation due to its authenticity in comparison with other religious scriptures.

Attribution of nonegalitarian ahadith to "non-Islamic" biblical and cultural sources is not at all unique to Arpaguş. It is a ubiquitous strategy in Islamic feminist engagement with ahadith. Discrepancies between the Qur'an and ahadith and the specific presence of misogyny within ahadith are explained by appealing to the ideas of corruption and foreign transplantation, particularly corruption from other religious traditions. Hassan adopts this strategy when she tackles widely held theological assumptions about the created superiority of men.[22] In addressing the question of how woman was created, she argues that the Qur'an's depiction of an undifferentiated humanity is more legitimate than and should take precedence over ahadith that echo the Genesis 2 account of Eve's creation from the rib of Adam. She similarly argues against prominent male interpretations of the events of the Garden, explaining that exegetes introduced incongruous details from ahadith reports, details that originated in biblical accounts. In other words, the existence of patriarchal and dehumanizing ahadith are explained— and explained away—by arguing that these accounts derive not from Islam but from other traditions and texts (primarily biblical texts and interpretations).

The hermeneutic of suspicion and the juxtaposition of the Qur'an and ahadith are forms of engagement with the hadith corpus. There is, though, a growing consensus that Islamic feminist interpretation needs to move toward deeper and more systematic engagement with ahadith.[23] The primary motivation for this is the simple fact that ahadith—especially in their specificity and tangible details— shape Muslim traditions, consciousness, and practice. If Islamic feminists and Muslima theologians aim to effectively advocate for egalitarian change, they must directly and deeply engage this source that shapes many traditional interpretations, as well as many on the ground perceptions and realities. Arguing for Qur'anic egalitarianism is part of the puzzle, as is juxtaposing the Qur'an and ahadith. Direct and deep grappling with the ahadith, reclaiming the ahadith, is another vital piece.

Underscoring the centrality of ahadith in Muslim life and practice, L. Clarke raises this precise issue and questions why "liberal" contemporary Muslims, including feminist interpreters, have "effectively abandoned hadith, leaving their opponents to harvest the field uncontested."[24] Exploring ahadith related to hijab and seclusion, she argues that liberals intentionally, yet detrimentally, deemphasize the ahadith. Liberals and feminists expect that ahadith will support conservative, androcentric, and patriarchal positions, and therefore do not engage deeply or comprehensively with this source. Ahadith are imagined to be an obstacle, not a resource, in feminist hermeneutics.[25] Ali voices similar concerns about the lack of depth and consistency in approaches to Prophet Muhammad's Sunna and ahadith; contemporary Muslims have "not been able to develop a uniform approach to his example. Instead, they alternate between praise, apologetics, and silence."[26] While most feminists do not wholesale reject ahadith, Ali argues that the dominant approaches of ignoring, making only "sparring reference," or depicting ahadith as secondary to or inconsistent with the Qur'an are insufficient.[27] She also, referencing wadud's and Barlas' early work, observes that Islamic feminists who prioritize the Qur'an will at times, and somewhat inconsistently, appeal to ahadith to support their egalitarian interpretations of the Qur'an. This is particularly the case in situations where the Qur'anic message is complex and troubling, for example, Qur'an 4:34. The meaning and implementation of this

Qur'anic verse is often restrained through reference to ahadith that describe Prophet Muhammad's ambivalent feelings about the verse and his personal nonimplementation of any form of "hitting."[28] Ali describes this as a defensive focus on what Prophet Muhammad *did not do*, rather than the construction of a positive model of behavior based on his actions.

From these critiques, Clarke and Ali promote the value and necessity of more thorough and substantial engagement with ahadith.[29] Clarke insists that, despite near surrender of ahadith, feminist hermeneutics is ideally suited for the challenges presented by the hadith corpus.[30] While existing approaches tend toward circumventing ahadith or only engage with them in a piecemeal fashion, there are several interpretive techniques that would be highly effective. She defers somewhat in directly advocating for any one approach—identifying her own positionality as a non-Muslim and respecting the agency of Muslim feminists—but she suggests some possibilities. These include excavation; comparing the Qur'an and ahadith; holistic treatment of ahadith; and focusing on "protest hadith."[31] Excavation refers to the identification and collection of ahadith on a particular topic. The process alone can be effective in pushing back against dominant—or "conservative"—portrayals of ahadith, superficial invocations of the Sunna or ahadith, and the overaccentuation of women-negative ahadith. Even a simple excavation can reveal "other voices and the possible outline of a different set of norms."[32] Clarke, herself, engages in the process of excavation when she compiles and examines ahadith related to hijab.[33] The potential effectiveness of this strategy alone underscores the superficiality of most contemporary (feminist and not) engagement with the hadith corpus. Comparison of the Qur'an and ahadith is already in play, yet Clarke appears to encourage comparison beyond simple juxtaposition and resultant dismissal. She maintains, for example, that deep comparison could effectively be used to reveal and destabilize the "recasting" and gendering of *fitna* (trial, affliction, temptation) that occurs in some ahadith.[34] With holistic treatment, Clarke advocates broadening the scope of engagement by placing women-focused ahadith in broader contexts, or comparing contradictory ahadith. Shaikh's exploration of The Book of Knowledge in Sahih Bukhari provides an example of this approach.[35] Shaikh analyzes the way human anthropology, inclusive of but not focused solely on women, is constructed in relation to the larger topic of religious knowledge. Finally, Clarke proposes the approach of focusing on "protest hadiths," which she describes as "a literature of resistance in subtle form within the scriptures," traces of which are preserved in the hadith corpus and hint at divergences between a more relaxed gender perspective expressed by Prophet Muhammad and a more restrictive, later perspective.[36]

Ali picks up on the themes of deeper engagement and a focus on tensions within the hadith corpus. She maintains that "Muslims spend far too much energy battling over the validity of a handful of hadith reports, or constructing elaborate (and disingenuous) apologia for past practices, or simply sidestepping sunnah altogether."[37] In lieu of these strategies, she proposes that contemporary interpreters revisit the distinction between "exemplary" and "exceptional" aspects of Prophet Muhammad's Sunna as articulated in early Islamic jurisprudence.[38] Ali is not suggesting that contemporary interpreters automatically accept the interpretative conclusions of early jurists. She uses the perspectives of early jurists to highlight debates and hermeneutical choices. She shows, for instance, that early jurists focused on specific *actions* in Prophet Muhammad's marital life not on the concept of marriage or on Prophet Muhammad's *statements* about marriage. Moreover, jurists disagreed about which aspects of the Sunna were exemplary (applicable in other circumstances and with other people) and which aspects were exceptional (restricted to Prophet Muhammad alone), and routinely (and selectively) invoked some ahadith over others dependent on their personal positions. Ali argues that contemporary interpreters could deploy similar strategies. Instead of debating the authenticity of women-negative ahadith or prioritizing declarative ahadith (statements as opposed to actions of Prophet Muhammad), they could explore Prophet Muhammad's personal martial behavior and freshly debate which actions should be classified as exceptional or exemplary. Perceptively, Ali notes that exceptional/exemplary debates permit deep and tensive engagement with the Sunna and ahadith but do not require direct attacks on or criticism of Prophet Muhammad.[39] She here responds to contemporary conceptions of the ahadith as an all-or-nothing package deal (accept them all or reject them), and as a list of directly applicable norms or practices.[40] She instead revives a more complex engagement with ahadith that recognizes various genres and the necessity of interpretation.

Ali does, however, broach the topic of the "disobedient prophet" as another way to reveal and engage tensions within the Sunna and between the Sunna and the Qur'an.[41] This approach focuses on moments in the Sunna when Prophet Muhammad appears to express discomfort with divine commands or attempts to mitigate against harsh punishments. Acknowledging the anxieties provoked by the idea of a "disobedient prophet," she emphasizes its long history and how it highlights competing views within the early Muslim communities, oscillation between multiple perspectives within the hadith corpus, rhetorical constructions, and diverse definitions of obedience. Chaudhry deploys this approach to explore the "complicated relationship" between Qur'an 4:34 and Prophet Muhammad's sentiments and actions, that is, between the divine command and prophetic example.[42] Building on Ali's distinctions between exemplary and exceptional, and between actions and statement, Chaudhry surveys diverse depictions of Prophet Muhammad's actions, feelings, and behavior. What is most significant about Chaudhry's approach is that her primary goal is to expose the complexity; she does not use the complexity or tensions as a basis for simply dismissing the ahadith or Sunna. She highlights it and asserts that the Sunna neither totally prohibits hitting, nor grants unbridled license to hit.[43] She also observes that the entire discourse in the Sunna is androcentric, focused on a husband's legal right to hit and personal choice to refrain from hitting. Notably, she describes the Prophet as "resistant" to hitting, yet not overturning dominant social hierarchies or challenging the legality of the practice.[44]

Chaudhry develops the notion of resistance into a general hermeneutical approach to the Sunna. Acknowledging other challenges presented by the Sunna and ahadith, she also emphasizes that interpretation of ahadith requires direct engagement with Prophet Muhammad's context. This leads to the challenge of reconciling the view of Prophet Muhammad as an "egalitarian man" with extensive descriptions of him as a man of his time, as a "patriarchal man."[45] In light of this, she considers the potential redemptive value of Prophet Muhammad's example in today's quest to promote egalitarianism. Ignoring ahadith is not a viable option, so she identifies two other possibilities: the anachronistic portrayal of Prophet Muhammad as a feminist; and the search within his contextualized example for "small acts of resistance" against male dominance and normativity.[46] She adopts the latter, and argues that, while it does not explain away, circumvent, or root out the overt patriarchy in many of these texts, it demonstrates the malleability of ahadith and the fact that they are—and have always been—open to multiple interpretations.

The theme of resistance appears repeatedly in approaches that aim to engage more substantially with ahadith. As mentioned, Clarke identifies the focus on "protest hadith" as one fruitful interpretative lens. Ali comments on the potential of exploring the "disobedient prophet." Chaudhry expands on this to focus on acts of resistance. Chaudhry, Tuksal, and Shaikh take resistance one step further and focus on examples of women's resistance as preserved in ahadith. Shaikh draws attention to the presence of "challenging and resistant women."[47] She singles out Aisha, Prophet Muhammad's wife, in particular, as an example not only of resistance but also of active "interlocution, interrogation, and interpretation" of the Qur'anic text.[48] Mernissi, Chaudhry, and Tuksal make analogous moves, highlighting respectively the manner in which Aisha challenges certain narrators of ahadith; "Aisha's hermeneutical strategy" for interpreting the Qur'an and communal practices; and the way in which Aisha's contestations are "true precursors to the concerns raised by women today."[49]

Critiques of dominant forms of engagement and new proposals all accentuate the need for hermeneutical approaches that are equipped to deeply and critically tackle the hadith corpus. These approaches, as is evident in some work, will not focus on neat or easy resolutions; they will be heavily invested in "excavating" what actually exists in the hadith corpus and in analyzing tensions, ambiguities, and discrepancies. They will aim to engage without sanitizing, surrendering, or depending on superficial renderings. They will seek to recover and center female agency and voice, and foster new relationships between the hadith corpus and contemporary communities.[50]

I close this section by returning to Clarke's contention that feminist hermeneutics are particularly well suited to the challenges presented by ahadith. Although she argues this, Clarke states, "[c]reative interpretation, including decisions about strategies and the measure of suspicion and imagination to be applied, are for those inside the tradition, and therefore outside the scope of this essay."[51] She, in a footnote to this comment, clarifies that the strategies to which she refers—creative interpretation, suspicion, and imagination—are approaches used in interpretation of the Torah and the Bible.[52] These particular methods have been largely advanced by the Christian feminist biblical exegete Elisabeth Schüssler Fiorenza. Clarke concedes that these methods "will not all necessarily suit Islam, for reasons not only of the different natures of the texts, but also possibly of reception by the audience."[53] Intriguingly, Clarke is not the only scholar to allude to the potential of comparative feminist approaches in relation to ahadith. Shaikh also references Schüssler Fiorenza when defining her feminist hermeneutical approach and critique of sexism.[54] Both Clarke and Shaikh indirectly engage Schüssler Fiorenza. Hidayatullah, however, explicitly engages her, seeking to "point out the powerful connections and synergy between Muslim and non-Muslim efforts to reclaim our various religious traditions as expressions of the full human and moral dignity accorded to women by God."[55] Comparing Islamic feminist Qur'anic interpretation and Schüssler Fiorenza's biblical interpretation, Hidayatullah identifies hermeneutical convergences, including retranslation, divine transcendence of gender categories, historical reconstruction of female agency, and foregrounding of women's experience. There are also significant divergences, the most pointed of which is the conception of the Qur'an as the Word of God that leads to an emphasis on critiquing interpretation rather than the text itself.[56] Due to this divergence, Hidayatullah argues that most Islamic feminist interpreters use only a hermeneutic of suspicion and do not venture into other strategies, such as Schüssler Fiorenza's hermeneutics of proclamation, remembrance, and creative actualization. Hidayatullah's observation is perceptive. These strategies are not used and may not even be suited to Qur'anic interpretation. However, returning to Clarke and Shaikh, there is another possibility. These strategies may be applicable to other forms of Islamic textual interpretation, particularly engagement with ahadith.

Biblical Exegesis: Strategies, Imperialism, Agency

Pursuing this nascent trajectory and as an extension of the analogical starting point of this book, in this section, I explore approaches and interpretations drawn from three Christian feminist biblical exegetes: Elisabeth Schüssler Fiorenza, Musa W. Dube, and Phyllis Trible. These exegetes struggle with the androcentric and imperialistic nature of the Bible, and the related marginalization of women and dualistic portrayals of other "others." They introduce concrete reading strategies that aim to expose power dynamics and rhetorical constructions, recenter women and others, and reconsider the boundaries of the official canon. Elisabeth Schüssler Fiorenza is a forerunner and prolific scholar in the fields of biblical interpretation and feminist theology. Born in Germany and Catholic, she competed her ThD at the University of Münster. Among many other books, she is author of *In Memory of Her* (translated into thirteen languages), *Bread Not Stone: The Challenge of Feminist Biblical Interpretation*, and *But She Said: Feminist Practices of Biblical Interpretation*.[57] Her research and teaching focus on hermeneutics, politics of interpretation, and biblical and theological epistemology. She is a cofounder and coeditor of the *Journal of Feminist Studies in Religion*, and is currently the Krister Stendahl Professor of Divinity at Harvard Divinity School. Musa W. Dube is a prominent Motswana (from Botswana) scholar and exegete, who earned her PhD in New Testament Studies at Vanderbilt University. She is the author and editor of multiple books—including *Postcolonial Feminist Interpretation of the Bible, Other Ways of Reading: African Women and the Bible*, and *The HIV and AIDS Bible: Some Selected Essays*—and her writing, research, and community activism focus on biblical studies, postcolonialism, hermeneutics, gender, feminist translation, and HIV and AIDS studies.[58] She has played a pivotal role in the Circle of Concerned African Women Theologians (the Circle), and in the Society of Biblical Literature's African Biblical Hermeneutics Program Unit. She is currently Professor of New Testament in the Department of Theology and Religious Studies at the University of Botswana. Phyllis Trible is a renowned biblical scholar and rhetorical critic, who earned her PhD in Old Testament at Union Theological Seminary. Her work focuses on rhetorical criticism, women and gender in scripture, and biblical exegesis, and she is the author of groundbreaking works, including *God and the Rhetoric of Sexuality* and *Texts of Terror*.[59] She is the Baldwin Professor Emerita of Sacred Literature at Union Theological Seminary, past president of the Society of Biblical Literature, and was, until 2012, University Professor of Biblical Studies at Wake Forest University Divinity School.

Elizabeth Schüssler Fiorenza: Women-Church, Conscientization, Hermeneutics

Elizabeth Schüssler Fiorenza defines feminist biblical interpretation as the endeavor to uncover lost aspects of texts, correct mistranslations, challenge and remove androcentric and patriarchal scholarship, and discover new meanings and symbols within biblical texts.[60] Connected to feminist theology, feminist biblical interpretation is a liberative approach that critically engages the "structural sin of patriarchy" and empowers the *ekklesia* of women (women-church), "the movement of self-identified women and women-identified men in biblical religion."[61] This movement is not separatist; it arises out of resistance to patriarchal co-optation of women and abandonment of biblical religion, and out of explicit solidarity with those most marginalized due to sexism, racism, and poverty. The women-church, for Schüssler Fiorenza, is the center and authoritative site of feminist interpretation of the Bible concretized in institutions, centers of learning, and even study circles that teach and practice rereading, and then enact those readings in rituals.[62]

As part of her definition of feminist biblical interpretation, Schüssler Fiorenza critiques common approaches to and understandings of the Bible. She notes that both "detractors and defenders of women's liberation refer to the Bible because of its ecclesial authority and societal influence."[63] While apologists and postbiblical thinkers diverge in whether this authority and influence should continue, they both view the Bible as a "mythological archetype"—as the "Word of God"—that has a fixed, universal meaning, rather than as a transformable historical prototype.[64] This view leads to lack of consideration of women's experience and detachment of the Bible from community contexts. Schüssler Fiorenza outlines three specific approaches that continue to embrace the Bible: the doctrinal, the historical-factual, and the dialogical-pluralistic model. The first is dogmatic and ahistorical. It views the Bible as the Word of God, insisting on its "verbal inspiration and literal accuracy."[65] The authority of the Bible is then deployed to bolster the Catholic church's teachings and creeds. The doctrinal approach cultivates a community that views the Bible in a consumeristic fashion, as a proof text or security blanket. The second approach—historical-factual—is a reaction to the doctrinal approach and an inversion of historical-critical scholarship; it depicts the Bible as a "book of the past" that is historically and factually true.[66] As such, any historical research that challenges biblical accounts or the canon can potentially undermine faith. The dialogical-pluralistic approach understands biblical texts as responses to original contexts and communal situations.[67] Schüssler Fiorenza argues that this third approach is insufficient because the Bible is not simply a collection of diverse, responsive pieces; it is a collection of diverse, contradictory, and oppressive pieces. Therefore, not every text of the Bible can or should be assigned the same authority.

Schüssler Fiorenza acknowledges that other exegetes resort to the idea of a "canon within the canon" in order to identify a critical principle on which to assess the rest of the text. She supports the necessity of identifying a critical, evaluative principle but claims that even the "canon within the canon" approach continues to uphold the Bible as an unchanging archetype. Since she rejects the archetype in favor of the prototype or "root-model," Schüssler Fiorenza cannot locate her critical principle within the Bible itself. She instead locates it within women's experience and the women-church.[68] This move, however, is not an abandonment of the Bible; it is a way to avoid abandoning any of the texts. Not all texts will be assessed positively, but all texts can act as a resource for critical feminist reflection.

She thus advocates for a new approach, the pastoral-theological paradigm, which seriously engages historical critical research and also seeks to determine what a text meant in the original situation and community to which it was addressed.[69] Biblical texts are deliberate responses to particular concerns and communities; biblical materials were "collected, selected and formulated so that it could speak to the needs and situations of the community of faith."[70] She describes her approach as a form of pastoral or practical theology; the pastoral task is one of "translating" biblical texts, critically and self-critically discerning the meaning and liberative value of texts for people today.[71] In line with her depiction of the Bible and critique of a canon within the canon, not all biblical writings will be theologically significant today. Biblical writings should be subjected to the critical and evaluative criterion of the contemporary community. This community is the location of hermeneutical translation, assessment, and interpretative activity.[72]

Beyond her critique of other approaches and description of the general pastoral-theological approach, Schüssler Fiorenza also outlines a set of specific hermeneutical reading strategies: hermeneutics of suspicion, hermeneutics of remembrance, hermeneutics of proclamation, and hermeneutics of liberative vision and imagination.[73] These strategies relate to different facets of feminist biblical exegesis, including "ideological suspicion, historical reconstruction, theoethical assessment, and creative imagination."[74] Schüssler Fiorenza emphasizes, though, that the strategies are not linear or sequential; they are ongoing, interrelated, and repeated throughout the process of interpretation. Moreover, the strategies aim to produce new or different readings of the Bible and to "interrupt" existing interpretations. She vividly captures this dynamic interrelationality by describing the interpretive process as a dance of interpretation.

For Schüssler Fiorenza, the dance of feminist biblical interpretation has an overarching goal; it is part of a process of "conscientization" in which the interpreter aims to cultivate critical awareness of sociopolitical, cultural, economic, and religious contradictions.[75] Conscientization ultimately aims to foster solidarity and transform relations built on subordination and oppression. It is facilitated through experiences of cognitive dissonance in which the normativeness, or common sense, of patriarchal readings is questioned. Breakthroughs and disclosures reveal the shaky foundation on which such "common sense" readings are built. Schüssler Fiorenza argues that the dance of interpretation implies a shift in the understanding of biblical texts and biblical interpretation. The Bible as "formative prototype" offers "paradigms of struggles and visions that are open to their own transformations through the power of the Spirit in ever new sociohistorical locations."[76] The texts are not set or fixed norms for all times and places. Biblical interpretation, as a result, is also reconceptualized. It becomes "a site of struggle and conscientization," not only of understanding texts *or* locating egalitarian texts.[77]

What are the characteristics of her four reading strategies? Schüssler Fiorenza begins with the hermeneutic of suspicion, defining it as a "searchlight" with which the interpreter critically explores her own interpretive assumptions and practices, other interpretations of biblical texts, and the Bible itself.[78] The hermeneutics of suspicion should be applied to both interpretations *and* the text. She dismisses the idea of presupposing a feminist or liberating character of the text, and thereby only deploying the hermeneutics of suspicion in relation to interpretations of the Bible. On the contrary, she grounds the hermeneutics of suspicion in the assertion that "*all* biblical texts are articulated in grammatically masculine language—a language which is embedded in a patriarchal culture, religion and society, and which is canonized, interpreted, and proclaimed by a long line of men."[79] The Bible, for Schüssler Fiorenza, is androcentric, male-centered, and therefore must be approached by the sleuthlike interpreter with a hermeneutic of suspicion aiming to destabilize the normativity of androcentrism and patriarchy.

Schüssler Fiorenza invokes the analogy of a quiltmaker to describe the hermeneutics of remembrance; the "quilt-maker . . . stiches all surviving historical patches together into a new overall design."[80] In response to characterization of the Bible as grammatically masculine and embedded in patriarchy, biblical texts that discuss women should not be taken at face value; these texts should be approached as indications of remnants that are "submerged in androcentric historical consciousness."[81] The goal of the hermeneutics of remembrance is to stitch together these remnants related to women and other marginalized people. This process identifies the submerged aspects, engages in historical reconstruction, and strives to reintegrate women and others as agents in the text. In doing so, it surfaces subversive and dangerous memory.[82]

The hermeneutics of proclamation is characterized by evaluation and assessment. Here, the interpreter is a "health inspector" who investigates the quality and potential harm of texts, subjecting them to ethical and theological evaluation to "determine how much they engender patriarchal oppression and/or empower us in the struggle for liberation."[83] Texts that are assessed to reinscribe patriarchy, domination, or exploitation cannot be affirmed or appropriated as the words of God; they should be proclaimed as and exposed as "the words of men."[84] If this exposure does not happen, the texts will continue to reinscribe and bolster the system of patriarchy. The hermeneutics of proclamation, however, is not only about identifying and distinguishing among poisonous and nourishing texts; it is also concerned with the sociopolitical contexts and circumstances in which even nourishing texts are deployed. Even feminist-neutral, feminist-positive, and other ostensibly nourishing texts (such as "love thy neighbor") can be deployed to sustain oppressive and often patriarchal relationships.[85]

The hermeneutics of liberative vision and imagination, Schüssler Fiorenza's fourth reading strategy, uses imagination and fantasy to "actualize and dramatize biblical texts differently."[86] Drawing on a range of creative expressions, media, and forms, this strategy aims to "elaborate and enhance" the remnants uncovered through the hermeneutics of remembrance.[87] It does so by retelling biblical stories from new perspectives and by giving voice to voices rendered silent within the texts. This is a creative and imaginative endeavor beyond simple recovery. Schüssler Fiorenza describes it as a valid and necessary strategy to "make present the suffering, struggles, and victories of our biblical foresisters and foremothers" and also to give women a sense of possibilities that have not yet been actualized and that are not preserved in the texts.[88] These imaginative retellings and elaborations must also be submitted to the suspicion and assessment of other hermeneutical approaches. Retellings are not all automatically egalitarian or nourishing.[89] This approach, though, aims to retell biblical stories but also to reshape patriarchal prayers and liturgy and create new feminist rituals.[90] Her emphasis on ritual is significant; she presents ritual enactment as a particularly potent arena of change within religion.

Musa W. Dube: Decolonial Biblical Interpretation and Semoya Spaces

Like Schüssler Fiorenza, Musa Dube is centrally concerned with the way the Bible facilitates relationships of domination. She maintains that the Bible played and plays a central role in supporting Western imperialism, colonialism, and missionizing in African contexts.[91] The Bible was used to subjugate other lands, other races, and other religions, and impose the images, ideas, religions, and economic and political structures of the imperial power. As a result, it is necessary to ask critical questions about the ethics and politics of the Bible, the relationship between imperialism and the Bible, and the ways we should "read the Bible given this history of its role, its readers, and its institutions."[92] These concerns and tasks are the project of postcolonial biblical interpretation. "Postcolonial," as used by Dube, is "a literary, technical term defining the setting, the use, and the classifications of texts."[93] The setting spans from early historical encounters with imperialism through colonialism to postindependence. The setting is also concerned with the search and struggle for decolonial, liberative possibilities. "Use" refers to the ways texts are read and then enacted to legitimate, collaborate with, or resist imperialism. As a classification, "postcolonial" refers to a set of texts "brought, born, and used in imperial settings."[94] Dube also invokes postcolonial to describe people—both colonizers and colonized—and the way their perceptions of each other are conditioned by imperial constructs and actions.[95]

Postcolonial biblical interpretation seeks to uncover—and potentially subvert—imperialism in the text and in readings of the text. In the African context, Dube states that this process begins by examining literary constructions of characters, geography, traveling/interactions in contact zones, gender, and material gains.[96] With characters, the focus is on dualistic, evaluative juxtapositions that sharply contrast colonizer and colonized. Geography can also be dualistic, with some "lands" presented as developed, light, and farmed, and others as dark, empty, and undiscovered. Bridging these two categories is the third, the traveler— the "authoritative stranger"—who enters the undiscovered land, encounters the devalued other, and identifies the inherent deficiency of the land and other.[97] Gender is frequently deployed in the dualistic juxtaposition of characters (especially the colonized indigenous woman), and also in descriptions of how dark, undiscovered lands are to be "entered," "penetrated," and subjugated. Dube describes such uses of gender as a male game in which women are used to articulate male views. She also highlights that the entering and subjugating of foreign lands and people have material gains, even if these activities are often cloaked in moral justifications. In sum, Dube contends that "colonizing texts present relationships of profound inequality, they are driven by expansionist aims, they exhibit fear of difference, they promote authority of certain traveling strangers, and they have the tendency to disguise their economic interests under moral claims."[98]

Dube underscores the continuing impact of these literary constructions. They legitimate white domination of black people and lands; devalue and stigmatize African religions, texts, and cultures; and result in unequal distribution of global power.[99] Biblical texts have historical contexts of origin, and they also continue to operate in and shape actions in contemporary contexts. Therefore, she asserts, that it is not enough to approach biblical texts only as ancient texts. This disconnects the texts from their contemporary impact and potential liberative roles. It also obscures the deep impact of imperialism, and thereby maintains imperialism. While Dube advocates the importance of connecting biblical interpretation to contemporary issues and concerns, she does not promote a strictly particularist approach. She acknowledges that universal interpretations prop up imperial domination but states that withdrawing into a particularist approach alone would be "almost unethical" as it would leave universal interpretations unchallenged and uncritiqued.[100] Postcolonial readers must analyze the unequal power relations that lead to the dominance of imperial universalist interpretations, and then formulate new, liberating strategies of interdependence.

These new strategies of interdependence are relevant to postcolonial feminist interpretation of the Bible. Dube emphasizes gender as a particularly important, yet frequently absent, topic in postcolonial discourse. In one way, women are subsumed in the juxtaposition of "white men" and "Africans."[101] In another way, gender is deprioritized under a "first things first" approach in which colonized men foreground resistance to imperialism without addressing internal patriarchy. These approaches are problematic as they do not grapple with gendered manifestations of colonization and imperialism. They avoid engaging with the reality that colonized women suffer from imperialism and two forms (colonizer-imposed and colonized-imposed) of patriarchy, while colonizing women suffer from patriarchy but often participate in or benefit from imperial subjugation.

Dube also critiques dominant formulations of Western feminism and feminist biblical interpretation for similar reasons. Western feminism "often brackets imperialism in its analysis of male texts, or operates within imperialist frameworks of power."[102] It does not always question white rule or imperialism directly, and thus works to maintain them. As part of this more general critique, she also directly engages key facets of Schüssler Fiorenza's work, including her reconstruction of women's history, the *ekklesia* of women, and practical application. Dube appreciates aspects of Schüssler Fiorenza's approach, but argues that Schüssler Fiorenza downplays historical imperial contexts; does not attend to manifestations of imperialism beyond patriarchy and kyriarchy; and embraces dualism, hierarchy, and universalism in some of her rereadings.[103] Dube, moreover, expresses concern about the *ekklesia* of women. The *ekklesia* of women, she argues, is alienating because it is a white, middle-class Christian feminist space. It also "dangerously befriends imperialism" in an attempt to occupy or claim the highest rank in Western male kyriarchy.[104] Western feminist biblical interpretation, therefore, does not go far enough. Feminist readers must become "decolonial readers"; they must cultivate awareness of the domination and exploitation of imperialism, and then consciously adopt decolonizing interpretative strategies to promote liberation of all.[105]

What are Dube's specific decolonizing reading strategies? First, she advocates for the side-by-side reading of multiple texts. This involves reading scriptures alongside of secular texts, and reading the Bible alongside of other oral, religious, and cultural texts.[106] She describes this approach as "boundary transgressing," intratextual, and protective against other forms of imperialism, such as anti-Semitism and Christian religious exclusivism.[107] To illustrate this approach, she examines a variety of texts, including Exodus, *Heart of Darkness, The Aeneid,* and the poem "The White Man's Burden." She formulates a series of standard questions in advance, referencing decolonial concerns, and then explores the questions in relation to each text. These questions include: What is the text's stance on imperialism?; Does the text promote travel to "foreign" lands, and if so on what rationale?; How does the text construct difference? As opportunity, dialogue, something to be condemned/evaluated?; and How does the text deploy gender to construct subordination?[108] What emerges from her posing of these critical questions to diverse texts is a map of literary-rhetorical trends in relation to power and difference. What also emerge are glimpses of ways to re-read the canon for decolonization. Speaking specifically of reading biblical texts and indigenous texts, she states that this "critical twinning" can become an anti-imperial act through its deliberate transgression of boundaries.[109]

Another concrete strategy Dube emphasizes is storytelling. Her interest in storytelling is connected to the preceding strategy of reading multiple and diverse texts. However, it especially seeks to reassert the value of oral texts and interpretative traditions; these texts and traditions are "vibrant and authoritative in the lives of women, and they need to be studied, analyzed, and reinterpreted for the creation of a just world and for the empowerment of women."[110] Storytelling permits the introduction of oral and cultural texts, and it is also a women's practice in many African cultures. Dube identifies various methods of storytelling, including reading the Bible alongside of African stories; retelling the same story multiple times with different characters and to address specific audiences and issues; retelling stories with group participation so that stories remain fluid and continually in process of being told; comparative explorations of biblical and African stories that assert the validity of multiple canons; retelling of stories using gender-neutral language to expose patriarchal and colonizing themes; and drawing on Trickster narratives to subvert status quo interpretations of stories.[111] These forms of storytelling seek to confront imperialism in both method of reading and in content of the readings. They resist being constrained to a single imperial canon and seek to "construct radically hybrid discourses of decolonizing."[112]

Storytelling as commentary is also a strategy that is open to scholars, the ordained, and lay members of a community alike. Dube argues that it is imperative to read with *and* learn from nonacademic readers.[113] Not only is this a pragmatic approach in recognition of the small number of African women trained in biblical interpretation in university settings, but it is also a prime way to "counteract the dominance of Western-oriented methods that are elitist and sometimes irrelevant."[114] Moreover, this reading together beyond academic contexts and credentials helps reveal novel nonacademic strategies of resistance and can help to further conscientize women readers to functions—sometimes hidden—of patriarchy in the Bible and in culture.

Reading with nonacademic readers points to another facet of Dube's decolonial approach: the creation of new feminist spaces in which contextual and international readings can be articulated. Drawing on her observations of women in African Independent Churches (AICs) who emphasize dynamic pneumatology, she refers to these spaces as *Semoya* spaces (*Moya*, meaning Spirit).[115] *Semoya* spaces are also a response to her critique of the *ekklesia* of women; *Semoya* spaces are constructed and seek to remain outside of patriarchal and imperial structures. This deliberate resistance creates fertile soil in which to plant new seeds of critical assessment, to continuously "hear God anew," to imagine and build radical equality, and to "promote and establish strategic coalitions among women of different backgrounds and situations, across borders, and beyond narrow identity politics."[116] Strategic coalitions and readings within a *Semoya* space are not for the colonized alone. Since all women are impacted by imperialism, all women must explicitly address imperialism. She does not imply that Western and white women have the same experience as "Two-Thirds" women; they are able to bracket out and benefit from imperialism. What she is asserting is they that should not do so, that they are ethically responsible for cultivating awareness of, confronting, and working in solidarity against imperialism.[117] This aligns with the ultimate aim of her various decolonial feminist reading strategies: the recognition of, respect of, and engagement with diverse "others."[118] She describes this objective as moving beyond a view of human difference as deficiency and toward a "liberative interdependence, where differences, equality, and justice for various cultures, religions, genders, classes, sexualities, ethnicities, and races can be subject to constant reevaluation and celebration in the interconnectedness of our relationships."[119]

Phyllis Trible: Genesis 2–3 and Woman's Agency

Genesis 2–3 depicts the creation of Adam and Eve, the creation of Eve from Adam's rib, and the disobedience and "Fall" of humankind. While many Christian feminist theologians focus primarily on the Genesis 1 account of creation, which depicts the creation of all humanity in the image of God (*imago Dei*), Phyllis

Trible directly engages the seemingly more problematic—from an egalitarian perspective—creation narrative.[120]

Trible acknowledges that Genesis 2–3 can be an example of how the Bible is hostile to women. Patriarchal readings are powerful and pervasive:

> So powerful has been the patriarchal interpretation that it has burrowed its way into the collective psyche.... We think we know what the text says, and we think it tells us that man was created first and woman last—and that the order of creation is a value judgment making her subordinate to him. She is his derivative, having come from his side. She is described as his "helper"; surely that means his assistant, not his equal. She seduces him and so is blamed for their disobedience. And we are told that she is cursed. She is punished by being subjected to the rule of her husband.[121]

Trible, however, contends that the text should be reread in order "to understand and to appropriate."[122] The latter is central to her exegetical project. She does not only cull the canon for egalitarian accounts but also appropriates some of the most difficult and disturbing biblical narratives.[123] She argues that women need not accept traditional, patriarchal exegesis; they can and should reclaim texts, rereading them as critiques of patriarchal cultures and interpretations.

Trible begins her rereading by arguing that *adham* (the term for Adam) is ambiguous. In one way, it refers to man and in another it refers to all humanity. Taking the more inclusive meaning as the initial meaning, Trible argues that *adham* is originally androgynous; "sexuality" manifest in the creation of woman is not the beginning of the story. Drawing on the literary structure of ring composition, she asserts that the later creation of woman is the "culmination" and "climax" of the narration.[124] Notably, the creation of woman is also the introduction of sexual differentiation for *both* male and female; from the original androgynous *adham* comes the "interrelated and interdependent" woman and man.[125]

Trible then tackles the description of God's creation of a helper from the rib of *adham* (Genesis 2:18, 20, 21–22). Highlighting the multiple meanings of the word for helper (*'ezer*), she focuses on the type of relationship that is encapsulated in the term. Juxtaposing the creation of woman with the creation of animals—that were not "helpers" for *adham*—this term connotes a beneficial relationship founded on equality. How then does this equality relate to the creation of woman from the rib of *adham*? Trible explains that just as it is Yahweh who decides that *adham* needs a helper, so it is Yahweh who creates woman from the "raw material" of the rib. In both actions, she stresses divine agency and diminishes male agency. She emphasizes that during creation man is in a "deep sleep." He "has no part in making woman; he is out of it. He exercises no control over her existence."[126]

Divine effort is required to create woman from the rib; the narration does not glorify the man. Man is passive and silent. Therefore, both man and woman are created by and depend on God.

The next topic Trible addresses is the act of naming, which reoccurs throughout Genesis 2–3. Recognizing that some exegetes opine that man's naming of woman (Genesis 2:23) indicates authority and power over woman, Trible pushes for a rereading of the text.[127] She claims that the language used is not naming language but the verb "to call" (*qara'*) as in "She shall be called woman."[128] She distinguishes this type of calling from other calling in Genesis 4 and Genesis 2 in order to argue that man does not actually assign a name to woman; "woman" is not a name per se but a common noun. Therefore, for Trible, this "calling" does not indicate authority of man over woman.

Moving from equality and no hierarchal relationship, she then tackles the part of the narration in which the serpent speaks to woman. She again directly addresses patriarchal speculations about the rationale for this targeted discourse; other exegetes connect it to the cunning, imagination, moral weakness, resentment, sexualization, and superstitious inclinations of women.[129] Trible, however, points out that the text does not state any of this. Revisiting what the text does say, she highlights the description of woman's creation as "good" (Genesis 2:18) and of human "physical, psychological, sociological, and theological" equality.[130] Trible though goes further and offers her own "female speculation" about why the serpent speaks to the woman and not man. Throughout the entire creation narrative, the woman is "the more intelligent one, the more aggressive one, and the one with greater sensibilities."[131] She describes the woman as a theologian and translator who assesses multiple possibilities related to the tree, and then independently and deliberately acts in light of these considerations. The woman is the agent in this account; she takes the initiative and the decision alone. Moreover, this decision is not haphazard but deliberate, conscientious, and informed. In contrast, man is a "silent, passive, and bland recipient"; he is given the fruit, eats the fruit, and makes no protest.[132] He is not a theologian, does not consider a range of possibilities, and does not make the decisions. Trible summarizes, "[i]f the woman be intelligent, sensitive, and ingenious, the man is passive, brutish, and inept."[133] She then emphasizes the extraordinariness of such portrayals within a patriarchal context, and clarifies that her reading is not meant to privilege women but to undercut patriarchal speculation and interpretations of the text.

What then is the outcome of this active and passive disobedience? Trible argues that after the distinctive actions, humanity stands together again, united in disobedience. Man blames God for creating woman who subsequently gave him the fruit; woman blames the deceptive serpent. The serpent, as a result, is cursed by God. Trible juxtaposes this "cursing" to the status of the woman and the man: "though the tempter (the serpent) is cursed, the woman and the man are not. But they are judged."[134] The judgment is a "commentary" on the effects of disobedience. Trible uses this phrase to stress that the judgments are not mandates or prescriptions; the judgments are *descriptions* of the state of humans "between creation and grace."[135] Thus, for Trible, the Genesis 3:16 statement that men will rule over women is not a permission but an indication of the state of shared sin. It is a symptom of alienation, discord, and inequality. In other words, it is not something God wills or desires. Notably, through this state of sin the woman becomes a slave, losing her freedom and agency. Trible then connects this to Genesis 3:20 in which "the man calls his wife's name Eve."[136] She distinguishes this calling from the earlier calling by a common noun; this calling is one of naming, of asserting power and rule. Amid shared sin, this naming is a corruption of equality and mutuality. Even after this corruption, though, the account concludes with a return to the androgynous *adham*, hinting at the possibility of a restored relationship of equality among humankind.

Knowledge, Critical Engagement, Reclamation: Muslima Theological Reflections

Clark, Shaikh, and Hidayatullah hint at the potential overlap in feminist exegetical strategies. Their intimations are confirmed by meaningful and rich convergences within hadith engagement and biblical interpretation. To start, there is the shared observation that women are marginalized or depicted in negative ways within some parts of these texts. These texts assert deep influence on communities and traditions, and they shape statuses, roles, and views of women. Due to the great impact ahadith and biblical accounts assert on society, institutions, and communal life, exegetes in both traditions strive to outline strategies for critically engaging the texts without dismissal or surrender, and without simply isolating a women-friendly canon within the canon. Some scholars certainly focus on identifying positive depictions of women, yet there is equal emphasis on the necessity of deeply and "suspiciously" grappling with not so positive depictions as well. This is evident in the common deployment of a hermeneutic of suspicion or skepticism in respect to the texts themselves (not just interpretations of the texts) and in the continued articulation of deliberate and multifaceted interpretive strategies.

While these convergences in concerns and even in methods exist, there are also notable divergences. The first is that the ahadith and biblical texts depart significantly in terms of form. Large portions of biblical texts and books are narrative, while many ahadith are not narrative in the same manner. Ahadith can be simple declarative statements or accounts of Prophet Muhammad's actions.

This divergence in form means that not all strategies for rereading texts will be seamlessly applicable. Some will not be at all, and some will need form-conscious modification. It is possible that more narrative driven strategies could be effectively extended to critical engagement with biographies of Prophet Muhammad (*sira*). The second divergence is related to form but also to ontological stature. Ahadith—even *sahih* ahadith—are not imagined to be the direct Word of God in the same sense assigned to the Qur'an. They are human accounts, subjected to screening and authentication. However, ahadith are attributed to Prophet Muhammad and therefore wrapped up in conceptions of his authority and stature. To critically analyze ahadith can, as Ali notes, provoke anxiety because it can be construed as critique of Prophet Muhammad even when it is not. The third significant divergence is that some Christians, especially evangelical Christians, espouse a view of the inerrancy and authority of the Bible that is, at least at first glance, more akin to perspectives on the Qur'an. This is what Schüssler Fiorenza refers to as the doctrinal perspective on the Bible as the verbally inspired and literal Word of God. While it is not my focus herein, there are potentially interesting comparative theological overlaps between a doctrinal view of the Bible and views of the Qur'an. I, though, place feminist engagement with ahadith in conversation with feminist biblical approaches that do not hold this view of the Bible or of all biblical texts; Schüssler Fiorenza, for example, labels some portions of the Bible the "word of man." I maintain that this is a richer—albeit always illuminatingly imperfect—comparative starting point, one that fosters valuable insights into reading strategies and one that is significantly less prone to mutual acts of imposition and horizontal violence.

Throughout this chapter, I have used the phrase "hadith engagement" in lieu of hadith interpretation or specific references to the use of ahadith in Qur'anic tafsir or legal formulation. I intend, with this, to draw attention to the fact that there are forms of engagement with ahadith that are distinct from (yet not wholly disconnected from) the use of ahadith in interpretative disciplines. Other scholars acknowledge this, drawing attention to the resilient embeddedness of ahadith in Muslim consciousness and to the fact that contemporary Muslims approach ahadith as a list of norms to be directly applied.[137] There are forms of engagement that occur outside of specialized fields. While I concur completely with Ali's view that contemporary egalitarian and feminist interpreters have much to learn from classical methodologies, I am also interested in hadith engagement more broadly.

To this point, my initial comparative theological reflection relates to the perceived goal of hadith engagement. In Muslima theology and Islamic feminist interpretation in general, the obvious overarching goal is to articulate interpretations that affirm the humanity, dignity, and equality of women. What, though, is the more specific goal related to ahadith? In exploring the various

Islamic positions, there are multiple goals, including prioritization of the Qur'an, deemphasis of the ahadith, rescreening of ahadith to delegitimize nonegalitarian texts, and searching for egalitarian precedent or women-positive portrayals. The intended goal clearly shapes the method used and the hadith texts that are examined. For example, the combined goal of prioritizing the Qur'an and delegitimizing nonegalitarian ahadith invokes the Qur'an as an external standard to the hadith corpus, occasionally depicts ahadith as secondary to the Qur'an, and relies on classical *isnad* authentication strategies. No one piece of this approach is wholly objectionable, yet I believe the overriding goal of hadith engagement needs modification.

Dismissal of ahadith is not pragmatic or theologically sound. Sanitizing ahadith is effective in highlighting problematic aspects of some ahadith but it is not a form of holistic engagement. It also relies on methodological rules articulated largely by male scholars. Both conclusions and methodologies should be subjected to a hermeneutic of suspicion. That does not mean all conclusions or methodologies will be rejected or deemed inappropriate simply because they were articulated by men but that they must be considered and evaluated for their latent assumptions. Biases and blind spots emerge not only in conclusions but also in the very strategies developed to arrive at those conclusions.

What then could be the goals of Muslima hadith engagement? In my view, there are three primary goals: knowledge, critical engagement, and communal reclamation. Knowledge, as the first goal, seems too obvious to even state. However, the dominant trend in much contemporary scholarly and public discourse is selective engagement with or invocation of ahadith. Islamic feminists do this both by focusing on nonegalitarian ahadith and in emphasizing ahadith that depict women-positive precedent. Other Muslims do this when they accentuate or recirculate particular nonegalitarian ahadith. In both scenarios, pieces of a much bigger corpus are emphasized, while the vast majority of ahadith are left unengaged and frankly unknown. Therefore, one goal is simply more knowledge of ahadith themselves.

Comprehensive knowledge is unlikely (particularly beyond specialists), yet it is possible to have a profound impact by broadening the foundation of knowledge even a small degree. Knowledge and exposure to content could assume a variety of forms, such as the thematic excavation work evident in Clarke on hijab and Chaudhry on hitting. A consistent underlying principle of such excavation and exposure should be that engagement takes place with "the good, the bad, and the ugly" of ahadith reports. Engagement should not be limited only to one genre: not just to deconstructing women-negative reports or to prioritizing women-positive reports. Some of the most powerful excavation work may not even use women and gender as the sole organizing thematic principle;

women and gender can be considered in relation to broader topics, such as Shaikh's work on knowledge and anthropology. Numerous similar projects can be undertaken with the goal of organizing existing ahadith reports in new ways—around new questions—and making them accessible to nonspecialists. Ahadith are deeply embedded in Muslim consciousness. However, it is perhaps more accurate to say that particular ahadith are deeply embedded (in positive and negative ways) in Muslim consciousness. Even before or outside of critical analysis, re-collections of ahadith effectively destabilize this embedded particularity. They use the existing investment into the value of ahadith, yet broaden the foundation of information. They place one hadith in a field of many or against a yet unconsidered background of other ahadith. This can effectively challenge overaccentuation of women-negative ahadith.[138] It simultaneously demands more critical and complex readings strategies from Muslima theologians. If the goal is no longer replacement of nonegalitarian ahadith with an egalitarian Qur'an or egalitarian ahadith, then Muslima theologians will need multifaceted strategies for critically engaging—yet not ignoring—diverse ahadith reports.

The goal of broadening the foundation of knowledge about ahadith must also extend to general knowledge about how ahadith are compiled and authenticated, different collections of ahadith, discrepancies among ahadith, and the relationship between ahadith and sociopolitical contexts. All of these topics can be highly specialized, and there is certainly a benefit to some Muslima theologians and Islamic feminists specializing in the study and interpretation of ahadith. Nevertheless, what I am advocating here is not specialization but a feminist investment in cultivating general awareness—or what Schüssler Fiorenza and Dube call "conscientization"—of these topics among Muslims more broadly. This may include, for example, cultivating general awareness that many jurists in fact used "weak" ahadith, even without specialized knowledge of which jurists did so, with which ahadith, and when.[139] The latter knowledge is invaluable, yet there is also much to be gained from more general "interruptions" of common ways of understanding and relating to ahadith.[140]

Another example of this is especially valuable to the second goal of critical engagement. This is cultivation of awareness of the space that exists between the Sunna of Prophet Muhammad and the written reports about his Sunna (ahadith). Again, this need not be overly specialized but generally communicated in relation to topics of comprehensiveness (what is preserved, what is not preserved), context, and the history of written compilation. Without this conceptual space, almost all feminist critical engagements with ahadith will be reduced to attacks on the Prophet and thus rendered pragmatically ineffective. In line with Chaudhry and Ali, this does not mean the Sunna will be left without critical engagement or contextualization. This topic is the focus of the following chapter.

With awareness of the space between Sunna and ahadith, though, the perceived "threat" of critical engagement is mitigated and the essential breathing room in which to evaluate, compare, and reclaim ahadith is created.

Existing critical engagements with ahadith overlap with Schüssler Fiorenza's and Dube's reading strategies in significant ways. As noted, the hermeneutic of suspicion—beyond simple juxtaposition of the Qur'an and ahadith, or avoidance of ahadith altogether—is employed by Islamic feminists to identify patriarchy and androcentrism in hadith reports. Tuksal exemplifies this in her exploration of "misogynistic reports." She not only identifies women-negative reports but also highlights various ways misogyny and androcentrism operate within individual reports. With the rib hadith, for instance, she argues that the hadith is not concerned with a women's perspective but "only treated with regard to the problems that her condition may cause to the man."[141] Her shining of the "searchlight" on these reports does not collapse all negative portrayals into one undifferentiated women-negative mass; she highlights particular modes of decentering and denormalizing women, and this uncovers—if not shakes—the foundations underlying these ahadith. While Tuksal does not dismiss these ahadith outright nor on the basis of reauthentication alone, she ultimately assesses them to be marginal in relation to the Qur'an's emphasis on human dignity. They are part of the hadith corpus, but she does not grant them the same level of authority as some other parts of the same corpus. This approach to evaluating and assessing ahadith reports is akin to the hermeneutics of proclamation.

Islamic feminists also deploy the hermeneutic of remembrance and hermeneutic of imagination, seeking to identify marginal female figures or remnants of women's perspectives within the existing hadith corpus. Clarke points in this direction when she describes the value of hadith excavation; by itself, it reveals other "voices" and norms longing to be heard.[142] Although she argues against the notion of ahadith as historical records, she states that ahadith preserve "at least a glimmer of historical truth" as well as "layers of emendations" arising from social concerns and debates in early Muslim communities.[143] Both of these characteristics lend themselves to acts of affective and creative interpretation, beyond simple discovery of egalitarian or women-positive reports. It is in this precise context that Clarke proposes the potential crossover of Schüssler Fiorenza's hermeneutics of creative and imaginative interpretation.

Mernissi provides one of the most well-developed examples of this approach. In addition to her critiques of hadith narrators and chains of narration (*isnad*), she reimagines and remembers the contexts in which verses related to hijab and segregation were revealed. While I will not outline all her observations, I do want to emphasize her portrayal of this strategy. She states that her approach is not a work of history nor an attempt to be the official narrative. Rather, it is a "narrative of recollection, gliding toward the areas where memory breaks down, dates get mixed up, and events softly blur together, as in the dreams from which we draw our strength."[144] She describes creative acts of remembering as the language of freedom and future liberation. She also draws astute attention to the fact that revisiting the past—"delving into memory"—is something that is strictly supervised, especially for Muslim women, as it has the tendency to reveal ways ahadith were used—fabricated even—to bolster political positions and power.[145]

Mohja Kahf provides another potent example of the possibilities of creative recentering of marginal women. In her theologically provocative and profound poetry, she—like Schüssler Fiorenza and Dube—gives actual voice to the thoughts, feelings, and concerns of women who are found on the edges of the hadith corpus. These women may actually be seen as central (as is the case of Hajar and Aisha), yet nonetheless their voices and concerns are not always preserved nor recorded. Kahf thus re-members Hajar in her struggles and fear, writing a cathartic letter to another marginalized woman, Sarah: "Dear Sarah, life made us enemies. But it doesn't have to be that way. What if we both ditched the old man?"[146] One of the unique facets of Kahf's approach is that she remembers into the contemporary context; she reclaims Hajar, Aisha, and other female figures with reference to history but also in terms that are evocative today. She deploys Aisha as a sort of historical prototype and reclaims her to address contemporary concerns and questions. She describes Aisha as the "professor,"

> the only woman of her generation with an endowed chair (for Shia, Um Salama occupies a similar position). She is the first woman on the Supreme Court—of Islamic religious authority. She is accepted, if grudgingly at times, by the Muslim old boys' club, the old *fuqaha* club, and that is an asset for the rest of us.[147]

This example distinguishes Kahf's approach from mere recovery of female precedent, something for which Aisha is often invoked. Kahf's strategy and creative expression goes beyond this to also capture the complexities and tensions of Aisha's authority in relation to men, androcentric norms, and other women.

These contributions identify androcentrism and misogyny, assess the authority of specific ahadith on that basis, and remember and recreate the voices and perspectives of marginal women. They are immensely valuable, and they further underscore the soundness of comparative feminist conversations centered on ahadith and biblical texts. The task is to continue to develop these types of critical engagement with the ahadith. When paired with excavation, these engagements will reveal and destabilize androcentrism, while simultaneously using ahadith as a resource for liberating reflections.

There are, though, a few extensions and considerations that are essential in critical engagement with ahadith. The first extension is an insistence on viewing hadith engagement and the struggles entailed in that engagement as valuable in and of themselves. Drawing on Schüssler Fiorenza's depiction of biblical texts as the "site of struggle and conscientization," we should be highly attentive to the various ways we attempt to diffuse struggle and moments of cognitive dissonance encountered in ahadith. Meaning, as we critique and reclaim ahadith, we should be careful not to sterilize or simplify the content. Chaudhry also warns of this when she critiques approaches that anachronistically and decontextually depict Prophet Muhammad as a feminist.[148] These strategies—along with dismissal and even reauthentication—eliminate frictions and tensions encountered in the hadith corpus. It is perhaps helpful to remember why Schüssler Fiorenza insists on this perspective. She argues that conscientization is *the* goal in feminist biblical exegesis. The goal is for feminist readers to use biblical texts to become increasingly sensitized to various manifestations of power, privilege, and dominance. Sensitization sets the stage for solidarity and transformation of contemporary oppressive relationships, including and beyond gender relations. Strategies focused only on interpretation or identifying egalitarian examples/precedent avoid the tensions and thus also the resultant sensitization. Some ahadith will be deemed less authoritative than others. And, appropriation and reinterpretation are vital to overarching egalitarian projects. Yet, there is also great value in the tensive encounter itself, in learning to see the nuanced displays of power and marginalization (even in hadith reports that at first glance appear to positively depict women), and in using this awareness to identify powerful moments of resistance and dissent. In short, conscientization means that the goal is not to clean up the canon but to use the tensions in the canon to become equipped to change oppressive relations today.

Conscientization cultivated through nuanced deconstructive analysis is valuable in and of itself. It is also invaluable in articulating constructive readings and appropriations of ahadith that avoid inadvertently reinscribing oppression, domination, or marginalization. In constructive engagement, appropriation, and reclamation of ahadith, conscientization requires us to apply suspicion or skepticism to hadith reports (both misogynistic and ostensibly women-positive) and to continuously reapply suspicion to—remain suspicious of—our own constructive interpretations. Conscientization becomes an continuing process of critiquing and rereading, all the while asking *who* a text/reading empowers and marginalizes, and *how* a text/reading empowers and marginalizes.

As noted, many Islamic feminist scholars identify the example of Aisha as a promising area of resistance and empowerment within the hadith corpus. She confidently critiques narrators of ahadith and interpretations of Qur'an and ahadith. The content of her positions and her methodology are ripe for Islamic feminist and Muslima appropriation. Her example, however, provides a clear illustration of the necessity of conscientization and the related reapplication of a hermeneutic of suspicion even to feminist appropriations. Scholars, including Clarke, Mernissi, and Ali, emphasize that ahadith are not simply factual reports; they may capture glimpses of history as well as debates in early Muslim communities. Therefore, when we encounter Aisha's example within the hadith corpus, we must raise questions about why she is presented in this fashion and also about how her example empowers and marginalizes other people, especially women.

Aisha Geissinger, in her work on Qur'anic exegesis and ahadith, introduces some such considerations. She argues that Qur'anic commentators used ahadith related to Qur'anic interpretation—including ahadith about Aisha—to construct the "abode of the wives of the prophet . . . an imagined space within which exegetical questions can be authoritatively resolved."[149] This abode was an interpretative construction that transcended time and place not a simple description of history. Moreover, she contends that many of the issues "resolved" within this space are related to gender and social hierarchical distinctions. In other words, the authority of the wives of the Prophet, including Aisha, is invoked to draw evaluative boundaries between groups of people. Geissinger's perspective thus at a minimum sensitizes us to the importance of considering rhetorical constructions of Aisha, the nature of her authority, and the implications of her authority for other women and other "others."[150] Conscientization and the application of the hermeneutic of suspicion do not render Aisha's example impotent; they sensitize us to complexities in the presentation of her and our subsequent deployments of her example.

Geissinger begins her discussion of the abode of the Mothers of the Believers by quoting from the tafsir of Yayha b. Sallam on Qur'an 24:30–31. In the exegesis, he uses ahadith—including from Aisha—to clarify proper "covering" and the distinctions in covering among free and slave women.[151] I cite this example to concretize Geissinger's observation about social distinctions and hierarchies being maintained. These distinctions are maintained through deployment of female agency and authority. Here, I cannot help but return to Dube and her insistence that it is not enough to focus on gender; we must focus on imperialism in all its manifestations. Extending and deepening Schüssler Fiorenza's call for conscientization, Dube insists on attentiveness to diverse and dynamic manifestations of domination and othering. Moreover, she critiques feminist "bracketing" of imperialism, as well as the "first things first" approach that prioritizes one form of oppression over another. Dube's perspective is especially relevant to Islamic feminism and Muslima theology. She voices the same critiques of "Western feminism" and colonial impositions that circulate within Muslim communities. Western feminism has blind spots. It does not always grapple with other forms of oppression outside of sexism nor with the fact that some women benefit from these forms of imperialism. Colonialism imposes ideas, texts, and categories in a violent, dualistic, and devaluing fashion. Dube's response to these realities is noteworthy. She argues that feminists—colonized and colonizing alike—must become "decolonial" readers who deliberately refuse to replicate imperialist assumptions, categories, and boundaries. One area where she stresses this refusal is in dualistic portrayals of and othering of groups of people. She includes, of course, men and women and is equally adamant about refusing imperialist othering across cultures, languages, and religions.

Based on Dube's definition of imperialism and her call for decolonial readings, I am compelled to revisit one of the dominant trends in Islamic feminist hadith engagement: the delegitimization of misogynistic and androcentric ahadith by attributing them to biblical and "non-Islamic" sources. This move is a form of horizontal violence. It is a form of imperialist and dualistic othering. The authenticity of nonegalitarian ahadith reports is undercut by tapping into negative stereotypes of external texts and traditions, and relying on constructs of authority that treat "non-Islamic" as a synonym for "illegitimate." As Hidayatullah observes, this strategy—that she calls a "rib-ectomy" of the Qur'an—seeks to "purify" Islam and the Qur'an of misogyny and of biblical influence.[152] This approach fails to address the reasons why nonegalitarian views have persisted within the Islamic tradition, and is also a repetition of the rhetoric of nonegalitarian Muslim interpreters who similarly argue for a "pure" Islam clearly distinguished from all other traditions and texts. Hidayatullah argues that Muslim feminists co-opt this particular set of "master's tools" to win a "short-term feminist gain for ourselves at the expense of other women."[153] The approach thus inscribes one form of othering in attempt to erase another. In doing so, it accepts imposed assumptions and boundaries, benefits from the marginalization of other traditions, and also forecloses significant interpretive opportunities.

One assumption accepted in this strategy is the superficial depiction of religious traditions as discrete and never-interacting. Neither history nor the Qur'an support this vision of wholly distinct religions.[154] It is a conceptual imposition designed to neatly order manifestations of religious diversity and interreligious interactions; it is also a view that props up the political and imagined idea of a singular orthodoxy. This strategy, however, goes beyond claims to wholly distinct and distinguishable traditions, and asserts the "ascendancy and superiority" of Islam to other traditions.[155] This assertion may play well within certain Muslim communities, but it is a form of dualistic othering.

Another curious feature of this strategy of purification via othering is the way it blatantly overlooks extensive and long-standing exegetical usage of accounts and details from Jewish and Christian sources, often as preserved in *Isra'iliyyat*. Hidayatullah draws attention to this and argues that delegitimization of this practice is closely tied to the tafsir of Ibn Kathir (d. 1373).[156] Ibn Kathir is not a shining example of decolonial or nonimperial interpretation; he was deeply invested in defining evaluative boundaries, specifically in relation to other religions and what he defined as "heretical" Muslim sects and practices. Co-optation of this view of *Isra'iliyyat*, therefore, is not apolitical or decolonial in Dube's sense. Moreover, if we adopt this methodology, we perpetuate power-infused othering and also reinscribe an interpretative methodology that has not led to egalitarian readings in relation to other forms of human difference. Why do we assume it would be effective and transformative with gender? It does resonate with contemporary postcolonial concerns about imposition and with depictions of non-Islamic as illegitimate. But, it does not have a track record of fostering inclusivity or centering those who are marginalized.

Attribution of nonegalitarian ahadith to other traditions and texts also displays a lack of substantial knowledge of other traditions and texts. It is accurate that some "misogynistic" ahadith are related to biblical texts or echo biblical accounts. The account of Eve being created from Adam's rib is found in Genesis 2. However, to simply reference this biblical text without broader contextualization to other biblical texts or within Christian exegesis is an irresponsible from of comparative engagement. It fails to grapple with the creation narrative found in Genesis 1, which depicts all of humanity being created in the image of God (*imago Dei*). It also does not attend to—and thus cooperates in and benefits from silencing—feminist grapplings with both of the creation narratives and interpretations thereof. There are no references made, for example, to Trible's skillful appropriation of Genesis 2–3, and rarely any made to extensive feminist scholarship on *imago Dei*.[157] There is an irony to arguing for egalitarian possibilities within one tradition while referencing only a superficial depiction of the challenging aspects of another. The irony is deepened because Muslim women scholars often face a very similar form of othering in interreligious conversations and dialogues. We are aware of it and its impact.

I have devoted significant space to critically unpacking the assumptions of this particular approach because I concur with and am challenged by Dube's demand for attention to diverse manifestations of dualistic othering. By presenting other traditions as juxtapositions to or corrupters of Islam, we agree to participate in dualistic othering and also facilitate and benefit from the oppression and suppression of liberative voices in other traditions. We, as feminist interpreters, cannot bracket this concern. Our unreadings and readings must be increasingly

conscious of various manifestations of power and marginalization and our potential facilitation or acquiescence to that marginalization. Beyond perpetuation of
othering, this strategy also agrees to "rules" of a game that we may not want to play
or benefit from playing. What if we did not agree to these rules?[158] I recognize
a limited pragmatic, on the ground value of promoting Islamic ascendancy and
tying that to egalitarian interpretations via juxtaposition with other traditions.
But there is something more valuable to be gained by troubling the "rules," by
revisiting—not just automatically devaluing—interreligious conversations and
even texts. This does not entail surrendering all evaluation or juxtaposition between different sources, but it would rule out delegitimization of insights and
sources on the sole basis of association with an "infectious" and "lesser" other.

Specifically, what I am suggesting is we revisit the way the hadith "canon" is defined. The amorphous nature of this canon is presented as a challenge in feminist
engagement with ahadith. There are various collections of *sahih* ahadith—such
as the six canonical collections of Sunni ahadith—and there are other collections
of varying authenticity and varying thematic foci. As Chaudhry notes, there are
also prominent ahadith that are not preserved in the *sahih* collections but appear
in Qur'anic exegesis (*tafsir*).[159] The extent of the hadith corpus is vast, and the
boundaries are ambiguous. The boundaries of the canon factor into feminist
critiques of ahadith. Some scholars do endeavor to identify a "canon within the
canon." Hassan, Mernissi, and Tuksal do so when they discuss reauthentication
of the *isnad* of various *sahih* ahadith. Without dismissing the validity of *isnad*
related critiques, the search for a canon within the canon does reify the notion
that all authority is found within the canon, even if only within a subset of the
larger canon. However, what if amorphous boundaries—and the long-standing
tradition of interreligious exegesis—are co-opted in service of egalitarian
interpretation?

Schüssler Fiorenza's and Dube's discussions of canon can assist in clarifying
the rationale and value of this co-optation. Schüssler Fiorenza critiques feminist approaches that seek to identify a canon within the canon, that seek to locate some biblical texts to use as a critical principle for evaluating other texts.
She argues against this approach because it reinforces the view of the Bible as
a mythological archetype, a source of unchanging norms. Since she recognizes
the necessity of evaluative discernment among biblical texts—this is the crux of
her hermeneutic of proclamation—she argues for a critical evaluative principle
grounded in contemporary women's experience in the women-church. Dube also
challenges a fixed and singular canon. Yet, she does so by arguing that there are
always multiple canons and that, in decolonial reading practices, these multiple
canons should be read in conversation. Dube retains a critical lens in respect to all
canons; the criterion of decolonialism is applied to all oral, cultural, and written

texts. But, this criterion is more effectively illuminated through engagement with multiple canons. The "critical twinning" of multiple canons through its built-in boundary transgression is protective against diverse forms of imperialism.

Muslima theologians can also benefit by reading across canons. Islamic feminist scholars already acknowledge this in one way; there is a dominant strategy of juxtaposing the Qur'an and ahadith. This is a form both of reading multiple canons and of locating the critical principle of evaluation outside of the ahadith corpus (often within the Qur'an). This practice, when rid of dualistic othering, can be extended to engage other canons, including biblical texts and feminist interpretations of those texts. Once the notions of impermeable boundaries of traditions and only corruption outside of the Islamic tradition are destabilized, then there is the possibility we will find valuable insights. Insights can be found in biblical texts themselves. The fact that some male exegetes used biblical details to bolster misogynistic interpretations does not mean that these are the only genre of details to be found.

It is worth emphasizing that this can be a practically beneficial reading strategy, but it is also a Qur'anically valid reading strategy. The Qur'an acknowledges other scriptures, including the Torah (*Taurat*) and Gospel (*Injeel*). The Qur'an also assumes some knowledge of narrative accounts and figures that it only alludes to in passing; this is not a peripheral aspect of the Qur'an but a common feature especially in reference to prophets and revelation. While Qur'anic exegetes have developed the theory of scriptural corruption (*tahrif*) to explain scriptural discrepancies and Qur'anic superiority, the reality is most Qur'anic exegetes who use the interpretive tool of *tahrif* only invoke partial *tahrif*, meaning they claim only some parts of previous scriptures are corrupted.[160] This means other parts are not corrupted. If the Qur'an references and praises other scriptures, and at least some portion of them are not "corrupted," then we can and should read these scriptures.

Another canon we should engage is feminist interpretations of those scriptures and, in the context of this book, specifically Christian feminist exegesis of the Bible. I examined Trible's reading of Genesis 2–3 because she provides a clear example of what there is to gain through such a feminist critical twinning. Trible addresses the more challenging biblical creation narrative, the one typically interpreted as describing woman as being created *from* and *for* man, and as precipitating the Fall. I deliberately invoke Hassan's description of this account to drive home the point. For Muslima theologians, Trible's rereading should be fascinating methodologically and in content. Methodologically, she does not shy away from this narrative; she explicitly argues for its appropriation by women. Trible does not argue that the Genesis 1 account is invalid or subservient to this account but insists that it is not enough to simply surrender the Genesis 2 account unchallenged. This perspective is worthy of consideration by Muslima theologians who juxtapose Qur'anic narratives of creation with ahadith reports. I agree with Qur'anic prioritization over the hadith reports, yet I also affirm that the embeddedness and prevalence of ahadith demands we do more than simply quarantine the hadith depictions. We need to reclaim them, to take ownership of them, to assert critical, creative, and imaginative agency within them. This leads to the value of Trible's actual rereading. Trible unexpectedly flips the assumed agency of the narrative; Eve becomes the center, the focus, the one who is active and independent. And in her autonomy, she makes deliberate choices, even if they have consequences. However, Trible also foregrounds another agent in this account: God. God makes Eve. It does not matter what from, it is God's will not the will of man. I draw attention to this particular move because it is wildly similar to the move many Islamic feminist interpreters make when arguing for egalitarian depictions of humanity. God relates directly to women. God created women directly. This direct relationship in multiple forms affirms the dignity of women and the corruption—or as Trible states, the sin—of hierarchical gender relations. We cannot holistically borrow Trible's re-reading, but we can certainly learn from it, in both its overlaps and divergences. In reading multiple canons, including feminist canons—and they deserve to be declared as canons—we will not accept every detail. With some, perhaps many, we may simply note the divergences and inconsistencies. This alone can be illuminating. In other situations, we will identify profound and strategically effective overlaps.

I have, in the process of discussing the goals of knowledge and critical engagement, touched on various types of reclamation. I want to focus in on one specific form of reclamation, reclamation that occurs in contemporary communal settings and beyond academic contexts. As Dube demonstrates, reading in community and with nonspecialists is indispensable for decolonial and nonimperial readings; she emphasizes this through her experiences with the Circle and in the idea of *Semoya* spaces. Schüssler Fiorenza also affirms the value of communal reading through the women-church, manifest not just as an invocation of women's experience but also in concrete settings, institutions, and centers where women read together.

With ahadith, communal, nonspecialist reading is similarly indispensable. Since ahadith are entrenched in communities, transformation of the relationship with ahadith must also take place in those communities. I am not dismissing academic and specialized scholarship on ahadith. These too are part of the bigger puzzle of egalitarian transformation. I am recommending a complementary strategy that seeks to empower communities—especially marginalized members of communities—to engage with ahadith in less superficial, less passive, and more faithfully suspicious ways. Such empowerment cultivates the soil in which diverse specialized interpretations can be understood, evaluated, and conscientiously enacted.

Communal reclamation upends one of the major challenges presented by the hadith corpus, the hyperspecialization of *usul al-hadith*. Most community members will not be or become specialists in ahadith; however, communal reading groups are an apt setting for the development of general knowledge of ahadith, as discussed with the first goal of Muslima hadith engagement. This basic knowledge alone interrupts dominant modes of hadith dissemination in Muslim communities, specifically citation of ahadith without discussion, use of ahadith as proof texts for various "authoritative" opinions, and overaccentuation of women-negative ahadith. In these modes of dissemination, community members, including women, are passive recipients of ahadith content or already interpreted "processed hadith."[161] They are not empowered or encouraged to claim an active role in engaging ahadith, especially in light of their contemporary contexts and concerns. Basic knowledge of ahadith—and not just the content of ahadith—in communal reading settings empowers nonspecialists to at least ask good questions about specialists' readings.

What might this communal reclamation look like? My proposal is very pragmatic. Communal reclamation should take place in concrete, actual community reading groups, in which diverse women come together to learn about ahadith and to learn from and with each other. As mentioned already, these reading groups should mostly be composed of women outside of academic contexts. Academics or specialists can participate in or even germinate these groups. They can also contribute constructively to the group by helping to cultivate the basic foundational knowledge of ahadith. Academics and scholars, though, should not act as resident experts. Expertise in these groups resides in the collective itself. Hadith reading groups should also be purposefully diverse, with particular attention to race, class, age, and geographical and political contexts. The more diverse the group the better if the objectives are to variously engage with ahadith, to claim ownership of ahadith, and to cultivate consciousness of various forms of entangled marginalization and oppression. Diversity among participants can also be extended to include interreligious members. The inclusion of interreligious members would protect against interreligious othering, and it would also directly facilitate the engagement of ahadith alongside of other canons. The Catholic feminist theologian Jeannine Hill Fletcher offers an example of the benefits of interreligious reading of texts in community settings. Reflecting on her experience at an interreligious dialogue, she reports that one participant recounted a story of Prophet Muhammad inviting a Christian king to convert to Islam. This invitation was refused, yet the king sent a young girl to Prophet Muhammad as a "token of friendship and good will."[162] Hill Fletcher connects this experience and account to Hidayatullah's writings on Mariyya the Copt, and then argues that accounts of Mariyya can be reclaimed as a source of insight related to feminist interreligious dialogue.[163] Specifically, she uses the example of Mariyya to open conversations about female bodies, male norms, binary constructions, and political investments in interreligious dialogue and engagement. Hill Fletcher—in a respectful, knowledgeable, yet critically engaged fashion—demonstrates some of the rich benefits of interreligious communal gatherings and reading of ahadith and multiple canons.

Hadith readings groups can arise informally or be attached to larger community institutions. In light of Dube's critique of Schüssler Fiorenza's women-church as too closely modeled on formal church institutions, it is likely that hadith reading groups will benefit from being affiliated with nondominant organizations or institutions. Women's mosques, inclusive mosques, and other third-spaces are some prime settings in which these groups can organize and develop. Such groups need not be completely severed from other institutions—and of course this would be pragmatically inopportune in terms of advocating for change—but nondominant organizations and institutions offer space within which to incubate and try out strategies that would be restricted in other settings.

Beyond membership and setting considerations, specific activities are effective in hadith reading groups. One activity is the formulation of and reflection on a series of standardized questions. Standardized questions address key themes related to women's presence, action, and characterization in ahadith, and are formulated with reference to the group's perceptions of how women are portrayed in ahadith. These questions are then asked in reference to portions of hadith collections. This is an important point. The questions could be posed to a single hadith, yet if the goal is to surface and map trends and even divergences among ahadith, then exposure to groupings of ahadith is essential. Notably, the power of this activity is grounded in the fact that the questions arise from women's own perceptions and experiences. The act of reading in light of those questions can confirm, complicate, or challenge perceptions and experiences. While questions should be generated in the groups themselves, some possible questions include the following: Are women present in these ahadith? If so, where and how are they present?; What characteristics and traits are used to describe women?; Do women talk in these ahadith?; Do women raise questions in these ahadith? Questions about what topics?; and What do women *not* do or say in these ahadith? An endless number of such questions exist, but they all function to cultivate awareness of the ahadith content in general and specifically to deepen awareness of the presence and depictions of women in ahadith accounts. As Shaikh and Clarke demonstrate, there is also a benefit to focusing more broadly beyond ahadith on women; encountering ahadith about women in more holistic contexts gives organic rise to juxtapositions, absences, and dynamics of power and centering/marginalization.

Another practical reading activity is for members of such groups to discuss where they find themselves and their contemporary concerns in ahadith reports. This raises the specter of androcentrism fairly quickly, but it also identifies new and meaningful connections with ahadith, new sites of reclamation, representation, and ownership. I am reminded of Ali's pointed and powerful dedication in her book on accounts of Prophet Muhammad's life story. Referring to the death of seven of his eight children, she writes, "[n]one of the miracles traditional sources ascribe to him [Prophet Muhammad] impresses me more than his having survived such loss."[164] The fact that Prophet Muhammad lost children is known and discussed. Yet, it is not commonly referenced as a locus of deep, emotive connection to his Sunna. Asking readers to identify a hadith that connects to, addresses, or captures part of *their* experience fosters deep connection with ahadith and also empowers and centers women.

The final reading activity I will propose is the imaginative retelling of the perspectives of people—especially women but also men, including the Prophet—that are not explicit or included within ahadith. In this activity, women are asked to imagine and creatively articulate what a person may have felt, thought, or desired. This activity can be concretized with reference to a hadith from the Book of Marriage in Sahih Bukhari that depicts a woman who offers herself in marriage to the Prophet.[165] The woman makes the verbal offer—notably in the third person—three times without response from the Prophet. Thereafter, a man interjects, asking the Prophet to marry her to him instead, and then ensues a conversation between the Prophet and the man about *mahr* (the bridal gift). Ultimately, Prophet Muhammad states that he has married the woman to the other man for the bridal gift of the man's knowledge of the Qur'an. It is not difficult to see there is a lot going on in this hadith. I frequently ask students to use this hadith as the basis for an imaginative retelling of the feelings, thoughts, and concerns of the woman. What was her motivation? What was she thinking? How did she feel? What emerges are diverse and considered accounts, some of which foreground her feminist precedent in asking him to marry her, some that are aghast at her not being explicitly involved in the decision-making process, some that imagine her expressing complete trust in Prophet Muhammad and his decision. Without privileging a sole reading of this ahadith, what I want to emphasize is that, in a group context without specialized skills, readers can surface multiple possibilities and then discuss the implications of and the motivations for their particular views. They are inevitably faced with an imaginative retelling they had not considered. This facilitates conscientization.

Communal reclamation of ahadith in nonspecialist community reading groups is a way to broaden the foundation of knowledge, cultivate critical engagement, and develop conscientization through hearing and reflecting on diverse perspectives. It is a pragmatic and decolonial strategy that shifts power to "living communities" and assists in fostering a "different and more critical relationship with the Hadith texts."[166] Many of the strategies discussed in this chapter seek to break the monopoly on deployment and interpretation of ahadith. At the same time, these strategies seek to foster ownership of and critical engagement with ahadith by women; they promote means by which women can contend with the complexity of ahadith, without dismissal, without sanitization, and with a sense of relevance, justice, and representation.

In concluding this chapter, I must underscore that reading alone is not enough. Rereadings must transcend the intellectual. This is partially accomplished in communal and nonacademic reclamation. However, rereadings also need to be concretized in action or embodied in practice. Often when we seek to reinterpret the Qur'an or ahadith, we do so to deconstruct other interpretations and for the pressing on the ground reality of modifying nonegalitarian formulations of Islamic law. Ahadith play an integral role in this, and we must continue this work. Ahadith also profoundly shape social norms and personal perceptions outside of legal imposition. They are stories and accounts told to children, woven into practice, coloring norms before norms are even consciously known. Because of this, rereadings of the Qur'an and of the ahadith must be embodied and enacted. We must teach our bodies new stories and new norms. One of the prime arenas for this is ritual. I return to this topic in the concluding chapter, but at this juncture it is necessary to stress that traction—transformative traction—requires integration into thoughts *and* the body. Even subtle allusions to derivative women and repeated decentering of women in ritual content and forms have an insidious impact. They convey messages that do not need to be spoken or codified; these messages are etched into the person. And, these messages may only be polished away through alternate, additional, or broadened ritual practices that strategically include and center women, women's experience, and women's concerns.

5

Bearers of the Words

MUHAMMAD AND MARY AS FEMINIST EXEMPLARS

SURAH AL-AHZAB, THE thirty-third chapter of the Qur'an, describes Prophet Muhammad as a "beautiful example": "Verily, in the Messenger of God, there is a beautiful example (*uswatun hasanatun*) for anyone who places their hope in God and the Last Day and who remembers God abundantly" (Q 33:21). This verse, along with others that encourage people to follow, help, and even obey the Prophet, provides a foundation of authority for his example, Sunna. The example or model of Prophet Muhammad is beautiful, excellent, and worthy of emulation. At times, his model is even labeled "perfect"; Prophet Muhammad is routinely described as *al-insan al-kamil*, the perfect man. The notion of the "beautiful example" or "excellent model" of Prophet Muhammad is widely accepted by diverse groups of Muslims, including Islamic feminists. When Ali, for example, revisits the distinction between exemplary and exceptional aspects of Prophet Muhammad's conduct, she does so within a larger framing of how Prophet Muhammad can be a "beautiful model" for Muslim husbands.[1] The preceding chapter, though, demonstrates that not every action or saying attributed to Prophet Muhammad is easily depicted as "beautiful."

In this chapter, I seek to examine the idea of Prophet Muhammad as a beautiful example through a feminist and Muslima lens. This emphasis is intimately connected to the content of the preceding chapter—the written ahadith that document aspects of the Sunna. Herein, though, I focus on assumptions underlying the theological idea of Prophet Muhammad as an exemplar and model worthy of emulation, specifically as an exemplar and model of emulation for women. I consider theological assumptions connected to the invocation of a historically male human as a universal exemplar, and to depictions of Prophet Muhammad as illiterate, sinless, and perfect. There is significantly less written on this topic—feminist grapplings with the maleness of Prophet Muhammad—when compared with the Qur'an and ahadith. Despite this, I maintain that the maleness of Prophet Muhammad and the implications of this maleness for emulation of his moral example should be a central concern of Islamic feminists and Muslima theologians. This chapter, thus, follows the analogical realignment around the Qur'an and Jesus. Yet, it is unique in that it seeks not only to build on extant discussions and approaches but also to introduce a new concern and site of feminist reflection. In this chapter, I do not contest the call to emulate Prophet Muhammad, nor do I dispute his role as a central exemplar. I do probe the gendered and sexed assumptions that factor into a person's ability to emulate him or follow his example.

I begin this chapter by exploring extant theological views of Prophet Muhammad as an exemplar, noting tensions between humanization and idealization, and introducing Islamic feminist interventions related to exemplariness, prophethood, and emulation. I then explore three Christian feminist perspectives on Mary and Mariology. Like Muhammad, Mary is the bearer of the Divine, the one who serves as a conduit for the Divine in the world. In this capacity—as bearer or conduit—theological debates arise about Mary's purity, virginity, consent, and participation in the process of revelation. Debates also arise about her depiction as a female ideal, typically in juxtaposition to the reality of actual women. Mary is centered as a theological exemplar and in popular religiosity. Her sex and gender, though, are also centered and debated. She thus provides an analogical parallel to Prophet Muhammad in her relation to God, but, as a female, she prompts consideration of gender and sex that does not always occur in relation to Prophet Muhammad. The three perspectives—from Elisabeth Schüssler Fiorenza, Elina Vuola, and Marcella Althaus-Reid—touch on Christian depictions and reclamations of Mary, and discussions of the way gender, ideal representations, and power are present in Mariology and Marian dogmas and practices. I conclude the chapter by exploring how Muslima theology can re-envision the "beautiful example" of Prophet Muhammad in light of discussions of gender, power, and the manner in which exemplars are often invoked to maintain the hierarchical status quo.

Prophet Muhammad: (Hu)man and Model

The innovative nature of my focus in this chapter impacts the structure of this first section. Since there is no extensive body of feminist theological reflection on the Prophet's maleness, I instead assemble a mosaic of relevant examinations, which discuss the exemplary nature of Prophet Muhammad, his central roles and characteristics, and aspects of veneration and emulation. I also engage Islamic feminist perspectives that broach components of this larger discussion, including prophethood and patriarchy, emulation of the wives of Prophet Muhammad, and the potential gender inclusivity of *al-insan al-kamil*. These perspectives begin to reveal the presence and function of gender within theological discourses on Prophet Muhammad.

Annemarie Schimmel provides one of the most comprehensive overviews of Prophet Muhammad as an exemplar and the practices surrounding his veneration.[2] Her largely descriptive account acknowledges diversity in interpretations and practices, and as such provides an invaluable base of knowledge. She focuses on both the beautiful example and the unique characteristics of Prophet Muhammad. In reference to the former, she stresses the humanness of Prophet Muhammad. Like all other prophets in Islamic tradition, Muhammad is a human, a servant of God, who never claimed any superhuman qualities. He is the mediator of God's message whose "only prerogative was that he was granted a revelatory experience."[3] His role was not earned or deserved; God chose him to be the "vessel" for God's revelation.

As the Chosen, or *al-Mustapha*, Prophet Muhammad's way of life (Sunna) and the ahadith that record parts of the Sunna are central in Islamic tradition; his example serves as a "uniquely valid rule of conduct for the Muslims."[4] He is to be venerated, and his Sunna imitated or emulated. While the coupling of veneration and imitation can simply be based on reverence and trust that Prophet Muhammad knew and displayed the best conduct, Schimmel emphasizes it can also "lead to an absolutely tradition-bound attitude, even in the minutest externals."[5] As an example, she cites al-Ghazali's insistence on following the general ethical and ritual guidelines of Prophet Muhammad's Sunna, as well as the specific ways in which he dressed, slept, and even put on his clothes. This form of veneration fosters a deep interest in all aspects of Prophet Muhammad's physical appearance (*shama'il*), behavior, and character. His physical beauty is an archetype of beauty, his care of his body is a model of action, and his preferences in clothing and consumption are studied and enacted. Elements of his physical being are even imbued with religious and spiritual significance that transcends imitation. Descriptions of his physical form (the *hilya*) and even his sandals (the *na'l*) are artistically rendered as potent symbols of blessing and protection.[6] Prophet Muhammad's spiritual beauty is manifest in his behavior and character. He exemplifies humility, kindness, and concern for the weak. In sum, his character is the Qur'an enacted.

Imitation of Prophet Muhammad (*Imitatio Muhammad*) accordingly focuses on replication of his actions, character, and physical appearance with the goal of spiritual and moral cultivation: "The imitation of the noble actions and thoughts that Muhammad, the 'beautiful model,' had taught his community by his personal example was meant to form each and every Muslim, as it were, into a likeness of the Messenger."[7] *Imitatio Muhammad* shapes each individual Muslim, and also creates a degree of uniformity throughout diverse—temporally, geographically, and culturally—communities. Muslim communities are not homogeneous, despite superficial claims to the contrary, but there are strands that run throughout and link these communities back to the Sunna of Prophet Muhammad. Moreover, even when there are vigorous debates over the content of the Sunna, there is rarely dispute over the beauty of his example nor the validity and necessity of some degree of imitation.[8]

Emphasis on Prophet Muhammad's physical appearance, behavior, and character center his humanity but also hint at the fact that there is something unique or exceptional about this particular human. He is chosen. He receives revelation from God. He is not just a servant but also a vessel for the Word. He is not just beautiful but an archetype of beauty. He is not just a model of moral uprightness, but he is the perfect model. The exceptional nature of Prophet Muhammad is formalized in theological assertions about his uniqueness and perfection. One central assertion is the doctrine of *'isma*, the claim that Prophet Muhammad is protected and free from all moral depravity and error; he has perfect, impeccable moral integrity.[9] While at first glance this may seem to be a reiteration of his moral character, *'isma* moves closer to the concept of sinlessness, incapacity for wrongdoing, and complete avoidance of all morally and religiously questionable actions. Schimmel states that no such doctrine existed in early Islamic history and that there have always been conflicting views on this topic. Nevertheless, over time the "doctrine of absolute sinlessness of the Prophet prevailed."[10] Prophet Muhammad's sinlessness and purity are also emphasized through narrations about the "Opening of the Breast," in which he is physically and spiritually cleansed in preparation for his roles as prophet and messenger. Doctrines on sinlessness, freedom from error, and purity help to explain why any questioning—or perceived questioning—of the righteousness of Prophet Muhammad's Sunna is a tensive and fraught endeavor.[11]

Prophet Muhammad is also described as *ummi*. This term is typically understood as "illiterate," that is, unable to read and write. It is also connected linguistically and conceptually with the notion of community (*umma*), more specifically a community of revelation.[12] Following this latter meaning, Schimmel associates *ummi* with the term "Gentile," suggesting it denotes a community (the Arab community) that has not yet received a prophet from God.[13] While my inclination is to foreground the communal implications of the term *ummi*, in much contemporary discourse the understanding of *ummi* as illiterate (unlettered) dominates and serves a particular function. Illiteracy emphasizes God's authorship of the Qur'an, Prophet Muhammad's inability to "write" revelation or borrow from other written scriptures, and Prophet Muhammad's passive role in the creation and reception of the Word of God. *Ummi* simultaneously acts as a proof of the prophethood of Muhammad, the miraculous nature of the Qur'an, and the omnipotence of God.

Although Prophet Muhammad's *ummi*-ness is a proof of his lack of agency in reference to the Qur'an, he is not deprived of all agency. He is, in fact, commonly connected with intercession in this world and on the Day of Judgment.[14] Intercession grows out of the notion that he is sent as a "mercy" to the worlds, and develops into discussions of intervention for his community on the Day of Judgment and the possibility of his intervention in this world in response to supplications, such as *tasliya* (supplications that ask God to bless Prophet Muhammad and his family). Intercession is not as pronounced in the Qur'an, which emphasizes individual accountability and the inability of any person to carry the burden of another (e.g., Q 7:15, 41:46, 6:164, and 35:18). As theological doctrine and popular practice, intercession is extensively debated, especially considering the unicity of God (*tawhid*) and Islamic prophetology, which insists on the humanity of prophets. While a popular depiction of Prophet Muhammad's exceptionality, intercession begins to blur the theological distinction between human and divine agency.

The Sufi concept of *al-insan al-kamil*, typically translated as the perfect man or human, also engages with Prophet Muhammad's uniqueness, perfection, and humanity. Tied closely to the thought of Ibn al-Arabi, *al-insan al-kamil* depicts Prophet Muhammad as the perfect manifestation of each and every one of the divine names or attributes. According to Ibn al-Arabi, people are unique because they are the only part of creation that can "comprehensively integrate and manifest the totality of God's attributes."[15] This ability, though, is potential; it requires actualization through spiritual, ritual, and moral cultivation. Humans embody diverse configurations of the divine names, and cultivation seeks to limit and balance each of these names. Prophets and friends (*awliya'*) of God manifest all the names in perfect equilibrium. It is in this context that Schimmel describes Prophet Muhammad, *al-insan al-kamil*, as "the suture between the Divine and the created world."[16] She hastens to add that despite his elevation to these "luminous heights," Prophet Muhammad remains a human, servant, and creature. Her comment points to tension that runs throughout the discourse on Prophet Muhammad as a (hu)man and unique exemplar. His perfection at times pushes him almost beyond the realm of humanity, at least humanity as lived and known by most humans.

Few Islamic feminists holistically explore the preceding aspects of Prophet Muhammad's depiction as an exemplar. There are, however, critical interventions related to prophethood, his Sunna, the extension of exemplariness to his wives, and *al-insan al-kamil*. As part of her larger "unreading" of patriarchy within

Qur'anic exegesis, Barlas engages the Qur'anic depiction of prophets in general and specifically Abraham and Muhammad. She contends that the Qur'an challenges patriarchy by refusing to depict prophets as surrogate fathers or surrogates of the Divine. The Qur'an "challenges the concept of father-right by refusing to sacralize the prophets as real or symbolic fathers."[17] In Abraham, she locates a model in which the prophet explicitly displaces father-right. Abraham is aware of his father's *shirk* (association of partners with God), confronts his father and rejects his father's authority, and undercuts the legitimacy of adhering to inherited patriarchal practices and traditions. Abraham's break with his father is central to and "the condition for the embrace" of God; patriarchy is an "impediment to faith."[18] Abraham is an exemplary believer and prophet due to his submission to God and his refusal to place human (male) sovereignty above God's sovereignty. Abraham is appointed as *imam* (leader) of the community of believers, a role that connects him to a community (*umma*) based on shared submission to God, not on patriarchal blood ties. Opposition to father-rule is also evident in the example of Prophet Muhammad. The Qur'an describes Prophet Muhammad as closer to the believers than their own selves (Q 33:6), yet it simultaneously stresses that Prophet Muhammad is not the "father" of any members of the community (Q 33:40).[19] While this is a rejection of symbolic fatherhood, it is also revealing that Prophet Muhammad loses his father before birth and loses all his sons in infancy. His patrilineal ties are destabilized. As with Abraham, Barlas argues that Prophet Muhammad introduces a new social community (*umma*), a "community united by a shared moral worldview rather than by blood, sex/gender, race, or age."[20]

Barlas, though, acknowledges that the Qur'an calls for believers to "obey" Prophet Muhammad. What does "obey" imply if prophethood is taken to be a challenge to and displacement of father-rule and patriarchy? Clearly, Prophet Muhammad is a role model, exemplar, and model for emulation for all Muslims. He is a role model as prophet and as a moral individual "whose character embodies the best of the masculine and feminine traits as we describe them."[21] Barlas asserts that Prophet Muhammad's moral character was unconventional according to the standards of his context and even of today. As an exemplar of this kind, the delicate balance between following (or emulation) and idolization is central. She cautions against any idolization or glorification of Prophet Muhammad as no prophet would seek to be worshipped, something due to God alone: "God is Ruler, Sovereign, Savior, not Muhammad."[22] Prophet Muhammad, like all prophets, is a human and therefore fallible. Barlas states—contrary to the doctrine of *'isma*—that the Islamic tradition rejects notions of infallibility. She offers as evidence the fact that the Qur'an corrects Prophet Muhammad at various times. Notably, rejection of infallibility is connected to her understanding of faith and moral responsibility: "Arguably, theories of exceptionalism and infallibility would undercut the Qur'an's own view of moral individuality and, in the end, it may be its view of human fallibility and unexceptionalism that makes Qur'anic epistemology truly antipatriarchal."[23] Barlas here hints at something to which I return later in this chapter: the theological connection between infallibility (or perfection) and male normativity.

Not every Islamic feminist is as convinced as Barlas of the absolutely antipatriarchal nature of prophethood or of the Sunna of Prophet Muhammad. In the preceding chapter, I examined Ali's and Chaudhry's approaches to ahadith. While they both focus primarily on interpretation of ahadith texts, their broader observations about Prophet Muhammad's Sunna are worth revisiting. Ali states the Prophet is an exemplar who provides a beautiful example, yet she seeks to embrace some of the tensions and complexities of that example.[24] One way she does so is by acknowledging that Prophet Muhammad at times felt "discomfort" with divine commands. While she does not draw this connection explicitly, discomfort certainly raises questions about simple portrayals of Prophet Muhammad as perfect and as only a passive vessel of revelation. Discomfort also surfaces in contemporary approaches to aspects of the Sunna—such as, child marriage—that are viewed as unethical and morally problematic.[25] Muslims tend not to dismiss the Sunna overall, and therefore "must attempt to accept the Prophet's action as blameless while reconciling it with their own discomfort."[26] This "tricky proposition" places Muslims in the situation of affirming that the "Prophet is the model of conduct for all Muslims while simultaneously believing that it would be wrong of a Muslim man to follow his example."[27]

Ali proposes two strategies for addressing discomfort. One is to accept Prophet Muhammad in his context and recognize his example as representative of that time. Contextualization can ease defensiveness and anachronistic evaluation of his example, although it does not always answer the moral question about the "goodness" of actions. The second strategy is the classification of Prophet Muhammad's Sunna into exemplary, exempt, and unique aspects.[28] In some ways Prophet Muhammad is an exemplar for other people; in some ways he is exempt from the obligations and responsibilities of other people; and in some ways he has unique or additional obligations, rights, and responsibilities. Ali's schema highlights that Prophet Muhammad is an exemplar for other humans but not in every aspect of his behavior or life. She uses this distinction to argue for exemplary/exceptional analysis of ahadith related to marriage, but it is also a useful lens for analyzing the presentation of Prophet Muhammad as a universal exemplar without critical consideration of the impact of exceptional and unique characteristics associated with his sex/gender and prophetic role.

Like Ali, Chaudhry situates Prophet Muhammad firmly in his historical and sociocultural context, and this leads to acknowledgment that he personally participated in patriarchal society *and* challenged some aspects of that society. While her descriptions align with common perceptions of Prophet Muhammad's exemplariness—as a receptacle of revelation, a perfect human being, and the embodied Qur'an—she also recognizes that his actual, contextual example is more tensive than these descriptors let on.[29] Chaudhry rejects flat depictions of Prophet Muhammad as a "radically egalitarian man" *or* "a fully seventh-century Arabian man."[30] Prophet Muhammad is both of his context and transcending it, resisting it in some ways. The "some" part is important; he does not resist patriarchy or androcentrism in all ways or at all times. He is not a "feminist" in contemporary terms. Chaudhry thus shifts her focus to "small acts of resistance" that help to reveal his rationale for interrupting patriarchy at all. She argues that resistance to patriarchy does not subvert or displace it but rather serves to protect the disempowered within a society.[31] In this reinterpretation, Prophet Muhammad's model assumes a new form; it is not just a list of specific actions to replicate but a model that justifies contextual interpretation and outlines strategies for moral reform within Islamic law and Muslim societies.

Notably, emulation is not restricted to Prophet Muhammad's model or Sunna alone. Muslims—specifically Muslim women—are also encouraged to emulate the wives of Prophet Muhammad, the Mothers of the Believers. Due to their proximity to Prophet Muhammad and their involvement in what Barbara Stowasser terms the "Quran-as-process," these women become models of ethical conduct and exemplars.[32] Their prestige does not match that of Prophet Muhammad, but they are granted an elevated status. The Qur'an, however, distinguishes Prophet Muhammad's wives from other women; they are "not like any other women" (Q 33:32). They are subject to stricter codes of conduct (such as not remarrying) and harsher punishments than other women. As Barlas explains, "they were required to be role models for the entire community and therefore carried a greater moral responsibility. As such, the Qur'an holds them to standards of behavior it does not require of others."[33] Despite this, Prophet Muhammad's wives have become models of female social behavior and codified legal precedent. Even the explicitly distinctive (and restrictive) obligations of the wives have been applied in general to all Muslim women.[34] Prophet Muhammad's Sunna is presented as "legally binding precedent for the community, but (in practice) mainly as constituted for male believers."[35] Likewise, the example of Prophet Muhammad's wives is glossed as being theoretically applicable to all people but really is applied only to women. The extension of emulation to the wives of Prophet Muhammad, in spite of the Qur'anic assertion of distinctiveness, may appear practical, based on common sense, and even as a move toward inclusivity. It provides concrete examples of women and their actions. It admits female figures, behaviors, and concerns into the realm of moral and esteemed action. At the same time, it vividly reveals the presence of gendered and sexed assumptions in emulation and veneration of Prophet Muhammad. If Prophet Muhammad's Sunna alone does not accommodate female experience, concerns, and obligations, then that Sunna is gendered and sexed.

The concept of *al-insan al-kamil* presents one possible way to contest and reconfigure gendered assumptions in the codification of the Sunna in Islamic law and ritual. As part of an exploration of the potential of Sufi constructions of theological anthropology in the reformation of Islamic law, Shaikh argues that *al-insan al-kamil* is a "standard for spiritual completion," which makes ungendered, identical claims on men and women. In other words, it is a standard applicable to and attainable by both.[36] It offers a depiction of human purpose based on explicit gender inclusivity, not hierarchical or patriarchal norms.[37] Ibn al-Arabi did not restrict any spiritual role or rank to men alone. Vice and virtue are equally accessible. Shaikh avers that his gender inclusivity can serve as a potent basis for reconstructing Islamic law but also recognizes some ambivalence in his perspectives, especially on the topic of prophetic mission. Ibn al-Arabi retains his insistence on the accessibility of spiritual perfection irrespective of gender/sex but also states that only men can attain "superlative perfection," a form of perfection associated with prophets and messengers.[38] General theological and interpretative consensus holds that only men can be prophets and messengers.[39] Ibn al-Arabi simultaneously contests and upholds this consensus. He identifies women, including Mary and Asiya (the Pharaoh's wife), who achieved a state of perfection, and he describes them as prophets (*nubuwaa*), that is, recipients of divine revelation. He nevertheless denies that women can be messengers (*rusul*), that is, people tasked with communicating and disseminating a message in the sociopolitical arena. His position aligns with Ibn Hazm, who argues that Mary was a prophet but similarly restricts female messengership.[40] This perspective, according to Shaikh, demonstrates how "patriarchal forms of power exclude women from particular positions of leadership."[41] Though she acknowledges male messengership may be a functional or pragmatic consideration based on context, she ultimately claims that it is a nonissue after the prophethood of Muhammad. Prophet Muhammad is the final prophet and messenger; there will be no others, whether male or female. Male superlative perfection and male messengership are now only theoretical. Therefore, today, stations of spiritual perfection are equally accessible to all. The unique stature of Prophet Muhammad as the *final* prophet resolves ambivalent presentations of gender in favor of inclusivity and equality.

Although Schimmel's writing on Prophet Muhammad is not comparative, she periodically interjects comparative references to clarify her observations. These interjections do not play a large role in her own writing; they are mentioned in passing—with the assumption that her audience will understand her references—and not developed in any detail. Yet, her comparative insights are striking because they are founded on the analogy of the Qur'an and Jesus. In explaining Prophet Muhammad's role as a human servant of God, she argues that it would be inappropriate to compare Prophet Muhammad and Jesus Christ. Her rationale for this assertion is that Prophet Muhammad and Jesus Christ are theologically and phenomenologically disparate. The Islamic comparison to Christ is the Qur'an: "The central position of the Koran [sic] . . . stands, phenomenologically, parallel to the position of Christ in Christianity: Christ is the Divine Word Incarnate, the Koran [sic] (to use Harry Wolfson's apt term) the Divine Word Inlibrate."[42] She makes another comparative reference when describing the common practice of hanging the calligraphic *hilya* in homes. She equates this to displaying images of the Virgin Mary. Both are intended to convey blessings and protection. Her comparison of the Muslim Prophet Muhammad and Christian Virgin Mary grows out of her insistence on the analogy of the Qur'an and Jesus Christ. This becomes vividly and provocatively clear when she connects Prophet Muhammad's status as *ummi* with Mary's virginity: "As in Christian dogmatics, Mary must be a virgin so that she can immaculately bear the Divine Word to its incarnation, thus Muhammad must be *ummi* so that "inlibration," the revelation of the Divine Word in the Book, can happen without his own intellectual activity, as an act of pure grace."[43] Schimmel here points to a fertile opening in comparative feminist theology: the comparative theological exploration of Prophet Muhammad and Mary in light of gendered presentations and norms. Mary's virginity is not just another theological assertion; it is a hotbed of Christian feminist critique, and theological and practical struggle. Comparison of the concept of *ummi* with the concept of virginity is an invitation to further unpack implicit gendered claims associated with doctrines about Prophet Muhammad's exemplariness and emulation.

Mary: Liberated and Liberating?

In Christian feminist theology, Mary, Mariology, and Marian dogmas are the subjects of extensive writing and critique.[44] Feminist theologians themselves passionately debate the egalitarian potential and liberatory value of Mary's historical and symbolic roles. Mary—largely as constructed in male-dominated theology—is at times deemed the epitome of the patriarchal feminine. As a passive, pure, virgin receptacle for Jesus Christ, she is a symbol so idealized, purified, desexualized, and removed from actual female experience that valorization of her oft comes at the cost of marginalization and stigmatization of other women. Dogmas of virginity, immaculate conception, and assumption distance her from women and make her a "toy" for patriarchal projection.[45] Conversely, other feminist theologians depict her as a relatable model of female experience, liberation, and divine care and mercy. In the specific context of Latin America, popular piety centers on her approachability, her familiarity with suffering, her intercessory ability, and her contextualization in local cultures (such as in visions of the Virgin of Guadalupe). Her ambivalent status, however, remains even in these contexts; she has been both the banner of conquest and of nationalistic liberation. Christian feminist theologians, therefore, debate whether Marian dogmas can be reinterpreted, whether Mary can ever be liberated from patriarchal theological constructs, and whether women who venerate Mary are reinscribing hierarchical domination.

In this section, I focus on perspectives from Elizabeth Schüssler Fiorenza (discussed also in the preceding chapter), Elina Vuola, and Marcella Althaus Reid. Elina Vuola earned her doctorate in theology in Philosophy of Religion and Theological Ethics at the University of Helsinki, Finland. Her research and writing focus on liberation theology and Latin American women's interpretations of the Virgin Mary, and she is the author of *Limits of Liberation: Feminist Theology and the Ethics of Poverty and Reproduction* among other chapters and articles.[46] She is currently the Professor of Global Christianity and Dialogue of Religions at the Faculty of Theology, University of Helsinki. Marcella Althaus-Reid, a pioneer of queer and indecent theology, earned her PhD at the University of St. Andrews in Scotland. Until her death in 2009, she was the Chair of Contextual Theology at the New College at the University of Edinburgh. Her research and writing focus on liberation theology, queer theology, and sexuality, and her books include *Controversies in Feminist Theology* (with Lisa Isherwood), *Indecent Theology*, and *The Queer God*. These theologians offer diverse perspectives on dogmas and practices surrounding Mary. While they arrive at different conclusions, they each acknowledge the ambivalent nature of Mary, fierce debates surrounding her potential as a feminist exemplar, and the central role of gender assumptions in the theological articulation of doctrines, dogmas, and practices related to Mary.

Elisabeth Schüssler Fiorenza: Mariology and the Dangerous Mary

Elisabeth Schüssler Fiorenza explores the topic of Mariology to highlight the shortcomings of hegemonic Mariology and the characteristics of alternative approaches. She also advocates for a new approach to Mary using the theological idea of the "discipleship of equals," which she defines as the enactment of a new, liberative vision.[47] According to Schüssler Fiorenza, hegemonic—or malestream—Mariology is a projection of the ideals of a celibate, male, priestly elite. It emphasizes perpetual virginity, sorrowful maternity, and humble obedience. In this formulation, Mary is a "model that must be imitated but can never be quite reached." [48] Hegemonic Mariology devalues women by emphasizing virginity, idealizing motherhood, valorizing obedience and passivity, and enforcing gender complementarity. It also affirms, legitimates, and "religiously internalizes" marginalization and structures of oppression. [49] For these reasons, even feminist theologians must be vigilant when formulating alternative Mariologies; we remain enmeshed in structures of domination, and it is therefore possible to implicitly reinscribe those structures. The "feminine style" or approach in itself cannot be assumed to be liberating. Women often internalize and reproduce hegemonic formulations, including Mariologies. In line with her perspectives on biblical exegesis, reproduction of hegemonic formulations is resisted through avoidance of essentialism and universalism, questioning of assumptions, and "permanent critical self-reflexivity." [50]

Beyond and in reaction to hegemonic Mariology, Schüssler Fiorenza identifies four alternative approaches and thereby provides an overview of persistent debates. The first approach she labels the Reformation approach. [51] This Protestant approach to Mariology rejects many of the accumulated dogmas and teachings about Mary, and attempts to return the focus to scriptural accounts and Christology. It arises in reaction to perceived excessive Catholic devotions to Mary, as well as the "almost unbridgeable chasm . . . between the historical figure, Mary of Nazareth, and the Queen of Heaven and mother of G*d celebrated in the cult of Mary." [52] Schüssler Fiorenza describes the Reformation approach as a historicizing approach that aims to craft a liberatory Mariology from below. It, however, falls short in that the rejection of ideals and dogmas, such as virginity, does not necessarily equate to challenging the underlying patriarchal and kyriarchal structures.

The second approach is the ideal-typical, which Schüssler Fiorenza connects to the Catholic Church and specifically Vatican Council II's reformulation of Mariology. [53] In response to Protestant critiques of Marian devotion, Vatican Council II sought to limit devotions and connect Mariology more closely to scripture. Mary thus was no longer depicted as Mediatrix (intercessor and bestower of divine grace) or coredempter alongside Christ. She became the "ideal representative and central symbol of a more human church oriented toward the world." [54] She became an archetypal model for a new humanity. Schüssler Fiorenza aptly observes that the proclamation of Mary as the archetype and mother of the church did not translate into ecclesial or social change. Women remained "second-class citizens in the Roman Catholic church insofar as they are not permitted to represent Christ and the church as ordained officials because of their sex."[55] Feminist theologians also embrace the ideal-typical approach, aiming to "universalize her [Mary] as the ideal type of woman and the paradigmatic model of submission in faith."[56] Mary becomes an exemplary disciple, poor woman, prophetic proclaimer, and mother of the oppressed. While women can relate to this view of Mary, Schüssler Fiorenza argues that feminist ideal-typical Mariologies at times resort to idealized elaboration, rarely transgress boundaries of official church teaching, and as a result do not contest hegemonic sex-gender constructs.

The doctrinal-mythologizing approach attempts to integrate Mary and ideas about a divine goddess into existing church dogma.[57] This approach centers Mary and attends to the enduring and intense devotion to Mary in practice. If the dogmas themselves can be reclaimed, the devotions can be sustained. Therefore, in this approach, the dogma of virginity is reinterpreted to stress "autonomy, integrity, independence, and self-determination of woman whose identity is no longer defined with reference to a man."[58] Schüssler Fiorenza asserts that these formulations tend toward idealism and apologetics, and remain deeply connected to ecclesial authority. Even reclamations and reinterpretations of central Marian dogmas cannot free sexuality or challenge the valorization of motherhood. Therefore, she does not deem such approaches liberative. Mary remains an exception, an idealized exception, not the rule, and thus she does not produce "transformative power for solidarity, justice, and liberation."[59]

The final approach is the popular religion or cultic-spiritual approach, wherein Mary is imagined as the quasi-divine mother of God. This quasi-divine mother is more than the human Mary; she is the "mother of all grace," the Mediatrix, a "revelation of divine goodness and the manifestation of redemptive power."[60] This perspective also appropriates sites and practices outside of Catholicism, and therefore goes beyond dogmatic boundaries. Schüssler Fiorenza argues that official Church institutions periodically try to "prune" these elements from belief and practice, but people on the ground continue to imagine Mary as divine and as sharing the functions of God and Christ. For Schüssler Fiorenza, the cultic-spiritual approach plays an important "corrective" role in reference to the patriarchal God.[61]

In response to her examination and critiques of other Mariological approaches, Schüssler Fiorenza outlines her own perspective, the "rediscovery of the struggle of the historical Mary" in light of the idea of the discipleship of equals.[62] She promotes a deconstructive critique and an imaginative interpretative enterprise consistent with her hermeneutics of creative imagination, and identifies two specific starting points for rediscovery. The first is the infancy narrative in the gospels of Matthew and Luke. These narratives reveal the desire of the powerful to eradicate "those who carry the vision of a different 'world order'—*basileia*—of justice and well-being."[63] Mary is the one who "carries" this vision. Another point for rediscovery is the visitation, the account of Mary visiting with and seeking solace from Elizabeth after the annunciation of Jesus' birth by the Angel Gabriel.[64] The visitation, and the announcing of the Magnificat thereafter, center Mary's agency, female solidarity, and liberation of all oppressed. Through these rediscoveries, Mary becomes "dangerous" to church and political authority. The dangerous memory of "the young woman, and teenage mother Miryam of Nazareth—probably not more than twelve or thirteen years old, pregnant, frightened, and single, who sought help from another wo/man—can subvert the tales of mariological fantasy and cultural femininity."[65]

Elina Vuola: Mary as Familiar and Beyond

Adopting an approach based more on ethnographic research than constructive exegesis and theology, Elina Vuola maintains that popular devotion to Mary among poor women is premised on the view that Mary is familiar with, yet beyond women's experiences. Based on this, she offers a multipronged critique of the Catholic Church, feminism, and liberation theology. Vuola observes that the Catholic Church plays a dominant and central role in Central and Latin America. Even though many people do not actually follow "official" teaching, the church remains "the main social and political institution shaping population policies and values around family, sexuality, and women."[66] The Church's teachings on these topics is, according to Vuola, patriarchal, sexist, and aligned with the notion of *marianismo*, that is, a system of thought that explains and legitimizes women's subordinate status and suffering. She also connects the Church's position on women to other forms of fundamentalism, which stress inherent cultural differences and depict feminism or women's rights as a threat and sign of social degradation. While she does not agree with this depiction of feminism, she does also critique what she refers to as a "feminist blindness" with respect to religion.[67] Feminist thinkers often dismiss the importance of religion and its liberatory potential for women or, conversely, depict it as the "sole signifier" of a woman's identity. Feminists fail to critically engage the "Janus-like face of religion," which simultaneously presents obstacles and offers tools for liberation.[68] In all perspectives, religious women are imagined to be passive victims, not active interpreters or appropriators of their traditions.

With liberation theology, Vuola contends that it has failed to articulate an alternative sexual ethics.[69] Although liberation theologians add the category of women to their work, they do not engage in critical analysis of the roots and experiences of oppression.[70] Vuola surveys multiple Mariologies, including those articulated by Octavio Paz and Leonard Boff, and finds that male liberation theologians tend to deploy Mary as a way to resolve male identity conflicts or exalt the feminine archetype by depicting Mary in an overly romanticized fashion. While liberation theologians condemn sexism, their framings of Mary are in tension with the condemnation. An exalted or fantastic view of Mary—in which her experiences are not like other women—cannot be expected to have an impact on the experiences of real women. The romantic view similarly "becomes a serious ethical issue if it prevents speaking of the real-life conditions of women, especially poor women."[71]

In response to these critiques, Vuola focuses her work on an "ignored space" between Church teaching, secular feminism, and liberation theology:

> I wish to look at the lacking but crucial space between official Catholic teaching, sexist no doubt, the more progressive and critical interpretations such as Liberation Theology, which has no explicitly feminist agenda, and the secular feminist discourses and practices which lump all things religious into one and the same basket of powerful and blatant sexism. What do we see in that ignored space?[72]

One observation about this space is that the relationship between women's popular devotion to Mary and *marianismo* is not direct and immediate; devotion to Mary does not necessarily translate into tacit consumption and affirmation of women's subordination. In fact, Vuola argues there is a "confusing interplay" between *marianismo*, the Virgin Mary, women, and oppression.[73] The Virgin Mary can indeed be a symbol of submission but is also connected to suffering, politics, and a host of varied (even conflicting) interpretations, or "competing Marys."[74]

Pushing back on reductive and ahistorical accounts of devotion to the Virgin Mary and *marianismo*, Vuola focuses on how and why women approach Mary and the interpretations they offer for this engagement. The Mary women approach is not a concept or a symbol but rather a Mary with a "very human (feminine) face" who is familiar with their "most intimate and real experiences."[75] Popular devotion is centered on the Virgin Mary who "affirms and shares but also transcends and is beyond human womanhood."[76] Mary is a woman like other women; she understands and has experienced what they have. Mary also goes beyond these experiences; she is a divine figure who combines humanity and divinity, or transgresses the liminal space between human and divine.[77] Vuola's description of Mary's familiarity and uniqueness highlights that these women do indeed relate to Mary, and that Mary is simultaneously beyond the ordinary.[78] Moreover, Vuola clarifies, that as both familiar and beyond, the Virgin Mary acts as a sort of "bridge-builder" and boundary crosser. She "keeps the impossible whole together" and embodies the "fusion/disappearance/crossing/

mixing of boundaries."[79] As a result, this Mary is a direct contradiction to pa-triarchal *marianismo*, which is "static and flat, leaving no space for ambiguities, contradictions, tensions, and points of identification."[80] In reference to Mary's virginity in particular, Vuola acknowledges a disassociation from sexuality when Mary is presented simply as a vessel rather than as an active agent. She argues, however, that virginity can—in line with perspectives on virginal pre-Christian goddesses—be understood metaphorically as a reference to integrity, autonomy, and resistance to patriarchal constructs.[81] This understanding of virginity would fit with popular devotion in which women do not imagine Mary as oppressive but as sustaining, attentive, and like them.

These understandings manifest in popular devotion to Mary as Mediatrix, intercessor and bestower of grace, and as *Mater Dolorosa*, the suffering mother whose lamentation allows women to suffer, cope, and act. Vuola stresses that love of and devotion to Mary is not sickness or delusion: "Women's intense love for and devotion to the Virgin Mary is (wrongly, I claim) seen as alienation or even some sort of sickness that women must be healed from."[82] Conversely, she validates the deep devotion of these women and argues that *imitatio Mary* (imita-tion of Mary) offers more to women than *imitatio Christi* (imitation of Christ).[83] Mary is an exemplar for all of humanity, including women and men. She is "an example of the possibility of human deification. . . . Human beings, women and men, can look at her as a model, as a predecessor, and strive for the same with her help."[84] Drawing on Grace Jantzen, Vuola describes Mary as a mirror and a horizon to move toward. For women specifically, Mary affirms that female hu-manity matters; the female body in itself is a starting point and center. Vuola emphasizes that these views of Mary and *imitatio Mary* are not proposals but rather observations about what women actually do and say.

Marcella Althaus-Reid: Mary, Queer of Heaven

Deeply skeptical of positive assessment of the liberative value of devotion to Mary, Marcella Althaus-Reid offers a pointed critique of Mariology and its role among women in Latin America, labeling Mary as oppressive and caustic and Marian devotion as "false consciousness."[85] In contrast with Vuola, she does not see the existence of extensive popular devotion to Mary as proof that devotion is liberating or affirming.[86] Althaus-Reid concretizes her reflections by recounting a conversation with a group of poor women in Argentina. She asked these women if they identified with Mary. They responded negatively, noting that Mary "has expensive clothes and jewels, she is white and she does not walk."[87] Mary was imagined as distant from their own experiences and realities, as passive, rich, and white. Nevertheless, Mary plays a large role in the lives of these women in popular devotion, but also, Althaus-Reid argues, in shaping ideas about femininity, sexuality, and the place of Latin American women. Mary and Mariology create internalized patriarchal oppression and consciousness built on "resignation, passivity and a lack of critical capacity to analyze the situation of oppression."[88]

Acknowledging that some women think they benefit from Marian devotion and Mariology, Althaus-Reid insists on the necessity of critically exploring the "hermeneutical circle of Mary," the history of Mary's role and deployment in Latin American contexts. Study of this hermeneutical circle reveals that Mariology has "roots in blood and violence" and continues to be "an instrument of a colonial project."[89] Althaus-Reid, like Vuola, explores the fifteenth-century Conquista that decimated original nations and women's bodies, and was literally fought under the banner of Mary. Exploring indigenous texts, references to female bodies, visions, and visual representations of Mary and other women, she highlights the way original languages, cultures, and feminine symbols were suppressed and eradicated. In their place, Mary, as a passive maintainer of the patriarchal order, was enshrined. This Mary, *La Virgen*, is no liberator of her "sisters." She oppresses other women, supports *machismo*, and cultivates disunity instead of women's solidarity; she is founded in inequality and thus perpetuates inequality and oppression.[90]

Althaus-Reid also critiques liberation theology's engagement with Mary. Liberation theology upholds the notion of an "ideal woman." The white, middle-class woman ideal is displaced in liberation theology by another ideal, that of the poor, uneducated, faithful Christian mother.[91] This new ideal fails to capture the complexities of women's struggles, concerns, and experiences. Theologians assume that starting with Marian devotion is akin to starting with materialist analysis of reality, or of what people are doing and experiencing in praxis. Althaus-Reid contests this assumption in two ways. First, she asserts that placing initial emphasis on reality and secondary emphasis on crafting theology—a hallmark of the liberation theology approach—does not analyze how reality is "conformed . . . what is excluded and what is included in that definition of reality."[92] As a result, liberation theology fails in Mariology to distinguish between oppressive and liberative aspects of dogma and practice. Second, she argues that Mary is not a materialist or historical starting point at all. She is more like an idea, gaslike substance, or simulacra than a woman; Mary is "fantastic and phantasmagorical."[93] Althaus-Reid does not deny the existence of a historical Mary but states that the historical Mary is theologically irrelevant. The Christian Mary is a symbol and part of a symbolic, theological discourse. Mary as a symbol is authoritative, but she does not represent or align with women's lived experiences. Mariology of liberation theology, moreover, fails to analyze economic concerns in relation to "genderised culture," and thus reinscribes ideas of "decency"—meaning, that which is viewed as proper—and fixed sexual constructions.[94] As a result, "native" articulations of Mariology, pioneered by and "approved" by male liberation theologians, are in fact equally as patriarchal as other articulations.

Althaus-Reid critiques other feminist approaches to Mariology, including that of Ivonne Gebara and Maria Clara Bingemer, for echoing liberation theology by upholding idealism and repeating the idea of Mary being affiliated with the poor. They do not critically explore how Mary is related to false consciousness, and whether Mary's biography actually contains actions demonstrating solidarity with the poor.[95] Gebara and Bingemer draw on the Magnificat to demonstrate Mary's solidarity with the poor and oppressed. Althaus-Reid, though, describes the Magnificat as a poem and underscores that Mary did not—unlike Jesus—give up her life in solidarity with others. Creative interpretation of Mary is valuable, but the areas in which her biography fails to align with liberation must also be acknowledged.[96] Marian devotion is pervasive in Latin America, but Althaus-Reid resists the conclusion that Mary is liberative simply because many women are devoted to her. Women can also be devoted to abusive husbands. Althaus-Reid pointedly asks: "If Mary is a symbol for the Latin American women's liberation movement, how is it that in 500 years we have seen exactly the opposite?"[97]

Rejecting Mary as a liberative symbol, she describes Mariology as a "machine" that produces false consciousness and perpetuates fixed economic and biological constructions of women. Women may reap some reward or benefit from Marian devotion, from "investing" in and reinscribing the Latin American "decency system."[98] The return on this investment, though, is frequently very poor, if not explicitly damaging. Focusing on virginity in particular, she describes Mary as the passive, humble, and "immobile receptacle" for the "seminal dissemination" of the Word of God.[99] Mary does not participate in the construction of divine speech; she is only the receptacle for the Spermatic Word, only a "toy sitting in the lap of that great ventriloquist God the Father."[100] Althaus-Reid observes that virginity is not a common experience of many women in poverty whose lives are shaped by violence and promiscuity. The Virgin Mary thus does not align with women's experience and does not foster empowerment beyond the "power to suffer."[101] The Virgin Mary is "theologically caustic" for poor women who marry young, are raped, and are victimized by incest. This even extends to the Virgin of Guadalupe, *Guadalupana*. Althaus-Reid argues that if we "lift up her skirt," we will see that she too hides and naturalizes the "phallus" of hegemonic patriarchy.[102]

Underlying Althaus-Reid's critiques is a central assertion about the purpose of theology: "Theology is a sexual act, a sexual doing, based on the construction of God and divine systems which are male and worked in opposition (and sexual opposition) to women."[103] Theology is implicated in and invested in the regulation of women's sexuality and sexual life, in articulating and enforcing a decency system. Theology must go beyond what she calls "vanilla Mariology" and question the "approved script on women and Christianity."[104] Theology and Mariology should be a process of conscientization that questions assumptions and given realities. The necessary response to existing constructions and false consciousness is a "theological indecenting of the Virgin Mary."[105] Theologians must reveal and challenge the hidden constructions of sexuality, gender, and heterosexuality within dominant Mariology and Marian devotion. As such, the Virgin Mary—the "decent" and patriarchal Virgin Mary—must be "boldly denounced," and the way in which sexuality and gender are constructed and controlled through the symbol of the Virgin Mary must be rigorously analyzed.[106]

Althaus-Reid ultimately does not surrender all hope of a liberated Mary, of a Mary that contributes positively to women's liberation, of a Mary that "walks."[107] A liberated and liberating Mary would require critical revision in theology and anthropology, beyond superficial changes in her visual depiction (that is, in skin color and clothes). A liberated Mary would need to speak in indigenous voices, modify constructions of femininity, and unmask Mary "the white upper class woman who has made of us passive supporters of a patriarchal system."[108] She offers two specific insights into "indecent" Mariology. First, she refers to Mary as the "Queer of Heaven" and explores the way in which queer theology proffers a unique approach to Mary. Queer here refers not only to sexuality but more generically to "a category of indecency: a zone of possibilities."[109] Drawing on personal accounts of the complexities of life and sexuality, she argues that a queer Mariology is focused on imprecisions and mismatches, rather than fixed definitions and dogmas. A queer framework uses theological imagination to challenge set ideas and assumptions, and therefore has deep transformative possibilities. Moreover, since it is "imprecise and mutable," it permits a broader range of identification and representation.[110] Queering Mariology is not simply about making weird or moving away from set ideas: "Queer is not oddity. Queer is precisely the opposite: it is the very essence of a denied reality that we are talking about here when we speak of 'Queering' or Indecenting as a process of coming back to the authentic, everyday life experiences described as odd by the ideology—the mythology—makers alike."[111] Althaus-Reid's second insight on indecent Mariology is connected to the presence of a variety of ambiguous Christ/Marys in diverse Latin American contexts. She invokes the idea of "cross-dressing" and argues that these Marys—such as *Santa Librada* in Argentina and *La Difunta Correa*—cross "sexual, class, and political borders."[112] These Marys are not official dogmas or formulations; they are dangerous memories invented by people on the ground. They are "loose canons" that demonstrate people's frequent lack of concern for official biographies and theologies, or resolution of theological contradictions. These Marys—diverse, multiple, border-crossing Marys—demonstrate that "[d]ogmas are dead master narratives, and people's popular theology discards them and modifies them according to time and social problematics."[113]

Gendered Emulation and a Prophetic Prophet: Muslima Theological Reflections

Prophet Muhammad and Mary occupy a strikingly similar theological space within Islam and Christianity. They are both intermediaries—even mediators—of the divine revelation. They are commonly—although not without tension—described as vessels, receptacles, and bearers of the revelations of the Qur'an and Jesus Christ. While Mary is the theological and literal "womb" for Jesus, it should not be overlooked that Prophet Muhammad is sent as a "mercy." Mercy (*rahma*) derives from the same root (*r-h-m*) as and alludes to the word *rahm* (womb). Based on this positioning, analogous theological doctrines and dogmas address their historical humanity, relationship with God, agency, and purity. These doctrines include *'isma*, virginity, *ummi*, immaculate conception, perfection, sinlessness, intercession (Mediatrix), and passive receptivity. Nasr, Madigan, and Schimmel place particular emphasis on analogical connections among purity, passivity, virginity, and *ummi*.[114]

The theological analogy between Prophet Muhammad and Mary is also evident in their central roles in ritual devotion and popular piety. Devotion to Mary is less pronounced—sometimes rejected—within Protestant communities, although some Protestant feminist theologians do reclaim her example and reconsider Marian devotion.[115] Veneration to and emulation of Prophet Muhammad, however, saturates Muslim communities. Its manifestations are not uniform, but there is broad agreement that his Sunna, his example, should shape moral character, social norms, and ritual practice. While there are convergences in devotion to Prophet Muhammad and Mary, a notable distinction also exists. There is great emphasis placed on emulation of Prophet Muhammad, emulation not only of general moral traits or broad themes but also of minute and specific details. Value is appended to praying as he did, dressing as he did, wearing clothes as he did, marrying as he did, speaking as he did. The small details matter. For some, they are the only "right" way to live, for others they are invaluable opportunities for spiritual and moral cultivation, for moving closer to God. Devotion to Prophet Muhammad does have an intercessory flavor (the role of Mediatrix), but emulation and imitation of his Sunna are heavily and consistently accentuated. It is this form of emulation that raises questions about and tensions related to change.

Another obvious distinction between Prophet Muhammad and Mary is one is historically male and one is historically female. They are both sexed and gendered but in different ways. Sex and gender impact their historical lives, theological and symbolic depictions, and the questions raised in critical feminist analysis and reclamation. Prophet Muhammad's position as a male in his context is not directly comparable to Mary's position as a female in her own. The contexts differ, the social conceptions of gender differ, and their respective power and privilege differ. Theologically, moreover, an idealized female symbol does not operate in precisely the same way as an idealized male symbol. Although both deploy gender and sex, critical feminist analysis poses distinct questions about how such symbols relate to people on the ground and to traditional notions of authority. As indicated at the onset of this chapter, the "maleness" of Prophet Muhammad is not a primary focus in Islamic feminism, despite contestations of patriarchal elements of the Sunna and tradition. There has been much more extensive and explicit Christian feminist analysis of gender and sex in relation to Mary. My goal is to draw on that analysis to probe the gendered assumptions and gendered limitations latent in descriptions of Prophet Muhammad and *Imitatio Muhammad*, and thereby articulate an alternative Muslima conception of his "beautiful model."

I begin with a simple fact: Prophet Muhammad is male. This fact is comparatively significant in relation to Mary but also immensely significant in relation to veneration, emulation, and reclamation of Prophet Muhammad's example. He is a male human. Sex and gender are in play; Prophet Muhammad is gendered and sexed. In his historical and social context—the context preserved in his Sunna—he is not beyond gender, nor is he representative of a neutral or universal human experience. He is representative of a particular type of human experience: male human experience. The presentation of male experience as normative, inclusive, or universal is commonplace, but this faulty and deceptive presentation is one of the central critiques of feminist thinkers and theologians. Prophet Muhammad's maleness must be acknowledged and addressed. His maleness does not mean that he is irrelevant to women. It *does* mean that we must consider the limits and boundaries of his relevance to women. Ali introduces the tripartite distinction of exemplary, exceptional, and unique aspects of his Sunna. I would add another component to this schema: the gendered exemplary. As a subcategory of the first classification, "gendered exemplary" draws attention to the reality that even within the exemplary conduct of Prophet Muhammad, there are variations and limitations associated with—among other things—sex and gender. Plainly stated, the exemplary is not uniformly or equally accessible or relevant to all people.

Prophet Muhammad is not only historically male. He is also symbolically and theologically male. Theological doctrines and teachings related to Prophet Muhammad are replete with gendered allusions and norms. Although notions of prophethood, perfection, and illiteracy may superficially present as neutral and unconcerned with constructions of sex and gender, they are in fact gendered and androcentric. They are invested in—or, at minimum, function to reinscribe—traditional constructs of what Althaus-Reid terms "decency." Barlas argues that prophethood is an explicit challenge to patriarchy as father-rule. She effectively demonstrates that Abraham and Prophet Muhammad destabilize and break with some norms of patriarchy. Indeed, prophets tend to challenge their people and societies. In Islamic prophetology, the message prophets are charged with communicating is never a message of holistic affirmation. Divine revelation rarely interrupts to pat us on the backs and affirm the status quo. Notably, however, Barlas does not address the glaring traditional consensus that all prophets are male.[116] I generally embrace her analysis of the societal challenge presented by male prophets, yet we must also acknowledge and contend with this consensus.

Shaikh broaches the consensus in reference to Ibn al-Arabi, who partially deviates from it to argue that women can be prophets but not messengers. His—and Ibn Hazm's—inclusive understanding of prophethood further illuminates the exclusive nature of the traditional consensus. Their perspectives also precipitate the question of why they distinguish between roles of the prophet and the messenger. In part, this distinction is textual; the Qur'an lists some women—including Mary—among the prophets and describes them as receiving revelation (*wahy*) in a manner akin to other male prophets.[117] The text, here, forces the inclusion of women as prophets but not as messengers. Conspicuously, the default stance is noninclusion of women; the authority of the Qur'anic revelation forces Ibn al-Arabi and Ibn Hazm to permit limited inclusion of women. The gendered distinction between prophets and messengers also is described as pragmatic or contextual; in patriarchal and androcentric societies, it would be ineffective and inappropriate for God to send a female messenger.[118] This pragmatic, contextual argument is reasonable enough. However, when appended to an unequivocal and universal exclusion of women from the role of messenger, it is no longer simply pragmatic. It is not just that female messengers in those contexts would have been impractical. It is that female messengers in any and every context would be impractical. What appears to be a pragmatic claim now assumes a normative function; it has moved from the realm of "was" to the realm of "can be."

Textual and pragmatic bases for female exclusion are not the only explanations of the dominant consensus. Both the consensus that excludes females from prophethood and messengership and Ibn al-Arabi's and Ibn Hazm's inclusive prophethood are legitimized through arguments based on purity, particularly the invocation of *'isma*.[119] *'Isma*, as moral impeccability and sinlessness, appears gender neutral. It appears as an idealization, yes, but not necessarily as a gendered or sexed doctrine. Within Islamic tradition, though, *'isma* is connected to both moral and physical purity (the latter, *tahara*). Since women generally experience menstruation, they are biologically incapable of continuous physical purity. They are, thus, deemed incapable of *'isma*, and as a result incapable of being a prophet and/or messenger. Without conflating the Islamic Mary with the Christian Mary, even the elevated righteousness, chosenness, and devout obedience of the Islamic Mary is not enough to convince most male scholars of her status as prophet or messenger. She is a model, but, on the basis of sex and gender alone, she can be nothing more. Georgina Jardim perceptively observes that debates over female prophethood and *'isma* reveal "androcentric assumptions of purity" and demonstrate how "biological differences between women and men have the final say in determining women's agency in traditional reasoning."[120] In addition to undercutting moral individualism, Barlas' rejection of infallibility—even with Prophet Muhammad—is tied to the entanglement of infallibility and purity with patriarchy and androcentrism.

The doctrine of *al-insan al-kamil* also emphasizes notions of perfection that are at times tinged with gendered assumptions. Shaikh explicitly engages Ibn al-Arabi's depiction of superlative perfection as the purview of males alone. She also acknowledges the complex presence and function of gender norms in other Sufi thought, specifically in the description of prominent Sufi women as "men." Shaikh examines various accounts of female Sufis—including Umm Zaynab Fatima, Fatima of Nisapur, and Rabia al-Adawiyya—highlighting their spiritual equality if not precedence over male peers.[121] One account of Rabia, from Farid al-din Attar, emphasizes that God does not look at externals but the intention of one's heart. In praising her, Attar writes, "when a woman becomes a man in the path of God, she is a man and one can no longer call her a woman."[122] Women who have advanced to the highest stations of spiritual perfection are here described as "quintessentially male." Shaikh acknowledges the possibility that this is a contextual or pragmatic description, but she also identifies it as evidence of male normativity, marginalization of women, and a theological anthropology "that cannot assimilate the category of femaleness into its ideal of human perfection."[123] Despite these ambivalences, she argues that *al-insan al-kamil* and other Sufi concepts can provide a spiritual basis on which to resist "the central patriarchal tenet that the male body is entitled to claim social and ontological superiority."[124] One way she justifies this perspective is through the finality of the prophethood of Muhammad. Prophet Muhammad, as the seal of the prophets (*khatam al-nabiyyun*), the final prophet sent by God, renders gendered distinctions purely theoretical. In practical terms, the gendered stations related to *al-insan al-kamil* no longer exist after the final prophet.

The invocation of finality is an effective argument within Sufi cosmology and Islamic theology. Yet, finality itself is not a neutral portrayal of Prophet

Muhammad, even though it is commonly asserted. It can be read as only descriptive, but it also plays a theological role in explaining the significance and uniqueness of Prophet Muhammad's message and role in relation to other religions and prophets. Finality is a theological doctrine. While other traditions assert significance and uniqueness through claims to singularity, superiority, and supersession, finality plays a central role in explaining the distinctiveness of Islam—more particularly, the Qur'an—in relation to other religious traditions and revelations. Finality carries a heavy theological load within Islamic theologies of religious diversity because of the pervasive Qur'anic insistence on multiple revelations and the similarities and consistency among revelations.[125] In other words, the revelation to Prophet Muhammad is not significant because it is new, unique, or inherently better. Great significance is appended to it being last and operating to seal and preserve divine revelation. I am convinced by Shaikh's insight in relation to the stations. I also want to be attentive to the interreligious function of this theological doctrine. It distinguishes Islam. Yet, it also entails judgment on the status of other revelations; the necessity of such "sealing" is often explained through corruption of previous revelations. It also entails exclusion; it excludes all traditions that fall temporally after the prophethood of Muhammad. As I argued in the preceding chapter, attentiveness to diverse manifestations of imperialism and hegemony is vital. Part of this is attending to the zone in which religious distinctiveness slips into religious superiority, especially in an effort to contest androcentrism.

A similar concern exists with the doctrine of *ummi*. *Ummi* reveals a tangle of interreligious and gendered assumptions. As indicated, *ummi* is typically understood in two ways: first, as illiteracy, and second, as referring to a person from a community that has not received divine revelation. The comparative feminist theological lens foregrounds the function of purity and passivity in both definitions. Prophet Muhammad is not the agent of revelation. Prophet Muhammad is a passive recipient of the revelation. The revelation is not "tainted" by the humanity and personality of Prophet Muhammad. The revelation is also not "tainted" by or borrowed from other traditions. Its purity and authority are thus defined by excluding both the personal agency of Prophet Muhammad and any encounter, reliance on, or interaction with other religious scriptures and traditions. It is based on this comparative overlap in passivity and purity that Schimmel connects *ummi* to the virginity of Mary. Nasr echoes this, even referring to Prophet Muhammad's "virginity of the soul":

> The unlettered nature of the Prophet demonstrates how the human recipient is completely passive before the Divine. Were this purity and virginity of the soul not to exist, the Divine Word would become, in a sense, tainted

with purely human knowledge and not be presented to mankind [*sic*] in its pristine purity. The Prophet was purely passive in the face of the revelation himself. He did not write the book but conveyed the Sacred Book to mankind [*sic*].[126]

Prophet Muhammad's virginal conception of the Qur'an is theologically parallel to that of Mary. However, he is not a woman, and purity, passivity, and virginity are not embodied in the same way. Nevertheless, from a critical Muslima perspective, the elevation of passivity, purity, and even symbolic virginity—untouched by personality and untouched by other traditions—is concerning. This is even more so the case because of the emphasis placed on emulating Prophet Muhammad. People are called to emulate his relationship with God and with the revelation. Some aspects of his relationship are unique (not emulable), but his passivity, receptivity, and unquestioning consent are considered exemplary. Even in Barlas' argument about prophets and patriarchy, it is noteworthy that the prophets' independence as manifest in rejection is at times—for example, in Abraham's near sacrifice of his son—correlated with receptivity and unquestioning consent.

When inscribed on male and female bodies, passivity, receptivity, and consent do not produce the same results. They are not gender-neutral constructs in a gendered and androcentric world. In this actual world, they are constructs of gendered "decency" that function to maintain the status quo and maintain privilege. Passivity, receptivity, and unquestioning consent in relation to the Divine have value, but we must critically scrutinize the way these characteristics bleed into and are co-opted in intrahuman relations. At times, these characteristics can be theologically and practically "caustic."[127] Women, for example, are taught—on the basis of *sahih* hadith—that angels (servants of God) will curse them if they do not consent to every sexual advance of their husbands.[128] Under divine threat, women are coerced into passivity, consent, and physical and emotional receptivity toward other humans—other humans that are conspicuously not enacting the same standards of passivity or receptivity.

All descriptions of Prophet Muhammad have a direct impact on emulation. This impact, though, is not always acknowledged or examined. What is the impact of maleness—historical and theological—on emulation, particularly female emulation of Prophet Muhammad? Idealized theological presentations of Prophet Muhammad are just that: idealized. For most humans, they are difficult if not impossible to attain. This is the case with unique aspects of his Sunna—such as receiving revelation—but also with technically exemplary and emulable aspects such as *al-insan al-kamil*. The latter do serve as aspirational goals, but they can also introduce distance between Prophet Muhammad and humans. As with

Mary, people are called to imitate that which is difficult if not impossible for them to ever imitate. Perfection and purity are not very relatable characteristics among humanity. There is a tension between the presentation of Prophet Muhammad as ideal and perfect and the call for detailed emulation. Perfection serves a theological function of preserving and stressing divine incomparability and agency, but it does not foster intimate human to (exemplary) human bonds. While Vuola and Althaus-Reid disagree over the liberative value of certain formulations of Mary, they both stress the centrality of relatability, familiarity, and tangible connections. Women need to see their struggles, concerns, and even likeness in Mary. Mary can be more than familiar, but she needs to be familiar as well.

In my experience, many Muslims do have a deep and intimate connection to Prophet Muhammad despite his general idealization and specific gendered idealization. Muslim women do find points of intimate and profound familiarity in his example, points of connection and resonance that sustain and comfort. Ali's reference to the loss of his children is one such example. But what are the bounds of these connections given Prophet Muhammad's maleness? Not every aspect of his life will be familiar or relevant. This may seem to be a shallow observation. However, remember the example Schimmel proffers of al-Ghazali. Emulation—and the moral and spiritual cultivation arrived at through emulation—is in the details. Every detail and every sliver of emulation is an opportunity for growth and proximity to the Divine. Without being overly essentialist, women are—by their very created biology—excluded from large swaths of these actions and behaviors. I will never be able to be a husband like Prophet Muhammad was a husband. I will never be able to be a father like Prophet Muhammad was a father. I will never perform ritual ablution on my female body in the way Prophet Muhammad performed it on his male body. These may seem like trivial points, but my argument is, in the existing understanding of emulation, gender and sex result in some people simply having more opportunities to engage in emulation. Does that mean that all men have the same opportunities? Absolutely not. Nor do all women have the same. But there is an inherent and fixed hierarchy in place; men will always have more potential arenas and forms of emulation. Women, in this system, will always be at a disadvantage. This observation is not new. It is the reason why many male scholars referred to women as having a "deficiency in religion."[129] Women did not pray all the time. They did not fast all the time. Because of sexual biology and gender, they did not have even the potential—never mind actual ability—to embody the Sunna to the same degree or extent as men.

I do not agree with this portrayal of women or of emulation. However, we must face it directly in order to move beyond it. We must also address two common strategies for circumventing it without challenging it. The first strategy is abstraction or generalization of the Sunna. This occurs, for instance, when Prophet

Muhammad's actions as a father are generalized to actions of parents irrespective of gender and sex. It also occurs when his actions as a husband are generalized to spouses. Abstraction can also manifest as somewhat amorphous or undetailed appeals to the good character and moral uprightness of Prophet Muhammad. These abstractions reference his positive treatment of people without wading into the specifics. Abstraction and generalization are strategies that address sexed and gendered limitations of the Sunna and also address contextual limitations of the Sunna. They allow the Sunna to be more broadly applicable and to remain relevant. I am not opposed to these strategies. However, they do not correct the disproportionate advantage of maleness in relation to the Sunna of a male exemplar. They extend the Sunna so non-male-identified persons can participate and relate. But, male persons retain the distinct privilege of participating in both a generalized/abstract Sunna and the detailed enactment of that Sunna. Their advantage remains intact. Moreover, the relinquishing of details and specifics that occurs with abstraction and generalization is not uniformly positive, even for Muslim women. It can obscure concrete details of the Sunna that are explicitly egalitarian, and it can deemphasize embodied enactment, which is, in my view, necessary and transformative. I personally experience cultivation through detailed emulation of aspects of the Sunna, and therefore do not want to forfeit each and every detail. I want critical and selective consideration of *both* the social and ritual Sunna. We cannot gut the entire Sunna, nor can we blindly reenact the whole without consideration of its gendered implications.

The second strategy for circumventing the sexed and gendered limitations of emulation is the invocation of the wives of Prophet Muhammad, the Mothers of the Believers. This strategy is another vehicle for extending the Sunna. Based on their proximity to and relationship with Prophet Muhammad, and despite the Qur'anic description of their distinctiveness, his wives become role models for moral/ethical norms and for legal precedent.[130] As Stowasser notes, this precedent is typically confined only to other women. The exemplary model of the Prophet's wives becomes a gendered corpus of jurisprudence. Yet, it also begins as a gendered maneuver, a sort of escape hatch or pressure release valve. When the edges of the Sunna are reached, exemplariness is extended to the Prophet's wives to avoid grappling with the gendered limits and boundaries of his own Sunna and resultant theological considerations. It is a way to fill in the gaps. The move to his wives' examples is cast as common sense and practical. But is this move common sense and practical? More significantly, is it theologically valid? Does it make theological sense to ascribe the same degree of authority to emulation of Prophet Muhammad—in his unique stature and roles—and emulation of any other human, including his wives? Of course, it can be argued that it is not the same degree of authority, that the examples of the wives are authoritative but less authoritative. Then, where does that leave women who are instructed to emulate their example and who live under Islamic norms and laws based on the wifely "sunna"? They are left emulating a less authoritative (and often more restrictive) practice, and again relegated by virtue of their sex and gender.

The "exemplariness" of the Mothers of the Believers is also more complex than typically acknowledged. The Mothers have not always been exemplary, sometimes are exemplary in their negative depiction, and sometimes are deployed as rhetorical devices to enforce Islamic boundaries and norms. Stowasser argues that early depictions within ahadith and Sunna focus on their portrayal as "ordinary women," often translated as "embodiments of female emotionalism, irrationality, greed, and rebelliousness."[131] Conspicuously, their ordinariness is juxtaposed to the extraordinariness of Prophet Muhammad. In early hagiographic accounts, they become inspirational figures, divinely chosen above other women, and participating in miracles connected to Prophet Muhammad. Their value here is relational; they are chosen by God for Prophet Muhammad, and their miracles serve to confirm *his* exemplariness. Later scholars introduce the notion of the wives as paragons of virtue and precedent-setting models.[132] Stowasser, however, draws attention to the type of precedent; the wives are paragons in safeguarding and enforcing dominant societal norms, in their social invisibility, and in their sacrifice. They signify themselves and more than themselves: "In ideal terms, they convey the essence of Muslim female morality as perceived and formulated by the medieval urbanized and acculturated theologians of Islam."[133] The essence of female morality according to these (male) theologians is segregation, domesticity, frugality, invisibility, and wifely obedience. Contemporary exegetes retain the emphasis on paragons of virtue but innovatively depict the wives as helpmates in Prophet Muhammad's cause and ideal models of "women's work" and female domesticity.[134] These portrayals positively spin some "ordinary" traits, such as jealousy. The wives as ideal women also become defenders of the cause and tradition, frequently defenders against change, innovation, and outside encroachment. As Jardim observes, "outside" encroachment manifests in diverse forms, including pre- or extra-Islamic Jahiliyya, non-Islamic social norms, Islamic sectarian divisions, and even "Western" imposition.[135] Therefore, while the contemporary presentation is more positive, it continues to conform to androcentric norms, and it functions to preserve conservative interpretations of Islamic tradition.[136]

In highlighting the theological implications, complex presentations, and hidden rhetorical functions of the Mothers of the Believers, I aim to underscore the way sex and gender operate in emulation, not to dismiss the value of these female exemplars. The examples and models of Khadija, Aisha, Umm Salama, Sawda, Hafsa, and others are valuable and relatable. However, their value does not negate the fact that they are being invoked to maintain an androcentric construction of exemplariness and of the Sunna. They serve to silence questions about Prophet Muhammad's historical and theological maleness. Moreover, the deployment of these female exemplars as Sunna-extensions undercuts their own independent authoritativeness. They are granted authority based on their relation and proximity to Prophet Muhammad, not on the sole basis of their exemplary model; they are "legitimized through their relationship to males as wives, daughters, or mothers."[137] These females do present exemplary models; they are powerful female exemplars. Their exemplariness deserves to be liberated from the additive role of filling in blanks in an otherwise normatively male Sunna.

The Sunna of Prophet Muhammad also deserves to be liberated from its truncated depiction. Gendered assumptions run throughout all the central descriptions of Prophet Muhammad and directly impact emulation. Descriptions entail constructions of gender, sex, and otherness. They often also entail notions of gendered (specifically androcentric) perfection. Gender is in play, descriptively and theologically. Yet, recognition of this is not an excuse for the dismissal of Prophet Muhammad. It is rather a critique of the way his example has been described, constructed, and glorified through exclusionary gendered rhetoric. Recognition of this is also not an excuse to gloss his maleness. He is male, and attempts to simply transcend his historical maleness will ultimately leave androcentrism intact. Prophet Muhammad is a male exemplar worthy of emulation by people. The question thus becomes: how do we reclaim and reinterpret his exemplariness and emulation without ignoring or reinscribing gendered assumptions and limitations? How do we reclaim Prophet Muhammad as a "beautiful feminist exemplar"?

One approach is to assert that Prophet Muhammad was a feminist and that at its core his Sunna is egalitarian. Though this approach is common in contemporary Islamic feminist discourse, especially popular Islamic feminist discourse, Chaudhry maintains that it is anachronistic and fails to address the reality that Prophet Muhammad was "comfortable" in the patriarchal context of his time.[138] He both participated in and challenged some aspects of his context. This observation—which Chaudhry arrives at based on in depth exploration of ahadith and the Sunna—leads her to focus on small acts of resistance and interruptions aimed at protecting disempowered members of society. These small acts do not holistically challenge or uproot social hierarchies or patriarchy.[139] Chaudhry thus reframes the Islamic feminist approach to the Sunna. Instead of asking why his Sunna is not perfectly egalitarian—or pretending that it is—she asks, "Why is patriarchy interrupted at all in Prophet Muhammad's practice?"[140]

This question points beyond considerations of his acts of resistance alone. It asks why someone with embodied privilege (for example, a male in a patriarchal context) would ever interrupt or destabilize that system. I contend that it is this destabilization of privilege—manifest in the theological and practical crossing of boundaries—that forms the kernel of Prophet Muhammad's model as a beautiful feminist exemplar. Prophet Muhammad is not female; he is male, and we must attend to the particularities of his embodiment, as much as we must attend to the particularities of female embodiment. Prophet Muhammad is not a feminist, nor is his example thoroughly egalitarian as defined in contemporary terms. However, Prophet Muhammad, theologically and historically, is someone who "troubles" the status quo. He does not eradicate the status quo, but he does not leave it fully intact either. A model focused on his "troubling" of the status quo addresses his specific embodiment, reframes theological accounts of his perfection and exemplariness, and outlines a model of emulation that attends to but is not limited by sexed and gendered norms.

To clarify my position, I return to Althaus-Reid and the notion of indecenting. Indecenting is her response to how Mary is often deployed in a hegemonic manner to reinforce and normalize "decent" constructions of sexuality, sex, and gender. Decent here does not mean good but hegemonically, patriarchally, and heteronormatively proper. Decency marginalizes, harms, and controls women. Althaus-Reid concretizes the process of indecenting by turning to queer theory and theology. Mary is only liberated and liberating as the boundary crossing, possibilities creating "Queer of Heaven." Queerness is a more authentic portrayal of the complexities and ambiguities of Mary. Interestingly, Ali also invokes queer theory to revisit gender in relation to the Qur'anic Mary and her role as a female exemplar. Ali describes the goal of queer theory as "undoing binaries and unsettling taken-for-granted categories, especially those that pertain to sex, sexuality, and gender."[141] The Qur'anic depiction of Mary when read through the lens of queer theory creates a new possibility outside of the more common and binary presentations of Mary as either the same as men, or as distinctive in her femaleness. The queer Qur'anic Mary is similar, different, subversive, uniquely maternal (giving birth without sex or a biological male), and disruptively relational (occupying roles not typically assigned to women). Referencing Althaus-Reid explicitly, Ali foregrounds the theological and social relevance of queer interventions: "challenging the presumed coherence and sacred nature of existing oppressive norms allows other forms of being and relating to emerge and flourish."[142] By engaging Mary's sex and gender—yet not fixing it within a "totalizing narrative"— these "other forms" emerge.[143]

Queer theory is equally relevant to Prophet Muhammad. As a theoretical lens, queerness permits a more robust, more complex understanding of the nature and value of his exemplary model. Prophet Muhammad's relationship with God is extremely "queer" in the theoretical sense. Boundaries of humanity and divinity are crossed, with Prophet Muhammad serving as a sort of bridge between the two. References to Prophet Muhammad's virginity, carrying, and bearing of the Word blur sex and gender norms. Tensions between an insistence on his humanity and dogmas of perfection and impeccability that transcend the human condition also challenge hard and fast delineations. In his historical context, boundary crossing and the challenging of binaries are also evident. Chaudhry and Ali highlight his resistance and even "disobedience." He participates in patriarchy but advocates egalitarianism. He obeys God, yet may not always like or enact every revelation. As Barlas highlights, he is born in a patriarchal context in which his patrilineal line is destabilized. He is also born in a powerful family, yet he himself is not powerful. He is protected through social and familial ties, yet also relegates social ties in favor of ethicoreligious ones. His example is ambiguous, complex, and resistant to well-ordered storylines. For Muslima theology, the ambiguity and boundary-crossing nature of his model is a strength; it creates a "zone of possibilities" that allows for the emergence of new norms.[144] These possibilities are not the approved script or repertoire of traditional religious authority—what Althaus-Reid might call "vanilla prophetology"—nor of patriarchal society. They are also not neatly or thoroughly egalitarian. These possibilities are dangerous, provocative, unsettling, and subversive. In short, they are prophetic.

By prophetic, I intend a specific meaning. Prophetic designates that which is situated in a particular context yet points beyond the constraints of the context. In Islamic prophetology, this is the basic reality of prophets. The Qur'an insists repeatedly that prophets are chosen from and sent to their own people, that prophets literally and figuratively speak the language of their people, and that nonhuman messengers (such as angels) would be ineffective among human communities (e.g., Q 10:47, 14:4, and 17:94–95). The prophetic is rooted in context; it is never found outside of human contexts in an idealized, utopian setting. It arises in the messiness of human context. Yet, as I have reiterated throughout, the prophetic has another aspect. It points people *beyond* the present condition. It does this eschatologically (in reference to the Hereafter) and socially, by drawing attention to the ways in which the social context of the prophet fails to align with central Islamic theological teachings about devotion to God, justice, and human dignity. The prophetic is enmeshed in context and points to—perhaps aggravates for—an ideal that has not yet been achieved. The prophetic aligns with Vuola's descriptions of Mary as being familiar and simultaneously beyond the experiences of women, as being a mirror and a horizon. It is in this dual role—as mirror and horizon—that the prophetic message and vision meet with fierce challenge and resistance. Prophets carry a new vision that is tangible yet troubling . . . in fact, troubling because it is so tangible. It is dangerous. The prophetic vision never conforms holistically to extant social hierarchies, but it speaks directly—loudly—to those contexts. Schüssler Fiorenza highlights the common tendency for the societally powerful and those who benefit from existing social hierarchies to attempt to destroy the new vision in Mary. The biography of Prophet Muhammad overflows with similar attempts to silence his message, delegitimize him through slander, ostracize him physically and socially, and even take his life. Rejection—as the Qur'an calls it—is the typical plight of the prophet; Prophet Muhammad is warned that he will be rejected as were the prophets before him (Q 26:all, especially 26:6).

Rejection, though, is not the only response. The prophetic vision will be supported and confirmed by some. With Mary, Schüssler Fiorenza centers the visitation of Mary to Elizabeth. If we look for a parallel to the visitation, do we find something similar in the Sunna? Where and to whom does Prophet Muhammad run when he is overwhelmed by the revelation of the Word, by the annunciation of Jibril, by his personal doubt, and by societal questioning? His "visitation" is twofold. First, he finds solace but also confirmation in his wife Khadija. Second—and notably on the advice of Khadija—the Christian monk Waraqa confirms Prophet Muhammad's experience and the revelation. The authority of the revelation, the veracity of his experience, the confirmation that it is of divine origin and not the product of insanity or delusion . . . all of this is confirmed across gender and religious boundaries. These events are often highlighted to stress the status of women or the interreligious connections in Islamic tradition. Yet, they are something more than this. These confirmations underscore that his vision—the prophetic vision—is one that will challenge assessments attached to such boundaries; the prophetic vision will not simply fall in line with extant social boundaries, notions of authority, and identity constructions.

It is helpful at this juncture to briefly revisit Barlas' argument about prophethood contesting father-rule. My perspective aligns with yet goes beyond hers. Prophethood does not just contest patriarchy. It troubles and destabilizes—fails to fully align with—social hierarches more broadly. The example of Abraham makes this clear. Abraham clearly challenges his father. His challenge to the norms of his people, though, is about more than father-rule; it is also about blind adherence to any inherited social norms and constructs. Abraham does not relinquish all such norms and constructs—he is in his context and of his context—but he becomes a model, in fact, *the* model (even for Prophet Muhammad) for critical evaluation of such norms. Strikingly, passive acceptance and adherence are not part this prophetic vision. The prophetic vision is challenging in its call for reflection, consideration, and logical assessment. It is challenging in its call to look at oneself *and* beyond oneself to the horizon of what is not yet but could be. The prophetic vision does not come to congratulate and confirm. There is thus a large degree of irony in the fact that those in power use the Sunna of the Prophet to maintain a status quo that facilitates their power and authority. What prophet ever did this? What prophet was sent to prop up the social elite and powerful, "those who cling too tightly to this world's comforts and their established value schemas"?[145] Prophethood as a reminder, as guidance, is fundamentally a social critique. What reminder is needed, what guidance required, if everything is acceptable as it is? If we endeavor to emulate the Prophet, should we not strive to emulate his *prophetic* example?

Emulation of the prophetic model of Prophet Muhammad requires us to be attentive to and aware of our social contexts and our specific positioning in those contexts. It calls for understanding how we are marginalized by, co-opted within, and benefiting from our investment in societal hierarchies. For Muslim women, this means direct contestation of patriarchy and androcentrism but also consciousness of how we implicitly conform to and benefit from systems of norms that exclude and marginalize others, including other women. Emulation of the prophetic model also calls for more than awareness. It demands that we use our particular positioning to challenge the status quo and resultant marginalization. No prophet ever came solely to draw attention to hierarchies. Action to destabilize and move beyond those hierarchies is central. Traditional theological doctrines stress the uniqueness of Prophet Muhammad's perfection. Here, I am emphasizing the exemplariness of his model of "perfecting," his example of troubling, destabilizing, and of being prepared to meet resistance, especially from those who "man" the helm of social hierarchies. The model of prophetic perfecting is not one of tame and compliant enactment. It can never be this because the prophetic model is not just what was done in the past, but it is also what must be done today to sustain the prophetic vision and carry it further toward liberation. The prophetic call is not just a call to replicate the past but also to imagine the future in every present.

This model of perfecting—without holistic and outright rejection, nor arrival at perfection—can be problematic. It can appear as complicit in or acquiescing to dominant systems. It would indeed be neater not to play any patriarchal, androcentric, heteronormative, ablest, and white privileging games. There is something deeply appealing in the idea that the ideal could simply manifest in the world. That God would and could simply make the ideal real. Theologically, this would align with the omnipotence and beneficence of God. It would also align with the way many people approach the content of the Sunna, that is, as a fixed and manifest ideal achieved in the past that needs only to be imitated in successive presents. I cannot, however, assert that this is the model found in Prophet Muhammad. His model is not ideal in the sense of achieving a fully liberated society without marginalization or dehumanization.

However, what his prophetic model offers may be more valuable than this to our actual, on the ground needs. He offers a model of how to begin the process of change and of how to sustain the process of change despite resistance.

His prophetic model also offers a somewhat uncomfortable, yet pragmatic, model of the messiness (perhaps, compromises) entailed in advocating for change. Again, the ideal of no compromise is so enticing. But is it realistic? Is it something we can actually enact? Or do we require a messy, complex, tensive model that forces us to contend simultaneously with our privilege, marginalization, human limitations, and desires for liberation and equality? The prophetic model is dangerously provocative because it is both enmeshed in and beyond the existing norms. It is a strategy for changing and challenging systems from within. Again, the romantic vision of exiting the system entirely looms large. Yet, are we able to do this, especially those among us who are most marginalized?

The prophetic model demands we use our positioning to move toward liberation and equality by strategically destabilizing dominant norms, including but not limited to sex and gender norms. Since we are not all positioned in the same way even if we share a social context, the manifestations of emulation will not be one-size-fits-all. If we attend to the specifics of embodiment, then we immediately recognize that emulation of the prophetic vision of destabilizing privilege will assume a variety of forms, none of which is automatically more valuable. To be concrete, male emulation will not be the same as female emulation of the prophetic model, not because of sex and gender, but because of distinct positionings in society. Additionally, my emulation—as a white, American, Muslim woman—will differ from emulation by an American Muslim woman of color. If I wish to enact this prophetic vision, then my whiteness requires me to decenter myself and challenge hierarchical constructions of race that privilege whiteness. I cannot relinquish my whiteness, and ignoring it would be superficial and frankly an option available only because of race-based privilege. Therefore, prophetic emulation calls me to recognize it, and then go after the structures that privilege me in that facet of my identity, to make room, to destabilize the social hierarchies of privilege. Although there will then be diverse manifestations of the prophetic model—multiple, even competing Muhammads—not every form of emulation will be prophetic. Emulation of Prophet Muhammad as a patriarchal exemplar, for example, is not and can never be prophetic. Emulation of a patriarchal exemplar is not even mere copying of his actions. It is participation in the maintenance and naturalization of antiprophetic social hierarchies. It is also valorization of the antiprophetic through association with the Prophet and God.

The prophetic model is a beautiful feminist exemplar, an *uswatun hasanatun*. This is not the only way to approach or understand the Sunna and centrality of emulation. It *is* a legitimate way to reclaim the exemplariness of Prophet Muhammad without neglecting his maleness or placing women at a disadvantage with respect to emulation and moral cultivation. Emulation of the prophetic model is a call to personal accountability and collective responsibility. It is also a way to retain emphasis on detailed, yet not blind or mechanical, imitation. The details can still matter; generalization is not enough. Moral cultivation is embodied, just as immoral marginalization is. But the details must be subjected to critical screening and assessment that probes how those details—big and small, prayer and putting on pants—either enforce, reinforce, or prophetically destabilize hierarchal norms.

6

Women in the World

HUMAN NATURE, CONSTRAINT,
AND TRANSFORMATION

TAWHID, THE UNICITY OF GOD, forms the foundation of many Islamic feminist theological claims to equality, agency, and voice. The absolute oneness and uniqueness of God rules out the legitimacy—although not the reality—of human domination based on biological sex or gender distinctions. Men do not stand in a more proximate or privileged a position in relation to God. Humans are endowed with freedom and capacity, and all stand in an undifferentiated relationship to God. God is distinct from, yet not distant from, all humans. Any claim to the contrary—any claim that seeks to automatically and inherently elevate men over women or usurp divine prerogatives—is a form of *shirk*, or association of partners alongside the one, unique God. *Tawhid* is also frequently coupled with other Islamic theological concepts, including *fitra* (human nature), *khilafah* (vicegerency), and *taqwa* (piety or God-consciousness), to underscore the moral and social equality of men and women.

In this chapter, I seek to explore and expand dominant formulations of egalitarian theological anthropology to consider the extent and reality of human freedom, especially in light of structural and systemic constraint. I begin by surveying existing Islamic feminist formulations of egalitarian anthropology—including my own work on religious diversity—which foreground *tawhid, fitra, khilafah*, and *taqwa*. I then engage Christian womanist and feminist perspectives on theological anthropology, embodiment, constraint, and survival from M. Shawn Copeland, Jeannine Hill Fletcher, and Delores S. Williams. These perspectives prompt important considerations about individual autonomy, systemic injustice, and possible responses to such injustice. I conclude the chapter by articulating a Muslima theological expansion of *taqwa* that centers Hajar and stresses systemic transformation through visibilization, conscientization, and prioritization of the marginalized.

This chapter and the final chapter of this book continue the comparative theological dialogue but are unique in that they do not propose a direct analogical starting point, as with the Qur'an/Jesus, Ahadith/Bible, and Prophet Muhammad/Mary. This chapter, though, does rest on the analogical groundwork laid in those chapters. As such, it circumvents typical discussions based on caricatures of the Fall and sin; I seek herein to listen to the theological accounting entailed in these Christian concepts and in the Islamic rejection of those concepts. My focus is not on adjudicating the divergence but on exploring the extent to which Islamic feminist theologies offer a substantive accounting of the existence and persistence of systemic constraint, especially in light of a generally optimistic theological anthropology.

Tawhid, Fitra, Khilafah, *and* Taqwa

Islamic feminists stress the importance of theological anthropology—theological perspectives on human nature, capacity, and purpose—in the pursuit of equality. The pioneering contributions of Riffat Hassan, amina wadud, and Asma Barlas center on theological anthropology, challenge nonegalitarian depictions of men and women, and articulate alternative egalitarian understandings of human creation and nature. More recent contributions, including those of Kecia Ali, Sa'diyya Shaikh, and Ayesha Chaudhry, emphasize the necessity of analyzing anthropological assumptions underlying Islamic law, ethics, and exegesis.[1] Even outside of explicit theology, theological anthropology is always in play. Particular—and often patriarchal, misogynist, and androcentric—anthropological conceptions shape laws, rights, ethics, and practices. Shaikh, therefore, asserts that legal reform cannot only be based on the pragmatic strategy of retrieving women's rights. Since these rights emerge out of specific conceptions of theological anthropology, retrieval alone is "constrained by reigning ideologies"; it can internalize and reinscribe various hegemonies even if the rights appear egalitarian or benevolent.[2] Islamic feminists must go beyond retrieval. They must engage in comprehensive structural critique aimed at revealing the anthropologies on which all laws and rights (even seemingly egalitarian ones) are constructed, interrogating the assumptions and implications of those anthropologies, and then seeking to critically rethink theological anthropologies.[3] Shaikh describes this shift from symptoms to structure as a necessary and "deeply productive" way to reframe the debate over Islamic law.[4]

Theological anthropology is concerned with the nature and purpose of human beings, but it is inseparable from core assertions about God. In Islamic feminist theology, the central such assertion is *tawhid*, the unicity of God, the oneness and uniqueness of God. God is not like any other thing; God is ontologically dispa-rate, while at the same time close and involved. wadud also describes *tawhid* as a "principle of equilibrium and cosmic harmony."[5] God's oneness and uniqueness serve to unite all else; everything is united in its distinction from and relation-ship to God. *Tawhid* is a central theological concept within Islamic thought; it is widely agreed on throughout the tradition. Its potential in feminist theological reconstruction stems directly from its recognized significance. Islamic feminist theologians seek to unpack and explicitly outline its implications in reference to God and also in reference to humans and interpersonal relationships. wadud ac-cordingly describes *tawhid* as the "starting principle and ethical imperative" of Islam, which can and should be applied to social and gender relations.[6] She argues that if *tawhid* was fully and actually implemented in human interactions, there would be a "single global community" without hierarchical distinctions based on race, gender, religion, sexuality, nationality, or class.[7] Therefore, beyond a the-ological assertion about the nature of God, *tawhid* is an authoritative "counter construct" to hierarchical and divisive social practices.[8]

Tawhid, as a counter construct, not only affirms the unity of all humanity but also delegitimizes certain possibilities for human beings. If God is one and wholly unique—distinct from humans and, in fact, all creation—then no part of the cre-ation can or should attempt to claim the prerogatives, power, and functions of God.[9] In other words, no human *is* like God, no human *can* act like God, and if any human attempts to do so or supports a social system that does so they are en-gaging in a form of *shirk*, association of partners (such as themselves, their group) alongside of the one God. The Qur'an identifies *shirk* as one of the greatest sins (e.g., Q 4:116).[10] Islamic feminists further specify this general warning and assessment: no *man* can legitimately claim to be like—or more like—God or attempt to wield power and authority over other humans. God alone has power and authority over humans. *Tawhid* or, as labeled by wadud, the tawhidic para-digm theologically challenges the legitimacy and authority of intrahuman domi-nation, including patriarchy, sexism, and androcentrism.[11]

Patriarchy, sexism, and androcentrism are connected to a dominant model of theological anthropology in which God sits at the top of a linear hierarchy with man and *then* woman placed in a descending order beneath God. In this model, women are depicted as inherently inferior, as more distant from God, and as being in an indirect or mediated (through men) relationship with God. As a direct and intentional critique of this dominant formulation of theological anthropology, wadud models the tawhidic paradigm as an invisible triangle or triad in which God is placed at the upper vertex, and man and woman are placed on the same level at the two base vertices.[12] Between God, woman, and man are dual-ended arrows indicating reciprocal and direct relationships between God and woman, God and man, and woman and man. The tawhidic model emphasizes the supremacy of God, a direct and similar relationship between all humans and God, and a human relationship that is "constructed horizontally, as one of mutual support and reciprocity."[13] Scholars use the tawhidic paradigm to contest the dominant hierarchical model, and to argue all humans stand in the same essential relationship with God. No human can—based on sex or gender—claim greater proximity to or affiliation with God. All humans are created by God, are objects of God's concern and mercy, and are subjects of God's judgment.[14]

A similar contestation of hierarchical intrahuman domination arises in Shaikh's reclamation of Sufi teachings in general and the specific teachings of Ibn al-Arabi. *Insan al-kamil* (discussed in the previous chapter) defines human beings—all human beings—as a unique part of God's creation, the only part capable of comprehensively manifesting the divine names. The divine names or attributes are typically classified as *jalali* and *jamali*, the former relating to God's majesty, power, and incomparability, and the latter to God's beauty, mercy, and similarity. Integration and manifestation of the divine names is *potential* in humans. It is actualized only through sustained spiritual practice and guidance designed to precisely limit and balance each attribute.[15] Shaikh emphasizes that divine power and majesty (the *jalali* attributes) should never be confused with human power or egoism.[16] Ibn al-Arabi, moreover, explicitly prioritizes *jamali* attributes in social and interpersonal contexts. Prioritization of *jamali* attributes thus offers a critique of "social hierarchies and discriminatory ideologies; it also rejects social structures that prize aggressive and other unrefined *jalali* qualities."[17]

In addition to explaining the human and ethical implications of central theological assertions about God, Islamic feminists also reclaim and assert equality based on exegesis of Qur'anic accounts of human creation and the events in the Garden. wadud's and Hassan's interpretations of these accounts have deeply impacted the field, and they continue to be widely referenced and upheld. wadud roots her groundbreaking exegetical argument for human equality in the account of human creation found in Qur'an 4:1: "People, be mindful (manifest *taqwa*) of your Sustainer, who created you from a single soul (*nafs*), and from it created its pair (*zawj*), and from the pair of them spread countless men and women far and wide; be conscious of God (manifest *taqwa*) in whose name you make requests of one another." On the basis of holistic interpretive methodology and linguistic analysis, wadud argues that the Qur'an describes the initial creation of humanity as a single, undifferentiated *nafs* (self).[18] This *nafs* is neither male nor female, although grammatically the term *nafs* is feminine. The creation account does not mention Adam or any male person as the initial creation. This is "noteworthy because the Qur'anic version of the creation of humankind is not expressed in gender terms."[19] From the single *nafs*, God intentionally creates the *zawj* (the pair). While *zawj* is grammatically masculine and has a variety of meanings, wadud favors the meaning of "pair" and emphasizes the theme of pairing throughout the Qur'anic text. She describes the pair as "two co-existing forms of a single reality, with some distinctions in nature, characteristics and functions, but two congruent parts formed to fit together as a whole."[20] The distinctions between the pair are divinely intended and "equally essential."[21] Barlas refers to this as the "ontology of the single self," and, like wadud, emphasizes how "men and women originate in the same Self, at the same time, and in the same way; that is, they are ontologically coeval and coequal."[22]

wadud also contends that, while the Qur'an acknowledges the distinctly female biological function of childbearing, it does not inscribe other cultural, social, and psychological functions of mothering. Her point in making this assertion is to again stress the absence of gender and gender-based roles in the Qur'anic presentation of the original human creation.[23] As noted in chapter 3, Hidayatullah critiques wadud's claim about the absence of gender roles, pointing to other Qur'anic verses—for example, Qur'an 4:34's reference to *qiwamah*—which appear to depict hierarchical social relationships between men and women.[24] Hidayatullah's critique raises important questions about the Qur'an and hierarchical social arrangements, questions that wadud herself revisits in more recent writings on *tawhid* and *qiwamah*. Therein, wadud acknowledges the problematic nature of Qur'an 4:34, and the way patriarchy has been privileged in exegesis, theology, and society. Yet, she argues that such privileging is no longer tenable given "our current understanding of human beings and human relationships with each other and with the divine."[25] Hidayatullah's critique and wadud's response, however, do not negate wadud's interpretation of the *original* creation as one founded in singularity, intentional pairing, and the absence of gender or gendered norms.

In the Qur'anic account of the events in the garden (Q 7:21–24 and Q 20:115–124), wadud highlights the themes of guidance, temptation, disobedience and obedience, divine forgiveness, and individual responsibility. The Garden was never intended to be the home of humans; "Allah's original plan in the creation of humankind was for man [*sic*] to function as a *khalifah* (trustee) on earth."[26] Adam and Eve are faced with the same challenge all humans will face in the world: the choice between obedience and disobedience. Satan—described in the Qur'an as an arrogant, disobedient jinn who refuses the divine command to prostrate before the human creation—tempts them, *both* of them, into disobedience. wadud pointedly describes their shared disobedience as a failure to *remember* the guidance of God. When Adam and Eve realize their error, they immediately repent and ask God for forgiveness. God accepts their request and also mercifully indicates that there will be another mode of guidance: divine revelation. The moral of this account, according to wadud, is that "any human might disobey through forgetfulness, the general nature of human weakness, and the temptations of Satan, but he who recognizes his error, repents, and asks for forgiveness, can and will be forgiven."[27] While wadud does not engage in explicit comparison, she underscores that it is both Adam and Eve who are tempted, disobey, repent, and are forgiven. The Arabic dual grammatical form is used in all but one instance in the Qur'anic accounts. The female is "never singled out as the initiator or temptress of evil."[28]

Hassan explicitly crafts her rereading of the events of the Garden in conversation with biblical accounts. I have in chapter 4 already expressed my concerns about comparative aspects of her interpretation, and explored Hidayatullah's critique of her approach as a "rib-ectomy" of the Qur'an that does not sufficiently grapple with the pervasiveness and persistence of ahadith reports.[29] Here, though, I want to focus on the content of her theological anthropology beyond its comparative posture and methodology. Hassan acknowledges that some Muslims "consider it self-evident that women are not equal to men who are 'above' women or have a 'degree of advantage' over them."[30] This perception is grounded in theology, and therefore can only be challenged by a theology of women. More specifically, Hassan identifies three primary theological assumptions that form the foundation of misogynistic and androcentric theological anthropologies. The first assumption is that man is the primary creation of God, and that woman is created from the rib of man. As a result, woman is viewed as "derivative and secondary ontologically."[31] The second assumption is that woman was the primary cause of or agent of the Fall and resultant expulsion. This assumption leads of notions of guilt being extended to all women, and thus all women being viewed with suspicion and contempt. The third misogynistic theological assumption is that "woman was created not only *from* man but also *for* man, which makes her existence merely instrumental and not of fundamental importance."[32]

Hassan challenges these assumptions by turning to the Qur'anic account of events in the Garden and asking how was woman created, if woman was responsible for the Fall, and why woman was created. These three questions lead her to some of the same conclusions already discussed in reference to wadud. She similarly argues original human creation was an undifferentiated humanity, but she uniquely asserts that even references to Adam within the Qur'anic text do not refer to a specific human, never mind a specific male human. "Adam" is conceptual shorthand for humanity.[33] By dismissing the soundness of some *ahadith*, she excludes any references implying creation of woman from the rib of man or from man in any way. She also rejects any Qur'anic basis for woman's unique culpability; disobedience in the Garden (*al-jannah*) was "a collective act not an individual act for which an exclusive, or even primary, responsibility is not assigned to either man or woman."[34] Like wadud, Hassan asserts that humans were destined to be in the world (to be vicegerents) and that the focus of the Qur'anic account is on moral choice. There is disobedience in the form of *zulm* (wrongdoing, inclusive of wronging one's self), but—invoking comparative theological language—Hassan asserts that there is no Fall or concept of original sin.[35] Humans, even after disobedience in the Garden, are not born "sinful" or in need of redemption or salvation: "Islam rejects the idea of redemption, of any intermediary between a believer and the creator. It is one of Islam's cardinal beliefs that each person—man and woman—is responsible and accountable for his or her individual actions."[36] Barlas echoes this observation; woman cannot be blamed for the Fall or original sin because there are no such concepts, no theological or ontological "rift," and therefore no resultant "otherizing" of woman.[37] In explicating the reason *why* woman was created, Hassan states that all of humanity was created in the "best of molds" (Q 95:4) to serve and worship God. Serving of God entails responsibilities to both God and other humans. This is the basis of vicegerency, a role and purpose that is not Qur'anically differentiated based on biological sex or gender. Men and women are "equally called upon to be righteous" and "stand absolutely equal in the sight of God."[38]

What are the anthropological takeaways from their exegeses? Some are readily evident. The first is men and women are created equally, and woman is not a derivative or binary opposite of man.[39] Another central takeaway relates to forgetfulness. Forgetfulness, as wadud stresses, is a core characteristic of human nature (*fitra*). As a diagnosis of the human condition, forgetfulness is variously manifest as simple forgetting, individual and collective arrogance (that is, forgetting God and *tawhid*, and thus thinking of one's self as independent from God and/or superior to other humans), and ingratitude (that is, lack of sustained awareness of God's nature, power, and sustenance). It is a particular theological explanation of why and how humans disobey guidance. As such, it is also a latent description of the basic orientation of human nature (*fitra*). The human *fitra* knows God and knows the difference between remembering God and rebelling. While not fixed or restrained, this is the starting point of human nature; the human begins with guidance, knowledge, and a perfect relationship with God. Qur'an 91:7–10 speaks of the undifferentiated, original *nafs*: "By the soul (*nafs*) and how God formed it and inspired it (to know) its own rebellion and God-consciousness (*taqwa*)! The one who causes it to grow in purity succeeds and the one who buries it fails!" These verses state that the original orientation of the *nafs* and *fitra* can be positively maintained or negatively interrupted. The God-inclined *fitra*, however, cannot ever be eradicated: "This is the natural disposition (*fitra*) God instilled in humankind. There is no altering God's creation" (Q 30:30 excerpt).[40] It can be buried or hidden, but in all people it remains as the essential core—the seed—that has the potential through guidance, repentance, forgiveness, and practices of remembrance to reawaken and grow.

Shaikh's exploration of "genderless" anthropological assertions within Sufism outlines one particular version of how human nature can and should be cultivated.[41] She highlights a general Sufi prioritization of the inner state of humans and emphasis on shared spiritual imperatives among all humans. The inner state of all humans is composed of *nafs* (soul), *qalb* (heart), and *ruh* (spirit). The first is the "lower self" in need of training and discipline. *Ruh* is the opposite of the *nafs*; it is the angelic self that draws a person toward God. Shaikh describes the *qalb* as the site of spiritual receptivity. Spiritual receptivity, while part of human nature, can be impeded (rusted or rendered opaque), and this is rectified only through the "polishing" practices of spiritual discipline and remembrance. For egalitarian anthropology, these concepts challenge the presentation of men as inherently superior and women as inherently inferior, and even the notion of human distinctions based on sex or gender. Moreover, the connection of egotism with the lower self presents another strong challenge to male superiority and humanly constructed hierarchies.[42] Such claims, views, and systems are "spiritual imbalances," products of a lack of spiritual discernment and cultivation.

The denial of the Fall and original sin is another central takeaway. This is not just a comparative or oppositional juxtaposition. While often phrased as such, it is also an assertion arising organically from views on the purpose and role of human beings. Islamic feminist theologians dismiss the Fall because they assert that vicegerency (*khilafah*) is the original and divinely intended role for each and every human irrespective of sex or gender; *khilafah* is "the basic teleology, or divine purpose, for human creation on the earth."[43] Humans did not invent or cause this role or purpose through their disobedience. This is why wadud, Hassan, and Barlas all frame the expulsion from the Garden as a necessary and even predestined part of human creation. The Qur'an indicates that humans were intended to be moral agents and stewards of the world: "The Sustainer said to the angels, 'I will create a vicegerent on earth'" (Q 2:30). The role of *khalifah* (vicegerent) is a trust (*amanah*) humans have been given and accepted from God.

Khilafah surfaces other components of Islamic feminist theological anthropology: specifically, the emphasis on free will, capacity, and responsibility.[44] To be a moral agent—to be *khalifah*—humans must be able to freely choose moral action. They must also have the inherent and nondifferentiated ability to identify, choose, and perform moral action. wadud emphasizes these abilities in her definition of Islam as "engaged surrender." She rejects the definition of Islam as submission because it implies coercion and limitation. Engaged surrender, however, captures the essence of *khilafah*; it "emphasizes the requisite role of human agency. It is a conscious recognition of choice and exercising that choice as an agent, not a puppet."[45] Engaged surrender also accentuates the continuous and dynamic nature of *khilafah*. *Khilafah* "binds human agency and divine will into the dynamic and enduring relationship that is always being exercised . . . in public or private human actions."[46] Due to their freedom and capacity, humans are responsible for maintaining and manifesting this relationship in the world. Responsibility is also egalitarian. As Barlas notes, the Qur'an "does not sexualize moral agency."[47] Men and women are held to the same standards of moral action and moral accountability. In sum, *khilafah* is an assertion about the basic egalitarian nature and purpose of all humans, but it is also a critique and authoritative claim.[48] *Khilafah* as critique challenges social structures, laws, and practices that limit the exercise of *khilafah*. *Khilafah* as authoritative claim legitimates Islamic feminist reinterpretations of the tradition as exercises in divinely granted moral agency.

If humans are created the same and equal, if they stand under *tawhid* in exactly the same Divine–human relationship of care, concern, and accountability, and if they are charged with the same human purpose, what is the basis of distinction among humans? Of course, human distinction will be tied to the degree of recognition of *tawhid*, of remembrance, of engaged surrender, and of actualization of *khilafah*. These ideas are often expressed through the integrative concept of *taqwa*, God-consciousness. *Taqwa* is an incredibly complex theological concept. While it is sometimes flattened into "piety" or "fear," *taqwa* is much more three-dimensional. *Taqwa* involves sustained and actively pursued belief, ritual action, social action, and moral action in light of and in constant reference to one's awareness of God; "*taqwa* is an orientation toward God, a constant awareness of God, that colors every facet of how one acts in the world."[49] Part of this coloring is that *taqwa* places a high value on social, familial, and intrapersonal relations but also indicates that these relations should never impede the relationship with God. In fact, many of the Qur'anic critiques of human forgetfulness and ingratitude are simultaneously *taqwa*-based critiques of the ways in which humans corrupt *taqwa* by prioritizing themselves, their social groups, their divinely created characteristics (including sex), and humanity in general over God.[50] *Taqwa* outlines "the unique balance for integrative moral action."[51]

Taqwa is referenced in numerous places in the Qur'an, a few of which have already been mentioned in this chapter. The Qur'an references *taqwa* in the account of creation from a single *nafs* (Q 4:1), in the depiction of the basic God-conscious nature of the *nafs* (Q 91:7–10), and in the postexpulsion description of "garments" of *taqwa* as the best garments for humanity (Q 7:26). *Taqwa* is also referenced in the description of the spread of humans throughout the world and their divinely intended human diversity: "People, We created you all from a single man and a single woman, and made you into ethnicities and tribes so that you should recognize one another. In God's eyes, the most honored of you are the ones most conscious of God (who manifest the most *taqwa*). God is all knowing, all aware" (Q 49:13). Collectively, these references reveal the centrality of *taqwa* in theological anthropology. The last verse plays a particularly central role in Islamic feminist theological anthropology. Drawing on this verse—a verse that explicitly indicates that human diversity is not the basis of assessment—Barlas asserts that *taqwa* is the *only* criterion of human differentiation.[52] *Taqwa* as the sole criterion delegitimizes intrahuman distinctions premised on, sex, gender, class, religion, race, and ethnicity, among other forms of human diversity. She clarifies that these are "lateral" forms of human diversity divinely intended to "enable mutual recognition."[53] They are not caused by disunity or degeneration. *Taqwa*, in contrast, differentiates hierarchically; it is a (divine) measure of individual, moral assessment. *Taqwa*, thus, functions to allow certain forms of assessment of human action but simultaneously discredits the collective linkage of such assessment to sex or gender. In other writings, I use *taqwa* and the lateral and hierarchal distinction to argue for a new model of religious diversity, one that envisions *taqwa* as crossing the boundaries of divinely intended religious communities.[54]

Taqwa also serves another function in Islamic feminist theology; it challenges the commonplace bifurcation between moral and social equality. While some Muslims happily pay lip service to the moral equality of all humans—and particularly of women—they often simultaneously invoke social, legal, and ritual models of inferiority, limitation, or complementarity: "They concede that the Qur'an treats women and men similarly, hence equally, in the moral realm (conceived as the realm of worship, or *'Ibadah*), but they argue that the Qur'an treats women and men differently, hence unequally, in the social realms by giving them different kinds of rights in marriage, divorce, and so on."[55] Pairing *khilafah* with *taqwa*, Barlas challenges this dual system, arguing that moral agency requires the observance of moral-religious and social responsibilities and obligations.[56] Even basic beliefs and ritual practices, such as prayer and fasting, are intimately tied to social practice. There are intrinsic links among the moral, social, and religious spheres. It is impossible to exercise *khilafah* or manifest *taqwa* in some mythological, nonsocial, moral realm. *Taqwa* thus directly challenges one of the most common, contemporary postures assumed in reaction to Islamic feminist theological claims to and embodied expressions of equality.

Based on their research among Muslim women in South Africa, Nina Hoel and Shaikh explore the intersections between theological anthropology and religious subjectivity. They specifically engage the theological concepts of *'abd Allah* (servant of God) and *khalifah* (moral agent, vicegerent).[57] Acknowledging the importance and empowering role of these concepts, they maintain that the concepts "need to be analyzed in relation to complex and embodied social contexts characterized by hierarchical gender power relations."[58] Hoel and Shaikh, for example, outline the ways in which servitude as a positive theological concept can be detrimental in situations of power and gender asymmetry. Even *khalifah* should be placed in conversation with the fact that some women do not have any control over their physical bodies. Hoel's and Shaikh's research highlights "implications for women's individual cultivation of religious piety and moral action when . . . capacities to act and make decisions . . . are bound up with symbolic and real patriarchal power."[59] Their research raises questions about human freedom and constraint.

The contours of Islamic feminist theological anthropology are extremely positive. Humans are created equal in the sight of God and in relation to each other. They are only distinguished from one another on the basis of *taqwa*, not on the basis of sex or gender. They can fulfill their purpose and choose to manifest *taqwa*. Their basic human nature begins in perfect relationship with God, and while this relationship can certainly be disturbed through forgetfulness and arrogance, the core *fitra* that inclines toward God can never be eradicated. Moreover, God provides abundant reminders (in scripture, in creation, and in humans themselves) to humanity that can awaken even a buried *fitra*. This is a very positive theological anthropology. In my view, it is also a theological anthropology that is phenomenally well rooted in the primary texts and sources, and phenomenally well suited to egalitarian argumentation. It is a theological anthropology on which I have based the majority of my constructive Muslima writing. This theological anthropology is beautiful, empowering, and human-positive. Yet, in line with Hoel and Shaikh, I am not sure it grapples sufficiently with the reality of some, if not most, women. My concern lies not in its theological rootedness. The roots are deep. My concern arises more from on the ground realities, particularly the situation of women and the implications of this theological anthropology for crafting an effective strategy for structural transformation. Is the beautiful, positive, optimistic theological anthropology founded on the intersections of *tawhid, fitra, khilafah*, and *taqwa* attentive enough—while not validating or yielding—to the realities of human constraint and limitation? If not, how might theological anthropology be expanded to be more attentive, while retaining the powerful and deep roots already articulated?

Embodiment, Freedom, and Survival

Like Islamic feminists, Christian feminist and womanist examinations of theological anthropology aim to critique hierarchical and androcentric depictions of humanity and articulate the value and equality of women. As is clear from the chapter on exegesis, biblical accounts of creation play a central role; Christian feminist and womanist theologians constructively engage with both the account of human creation as *imago Dei* (in the image of God) and the depiction of disobedience and the Fall. On these bases, they outline a variety of models of theological anthropology, including what Ruether labels egalitarian, liberal, and androgynous models, and explore the nature of individual and structural sin and evil.[60]

In this section, I engage with the perspectives on theological anthropology articulated by M. Shawn Copeland, Jeannine Hill Fletcher, and Delores S. Williams. M. Shawn Copeland is Professor of Systematic Theology at Boston College. She earned her PhD in theology at Boston College/Andover Newton Theological School, and her research interests are theological and philosophical anthropology, embodiment, political theology, and African American intellectual history. She is the author of *Enfleshing Freedom: Body, Race, Being*, and is a former convener of the Black Catholic Theological Symposium and former President of Catholic Theological Society of America.[61] Jeannine Hill Fletcher is Professor of Systematic Theology at Fordham University in the Department of the Theology. She earned her ThD in systematic theology at Harvard Divinity School. Her research and writing focus on issues of religious diversity, religious identity, Christian cultural diversity, race, and gender, and she is the author of *Motherhood as Metaphor: Engendering Interreligious Dialogue* and *Monopoly on Salvation? A Feminist Approach to Religious Pluralism*.[62] Delores S. Williams is a Presbyterian womanist theologian whose work centers on historical and present testimonies of black women, race, gender, and culture. She earned her PhD at Union Theological Seminary and, prior to her retirement in 2005, was Associate Professor of Theology and Culture at Union Theological Seminary in New York City. She is the author of *Sisters in the Wilderness: The Challenge of Womanist God-Talk*.[63] These three theologians focus specifically on issues of freedom, suffering, embodiment, and constraint in relation to theological anthropology. Copeland and Williams do so by foregrounding the atrocities *and* survival strategies of black women in slavery and postslavery contexts. Hill Fletcher contributes an explicitly comparative perspective. Together, these contextualizations present a significant challenge to other Christian theological anthropologies and provide an invaluable dialogical lens for *Muslima* reflections on the extent of freedom and capacity.

M. Shawn Copeland: Black Women, Embodiment, Solidarity

In her constructive critique of Christian theological anthropology, M. Shawn Copeland centers embodiment, specifically the embodied experiences of black women. She argues, on this basis, for reconsideration of the human subject of theological anthropology, the nature of freedom, and the praxis of solidarity. Embodiment should be a central concern of theological anthropology because "[i]n and through embodiment, we human persons grasp and realize our essential freedom through engagement and communion with other embodied selves."[64] We do not exist outside of our bodies, and we inhabit diverse social and physical bodies. As a result, focus on the body, on concrete and diverse bodies, raises important theological questions and challenges dominant anthropological assumptions: "The body provokes theology. The body contests its hypotheses, resists its conclusions, escapes its textual margins."[65]

According to Copeland, each and every body is implicated in a web of "body commerce, body exchange, body value."[66] The embodied experiences of black women in slavery are a particularly vivid and effective means by which to reveal this web and confront the manner in which Christian theology is entangled in it. Copeland asserts that "the full meaning of human freedom (religious, existential, social, eschatological) can be clarified only in grappling strenuously with the 'dangerous memory' of slavery."[67] She thus explores social and physical dimensions of racism and slavery. She surveys the invention of race in Enlightenment thought; the association of whiteness with reason, intelligence, and civilization and blackness with unreason, savagery, and ignorance; the development of quasi-scientific theories and racial taxonomies; and the manner in which racism facilitates a "horizon of knowledge" that normalizes bias and renders the "other" invisible or hidden.[68] Copeland underscores that these ideas, theories, and worldviews have very real and potent impact on black women's bodies. Race is a social construct, but it manifests in and fosters racist and dehumanizing actions. Racial privilege, for instance, aims to render the racial other invisible, but if that other contests the system—steps out of place—"they are subordinated literally to surveillance, inspection, discrimination, assessment and containment."[69] The physical damage of racism and slavery is extensive and pronounced. For black women, it includes objectification of their bodies and physical impact on their bodies.[70] It involves control of property, production, and reproduction, severing of biological and familial ties, and sexual violence and the "silent collusion" of white women in that violence. In short, Copeland demonstrates that the "libidinous economics of the plantation quite literally reduced black women to body parts," parts that men used, parts that were sold, and parts coerced to care for their oppressors.[71]

While Copeland recounts the damage in detail—deliberately making it visible—damage is not the whole story. Black women under slavery sought freedom and resisted despite the many horrors; they sought ways to free their minds and spirits and to reclaim their bodies. These ways included "stealing" education, imagining God as the source of freedom, praying for a different future for their descendants, backtalk and "sass," purchasing freedom, and physical fighting.

In short, they "nurtured a sense of themselves as subjects of freedom."[72] With emancipation, freedom assumed new dimensions, as well as distinct demands and challenges. Copeland references Toni Morrison's depiction of The Clearing in *Beloved*, and argues that emancipation became a time for healing and growth, a time to love themselves and "enflesh" freedom.[73] She connects this "enfleshing" to the marked body of Jesus. Jesus lived and died under the rule of empire, yet preached and embodied an alternate vision of *basileia tou theou*, the reign of God. His alternate vision was both resistance and a desire for new relationships and practices of solidarity: "Jesus invites all who would follow him to abandon loyalties to class and station, family and kin, culture and nation in order to form God's people anew and, thus, to contest empire."[74] Additionally, the body of Jesus the Christ "radically clarifies" the meaning of worldly embodiment; his self-disclosure becomes the "paradigm for all human self-disclosure in contexts of empire and oppression, exclusion and alienation, slavery and death."[75] It manifests love, compassion, and inclusion, and it refuses silence in the face of suffering.

Copeland's exploration of racism, slavery, and emancipation seeks to "unsettle and problematize" typical assumptions and goals of theological anthropology.[76] Christian theological anthropology is grounded in Old Testament accounts of human creation, the fall, and the first humans. These accounts provide a "paradigm of human nature" based on three convictions: that humans are created in the image and likeness of God (*imago Dei*), that humans are unique in the cosmos, and that humans are created to be in "communion" with other beings.[77] Copeland argues that slavery desecrated and deformed each of these doctrines of the human person. As such, granting hermeneutical and theological privilege to "black-embodied-being-in-the-world" reveals the inextricable link between the body and freedom, the shaping of the body and freedom by a complex matrix of power relationships, and the "struggle to achieve and exercise freedom in history and society."[78] This hermeneutical privileging also challenges the European Enlightenment "turn to the subject," which emphasized a supposedly free, rational, human. While presented as emancipatory and universal, the Enlightenment subject was in fact neither.[79] The turn to the subject coincided with and justified domination, imperialism, and genocide. Moreover, while it was presented as general, the characteristics of this subject were rooted in white, male, bourgeois European embodied experience.

Based on her centering of black women's embodiment and critique of the Enlightenment turn to the subject, Copeland proposes a new anthropological subject: exploited, despised, poor women of color. This move is not simply an effort to include overlooked experiences, nor to restate earlier models—sometimes proposed even by feminist theologians—of theological anthropology based on androgyny, unisex ideals, or complementarity. Copeland rejects these models and argues that androgyny and unisex ideals are—like the white, male subject—equally grounded in Enlightenment notions of an "autonomous, isolated, individualistic, and acquisitive" human being.[80] She does not intend for this new subject to foster essentialization, alienation, or exclusion. The new anthropological subject, in contrast, provides a more robust, realistic, and responsible model of a human being; it is a model of a human who is made by God, situated in social relationships with other humans, "capable of working out essential freedom in time and space," unafraid of difference and interdependence, and willing to engage in the necessary daily struggle.[81]

Copeland also redefines the role and nature of solidarity. Solidarity is not just a helpful add-on to connect discrete individuals. Solidarity is the only way that we—all of us in our particular positioning and embodiment—can realize our full humanity: "If personhood is now understood to flow from formative living in community rather than individualism, from embrace of difference and interdependence rather than their exclusion, then we can realize personhood only in solidarity with the exploited, despised, poor 'other.'"[82] This genre of solidarity is more than distribution of material and cultural resources, more than identification with a social group, and more than identity politics. It is a "set of body practices" aimed at healing, creating, and maintaining "responsible relationships" based on obligations arising from "basic human creatureliness."[83] She connects the praxis of solidarity with the cross of Christ and the Eucharist; ultimate and enacted solidarity involves loving self-donation, willingness to shoulder responsibility, and "the intentional remembering of the dead, exploited, despised victims of history."[84]

Jeannine Hill Fletcher: Relationality and Constrained Creativity

Jeannine Hill Fletcher describes theological anthropology as the "most fundamental theological fruit"; theological anthropology shapes self-perception, ideas of what it means to be human, understandings of God, and Christology.[85] As theology and explications of theological anthropology have largely been male endeavors, she seeks to "think from the experience of women" to identify corrections, challenges, and new insights into theological anthropology.[86] It is not only feminist and women's insights, however, that have been excluded from theological anthropology but also insights from other faiths. Hill Fletcher asserts that the religious diversity of our lived experience is also a theological resource capable of revealing new possibilities and contributing to the struggle for a just world. In this combination of concerns, her work is an example of feminist theological anthropology and also a form of comparative feminist theology.

Hill Fletcher situates her reflections in relation to dominant formulations of modern theological anthropology. Specifically, she seeks to test the universality of Karl Rahner's description of humans as knowers, doers in freedom, and lovers.[87] To do so, she draws on three interreligious "feminist" sources: the missionary Maryknoll Sisters in China; the secular, transreligious movement for women's rights; and a Philadelphia multifaith women's group. These feminist resources present a distinct challenge to modern theological anthropology; they depict the human condition as one in which "relationality precedes the individual, constraint challenges our freedom, and interreligious knowing is recognized as a new form of sacred knowledge."[88]

Relationality contests the idea of the "individual as the site of agency and identity."[89] While modern theological anthropology imagines the human person to be free, autonomous, and independent, even capable of reaching outside of their own selves or conditioning, the reality is each individual is born into and found in a "web of relationships and responsibilities."[90] Feminist theology and women's experience reveals that relationality, sociality, and intersubjectivity precede and condition our human self; we never exist outside of this web. Hill Fletcher describes these webs as fluid and dynamic, and as shaping our self-understanding. In this context, she introduces the metaphor of motherhood to capture the way we are all "constituted by our relationality."[91] She emphasizes that this symbolic motherhood is not intended to be essentializing, nor is motherhood the only or first experience of relationality. Her contention, though, is that motherhood—broadly defined and diversely "complicated" by class, race, education, nationality, and culture—illuminates central aspects of our embeddedness in relationality.[92] One such aspect is what Hill Fletcher calls the "calculus of concern," the making of decisions about distribution of limited resources and negotiation of competing concerns and needs (including our own and those of others). Motherhood underscores that relationality requires us to relinquish some self-concern in order to care for others. This relinquishing is the basis of solidarity, and the negotiated "balance of self-concern and other-centeredness is the nature of what it means to be human."[93] Yet, Hill Fletcher acknowledges that relationality has, what she calls, a "shadow side." We are conditioned by limited resources, even while we are resourceful in attending to multiple and diverse concerns. Relationality therefore should not lead to a typically gendered romanticization of self-sacrifice. She upholds the value of self-sacrifice but argues against exploitative expectations of care and for the increasingly wider distribution of self-sacrifice.[94] Relationality can also be selectively cut; we cannot escape relationality altogether, but we can "refuse" other humans, refuse to recognize or attend to their concerns or humanity. Theologically, such

such self-centeredness aligns with the notion of original sin. It is a refusal of "the multiple relationships and responsibilities of interconnected humanity. Writ large in the public disparities, deceits, and refusals of care for the least, sin is reflected in discrete decisions and in the intersecting systems that fundamentally structure our societies of separations."[95] Hill Fletcher clarifies that sin can be both self-referential willful ignorance of relationality *or* structural ignorance, in which constructed systems privilege one group of humans over another on the basis of race, gender, sexual orientation, religion, class, et cetera.[96] She vividly refers to ignorance and neglect of relationality as "de-creation." Hill Fletcher also connects relationality to a Christology based on the "mother-care of Christ." This Christology centers self-giving, nurturing, attentiveness, awareness of one's own vulnerability, and restructuring of "one's interests and privileges in solidarity with the other."[97]

Modern theological anthropology not only emphasizes the individual but also emphasizes the autonomy and freedom of each individual. Individuals are presented as agents who can freely exercise choice. While she challenges this presentation with the notion of constrained creativity, Hill Fletcher recognizes that many women's rights and feminist movements have claimed and capitalized on this view of the human being as self-directed, able to transcend oneself, and able to make unencumbered decisions about and for oneself.[98] The struggle for women's rights, however, contests this description, offering example after example of women "constrained by social expectations, barred from political action, excluded from education and the possibilities for knowledge."[99] For women, freedom without any constraints is an illusion. Hill Fletcher therefore revisits the emphasis on unlimited, unconditioned freedom, and argues that humans are more accurately defined by our creativity within particular embodied, social, racial, material, and religious limits and our "courage" to deploy that creativity.

With specific reference to religious norms and limits, she emphasizes that religion can be and is frequently used to police female creativity by outlining and enforcing gender norms. She thus ponders whether the "master's tools of religion can sufficiently dismantle the master's house of sexist and androcentric religious and social practices."[100] Sacred stories, for example, can function both as androcentric idols or feminist models. She specifically revisits the account of Eve and—somewhat akin to Trible's rereading in chapter 4—presents Eve as a knowledge seeker and boundary transgressor, who nevertheless remains situated in relationality and the associated constraints. Hill Fletcher clarifies, though, that constraints are not ontological realities. While humans are always characterized by some constraint, no particular system of constraint is fixed, static, true, or universal.[101] Notably, in reclaiming Eve, Hill Fletcher references other interreligious feminist perspectives, including that of Riffat Hassan, and argues that interreligious perspectives are an important resource in reclaiming sacred stories.

As with Hassan's reclamation of the Qur'anic Eve in distinction from Jewish and Christian presentations of Eve, interreligious feminist perspectives reveal new ways—new tools—for engaging texts and traditions.[102]

The final area of theological anthropology Hill Fletcher explores is knowledge, and the presentation of humans as distinctive in their capacity for thought. Feminist theory, the women's multifaith group, and Thomas Kuhn's theories on paradigms, however, challenge the idea of disembodied reason or universal knowledge. Humans are situated in "economies of knowledge" that shape how and what people see and know.[103] Hill Fletcher does not just highlight the existence of diverse, multiple, and shaping economies. She also emphasizes that women are often structurally excluded from participating in the economies of knowledge that shape their experience.[104] They are, for example, excluded from education, ordination, and consideration as experts within religious traditions. She argues that this reality led first- and second-wave feminists to focus on becoming "authoritative" within the dominant economy of knowledge by gaining access to education and training. She also highlights the impact on interfaith dialogue, wherein women are often excluded because they do not hold leadership roles or are not perceived (self-perceived) as experts. Another feminist response to exclusion from dominant economies of knowledge is the articulation of alternative economies; feminists underscore the multiplicity of economies, seek access to existing economies, and simultaneously outline new sources and modes of knowing, often those connected to oral traditions and embodied ritual.[105]

The realization that economies of knowledge shape our existence, are multiple, and are exclusionary requires us "to interrogate our own systems of knowledge for the part they play in guaranteeing material well-being or withholding it."[106] According to Hill Fletcher, knowledge systems are not power neutral, and they have material and practical outcomes. Theologically, she links this interrogation with the notions of salvation and eschatology. Identifying shortcomings within exclusivist, sameness only, and particularist approaches to theologies of religious diversity, she presents an alternative, interreligious eschatology. This eschatology recognizes the ineffable within and beyond Christianity, and understands the religious other (she-who-is-neighbor) as playing an intimate role in an ever deepening and "salve-ific" relationship with God and humanity.[107] Interreligious engagement thus becomes as alternative economy of knowledge and a theological resource in light of human constraints and creativity.

Delores S. Williams: Hagar and Survival, Quality of Life

In her articulation of womanist theology, Delores S. Williams, like Copeland, places the faith, experiences, thought, and life struggles of African Americans at the center of exegetical and theological exploration. She describes this move not simply as cathartic but also as motivated by theological rationales. Womanist theology seeks to provide theological resources that respond to the experiences and challenges facing African American women, and it provides a "theological corrective" to the suppression of black women's voices in churches and thought.[108] It is a prophetic voice that "attempts to help black women see, affirm and have confidence in the importance of their experience and faith for determining the character of the Christian religion in the African American community."[109] At the same time, womanist theology articulates a broader challenge to all modes of oppression. Womanist theology overlaps with but is distinct from both black liberation theology and Christian feminist theology. Specifically, in relation to the former, womanist theology is distinguished by its critique of black liberation theology's participation in making some experience "invisible," its challenge to doctrines of redemption and salvation based on "bloody surrogacy," and its introduction of new ethical concerns.[110]

New ethical concerns arise, according to Williams, because of a shift in focus from the topic of liberation to the topic of survival. Speaking explicitly about African American biblical appropriation, she identifies two dominant traditions: the liberation tradition and the survival, quality of life tradition.[111] The former is characteristic of black liberation theology. Drawing on accounts of Jesus, Moses, and Paul, it emphasizes the "liberation of the oppressed" and depicts "God relating to men in the liberation struggle."[112] The central, normative claim in this tradition is God is the one who liberates. The survival, quality of life tradition—within which womanist theology is situated—differs markedly in that it centers female agency in the person of Hagar, and describes God's response not as liberation but as presence and participation in survival.[113]

In the Genesis account (16:1–16 and 21:9–21), Hagar is a female slave, surrogate mother, and single mother brutalized by the desires of her owners.[114] Her motherhood is coerced, and her experience is one of profound insecurity. When Hagar runs off into the wilderness to escape brutalization, she is told—by the angel of the Lord—to return. Hagar does not have the resources required for survival, so God saves her and her child by ordering her to return to Sarai and Abram. This is "no liberator God" but a survival God.[115] Williams argues that what appeared as a "curse" was required for her future survival, and that Hagar's compliance with the divine order "after her self-initiated liberation demonstrates her faith and her radical obedience to her God."[116] After the birth of Issac, Hagar is expelled. Again, she finds herself without resources and relational protection. Yet, again, God calls to her, acknowledges her and Ismael's plight, and promises they will become a great nation. Williams states that God remained with them as the child grew and sustained them in relative autonomy.[117] In all of her experiences—as surrogate and single mother, as slave, as homeless and without resources—Hagar had "serious personal and salvific encounters with God—encounters which aided Hagar in the survival struggle of herself and her son."[118] God does not grant liberation, but God here is involved in survival and development of quality of life. God, in Williams's reading of Genesis, is present in Hagar's struggle, helping to make "a way out of no way," and fostering hope amid oppression.

Hagar's experiences of struggle, of divine encounter and involvement, of survival, of female agency, and of hope are closely parallel to the experiences of African American women.[119] Williams draws specific connections between motherhood grounded in "god-consciousness and God-dependence," coerced and voluntary surrogacy, and blackness in a world of "white racial narcissism."[120] She gives special attention to the "wilderness experience," stating there is nothing else that so closely links African American women and Hagar. She defines "wilderness" or "wilderness experience" as "a symbolic term used to represent a near-destruction situation in which God gives personal direction to the believer and thereby helps her to make a way out of what she thought was no way."[121] Within struggle, often alone, with only the help of God, women find a way to deal with destructive situations. Williams surveys depictions of the literal wilderness, highlighting its associations with religion, spirituality, and healing transformation within spirituals and among slave narratives. She acknowledges that these positive associations were challenged by largely white depictions of the wilderness as the opposite of civilization. After slavery, Williams observes that wilderness came to be associated with one of two things: religious experience, or economic insecurity and new oppressions. While distinct, Hagar aligns with both wilderness experiences; she is at first still a slave, and then with freedom—after expulsion—is faced with new challenges.[122] The symbolism of "Hagar-in-the-wilderness" thus illuminates key aspects of African American women's experience. It is a symbol of the bonding of the spiritual and political. It also provides a "realistic model of non-middle-class black womanhood" that "affirms such qualities as defiance; risk-taking; independence; endurance when endurance gives no promise; the stamina to hold things together for the family (even without the help of a mate); the ability, in poverty, to make a way out of no way; the courage to initiate political action in the public arena; and a close personal relationship with God."[123] Hagar symbolism defines "death-dealing" circumstances as oppression and validates a diversity of resistance strategies that do not necessarily accord with "proper" roles or expectations of women.[124]

The relevance of Hagar's story and Hagar symbolism is confirmed by the long-standing and extensive history of appropriation of Hagar within African American communities, expressions, and thought.[125] Williams seeks to further develop this appropriation in womanist theology, highlighting three primary areas of significance. The first is that appropriation of Hagar and the survival, quality of life tradition "establishes *a continuity of tradition about God*."[126] Examination of patterns and practices related to Hagar reveal how ideas and beliefs are communicated within the tradition and African American community. Additionally, uncovering female-centered traditions focused on survival—not solely on liberation as in many androcentric traditions—expands understanding of how God acts in the world in relation to people. Williams does not dismiss a liberation emphasis holistically; liberation is relevant to and consistent with some experience. She does, however, contend that the addition of the survival, quality of life focus opens and extends theological possibilities; it "affirms God's freedom to act in many different ways in response to a community's life and faith."[127]

Hagar appropriation is also significant to womanist theology because it introduces a new methodological level of interpretation. Williams describes this new level as "proto-gesis," consisting of interdisciplinary examination of diverse "deposits of culture" that reference Hagar, including spirituals and literature.[128] Examination occurs prior to and uncovers questions that will shape historical critical analysis. Finally, Hagar appropriation illuminates the connection between faith and politics. Hagar's political way of acting, her resistance, endurance, and inability to say no to God are all connected to her faith in God. Williams describes this as a "triumphant faith statement" that envisions God as a "co-worker" in the struggle.[129] In sum, Hagar expands understandings of theology, interpretation, and divine and human action. Thus, while Williams does not explicitly situate her work on Hagar in reference to theological anthropology, these emphases indicate the relevance of her work to this topic.

Transformative Taqwa: *Muslima Theological Reflections*

It is immediately evident that Muslim and Christian perspectives overlap in the way they center the question of theological anthropology. Theological anthropology is deeply connected to all other theological assertions, and it has also been a prime playground for misogynistic and androcentric declarations about human nature. As a result, theological anthropology must be subjected to critical scrutiny and must be articulated in relation to the experiences and concerns of diverse women. Textual references and accounts of human creation are also key in the articulation of perspectives in both traditions. While the content and related challenges and opportunities presented by those textual references differ, Islamic feminists and Christian womanists and feminists reclaim textual references to assert female equality, agency, and relationship with the Divine. Conceptions of the Divine and of the human–Divine relationship, however, are markedly different. Islamic feminists invoke *tawhid* and the ontological disparateness of God to assert their equality with all other humans, while Christian womanists and feminists foreground *imago Dei*, creation of humankind in the image and likeness of God. That is to say, Islamic feminists claim equality through *dissimilarity* with God, and Christian womanists and feminists claim equality through *similarity* with God. This distinction, while theologically profound, should not be confused with the caricature of a distant, transcendent Muslim God and a personal, immanent Christian God. It is more complex and intriguing than that. God for Islamic feminists is nonpersonal (not a person or like any person) but incredibly close to humans—as Qur'an 50:16 states, "closer to them than their jugular vein"—and constantly involved. Another clear area of differentiation is the account of the Fall and the notion of original sin. Islamic feminists distance themselves and Islamic thought from both in an attempt to undercut female culpability and foreground divinely intended human vicegerency (*khilafah*). Christian womanist and feminist theologians do not necessarily reject the Fall or original sin, but they reclaim them in relation to *imago Dei* by emphasizing female agency and by framing original sin as structural not just individual. Original sin, and sin more generally, is linked with the existence of oppression, dehumanization, and injustice in the world.

The themes of visibility and invisibility recur throughout the writings of Copeland, Williams, and Hill Fletcher. In crafting their theological anthropologies with a particular focus on the limits of human freedom and choice, they introduce a critical analytical lens that asks: what does this theological anthropology render visible, and what does it render invisible? Copeland and Williams challenge the way some theological anthropologies—even those of black liberation theology—render the experiences of black women during and after slavery invisible. They insist that when these experiences are centered (that is, made visible), they offer a necessary theological corrective. I aim to explore this question about visibility and invisibility in relation to the dominant Islamic feminist theological anthropology. However, before turning to that, I must acknowledge the complexity of my engagement with the work of Copeland and Williams—and later in this chapter, wadud—specifically their descriptions of the horrors and dehumanization of slavery, of the continued legacies of slavery and racism in the United States, and of the strategies of survival and hope of black women. These are not my experiences. And, I am embedded in a system in which I benefit in my whiteness from the legacies of slavery. I attempt to approach their work with upmost respect and a sustained, productive ambivalence about appropriation. As with the rest of this book, I attempt to listen attentively, to hear deeply, and to take seriously the challenges and correctives they offer based on their experiences. These correctives are profound and push me to reconsider how I formulate my own views on human nature, freedom, and social interactions. This reconsideration begins with the question of visibility and invisibility.

What does Islamic feminist theological anthropology render visible, and what does it render invisible? What is made visible by the dominant concepts of *tawhid, fitra, khilafah*, and *taqwa*? And what is hidden, concealed, or left without consideration? First and foremost, all of these theological assertions emphasize the foundational value of each and every human being in relation to God and in relation to each other. While each concept has distinct nuances, they all weave together with this primary objective. They all work to assert universal human equality, capacity, and responsibility. This is vital in combating misogynistic, patriarchal, and androcentric normativity within Islamic traditions and Muslim practices. It is a theological corrective that asserts women's equality; it makes the claim to equality visible. At the same time, it offers a critique of non-egalitarian views and practices, designating them as deviations and corruptions of the ideal human–human and human–Divine relationships.

The key word here is "ideal." Islamic feminists visibilize the *ideal* theological anthropology. I have already stressed the empowering value of this, and I myself make the same ideal claims. However, claims to an aspirational ideal are not the same as attending to the descriptive reality on the ground, the real. Copeland and Williams stress the importance of "realistic" models of theological anthropology. A realistic model is not simply an embrace of whatever the on the ground reality may be; it is not just description. A realistic model, though, needs to be in conversation with the descriptive, embodied reality, particularly the descriptive reality of the most marginalized in any society. If a model of theological anthropology is too distanced from or out of touch with the reality on the ground, then no matter how many beautiful claims it makes to equality, freedom, and responsible relationality, it can serve to further marginalize. A theological anthropology of freedom, choice, and capacity can be irrelevant and oppressive to those who are not free, cannot choose, and are not capable. Hoel and Shaikh point to such a disconnect in their analysis of the relationship between *'abd Allah* and *khilafah* and actual religious subjectivity. They also emphasize that these ostensibly liberative and egalitarian theological concepts manifest in unexpected ways within real social structures of power and limitation, that is, within conditions of relationality and constraint. These concepts alone thus do not rule out the manifestation of social inequality. They can even facilitate and perpetuate it.

Do other Islamic concepts—particularly *fitra* and *taqwa*—address constraint and relationality? They critique constraint clearly. And, they distinguish between acceptable and unacceptable forms of relationality. *Fitra*, though, also promotes a fairly robust idea of unrestrained autonomy and individuality. One way it does so is through connection to Abraham. The sole Qur'anic reference to *fitra* in Qur'an 30:30 implicitly invokes his example; Abraham, in many ways, becomes the exemplar of a *fitra*-based theological anthropology.[130] The Qur'an describes Abraham in this way, and then uses his story to explicate the contours of what it means to naturally incline toward God, to be *hanif* (Q 30:30). Abraham knows God and obeys God. Abraham comes to know God primarily through the actualization of his *fitra*, as manifest in his rational reflection on the natural and cultural world surrounding him. Reflecting on the stars, moon, and sun, he reasons that God could not be like any of these things but must be greater than each of them (Q 6:75–89). Abraham also reflects on the practices and beliefs of his father and society. He sees them worshipping "idols" that cannot speak, respond, or help. He, based on his *fitra*-derived understanding of God, rejects these practices, his father, and the ways of his people (Q 6:80–81, 21:63–67). Drawing on Hill Fletcher, Abraham's *fitra* and natural capacity enable him to escape—cut constraints from—both his context of relationality and his sociocultural economy of knowledge. And this ability is extensively praised. Abraham is the model of faith, the model even for Prophet Muhammad (Q 6:123).

As the model, Abraham is contrasted with the *mushrikeen*, those who engage in *shirk*, those who associate partners with God (e.g., Q 3:67, 3:95, 6:69). Superficially, it appears this contrast is merely one of monotheism versus polytheism. However, the Qur'anic discourse is focused on Abraham's unrestrained ability to disassociate from the societal, cultural, and religious norms of his people and community. The *mushrikeen*, in contrast, are critiqued as those who "cling" to the ways of their forebears (e.g., Q 37:69–72, 43:22). Moreover, the Qur'an indicates that such clinging is not an acceptable excuse for people whose *fitra* and *nafs* are created with an ingrained knowledge of and relationship to God:

> When your Sustainer took out the offspring from the loins of the Children of Adam and made them bear witness about themselves, God said, "Am I not your Sustainer?" And they replied, "Yes, we bear witness." So, you cannot say on the Day of Resurrection, "We were not aware of this." Or, "It was our forebears who, before us, ascribed partners to God, and we were only the descendants who came after them. Will you destroy us because of the falsehoods they invented? (Q 7:172–173)

The exemplary model of Abraham emphasizes that *fitra* is actualizable irrespective of the embodied realities of relationality and constraint. Relationality and constraint are not valid excuses for lack of actualization. The Qur'an indicates individuals will be held responsible for their actualization of *fitra* and *taqwa*. I confess that I find this Abraham-centric theological anthropology of *fitra* beautiful and empowering. It validates basic individual human integrity irrespective of context. It elevates the female individual who is so often obscured and relegated within collective societal and communal structures. It validates the assertion of agency within and in contestation of dominant structures. Yet, I also see now that it fails to grapple sufficiently with constraint.

As a result, the dominant *fitra*-centric theological anthropology can function as a sort of theological rugged individualism. If humans are all equally free, capable, and responsible, then they should be able to actualize their freedom and capacity, and they should be held responsible for not doing so. To be clear, no Islamic feminist theologian states this. But, just as Hill Fletcher addresses the "shadow side" of relationality, there is also a "shadow side" of individualism. Copeland, for instance, links the assertion of the free, autonomous, and isolated individual subject with the "shadow sides" of genocide and imperialism. In the United States, this shadow side is alive and well. "If you just work hard enough, you can be anything you want to be." "If you live in poverty, it is because of your personal choices and, perhaps, your individual laziness and dependence." These myths frequently ride along with autonomous individual-affirming theological anthropologies, and they result in marginalized individuals being exclusively blamed for their own marginalization.

Another significant byproduct of this anthropology, one that is manifest in Islamic feminist theologies, is a heavy reliance on the power of knowledge to rectify human oppression, wrongdoing, and deviations from *tawhid* and *taqwa*. The cause of oppression, wrongdoing, and deviations is often depicted as lack of knowledge. Of course, this diagnosis fits well with the anthropological emphasis on human forgetfulness, which breeds arrogance and ingratitude. The idea is that if people just remember, just know, then they will behave differently. Knowledge is undoubtedly part of the issue, but constraint and embodiment force us to consider other questions about conditioning of behavior and, more importantly, change of conditioned behavior. When Hill Fletcher invokes Kuhn's paradigm shift, she is not only interested in knowledge. She is foregrounding the conditional and communal nature of knowledge production, enactment, and reification. An autonomous, individual, and positive theological anthropology—which is empowering and dissonance producing—can eclipse the complexities of communal constraint. Islamic feminists, myself included, have capitalized off asserting the inherent value, capacity, and responsibility of each individual through the concepts of *tawhid*, *fitra*, and *khilafah*. Now, we must attend to the shadows cast by our assertions.

In addition to the exemplary depiction of Abraham, the Qur'an does broach the topic of embodied and material constraint. Qur'an 4:97 depicts a conversation between angels and humans who have engaged in evil during their lives.

These humans, at the moment of death, attempt to excuse their wrongdoing by claiming they were oppressed (*mustad'afeen*) in the world. The angels, as servants of God, respond with a question: "Was God's earth not wide enough (spacious enough) for you to move yourselves away?" The Qur'an presents these people as falsely claiming oppression as a constraint on their decision-making ability, on their ability to choose righteousness and *taqwa*. They are then compared to people who are really constrained, the "truly helpless men, women, and children who have no means in their power and no way to leave" (Q 4:98). The latter are not held accountable like the former. They are not free to choose, do not have the means to act in prescribed ways, and accordingly are not answerable in the same manner. This is a Qur'anic accounting for constraint and limitations on freedom and capacity.

This accounting is echoed throughout Qur'anic exegesis, jurisprudence, and ethics. People who are not actually capable of performing certain ritual, legal, and ethical obligations are not held accountable—by God or society—for those obligations. For example, a person who cannot stand while praying is exempted from the standard obligation of standing while praying. The real physical and ability-related constraint validates the exemption. This is a fairly innocuous example, but there are others that are more challenging. A woman is not required (permitted?) to pray or fast during her menstrual cycle. A poor person is not required (not able?) to pay zakat, the obligatory charity on accumulated wealth. And, a slave is not punished to the same degree as a free person. All these examples attend to the reality of constraint and agency. They are responsive to embodied realities. They are variously depicted as necessary accommodations, merciful responses, and contextual adjustments. Therefore, even with the heavy emphasis on autonomy and individuality in *fitra*, there is some attention to conditions and systems of constraint.

My concern, however, is that attending to constraints is not the only issue. Attending to constraint does not challenge or seek to undo constraint. Not every constraint is one that can be undone; there are diverse varieties of constraint. But some, even in these brief examples, relate to broader systems of human hierarchy (particularly gender, class, and race hierarchies) that Islamic feminism and Muslima theology seek not only to attend to but also to destabilize, even eradicate. Do exemptions and modifications challenge underlying systems? Exemptions and modifications may appear to be *or* be necessary, fair, or merciful within a dominant system. But, exemptions and modifications are also ways to keep the dominant system intact; they are ways of servicing the system. Exemptions and modifications also reveal the normative assumptions of that system. If women are granted an exemption from ritual prayer because of menstruation, then the overarching ritual system is based on a male norm.

Constraint-based exemptions have significant implications for *taqwa*. As outlined, *taqwa* is deemed the only legitimate basis of human distinction. Distinctions following other criteria—sex, gender, race, religion—are unacceptable and distort *tawhid* and *khilafah*. *Taqwa*, though, is not a vague concept.[131] *Taqwa* is manifest in belief *and* in ritual and social action. Some central avenues for expressing and cultivating *taqwa* are prayer, charity, education, and familial relationships. We do not all have the same opportunities and possibilities for expressing *taqwa* in these various areas, and divergence in opportunities is not just a result of individual or biological particularities (such as childbearing). Opportunities are shaped by the existing—often non-*taqwa*- and non-*tawhid*-aligned—structures and systems. We strive for *taqwa* within structures and systems—such as androcentrism, poverty, and white superiority—which impinge on and constrain some people's abilities to manifest *taqwa*. Responsiveness to material limitations and constraints in the form of exemptions, while pragmatic, means that those most constrained will be those most exempted and thus those with fewer avenues to express and cultivate *taqwa*. The exempted are not blamed. They are not held accountable. But they are excluded, and the system is left intact. If *taqwa* remains the only legitimate basis of distinction, and some humans have more possibilities and opportunities to manifest *taqwa*, then a cycle that privileges some over others continues.

I am, of course, not arguing that exemptions and modifications simply be cast aside and everyone left to their own devices irrespective of the reigning system. To do so, without any change to the underlying system, would align with the mythological rugged individualism I have already critiqued. My question is about changing the system, about moving from the *real* closer to the *ideal* that Islamic feminists and Muslima theologians have identified. *Taqwa* theoretically delegitimizes other hierarchies of evaluation. It also provides a potent challenge to the bifurcation of moral and social equality; beliefs and actions are intertwined and must be enacted in social contexts and relationships. But, does *taqwa*—as currently articulated—provide a moral impetus for changing extant systems of human hierarchy? Or to put it a different way, can *taqwa* provide an impetus, an imperative even, for active and conscious cultivation of the conditions in which other people can exercise a less constrained and more creative form of *khilafah*? I am not willing to surrender the liberative and empowering aspects of the tawhidic paradigm, *fitra*, and *khilafah*. I am also fully invested in the critique and moral-social integration of *taqwa*. I am interested, though, in exploring ways to expand these foundations of theological anthropology to simultaneously attend to the real, aim for the ideal, and impel the gritty and continuous work of transforming structural and systemic constraints and injustice.

A hint toward these expansions lies in an overlap in the writings of Copeland, Williams, and wadud. Like Copeland and Williams, wadud also invokes African American experience during and after slavery in her reflections on theological anthropology. In a more recent essay arguing for the precedence of the ethics of *tawhid* over the ethics of *qiwamah* (male authority as protectors and maintainers of women), wadud contextualizes her development of the tawhidic paradigm in relation to the historical legacy of African American Muslims.[132] She focuses in particular on the way slavery and postslavery realities precluded *qiwamah* of males over women. Men were not capable of being protectors and maintainers of women because of the constraints of slavery and the postbellum period. Despite this descriptive reality, she observes that many African American Muslims retain a "tenacious romantic attachment to the illusion of male power and privilege presumed to be a part of the qiwamah construct."[133] This illusion of *qiwamah* serves as a counter to the violence perpetrated against black men and women. However, wadud—invoking language very similar to Williams—argues that the illusion of *qiwamah* as an ideal conflicts with the actual familial and economic "survival mechanisms" employed.[134] Male *qiwamah* is projected to all men irrespective of their own actions and capacity. At the same time, women's contributions to the family's survival are obscured and devalued through the invocation of common Islamic tropes about women's roles and responsibilities within the family. Specifically, the trope that a Muslim woman's money is hers alone without any obligation to contribute to familial maintenance is bandied about, while the majority of women actually contribute to the family. wadud's goal in highlighting this reality and disconnect is to undercut the contemporary and contextual legitimacy of a familial model based on *qiwamah*. She also is drawing attention to constraints, embodied realities, and the manner in which normative ideals can be detached from both and thus perpetuate injustice.

While not explicitly focused on theological anthropology, wadud echoes a similar perspective in earlier writings on motherhood and the specific experiences of African American female heads of household. Reflecting on limitations on the "freedom, dignity, and human potential of those enslaved," she claims that common Islamic tropes or idioms glorifying motherhood are the "nemesis" of women whose struggle and experience does not align with the normative, ideal depiction.[135] The "paradise" that supposedly lies at the feet of the mother becomes a "living hell for many single female parents, or women with disabled or un-able fathers, husbands, and brothers in a Muslim community that pretends such an idiom is a statement of fact and therefore ignores the agony of these women making them *invisible*."[136] wadud describes these idioms as misogynistic fantasies enshrined in a social and legal system that does not attend do, does not recognize, and therefore does not support single female heads of household. The promotion of disembodied, decontextualized ideals of motherhood and family overlooks the reality, and therefore results in additional burden on women who carry both the weight of the real (that is, the need to survive) and the weight of the ideal (that is, the expectations of a system that judges them but does not support them). On this basis, similar to her argument about the illegitimacy of *qiwamah*, wadud advocates for the acceptance and systemic integration of egalitarian and flexible family structures that do more than just ignore reality.[137] It is how wadud concretizes her position that is of great significance in this project.

In a theologically provocative overlap with Williams, wadud articulates her perspective through another paradigm: the Hajar paradigm.[138] She invokes the experience of Hajar as the basis for constructing familial models that both attend to reality *and* seek to actively undo injustice. She identifies a parallel between single female heads of household and Hajar, who runs back and forth between the hills of Safa and Marwa seeking sustenance for her son. All burdens fall on her shoulders, and those burdens are not eased or removed by the "magical rhetoric of 'with Allah's help.'"[139] wadud does not dismiss God's help but emphasizes the vacuousness of idioms, the necessity of survival, and her definition of Hajar-esque faith as a "partnership" with God requiring personal action and divine involvement.

While many of these emphases are comparable to Williams', there is a notable difference relating to the position of Hajar/Hagar within the broader traditions. Hajar is imagined to be the foremother of the Islamic tradition. This positioning does not erase the abuse, abandonment, and struggle she faced and endured. Yet, it does mean she is not a marginal figure within the hagiography or self-definition of the tradition. Her centrality within Islam is best evinced in the preservation in hajj (the obligatory pilgrimage to Mecca) of her survival-focused running between Safa and Marwa. This rite—*sa'i*—is something that all pilgrims must perform in order to complete the pilgrimage. As wadud notes, her struggle is centered and preserved "liturgically."[140] But, this is where things get interesting. Although Hajar is centered—in the middle of the Islamic theological and ritual world—she has nonetheless been rendered invisible in Islamic social practice and law. Muslims literally walk and run in her footsteps, but wadud bemoans that fact that few actually reflect on Hajar's experience and manifestation of engaged surrender.[141] Moreover, the legal system ignores her example and circumstances, and is built on the false and facile presumption that "a woman will never, for any reason, become responsible for providing for and protecting herself and her offspring."[142] The Hajar paradigm is a challenge and corrective to this system, a system within which Hajar herself would be considered deviant. wadud's assertion here parallels Williams' view on "proper" roles and Hill Fletcher's perspective on the way religious norms are often used to constrain creativity. The Hajar paradigm offers a historical precedent, concrete attentiveness to constraints and strategies of survival, and an insistence on collective, communal responsibility for modifying dominant ethical and legal models of family. With the latter, wadud argues that there is no singular, natural, or inevitable family structure. Family structures in and of themselves carry no essential value.[143] Value is assessed based on the actions of, equality of, and support provided to all individuals within a family, that is, on the basis of *taqwa*.

Hibba Abugideiri also connects Hajar, social structures, and *taqwa*. Writing about the leadership of wadud, Amira Sonbol, and Sharifa Alkhateeb in the "Gender Jihad," Abugideiri states that Hajar is in fact a symbol of *taqwa*, an embodiment of *taqwa* in her God-consciousness, perseverance, struggle, and active female agency.[144] Hajar's model of *taqwa* moreover is a "tool of reform" for Muslim women leaders, a tool that inspires them to "correct the wrongs of society."[145]

Building on the Hajar paradigm and Abugideiri's connection of Hajar, *taqwa*, and change, I propose one way to expand the dominant Islamic feminist theological anthropology—specifically *taqwa*—is to root it even more deeply in the example of Hajar, to make Hajar the exemplar of theological anthropology. What would an Islamic Hajar-centered theological anthropology look like? What would be its implications for the pivotal and integrative concept of *taqwa*? I will, throughout the remainder of this chapter, explore expansions to *taqwa* arising from consideration of and responsiveness to Hajar as an actively creative, relational, constrained, and embodied model of human nature. Hajar's model, a *taqwa*-centric model, provides an illuminating counterpoint to the Abraham *fitra*-centric model, which somewhat exalts autonomy and capacity for removing constraints. Hajar does not present a wholly distinct model of theological anthropology; she is also a model of *tawhid, fitra*, and *khilafah*. But, her actualization of *tawhid, fitra*, and *khilafah*—that is, her manifestation of *taqwa*—provides a more robust accounting for human experience, aspirations, agency, and collective responsibilities.

Before turning to the ways Hajar's example expands the concept of *taqwa*, I must explicitly address some of the standard ways in which Hajar's example is reduced in Muslim discourse. She is often presented as just a mother, just a woman, or just an appendage to the story and life of Abraham. She is, among other things, a mother and a woman. Motherhood and womanhood certainly color her experience and example but neither confines the relevance of her example to mothers and women alone. Confining her in such a way is a testimony to androcentric normativity in Islamic thought and practice. It is also a strategy for avoiding the collective demands placed on all of us when we truly encounter her example. Her example forces us to see and engage with racism, slavery, violence, patriarchy, struggle, and abandonment. Hajar, moreover, is anything but an appendage, even though she is deeply, viscerally entangled in webs of relationality. Hajar is also often presented as an exemplar of absolute faith and trust in God. I embrace wadud's depiction of her relationship to God as an active partnership. Hajar faithfully and deeply relied on God. I do not accept that that faithful and deep reliance removed her fear, pain, struggle, and even anger. It also did not remove her agency and the necessity of her action. The presentation of her as an exemplar of faith, however, sometimes functions to mute her struggle, her human emotions, and her agency in survival. The implied message is that acknowledgment of struggle—struggle that God knows of and Abraham is involved in—is an affront to or contradiction to deep commitment to God. This message is amplified with Hajar because she is the foremother of the tradition; her struggle is piece of the larger story leading to the Islamic tradition. Any intimation that her situation of abandonment and suffering was problematic can be taken as an assault on the broader narrative of origins. This messaging is part of the gap between ideal rhetoric and reality. We need a model of theological anthropology capable of accommodating humans—in their messy, beautiful humanness—and God. Hajar *is* an exemplar of faith; her example is just more complicated—and thus more realistic, relevant, and stimulating—than typically presented.

How are *taqwa* and theological anthropology expanded based on the model of Hajar? I am interested not only in what Hajar is and does but also in what we learn from and are called to do in light of Hajar's example. To begin, Hajar is active. This is not a wholly exceptional expansion of *taqwa*. As I have emphasized, *taqwa* requires ritual and social action. *Taqwa* cannot be manifest devoid of such action. Hajar's model, though, pushes this further. She does not just perform particular prescribed actions or abstain from performing other specified actions. She asserts agency. She runs. She struggles. She survives. There is persistence, a sustained quality of agency in her example. Moreover, she is not only active in relation to other people or her context. Her entire relationship with God is active. Hajar is a model of wadud's engaged surrender. She is not passive, submissive, or simplistically obedient. She exemplifies the continuous and dynamic nature of vicegerency (*khilafah*). *Taqwa*, thus, becomes a reference to sustained, persistent assertion of personal agency. This assertion should not be confused with complete individual autonomy, the absence of relationality. Hajar is not autonomous or unconstrained. She is constrained in many ways, but she is an agent always. Hajar's agency manifests in what Hill Fletcher refers to as constrained creativity. Within constraints, she seeks creative means to survive even when those means seem impossible. When the few supplies she is left with are gone, she runs *and* implores God. She acts *and* she calls on God for assistance. *Taqwa* requires both, and it requires both simultaneously and continuously.

Hajar's exercise of constrained creativity is the very means of her survival. Whereas with Abraham, *fitra* is manifest as reflection and discernment, followed by extrication from constraints, Hajar presents another model. Her *fitra*—her innate knowledge of and relationship with God—spurns reflection and discernment, followed by creative action in light of very real constraints and relational obligations. Creativity and responsible relationality become central features of *fitra*, features that must be enacted in the real world. As Williams and wadud stress, Hagar/Hajar's creative action is not "proper" or aligned with the "norm." Her survival depends on her "deviance" from such norms. Norms and proper roles are not even viable options. This is a description of Hajar's experience and the experiences of some African American women. wadud, however, stresses Hajar's "deviance" for another reason: to delegitimize the dominant norm itself, including the norms of *qiwamah*, idealized motherhood, and a patriarchal family structure. Hajar cannot manifest *taqwa* within these norms; she cannot even survive within these norms. Hajar's creative deviance, therefore, is a challenge to the value and authority of singular and static norms of action and relationship. Hajar's creativity is not an impediment to *taqwa*; it is a necessity for manifesting *taqwa* amid the reality of constraints. *Taqwa*—as a social manifestation—must attend to social constraints and relationality. The cultivation and expression of *taqwa* are severely deformed and truncated when forced into static, singular norms of action and relationship. The great irony is that these norms are often invoked as *the* singular Islamic tradition, and deviation from this fixed tradition is shunned. Without the creative, *fitra*-inspired "deviation" of Hajar, there would be no tradition at all.

Another expansion of *taqwa* arising from the centering of Hajar relates to structural and systemic transformation, that is, moving from the real closer to the ideal. *Taqwa* is creative agency *within* constraints and relationality. There will never be a completely unconstrained or nonrelational context. That is a privileged myth. We are not autonomous individuals, and moreover *taqwa* is not about autonomous individuality. It is distinctively social and relational. But, as Copeland argues in her redefinition of solidarity, there is the possibility of creating and maintaining more responsible relationships among people. These relationships do not do away with the constraint of relationality, but they seek to consciously reconfigure it. Hill Fletcher echoes a similar sentiment about dynamic possibilities within constraint and the potential of restructuring one's own "calculus of concern" for the other. I acknowledge Williams' assertion that Hagar's experience is about survival, quality of life, not about liberation from oppressive systems. This accords in many ways with the Islamic story of Hajar.

Placing Hajar in conversation with *tawhid, fitra,* and *khilafah,* however, moves me to assert that humans are *capable of* and *called to* transform systems of inequality and oppression. Divine liberation from these human systems does not appear to be the reality of human history. Yet, human transformation is intimately tied to the capacity of *fitra* and the teleology of *khilafah*. It is what we are called to do. Since we are located in nonideal systems—systems that do not align with the tawhidic paradigm—our obligation cannot simply be maintenance of the status quo. Nor can we ignore reality while paying lip service to romantic tropes and norms. This is not only unrealistic but also exclusionary and oppressive. It does not acknowledge the reality, respond to it, or seek to transform it. We also cannot just acknowledge the reality and assert an ideal alternative. Our obligation is structural and systemic transformation with the goal of creating the conditions within which more and diverse people can better manifest their vicegerency (*khilafah*). This transformation, importantly, cannot solely seek to exempt or accommodate people into the existing social system. The systems themselves must be challenged and transformed. Challenging and transforming become central modes of manifesting *taqwa*.

What does this transformative *taqwa* look like? Copeland points to one step in her explication of the reason why she details the horrors and violence of slavery. She states that she does so as an act of "intentional remembering of the dead, exploited, despised victims of history."[146] Williams and wadud make a similar move with Hagar/Hajar and the experience of African American women. They render the experiences visible. And in doing so they render the inhumanity of dominant systems of violence and oppression visible. For many, these experiences are already visible, well known, and embodied. For others, they are unknown, unacknowledged, and often ignored. For the latter, the challenge is to see what is being made visible without defense, dismissal, or minimization. It is only by truly seeing that those with privilege can ever hope to engage in solidarity.

For this reason, I suggest a reconfiguration to the standard translation of *taqwa* as God-consciousness. *Taqwa* is God-consciousness, but it also has to be social conscientization. Social conscientization is not the same as acting in the social realm. This social component of *taqwa* is widely asserted already. What I am asserting is different. While social action certainly remains important, *taqwa* also requires that we deliberately seek to become more aware of the systems and processes of marginalization within our societies. Good actions are not enough. *Taqwa* demands awareness. *Taqwa* as God-consciousness and social conscientization is connected to *fitra* in an intriguing way. *Fitra* is described as equal, capable, conscious of God, and conscious of the distinction between good and wrong. As discussed, human forgetfulness is the primary explanation for humans' failure to live up to the positive view of human nature expressed through the concept of *fitra*. The *fitra* can be buried, covered, hidden. Our natural knowledge can be buried, covered, hidden. Conscientization is a call to engage in the process of uncovering and polishing our *fitra*, of remembering our relationship to God and to other humans, of refusing false notions of independence from God *and* from other humans, *and* of rejecting the arrogance of indifference in relation to systems of privilege and oppression.

In addition to visibilization and conscientization, transformative *taqwa* requires targeted action. This action includes the obligatory actions of Islam, such as prayer, fasting, charity, et cetera. These actions are important and play a role in transformative *taqwa*. Nevertheless, as discussed, they can also perpetuate the status quo in two ways: through romantic and detached normative ideals and through systems of exemptions. Transformative *taqwa*, therefore, requires that all actions be assessed in light of a specific criterion: the concerns and needs of the marginalized and oppressed (*mustad'af*). As noted, Esack invokes this same criterion as a hermeneutical key in his Qur'anic liberation theology.[147] He argues that, in the struggle to restructure society in line with justice, preference must be given to those who are oppressed by others, to those who are oppressed by the "behavior or policies of the arrogant and powerful."[148] This preference is a conscious denial of objectivity. In systems of constraint, there is no value to objectivity; objectivity can be oppressive. According to Esack, preference for the *mustad'af* is also a quest to respond "creatively" to suffering while recognizing the agency of those who are marginalized. Notably, he connects such preferential and transformative action to Qur'anic demands for *taqwa*; the Qur'an emphasizes the "need for a community and individuals deeply imbued with *taqwa* who will carry on the prophet's task of transformation and liberation."[149] To strive for transformative *taqwa* is to follow the example of Prophet Muhammad. Transformative *taqwa*—as visibilization, conscientization, and actionable preference for the marginalized—is prophetic.

I conclude this chapter by highlighting one other key aspect of Hajar's re-centering in theological anthropology. Hajar is embodied; her experiences highlight the reality and complexity of life, struggle, and hope. Hajar is also embodied ritually. Hajar's physical actions are preserved in the rites of hajj. As part of the larger discussion of egalitarian theological anthropology and of transformative *taqwa*, her ritual embodiment cannot be ignored or downplayed. A female, a mother, a black woman is preserved in her particularities at the center of Islamic ritual. This preservation raises important questions about the role of ritual in transformative *taqwa*, and the role of women in ritual practice. These are the subjects of the final chapter of this book.

7

Enacting Equality

RITUAL PRAYER, TRADITION, AND COMMUNITY

IN 2005, AMINA WADUD led a mixed-gender congregational prayer in New York City at the Cathedral of St. John Divine. The prayer—promoted as the "first" of its kind but not the first or only of its kind—aroused vigorous debates within and beyond Muslim communities. It was a concrete and embodied enactment of Islamic feminist assertions of egalitarianism, and it stirred conversations about inclusion, tradition, authority, and change. Detractors argued the prayer was a deviation or negative innovation (*bid'a*) that was never performed in Prophet Muhammad's lifetime. Some proponents sought to validate their stance by drawing on ahadith indicating precedent for such rituals, while others— amina wadud included—emphasized theological equality of humans as the basis for female leadership of mixed-gender congregational prayer. Since 2005, other initiatives aimed at creating more inclusive and women-friendly worship settings and experiences have arisen. These range from attempts to ensure female access to and equal facilities at mosques to calls for female representation on mosque boards to creation of gender and LGBTQI+ inclusive communities to the creation of female-only mosques, such as the Women's Mosque of America in Los Angeles.

In this chapter, I contextualize woman-led prayer within broader discussions of authority, tradition, and change. I begin with an exploration of Islamic feminist discourse on woman-led prayer, female leadership, and androcentric ritual norms. While I touch on the precedent-based arguments made in favor of woman-led prayer, I am more interested in the theological and social assumptions underlying exclusion and promoting inclusion. I then engage Christian feminist approaches from Delores S. Williams, Elizabeth A. Johnson, Rosemary Radford Ruether, and Traci C. West that grapple with notions of community, male imagery of God, tradition, and ritual. While it certainly would be possible and interesting to focus only on worship and ritual leadership by women in this comparative theological section, I have chosen to engage more broadly in order to unearth latent theological assumptions impacting ritual manifestations.[1] I conclude the chapter by returning to Muslima theology and arguing for the necessity of embodied egalitarian ritual, a dynamic view of tradition, and reassertion of the transformative space between ideal and real community (*umma*).

Ritual Prayer, Inclusion, and Gendered Assumptions

As Juliane Hammer aptly expresses in the subtitle to her book on American Muslim women, the 2005 prayer—and by extension, woman-led prayer—is about "more than a prayer."[2] It *is* about prayer, *and* it is also about interpretative authority and voice, reclamation of texts and tradition, embodiment of equality, and communal inclusion. Woman-led prayer (which I use herein to indicate woman-led prayer in mixed-gender congregational settings) is a symbolic act, a challenge to androcentric norms, and an assertion of full humanity. There are many reliable and accessible sources written on the 2005 prayer in New York City.[3] It is not my intention to rehash or survey the diverse perspectives on that prayer or woman-led prayer in general. I focus on Islamic feminist discourse outlining the need for woman-led prayer, the way such prayer is intertwined with broader concerns about inclusion and authority, and the related assumptions about gender, tradition, and change.

While there are historical precedents and classical scholarly opinions (including Ibn al-Arabi) that validate woman-led prayer, the dominant practice has been and remains exclusive male-led congregational prayer in mixed-gender settings.[4] There are communities and groups in which woman-led prayer is increasingly common, including inclusive mosque settings, third space settings, female-only mosques, and more informal gatherings. In the United States, though, most mosques do not engage in or even consider woman-led prayer. Islamic feminists who advocate for and enact woman-led prayer do so to explicitly challenge this gendered exclusion.

A central basis for their challenge is the theological anthropology emphasized in Islamic feminist exegesis, legal examination, and theological articulation. As examined in the preceding chapter, these anthropologies are grounded in the tawhidic paradigm, *khilafah, taqwa*, and a rejection of bifurcation between the moral and social spheres. wadud accordingly describes her role as *khateebah* (giver of the sermon) at the Claremont Road Mosque in South Africa in 1994 as a challenge arising out of *tawhid* and the tawhidic paradigm: *tawhid* provides the "ethical rationale for reciprocal relations between women and men in all aspects of society: familial, political, and spiritual functions, roles, and contexts."[5] Since women are fully human, in direct relationship with God, and equally capable of and responsible for *khilafah*, Islamic feminists argue that there is no theological justification for a gender- or sex-based restriction in leading the central ritual obligation of prayer (*salat*). Automatic exclusion of women from this role based on biology—not qualifications or competency—is an affront to their equality and humanity, as well as to *tawhid*.[6]

Building on Shaikh's *tafsir* of praxis, Hammer describes woman-led prayer as "embodied *tafsir*."[7] Embodied *tafsir* underscores the direct link between woman-led prayer and decades long efforts in Qur'anic exegesis and reclamation, as well as the central insistence that exegesis must be translated into ritual, social, and political action in the world and in relation to real bodies.[8] Woman-led prayer is a ritual "embodiment of the oft-stated spiritual equality."[9] Hammer's wording here is significant. Equality is frequently asserted even by those who deem woman-led prayer to be unacceptable, a corrupt innovation (*bid'a*), or detrimental to the community. The juxtaposition of the assertion of equality and the biological criteria of exclusion from prayer leadership illuminates the precise disjuncture between moral, social, and ritual equality proponents of woman-led prayer seek to challenge; it is "equality" that exists only as an assertion but does not manifest in actual social or ritual actions in this world. The holistic exclusion of women from central ritual spheres "signals, not only the continued gendered view of humanity in the social sphere, but also the marginalization of women's experiences and corporeality as women from centres of religious worship."[10]

As a deliberate and symbolic challenge to marginalization and exclusion, woman-led prayer is intertwined with broader trends in Muslim religious communities, institutions, and mosques.[11] Many Muslim women in the United States have experienced exclusionary practices and oppressive behavior in such settings. In mosques in particular, exclusion ranges from the lack of a female prayer area to inadequate prayer spaces to neglect of female concerns and needs in educational and pastoral contexts to explicitly hostile behavior.[12] Exclusion also manifests in a lack of leadership roles and decision-making involvement in mosques; in many mosques, women do not have an official role, do not sit on boards, and thus do not formally participate in mosque governance. Diverse efforts, such as Aisha al-Adawiya's Women in Islam, Inc. and Hind Makki's SideEntrance Tumblr, aim to increase awareness of women's marginalization in mosques and to achieve concrete improvements, including designated female prayer areas, women's participation in programming, and women's participation in decision-making.

Some advocates for "women-friendly mosques" distance themselves from woman-led prayer, arguing against it explicitly or claiming it is not a central issue. Hammer, however, contends that woman-led prayer actually sits in a direct and dialectical relationship with broader inclusion issues. It arises out of these concerns, and it has served as a "catalyst" for conversation and action on these concerns.[13] After the 2005 prayer, many organizations and mosques were compelled to address inclusion issues. It is true that they have often done so without considering woman-led prayer or mentioning the main people involved in the 2005 prayer.[14] It is also true that steps toward inclusion—whether in the form of allowing women to pray in the main prayer space, allowing women to give programmatic (nonritual) talks, or encouraging greater verbal inclusion from male leadership (e.g., addressing not just "brothers" but "brothers and sisters")—have further highlighted the marginalization of women. These measures are absolutely valuable, but they also highlight the norm and locus of authority; they "highlight women's exclusion from Islamic religious authority and participation in the mosque."[15] Woman-led prayer is not just a random "blip" or unrelated phenomena. It is part of "long-standing, ongoing and complex negotiations over gender norms within an inescapably diverse and indeed pluralistic 'imagined community' of global Islam."[16] Portraying woman-led prayer as random, unrelated, or peripheral seeks to delegitimize its organic connection to intellectual work and activism and to the tradition.

Such portrayals also miss the fact that woman-led prayer is tied directly to the crucial importance and function of congregational *salat* in Muslim communities. Some opponents of woman-led prayer and some supporters of broadening women's leadership and inclusion maintain that leading from the *mihrab* (prayer niche) is a relatively inconsequential position.[17] Technically, anyone—more accurately, any male—with basic knowledge of prayer rules and of the Qur'an can lead the congregational prayer. Yet, many Islamic feminists emphasize the central role congregational prayer plays within Muslim communities. The first function of congregational prayer—and certainly one that would not be debated—is to gather, unify, and shape the community. As with many obligatory Islamic rituals, congregational prayer has an essential communal element. Friday congregational prayer is "the center of Muslim religiosity. . . . Muslims come together as a community and turn collectively toward God. The form of the prayer affirms the community's identity."[18] The communal functions are even more emphasized within Muslim minority contexts, such as the United States, where mosques are frequently the only institutional manifestation of Muslim communal identity.[19] Mosques, mosque activities, and use of space within mosques, therefore, are expressions of communal identity at the same as they are shaping communal identity. Communal identity is shaped verbally, nonverbally, and spatially. It is for this reason wadud describes mosques as "an important site to initiate change and mark transitions in the context of the Muslim community."[20]

Congregational prayer leadership, moreover, is significant because it is through such leadership, and especially delivering of the sermon (*khutbah*)—that is, speaking from the *minbar* (pulpit)—that knowledge, information, and perspectives are shared throughout the community. The *minbar* is a "critical instrument of public speaking, teaching, and discourse production."[21] When women are barred from this role, their concerns and perspectives are unlikely to be centered, emphasized, or represented.[22] Mattson claims that even the most compassionate or insightful man will, at minimum, overlook concerns and issues. Perspectives voiced by males—even diverse males—are "not neutral, nor necessarily responsive, to the realities of experiences of women, although they are commonly presented as such."[23] Beyond centering and attending to a broader range of concerns, the *khutbah* is also connected to the production and communication of authoritative knowledge. If all women are automatically excluded from this role—from the role of giving the *khutbah*—then they are automatically excluded from one of the most central and authoritative sites of knowledge production. While Mattson rightfully notes that there are other forms of leadership open to Muslim women outside of mosques and traditionally Islamic institutions, the reality remains that in the United States mosques and congregational rituals continue to be the central loci of religious authority.[24] Other forms of leadership do not carry the same degree of symbolic or religious authority. This is especially apparent among Islamic feminists, many of whom are routinely discredited because their production and sharing of knowledge is rooted in the academy and not only, or authoritatively, in the mosque.

wadud and Silvers stress that woman-led prayers and woman authored and delivered *khutbahs* are also beneficial to the broader community.[25] Woman-led prayer, thus, is not only about including women or permitting female access. It is also framed as a broader concern for the moral, social, and spiritual development of the community as a whole. Women's access to central communal rituals can actually enhance *all* members' experience by offering new content, new perspectives, and new forms of representation that provoke thought and foster deeper and wider commitment to God and to other humans. Silvers, specifically, argues that woman-led prayer results in female role models; renders women visible, which is vital since much disrespect is connected to female literal and metaphorical "invisibility"; and habituates community members to viewing women as worthy, knowledgeable, and authoritative.[26] The community is enhanced through content *and* also through the physical representation of a woman in the central role.

Implied in these arguments for the importance of woman-led prayer is a critique of the exclusion of women from the role but also a critique of the underlying androcentric normativity of these practices. Ritual congregational prayer—including spatial organization, leadership, and content—is linked to gendered assumptions depicting the male as the center of the community and as the human norm of behavior. Ritual prayer is "the foundation of Muslim religiosity," and ideally it should function to underscore the equality of all people before God.[27] However, "the performative practice of prayer is embedded in patriarchal cultural norms in which only men are empowered to lead the prayer and have the power to express themselves through public piety."[28] Androcentric norms privilege men, while working to invisibilize and control the bodies of women. Islamic feminists seek to reveal and problematize these gendered assumptions.

Gendered assumptions and androcentrism manifest in the spatial arrangements during prayer and within mosques. In analyzing the debates surrounding wadud's 1994 *khutbah*, Nina Hoel emphasizes "assumptions regarding women's sexuality that inform the politics of religious exclusion/inclusion."[29] She, on the basis of this analysis, reveals that androcentric assumptions and notions of gender complementarity underlie many reactions to the 1994 *khutbah*. Although the *khutbah* generally aligned with the mosque's broader vision of equality, the *khutbah* received a lot criticism. This occurred because wadud destabilized and created a "fissure in the customary workings of the mosque space as a sacred space of worship."[30] The sacred space of the mosque is normatively male; if and when women are "allowed" to attend, they are confined to specific—often peripheral—areas and spaces within the mosque. The sacredness of the mosque space is entangled with this gendered spatial arrangement. Therefore, any change or challenge to this arrangement is seen as a threat to the purity and sacredness of the mosque. wadud not only gave the *khutbah*—placed a female body in a male space at the *minbar*—but her presence also provoked a change in the location of other women in the mosque.[31] They had prayed in a balcony but moved to and remain in the main prayer space. While the Durkheimian language of defilement is not as common within Muslim communities, the language of innovation (*bid'a*) communicates the same concern. *Bid'a* uses "tradition" to reject as deviations any changes to normative androcentrism. Tutin Aryanti similarly describes mosque space as explicitly political; power is "produced and asserted" through spatial restrictions and architecture within mosques.[32] Spatial restrictions and architecture are nonverbal tools that facilitate specific and defined social relations, and, in turn, these relations are practiced and reproduced within the mosque setting. Aryanti insightfully observes that mosque spatial arrangements are typically "regarded as natural and innocent—even when women are clearly absent—and such an assumption has resulted in further gender discrimination."[33] Not only do spatial arrangements assert an inherently gendered ideology but that ideology is also masked by the presentation of it as the *only* natural, traditional, and acceptable option, irrespective of historical and contemporary contextual realities.

Gendered assumptions are also manifest in the common accusation that woman-led prayer foments *fitna* (dissension or disorder) within Muslim communities. *Fitna* is connected to notions communal unity and a fear that the Muslim community will fracture through disagreement. However, *fitna* has gendered associations as well; it is linked to concerns about modesty and sexuality.[34] One of the most common rebukes of woman-led prayer is it places women in front of men, thus compromising women's modesty, distracting men from prayer, and introducing the temptation of illicit sex. Elewa and Silvers acknowledge that it may seem like a large leap from woman-led prayer to fornication or illicit sex, but historical and contemporary discourses on woman's physical presence in the mosque—not even leadership—repeatedly make this connection.[35] To be completely clear, the validity of women's corporeal presence in the mosque is being assessed based on the impact it has on men's spirituality and capacity for control.[36] Women are instructed to and compelled to conceal their bodies, render themselves invisible and silent, in order to not distract men. Practices of gender segregation and exclusive male leadership are thus imagined to be "preventative and indeed necessary means of control that condition and enable men's cultivation and expression of religious devotion."[37] This perspective not only saddles women with the "onus of sexual morality" but also paints a somewhat dismal picture of men's ability to control themselves and cultivate spirituality.[38] Woman-led prayer is a direct challenge to normative androcentrism and this particular gendered view of theological anthropology and spiritual development. Islamic feminism and woman-led prayer seek to shift the discussion from a focus on women's sexuality and bodies to a focus on women's spirituality and humanity.[39] When women are excluded unequivocally from prayer leadership and marginalized in mosque spaces and knowledge production, their full humanity and equality are not recognized. Woman-led prayer is thus a "human enactment of moral agency, an expression of gender justice, and responsive to the right to participate as equally enfleshed, sexual, and spiritual subjects in the production of religious meaning and meaning-making."[40]

Reflecting on her experience giving the *khutbah* at the Claremont Main Road Mosque, wadud probes the way gendered assumptions relate to the form and content (or substance) of female religious leadership. She expresses frustration over the fact that the form of the *khutbah*—meaning herself as a female in the role of *khateebah*—received the bulk of attention, while the content of her actual sermon received minimal comment even among most "progressive" participants.[41] She identifies a similar reaction to the 2005 prayer in New York City.[42] Her frustration stems from the importance she personally assigns to the topic of the *khutbah*— Islam as engaged surrender—but it also stems from the realization that the dominant model of Muslim religious leadership is inherently gendered. wadud felt her full humanity and the particulars of her identity could not simultaneously manifest in the normative religious leadership model. Even in a context that embraced her in the role of *khateebah*, she could only be leader *or* woman.[43] Male normativity, she asserts, is present in both progressive and conservative approaches to women's leadership. Progressives embrace female leadership but have not fully grappled with the "relationship between biology, the politics of ritual, and the legal stipulations given historically."[44] Conservatives foreground femaleness yet refuse to engage topics of female marginalization in ritual and leadership.

wadud, therefore, asserts that it is not enough for women to simply have access to and step into the predefined male model (form) of leadership: "No mere performances in the center will reconstruct status quo. Therefore, the task is not so much for women to claim that center space as legitimate for female agency. Instead, the whole of the community must enter into the margins with women to affirm the place where women's lives are experienced."[45] She emphasizes that it is necessary for the substance (content) of female leadership to receive attention. She is not proposing doing away with the ritual format; she is advocating for serious embrace of multiple centers of knowledge and experience. Her participation in woman-led prayer testifies to this. She largely upholds the traditional format of congregational prayer.[46] And while the content of her 1994 sermon is not provocative, it is replete with images drawn from and references to female experience. When she describes Islam as engaged surrender—a completely illuminating, yet unprovocative statement—she concretizes this with reference to her own experiences as a woman; she explains "Islam as engaged surrender from the perspective of being female, mother, and wife."[47] In sum, wadud's critique of androcentric norms is threefold. She critiques the exclusion of women from ritual leadership. She critiques the inclusion of women within a male norm of ritual leadership, as evinced through the sole focus on her bodily presence (form) in that role rather than on content of her sermons. And, she draws attention to the fact that her invocation of female experience in the content (substance) of her sermons can appear overly particular, odd, or not applicable to all people. This latter occurrence is also a clear indication of androcentrism. Male experiences are often taken as generic and applicable to the whole community. Male normativity will only be fully destabilized when female experiences are envisioned as equally relevant and equally capable of informing broader understanding. Ironically, this can only occur through the habituation that Silvers argues arises out of women assuming ritual leadership roles in congregational settings.

In addition to gendered assumptions, the discourse on and reactions to woman-led prayer reveal diverse and sometimes conflicting assumptions about tradition, authority, and change. Hammer highlights a "discursive disconnect" among proponents and opponents of the 2005 prayer.[48] While organizers and participants in the prayer tended to highlight the symbolic meaning of the prayer as a reclamation and assertion of human equality, many opinions focused on the event's legal (im)permissibility. Woman-led prayer is not mentioned—to prohibit or permit—in the Qur'an, but Sunni juridical consensus has generally opposed woman-led prayer in mixed congregational settings. Opponents of the prayer invoked this consensus to delegitimize the prayer without engaging theological, sociological, or spiritual rationales for the prayer. Part of this discursive disconnect comes from different views on the nature of the prayer.[49] Some see prayer as a form of ritual worship (*ibadah*) that is legally unchanging. Therefore, the correct posture in relation to prayer is detailed and unquestioning imitation (*taqlid*).[50] Advocates of woman-led prayer do not holistically dismiss this—they maintain most formal specifics of prayer—but they also stress that prayer is not just a legal dictate. Prayer has spiritual, sociological, and moral implications as well.

Beyond a disconnect between legal and symbolic, there is also a disconnect related to understandings of the nature of legal tradition. Islamic feminists (as should be clear at this point in this book) recognize the role of the legal tradition but also argue that juridical perspectives were articulated largely by men in often patriarchal contexts and cultures. Juridical perspectives are not revealed, not articulated in a cultural vacuum, not inclusive of female perspectives, and not neutral. Legal opinions on woman's prayer leadership, specifically, are tangled together with misogynistic views of women as inferior in intelligence, physical stature, ritual performance, and lineage; references to ahadith on women's menstruation related "deficiency" in religion; and claims to male superiority.[51] The exclusion of women from prayer leadership grows out of this soil. Ironically, many contemporary scholars who invoke the singular, unchanging legal "consensus" barring woman-led prayer strategically disassociate it from these perspectives, which are not as palatable today. Silver thus highlights the human production of Islamic law (*fiqh*); *fiqh* "developed out of a human struggle to interpret the Divine intent from our sacred sources, the Qur'an and Sunna. But there is nothing sacred in the scholars themselves."[52] Expressing her personal love of the legal tradition, she argues that it cannot be granted infallibility or unquestionable status. Silvers contrasts her perspective on law with the perspective of others who "honor the legal tradition by refusing to question it even in the face of social wrongs that they themselves admit."[53]

Islamic feminists also emphasize that legal tradition is diverse and full of varying opinions. The invocation of a singular and fixed legal consensus is an oversimplification restricting discussion of dissenting opinions and of change.[54] It draws boundaries around the "true" Islam, including and excluding as it does so. Hammer observes that such invocations of *the* tradition or *true* Islam derive authority not only from a connection to previous perspectives or precedent but also because of their "congruence" with the expectations of the listeners or receivers of the ideas.[55] Aryanti offers a confirmation of this in her writing on mosques in the Indonesian Muhammadiyah Muslim community. In this community, woman-led prayer in mixed congregational settings is legally permissible. This legal permission, though, is not widely communicated to members of communities, and when it is, community members are often "shocked" and argue that there is "no reason or urgency" for woman-led prayer.[56] The urgency in the Indonesian context, especially in the Muhammadiyah context which includes women's mosques, may differ from the United States. However, Aryanti's observations raise important questions about the relationship between legal consensus and communal opinions. Authority can have less to do with perpetuating a singular, unquestioned, unchanging form of thought or practice, and more to do with a self-perpetuating cycle of expectations. The issue here is that the cycle has been and remains androcentric and patriarchal. Androcentric and patriarchal content, laws, and views are received as authoritative because they align with the dominant practices and expectations on the ground.

Interrupting this cycle is one of the reasons why woman-led prayer is an important, radical, and legitimate action.[57] It is an action, though, that will be unlikely to emerge without an intentional push or concerted effort for transformation. Transformation, according to wadud, should be "collective and conscientious" and will require the solidarity of those who currently occupy positions of ritual authority.[58] Practically, wadud argues that woman-led prayer should be decided within individual communities based on a leader's qualifications and character, not sex or gender. Silvers echoes wadud's insight that transformation will require a deliberate push and will meet resistance. She calls for participation in woman-led prayer as a form of "civil disobedience" designed to highlight women's exclusion and raise consciousness.[59] Drawing a parallel to civil rights movements and their use of civil disobedience, she stresses that it is not typical for dominant groups to freely and without provocation relinquish power and privilege: "Just like whites, Muslim men have not been eager to give up their *legislated* privilege to stand in front of women in prayer and to lead women in other matters."[60] While she insists on the necessity of such acts now—in this moment—she also challenges legal scholars to engage tradition in order to find a way to legally justify woman-led prayer. Jurists have done so on other topics, such as slavery, that are explicitly discussed (not outright prohibited) in the Qur'an; therefore, legal justification of woman-led prayer, which is not explicitly mentioned at all in the Qur'an, should be as (if not more) possible. wadud and Silvers highlight the need for specific, pragmatic, and transformative change. They also draw attention to the importance of communal involvement and investment in that change, while recognizing the reality of ingrained privilege and deep resistance.

Bubbling beneath the surface of discussions of and reactions to woman-led prayer are questions about God, about human nature, about tradition and Sunna, and about the role of ritual in relation to norms and authority. These topics shape reactions and openness to woman-led prayer. How can we further emphasize what is at stake in the rote exclusions of women from this role? Can a more nuanced understanding of ritual, tradition, and community help in this process?

Black Church, Male Symbols, Tradition, and Ritual

Women's participation in ritual and liturgy is also a central issue within Christian feminist, womanist, and mujerista theologies. There is extensive scholarship on these topics, including concrete spatial, content, leadership, and symbolic reformulations of Christian worship. Due to the nature of ritual Islamic prayer (*salat*) and the concerns voiced by Islamic feminists, however, I have chosen to explore a mosaic of Christian perspectives on community, change, tradition, and ritual exclusions in hopes of identifying helpful theological and practical extensions of existing Islamic feminist insights, extensions that will assist in further visibilizing the necessity of female inclusion.

The Christian perspectives in this section come from Delores S. Williams, Elizabeth A. Johnson, Rosemary Radford Ruether, and Traci C. West, two of whom (Williams and Ruether) I have discussed in earlier chapters. Elizabeth A. Johnson is Distinguished Professor of Theology at Fordham University, where her research and writing focus on systematic theology, creation and ecological ethics, suffering, and interpretations of Mary. She earned her PhD in theology from Catholic University of America, and she is the former president of the Catholic Theological Society of America and the American Theological Society. She is the author of many books, including *Ask the Beasts: Darwin and the God of Love, Truly Our Sister: A Theology of Mary in the Communion of Saints,* and *She Who Is: The Mystery of God in Feminist Theological Discourse.*[61] Traci C. West is Professor of Ethics and African American Studies at Drew University Theological School. She is an ordained elder in the New York Annual Conference of the United Methodist Church, and she earned her PhD in Ethics from Union Theological Seminary. Her research and writing focus on Christian social ethics, sexism, racism, gender violence, and sexuality, and she is the author of *Disruptive Christian Ethics: When Racism and Women's Lives Matter* and *Wounds of the Spirit: Black Women, Violence, and Resistance Ethics.*[62]

Delores S. Williams: Black Church and African American Denominational Churches

In her work on womanist theology and appropriation of Hagar, Williams draws a pointed distinction between the Black Church and African American denominational churches. William asserts that the Black Church does not exist as an institution. The Black Church is a core symbol within the African American Christian community; the Black Church is the "heart of hope" that cannot be made respectable, elite, racial, male, heterosexist, or political.[63] It is "community essence, ideal and real as God works through it in behalf of the survival, liberation and positive, productive quality of life of suffering people."[64] Denominational churches do exist as institutions; they are visible, but they are not the Black Church. According to Williams, the "fallacious merging" of the Black Church and denominational churches works to obscure the "sins" against black women and others that are prevalent and habitual within denominational churches. These sins include sexism that refuses females leadership roles, immoral models of male leadership, teachings that indoctrinate women and other marginalized people into self-sacrifice, homophobia, sexual and emotional exploitation of female members, and failure to use community resources to address pressing community issues, including poverty, homelessness, and hunger.

Not all African American denominational churches equally participate in these sins; Williams acknowledges the important and effective work of some. Nevertheless, she emphasizes the need for deeper consideration of black women's experience. She asks, for example, what do denominational churches do "to motivate self-love and self-esteem among black women."[65] How often do preachers and leaders explicitly address oppression, exploitation, and violence targeting black women? How often are men called to treat women better and to be more responsible in all relationships? Posing these questions leads to recognition that while black men battle against racism, they are "thoroughly bonded in their affirmation of the subordination of women."[66] Williams warns against the invisibilization of gender oppression that commonly occurs in a first-things-first approach focusing solely on racism: "sexism affords as much bondage as racism."[67]

Recognition of male acquiescence to female subordination can impel a women's movement within churches, yet at the same time Williams recognizes how deeply women are indoctrinated into their own subordination. Indoctrination can produce a lack of woman-to-woman solidarity. Lack of solidarity is also "tied to male-dominated and androcentric character assigned to the liturgy and to the thoroughly masculine character assigned to the deity the church women have been taught to worship and celebrate."[68] Therefore, attentiveness to the experiences of black women is not all that is required. Core theological doctrines must also be critically explored to determine if and how they support racial, sexual, and class-based oppression. Williams describes this as a continuous process of "revaluing value" with the goal of rooting out all modes of oppression.[69] Beyond deconstructive critique, she asserts that black women in denominational churches also need a doctrine of resistance and resistance rituals. Their experiences and struggles against oppression should be incorporated into liturgies, worship, and interpretative practices. This is evident in her appropriation of Hagar; Hagar is content, reading strategy, doctrine of resistance, and embodied practice.

Elizabeth A. Johnson: Male Symbols, God, Change

In *She Who Is*, Elizabeth A. Johnson tackles what she defines as traditional speech about God, assessing such language to be "humanly oppressive and religiously idolatrous."[70] It is oppressive in drawing concepts of God primarily from the reality of male rule, and it is idolatrous because of the way in which it presents these concepts as the best or only way to portray the Divine. Classical theism and the associated traditional forms of speech about God—including Father, Son, King, and Lord—stress transcendence, hierarchy, and analogies to an earthly monarch, while downplaying divine immanence, confining the mystery of the incomparable Divine to a fixed set of symbols, and formulating theological claims about God and humanity based on male experience alone. In sum, Johnson critiques traditional theological formulations for being exclusive, literal, and patriarchal.[71] The result of this is a "two-fold negative effect" in which classical theisms end up failing humans and failing the divine mystery.[72] In reference to humans, language and symbols are never just language and symbols. They have social and psychological effects and are internalized by those who hear and see them. In Johnson's words, "the symbol of God functions."[73] It legitimates social structures and shapes the religious identity of women through subtle and not so subtle conditioning. In reference to divine mystery—that is, God—classical theism fixes the dynamic and incomprehensible nature of this mystery in a limited repertoire of symbols surrounding the construct of God-He.[74]

Recognizing the theological and human impact of this limited set of symbols, Johnson probes other possibilities. She discusses alternate linguistic and symbolic options.[75] Johnson acknowledges other options—including God/dess and Word—but ultimately makes a pragmatic argument for retaining the term "God." Building on Martin Buber, she holds that the word "God" can be redeemed from its historical contamination with male imagery and transformed in light of women's experience. However, even this decontaminated and transformed version of "God" is not sufficient because of its nonpersonal character. In

Johnson's view, the term "God" expresses divine incomprehensibility but glosses the personal character of the Divine and the relationship between the Divine and the world.[76] Moreover, use of "God" alone does not grapple with the question of whether language and symbols of God can be drawn from women's experience; rather, it skirts the question by asserting a God beyond all such human categories.

Johnson, consequently, advocates for introducing female images and language to "shatter the exclusivity" of male personal symbols.[77] Introducing female images and language runs the risk of being taken literally (one of her critiques of classical theism) and the risk of being deployed stereotypically, that is, using only stereotypical ideas about women as caring and nurturing. Despite these risks, she emphasizes the crucial role personal images and language play in mediating experience of the Divine and of the world; they are not dispensable or secondary. The task is to expand—even balance—the repertoire through female symbols and imagery. Johnson further justifies this by asserting that the image of God (*imago Dei*) is found in women, that symbols of the Divine are diverse, changing, and flexible, and that "fundamental aspects of the doctrine of God" have been overlooked.[78]

How might female symbols and imagery be effectively introduced? Johnson explores three possible approaches.[79] The first is attribution of feminine traits, such as nurturing and mothering, to God. She argues that the dominant God-He symbol is enhanced by the addition of such traits. However, this approach does not decenter male imagery or masculine qualities assigned to God. Feminine traits are simply added to dominant male symbols. Feminine traits remain subordinate to the core male symbol, and they also reinscribe stereotypical and binary depictions of male and female. As such, this approach does not move speech about God in a "more inclusive and liberating direction."[80]

The second approach is the attribution of feminine dimensions to a Trinitarian God, commonly in the portrayal of the Holy Spirit as feminine. This is a more substantial incorporation of female symbols, and it draws on scriptural—for example, Genesis 1:2 and Luke 1:35 and 3:22—and early Christian depictions of the Spirit as female and motherly. Johnson expresses concern about this approach because the Holy Spirit is often imagined as amorphous, unclear, and subordinate to the Father and the Son, the male persons of God. These characteristics are oversimplified and stereotypically associated with females and the feminine. At the same time, they are descriptions of female and feminine that do not reflect, or arise out of, the lived experience of actual women. While introducing a female dimension, this approach fails in challenging patriarchal depictions of God and women. Thus, it does not provide a new way of speaking about God that empowers or develops women—in their complexity and diversity—as *imago Dei*, the image of God.

The third approach—and the one that Johnson ultimately adopts in her articulation of God as the relational, living She Who Is—is speaking about the Divine in "images taken equivalently from the experience of women, men, and the world of nature."[81] This approach retains personal language about God but is distinct from the other two alternatives in that female language is used to refer more holistically to God, rather than as a trait or dimension. Use of female images and language does not replace male images but is used simultaneously and interchangeably. Johnson claims that such usage is valuable because it affirms the notion of the female as a full expression of *imago Dei*, and because it does not uphold stereotypes about women or male redemptive action in the world. While Johnson identifies equivalent imaging as the ultimate and best option, she asserts that this option may not be immediately possible because "female religious symbols of the divine are underdeveloped, peripheral, considered secondarily if at all in Christian language."[82] Due to historical dominance and institutionalization of male imagery, it is necessary to uncover and then use more female imagery as a sort of intentional correction or intentional disruption of the existing system. Use of more female imagery will jolt awareness of the dominance of and reliance on male imagery and formulations of God-He. This is a necessary first step toward the ultimate goal of equivalent images.

Rosemary Radford Ruether: Tradition, Experience, Crisis

Rosemary Radford Ruether, in her early survey of the methodologies, sources, and norms of Christian feminist theology, offers a clear explication of the role of human experience in relation to tradition and community.[83] She challenges assumptions about the novelty of feminist invocations of experience, as well as about the singularity and unchanging nature of religious tradition. Ruether argues that the invocation of experience is not at all unique to feminist theology. This perception is a "misunderstanding of the experimental base of all theological reflection."[84] There is no theology or tradition that does not involve and rely on human experience. Human experience—including experience of the Divine, of self, of community, and of the world—is the "starting point and ending point of the hermeneutic circle"; theology and tradition are rooted in and renewed through experience.[85] Traditional symbols are authenticated or devalued based on their capacity to respond to and explain experience. Ruether, though, acknowledges that authority structures within traditions seek to invert the relationship between tradition and experience; they attempt to "make received symbols dictate what can be experienced as well as the interpretation of that which is experienced."[86] While this is a common strategy, Ruether states that it is bound to fail. Religious symbols and traditions that cease to respond to experience die. The uniqueness of feminist theology, therefore, is not its use of experience as an authoritative and necessary criterion but its centering of female experience. Female experience has been excluded and marginalized, while male experience has been presented as universally normative.

To further illuminate the dynamic and ongoing dialectic between experience and tradition, Ruether offers a simplified yet helpful model, which she calls the hermeneutical circle of past and present experience.[87] The first stage in this model is the revelatory experience, a breakthrough experience typically starting with an individual, a prophet, teacher, or savior. This revelatory experience is then appropriated and promulgated by a formative group or community. Ruether emphasizes that no matter how important the individual recipient of the breakthrough may be the "revelatory experience becomes socially meaningful only when translated into communal consciousness."[88] Without the formative group, the revelation will never become tradition. She also argues that the formative group "mediates" revelatory experience through existing cultural symbols and traditions. There is no cultural vacuum or tabula rasa. The uniqueness of the revelatory experience, therefore, is not holistic originality but the way it is able to "combine and transform earlier symbolic patterns to illuminate and disclose meaning in new, unexpected ways that speak to new experiential needs as the old patterns ceased to do."[89]

In the third stage, the formative community "gathers" the historical community. Ruether explains that oral and written teachings—more than one—develop within the formative community, and eventually a group of leaders invested in controlling this development emerges. These leaders develop and impose criteria to determine correct (orthodox) interpretations and, on this basis, seek to eradicate that which has been deemed incorrect, deviant, or heretical. This process of control and policing of tradition often coincides with the identification and canonization of a body of authoritative texts, that is, Scripture. Other texts and teachings are not eliminated, but they are marginalized and suppressed. Once Scripture is canonized, subsequent tradition is composed of reflection on Scripture and correction through reference to the authority of Scripture. "Orthodox" authorities "seek to clothe themselves in past codified tradition that provides secure access to divinely revealed truth."[90] Despite attempts to do this, it is never possible to holistically ignore present experience. While many scholars—even the orthodoxy—claim to just teach what has always been the tradition, there is a continuous process of revision in light of their experience. The received ideas of tradition are constantly tested by experience, and if they continue to develop they will remain responsive to that experience. Tradition remains alive as long as it "continues to speak to individuals in the community and provide for them the redemptive meaning of individual and collective experience."[91]

However, this does not always happen. Traditions and traditional teachings do not always respond to, or respond effectively and sufficiently to, the present experiences of individuals and communities. When this happens, a crisis of tradition ensues.[92] Ruether identifies various levels of crises, ranging from the view that some interpretations of the tradition are corrupt to the view that institutions—but not original sources—are corrupt to the view that the entire religious heritage is corrupt. The first view leads to new interpretations and articulations of theology. The second results in the "myth of return to origins" which seeks—according to Ruether, impossibly—to go back and behind all institutional development to the original founder and revelatory experience. The latter results in the search for an alternate system of authority that can be used to critique the corrupt tradition while simultaneously avoiding a merely subjective experiential assessment.

Traci C. West: Ritual, Norms, White Superiority

In outlining practical applications of her "disruptive Christian ethics," Traci C. West explores liturgy and ritual. She stresses the importance of ritual, yet also critiques the manner in which it can absorb and sustain white privilege and superiority within both majority white and majority people of color congregations. West describes Sunday worship as a forum for people to "publicly rehearse what it means to uphold the moral values they are supposed to bring to every aspect of their lives."[93] Sunday worship is a ritual reminder, rooted in Christian tradition, that can either challenge or reinforce norms—such as white privilege and superiority—of the broader society. Due to this function in relation to norms, West contends that public Christian ritual is a central arena for enacting liberative ethics. Liberative ethics need to be rooted in the "concrete practices of Christian faith communities."[94] In much the same way that people make choices about which societal norms are promoted, similar choices about norms can and should be made within the communal rituals of the church.

To concretize her discussion of manifestations of explicit and implicit white privilege within Christian communities, West describes several personal experiences visiting predominantly white congregations outside of her home church. Her visitation to these churches arose out of her own "spiritual cravings and theological ideals"; she expresses her longing to participate in church life.[95] However, her cravings and ideals at times clashed with the "racial realities" she encountered within church settings. She describes interactions with congregants in which she was asked where she lived, was told she must be a visitor, and was praised for having singing ability, of which she, self-descriptively, has none. These experiences and the repetition of such experiences made her aware of being a "racial outsider," and her entire experience within those settings was thus "saturated by race."[96]

Acknowledging that there are always diverse and multiple factors beyond race, including sex, gender, and class, in play within church settings, West focuses on white privilege and superiority. She stresses that white superiority and racist socialization are ingrained through daily routines and habits, and that they are effectively perpetuated by denial that racism or superiority exists. Both within society and within the church, denial shuts the door on analysis of the potential manifestations of racism in the content or form of actions and ritual.[97] White privilege arises out of white superiority and manifests in the distribution of power and resources, in the choice to not think about race, and in the presentation of white people as the "normal" or unraced human. White privilege surfaces in worship in a variety of ways, including presentations of "us and them," mission language, depictions of the specialness of Christians, intercessory prayers, prayers of thanksgiving for the blessings *we* have received, and prayers for the "less fortunate." These practices are not neutral; they teach and socialize. Specifically, West states that they teach "a sense of privilege that easily merges with racial messages about privilege in the broader culture."[98] She does not dismiss the practices of giving thanks or helping others, but she problematizes notions of entitlement and assistance that do not require reflection on or relinquishing of one's own racial or class privilege.

Notably, West insists on the necessity of rituals: "[w]e need rituals. They celebrate, promote, and create patterns of behavior. Rituals provide a sense of stability and of possibility."[99] However, she seeks to unpack the function of rituals. Drawing on the work of Tom Driver, she distinguishes between ritualizing and ritual. The former consists of making new ritual forms in response to needs, events, and concerns within a community. The latter relates to known practices that are symbolic, repeated, and function to "preserve and even sacralize established patterns of behavior and attitudes."[100] Without ritualization, ritual becomes completely static and unresponsive. Without ritual, ritualization loses its connection to the broader tradition. In West's view, white privilege as a societal practice has pronounced ritualizing ability; it adapts to numerous situations and forms, both explicit and implicit. Within Christian church contexts, the ritualizing function of white privilege can attach to the rituals of worship. She offers the example of communion and atonement theology in which our sins are taken away by the sacrifice of the body of another. Christians, though, can be resistant to probing the presence of white privilege within ritual forms. One reason for this is the view that worship ritual is an expression of the universality of Christianity.[101]

Common practices unite the broader Christian community across national and theological boundaries. Claims to universality also encourage people to pretend as though race and culture do not matter within the ritual space: "[p]articipation in worship practices falsely labeled culturally neutral constitutes a specific practice of denial that can foster white disassociation from the reality of racist inequality, how people are implicated in it, and what its costs are."[102] The appropriate response to this reality is not abandonment of ritual but articulation of rituals that intentionally destabilize and challenge the norms of white superiority and privilege.

Such rituals are not only required within majority white congregations. West maintains that they are also necessary within congregations made up primarily of persons of color. Persons of color are socialized into white superiority; they are "always contesting, negotiating, and creating the meaning of their racial identities, especially in reaction to the boundaries and stigmas marking them as inferior."[103] Socialization into white superiority and the resultant "distortions of personhood" can be internalized and thus manifest in the worship context even without the presence of white people.[104] West identifies various manifestations including racial self-silencing to ensure invisibility, misrepresentation to fit stereotypes or gain power within racial hierarchies, acquiescence to white privilege, and replication of hierarchies within the community. She also problematizes the strategy of exceptionality, in which a person consciously tries to avoid racial stereotypes. Recognizing the importance of honoring achievements within communities of color, she highlights the socioeconomic exclusivity of some such efforts: "poor black single mothers who have achieved amazing feats of struggle and survival on public assistance will most likely not be among those celebrated for accomplishments or for gifts of courage and tenacity."[105]

West also draws attention to the discriminatory treatment of women in black churches. Women are sometimes denied access to leadership roles on the basis that they are only for men, and even "physically barred" from parts of the ritual space—such as the pulpit—for fear of contamination or desecration.[106] West describes this treatment of women as a reproduction of the inequality that black people experience in the broader society. Discrimination against women in black churches is often not acknowledged or discussed because of a "concern that such open criticism of black religious tradition undermines its historical role of maintaining unity and cohesion in the black community that enables resistance to white domination."[107] There is a very real fear that white people will co-opt any such criticisms as proof of black inferiority or at least as a distraction from reflecting on inequality in the broader society. Despite this threat, West argues that form and content in ritual practice are inseparable, meaning the content cannot be disconnected from rules about who, how, and where that content is delivered. Moreover, the form itself can carry *implicit* content that contradicts the *explicit* content: "There is a powerful moral message in preaching and teaching about God's inclusive love within exclusive traditions that rule out certain groups of people as innately ineligible to do that preaching and teaching. This worship conveys moral hypocrisy, and cultivates a spiritually comforting routine for denying that hypocrisy."[108]

In response to the challenges of white superiority and other forms of inequality within worship, West reiterates that choices about liturgy are in fact already and always being made. Choices, for instance, are made about music, prayers, hymns, space, and decor. These choices can serve to either nurture or challenge white dominance. Turning to multicultural theory, West outlines concrete strategies for making choices that challenge dominance. These include basic knowledge of diversity to contest binary and simple depictions, a shift away from presenting American and European people as the primary agents of history, and the exploration of diversity as a spiritual resource that expands our understanding of and relationship with God.[109] There are endless possibilities for ritualizing nondominant expressions within liturgy, but West emphasizes the necessity of intentional and deep reflection on race and power. The rituals will not matter if this does not transpire. Worship rituals need to engage the privileges that society grants and the disproportionate way in which those privileges are granted.[110]

Embodied Equality and Transformative Community: Muslima Theological Reflections

Christian perspectives on community, change, tradition, and ritual overlap with existing Islamic feminist discourse in several striking ways. Christian and Muslim scholars, to begin, both seek to better explain the political and dynamic nature of tradition; rather than a fixed, ahistorical entity, they foreground processes of development and change, the role of experience, and internal diversity of perspectives and practices. Ruether, however, makes a unique observation about crisis of tradition. The notion of crisis is not explicitly invoked in discussions of woman-led prayer, although it is present in other Islamic discourse, something I revisit later in this chapter. Another area of consonance among Christian feminists and Islamic feminists is the insistence on the role and importance of ritual and symbols. Ritual and symbols are expressions of the community, and they work to shape the community. The exclusion of women and female symbols, therefore, not only reveals historical androcentrism but also perpetuates future androcentrism.

While Christian and Muslim scholars agree on the centrality and active nature of rituals, the rituals and liturgies differ. I do not explore details of ritual and liturgy, but Johnson surfaces one crucial divergence connected to theological perspectives on divine ontology. She bases her critique on two facts: the predominant usage of male language and symbols to represent God and the centrality of the assertion of a personal God in Christian thought. Neither of these facts is emphasized in Islamic feminist discourse. There is some discussion of using the pronouns He, She, and It in English to destabilize the overdependence on He alone.[111] Yet, male language, especially personal titles such as Father and Son, are not used and thus do not present the same concern. Moreover, as discussed in the preceding chapter, Islamic feminists generally do not assert a personal God. The theological challenges surrounding male language and symbols thus differ. One final point of divergence within the perspectives I have surveyed is that both Williams and West discuss race in addition to gender. Most Muslim communities in the United States do not face the challenges of predominantly white congregations—Muslims in the United States are majority people of color—but they do face challenges associated with intracommunity racism, with structural white supremacy, and with first-things-first approaches. Race is another system of exclusion and marginalization within Muslim communities; it is often denied, but—like gender—it actively colors views on authority, leadership, and knowledge production.[112]

Women-led prayer leadership is certainly not the only issue or manifestation of equality possible within diverse Muslim communities. However, it is a concrete manifestation of tensions related to embodied equality, even in situations when theoretical or theological equality is affirmed. Woman-led prayer leadership connects directly to a larger claim asserted throughout this project: that experience and embodiment matter. Experience and embodiment matter not only as ideas and as sources of information but also as sites of transformation. In other words, female prayer leadership is not just "proof" of equality. As wadud indicates, it is not always even this. Woman-led prayer leadership is a mode of transformation, a ritual enactment designed to foster awareness, expand understanding, and sensitize us to the limits of existing manifestations of equality and the latent theological and gendered assumptions underlying dominant practice. In the remainder of this chapter, I highlight some of these limits and assumptions in relation to ritual, tradition, and community to further underscore just what is at stake in conversations about woman-led prayer and to identify some pragmatic strategies for continuing the conversations.

Ritual prayer (*salat*) is important and valuable. No critique or extension that I propose undercuts this basic assertion. It is, in fact, my commitment to and experience with the value of ritual prayer that prompts my concern about inclusion and latent theological assumptions. My concern would certainly be mitigated if the role and function of prayer were more peripheral in my thinking and being. It is not. I have experienced the beauty of congregational prayer, the individual cultivation of habitual, ritual prayer, and the unifying force of a shared (across generations and geography) practice. I have entered mosques around the world knowing what to expect. I have felt the power of standing shoulder-to-shoulder in community with strangers who are somehow familiar. I have experienced and continue to rely on the polishing of prayer. At the same time, I have been on the receiving end of the rote exclusions and gendered assumptions of congregational prayer. These experiences range from being told that there is no prayer space for women to being directed where to stand and where to enter a mosque to murmurs of *astaghfirullahi* ("I seek forgiveness from God") when my gendered body was not in the "proper" place to enduring *khutbahs* and leadership by male individuals who were significantly—and noticeably—less qualified than the woman sitting next to me. My love of and commitment to prayer make the latter experiences even more glaring and tensive. While critiques of gendered exclusions in ritual prayer are often cast as lack of commitment, the reality is that, for myself and many others, they are directly tied to commitment and deep experience with prayer.

Commitment and experience teach that ritual prayer is not a neutral activity. The community setting is not neutral and neither is the prayer itself. Ritual prayer is intended to do something. It has agency. Throughout Islamic history, *salat* is discussed in terms of legalistic stipulations. It is, however, more significantly connected to enduring discussions of "the ethically formative powers of human behavior, the individual's ability to discipline the psyche, and the ways in which human interactions with the divine mirror and shape this-worldly relationships and hierarchies."[113] Ritual prayer, thus, does something to the person involved. It has potency. Islamic feminists emphasize the way ritual prayer expresses and shapes community identity. Ritual prayer also—drawing on West—creates a certain type of person. Ritual prayer is active, inscribing, and formative. It is not simply that a person arrives fully formed and committed and then undertakes prayer as a choice based on that formation and commitment. Prayer itself also shapes the person who engages in it. It is not just a confirmation of what is already assented. There is an active dialectic between the ritual of prayer and the person who establishes the habit of prayer. Again, this is not a debated point. It is the very rationale for habitual and standardized *salat*.

West's perspective aligns with customary Islamic perspectives on prayer. However, she offers an important caution. Social and contextual norms can be grafted onto the ritual, especially in congregational settings. More accurately, social and contextual norms are *always* grafted onto the ritual in some way in congregational settings. Choices are always made in liturgy and ritual. These choices can be explicit or implicit, verbal or nonverbal, spatial or symbolic. Choices are also made about what and whom to include and what and whom to exclude. Making choices is unavoidable; it is impossible to have congregational ritual without choices or contextualization. Choices, however, are never neutral or simply what has always been done. Congregational ritual, therefore, either *actively* nurtures or *actively* challenges contextual norms. There is no neutral, ahistorical ritual performance. While congregational *salat* is often presented as such, it is not. Choices are made about leadership, about content, about spatial arrangement, about facilities, even when the general form of prayer remains largely the same. Each and every one of these choices is an opportunity to reinscribe dominant norms—in this situation, androcentric norms—or consciously challenge those norms in pursuit of a more egalitarian community. The assertion that they are neutral is factually inaccurate. Congregational *salat* has historically been used to assert political authority, to espouse particular theological creeds, and even to inculcate women into specific domestic ideologies.[114] Intriguingly, in reference to the latter, Marion Katz observes that modern reformers urged women to attend congregational prayer with a twofold purpose: to correct "deviant" understandings of Islam cultivated outside of the mosque and to inculcate women into participation in reform movements. The point is that neither the ritual of prayer nor the choices surrounding the congregational enactment of prayer are neutral. Careful theological and ethical attention, therefore, should be paid to the choices that are made, to who benefits and does not from those choices, and to how those choices do or do not actually cultivate *taqwa*—transformative *taqwa*—in all members of the community.

Assertions of the neutrality of congregational prayer and male-only congregational prayer leadership attempt to mask theological and ethical implications. Male-only congregational prayer leadership ascribes characteristics to God and to human beings. It is worth, in my estimation, considering whether those characteristics are ones we would explicitly affirm. Islamic feminists argue that male-only congregational prayer leadership and androcentric and misogynistic assumptions violate *tawhid* and are therefore idolatrous. The language of idolatry also appears in Johnson's description of exclusive and literal Christian use of male symbols and language. I have noted that Johnson arrives at this assertion based on divine ontology and symbolic practices not prevalent in Islamic thought; God is not imagined as a person, nor are familial and male titles invoked to reference God. I am provoked by Johnson's analysis, however, to reconsider this statement. No, God is not described as a person or as personal. There are, in fact, extensive debates in Islamic theology (*kalam*) over the mere claim of anthropomorphism. And, while titles such as Lord (*rabb*) and King (*malik*) can be defined as hierarchical or even patriarchal, they are not the same as "father" and "son." Nevertheless, is it possible that there is a latent conception of God as male in Islamic thought and Muslim practice? This is not explicitly stated. But, is it operative? At a minimum, it seems that God is widely conceived of as being on the side of men, as privileging men in terms of leadership and authority. Is this the God we assert? It is tempting to simply discount this question by invoking gender complementarity and arguing that men have privilege in some areas while women are privileged in others. But even with complementarity, is this the kind of God we assert? A God that would automatically disqualify a woman who has vast pastoral and leadership gifts to offer to the community? Automatically exclude her because of genitalia and biology? The best assessment of latent views of God is found in the way those views shape actions and representation.

It is also worth recalling that even notions of gender complementarity have not been static or sustained throughout the tradition. Scholars, including al-Nawawi, did not ground their positions on female exclusion from prayer leadership in arguments of gender complementarity (including the idea of female domesticity).[115] They based it on notions of inherent female inferiority, inherent male superiority, and concerns about female-precipitated *fitna*. The unexamined perpetuation of female ritual exclusion under a new explanatory veneer can have unintended theological consequences. The claim that female exclusion is divinely intended cannot help but say something about the type of God in play. The perpetuation also raises an important question of who really benefits from the disassociated invocation of legal exclusions. In other words, why would the legal rulings of past scholars be invoked today under a new explanation, instead of the original explanations? If legal rulings that exclude women from leading congregational prayer are the only option and only divinely authorized option, then why avoid the original human explanations of those options? My suspicion is that straightforward misogyny and androcentrism are much less palatable and acceptable today in the US context. Moreover, original explanations for legal exclusion unambiguously reveal the role that gendered and sexed assumptions play in the supposedly "neutral" prayer and prayer leadership. Invocations of gender complementarity—distinct but equal, or as better known in the US context, separate but equal—provide a buffer to this revelation.

The notion of *fitna*, though, has not completely disappeared from contemporary arguments against woman-led prayer. Today *fitna*, as dissension caused by sexual temptation or distraction, is offered as an explanation for why women are not permitted to pray (stand?) in front of men and by extension not permitted to lead mixed-gender prayers. This explanation is—unlike gender complementarity—consistent with the explanations offered by past legal scholars.[116] Based on her survey of legal positions, Katz states that beginning in the eleventh century, *fitna* was "established as the central rationale for limitations on women's mosque attendance."[117] *Fitna* replaced earlier rationales based on seniority as the central criteria in defining the possibility and extent of women's access to mosques. *Fitna*, therefore, was primarily about access to the mosque (mosque attendance), not about female space *within* the mosque or female prayer leadership. Katz observes that *fitna* resulted in two distinct scholarly approaches: one that forbade female mosque attendance altogether, and one that stipulated female behavioral norms designed to avoid *fitna* if women did attend the mosque.[118] The acceptance of *fitna* today as a legitimate explanation of gendered spatial arrangements and leadership exclusions is somewhat problematic. While aligned with past legal explanations, it nevertheless covers over the origin of this explanation, that is, the exclusion of women from mosques altogether. Is it possible to accept female-produced *fitna*—even in a watered-down version—as the explanation for gender segregation and male leadership within a mosque and simultaneously avoid reinscribing the associated debates over whether women should be in the mosque at all? I, of course, do not support women's exclusion from the mosque. I do however wonder whether some inclusion efforts inadvertently normalize *fitna*-based assumptions about women, men, and God.

Fitna-based arguments not only have roots in assumed female exclusion from the mosque but also evince conflation between descriptive and prescriptive views. *Fitna* is based on the idea that men are attracted to and distracted by women. Women are attractive, even deceptively tempting. And, as a result, women should not be in front of or even visible to men in a space in which men are supposedly attempting to focus on spiritual concerns and development. Occasionally, the importance of not compromising women's modesty by having them in front of men is also mentioned. My question is: is this a descriptive or prescriptive position? Is this a description of reality on the ground, a description of the natural feelings, interactions, and possibilities among men and women? Or is this a prescriptive statement about what should be, about the desired ideal, about normative expectations? *Fitna* appears to be a description (men's attraction to women/women's attractiveness to men) that is used to legitimate and enforce a prescriptive ideal (male-female gender segregation and male leadership). Many people who appeal to *fitna* present it as the natural (not necessarily meritorious) behavior of humans. This is just what men are like; they are easily distracted by women in a place of worship. Even if they do not assign women the full responsibility for causing *fitna*—they may equally stress man's susceptibility to sexual distraction—it is presented as a description of something that actually happens. This normalization and naturalization of *fitna* legitimates the supposedly pragmatic and necessary response of male-female gender segregation and male-only leadership.

There are some issues with this presentation of *fitna*. To begin, *fitna* is not a realistic presentation or description. It overlooks several realities, such as the fact that women are also attracted to men (who almost always stand in front of them), that men are attracted to men and women are attracted to women (who stand next to them), and that not all people identify within the male-female binary. I am aware that some would like to downplay or even deny these realities. However, they are realities. If spatial segregation and leadership in the mosque are just pragmatic responses to descriptive realities of sexual attraction and gender identity, then the current arrangement overlooks some significant facets of this. Not only is it androcentric through and through, it is also heteronormative and binary. A pragmatic spatial and leadership response to the *real* situation would need to be much more complex and nuanced than dominant forms. I am not advocating for this. I do not agree that sexual attraction and gender identity should be the basis of determining ritual format and leadership. I am highlighting it to stress the ambiguity (perhaps superficiality) surrounding *fitna* as an explanation for gender segregation and women's exclusion from prayer leadership.

If *fitna* is not an accurate description of the reality of sexual attraction and gender identity, then is *fitna* a prescriptive position? It does attempt to delineate "proper" and "improper" attraction and interaction. Its disconnect from reality also hints at this possibility. However, how can *fitna* possibly be a prescriptive ideal? It is not ideal behavior or interaction. *Fitna* is an inaccurate, androcentric pseudo-description of less than meritorious human behavior. How can this be the criterion used to define the most potent, unifying, identity expressing, people shaping ritual in Islam? While I am fully on board with pragmatic attentiveness to experience and on the ground realities, should these formative rituals and roles of leadership not be defined by more accurate, more *taqwa*-concerned criteria? Should prayer leadership not embody and inspire toward the ideal? Or perhaps, this is the issue. Perhaps male-exclusive prayer leadership does embody some people's ideal, an androcentric ideal. If this is the case, we must confront the explicit role of androcentrism and misogyny in shaping congregational prayer leadership, rather than explicitly or implicitly consenting to the explanatory crutch of *fitna*.

One way to circumvent critiques of *fitna* and its pseudo-descriptive nature is to invoke "tradition" to legitimate male-only prayer leadership. Male-only leadership is "what has always been done;" it is *the* consensus of *the* tradition. Tradition, thus deployed, is a strategy to delegitimize other possibilities and even to squelch discussion of other possibilities. As noted, Islamic feminists challenge both the depiction of legal consensus and the overarching understanding of tradition as singular, unchanged, and unchangeable. They argue that tradition is articulated and developed by people, responds to diverse contexts, and comprises varying opinions and debates that are muted under the rubric of a singular, static tradition. In their critique and redefinition of tradition, Islamic feminists align with Ruether. She similarly challenges the construct of a static tradition. In her hermeneutic circle of past and present experience, she also emphasizes the role of human experience, its relationship to orthodoxy, and the crises that ensue when human experience is ignored. Islamic feminists certainly understand the role of experience. When they stress that primarily male scholars in patriarchal contexts articulated legal opinions, they are stating that those scholars' experiences and frames of reference are particular and diverge from other experiential frames.

What Ruether offers is an argument about the detrimental impact—even impossibility—of ignoring human experience. It is not just that experience is always in play. Nor is it just that some (male) experience has been privileged. It is that experience must always be in play for the tradition to continue to thrive. Yes, orthodoxy will attempt to invert the relationship between tradition and experience, aiming to condition and dictate experience based on the parameters of earlier tradition. This is such an illuminating description of the debates on woman-led prayer. Not only is the legitimacy of woman-led prayer flatly denied but so also is the legitimacy of the experiences that prompt the discussion of woman-led prayer. The experiences of wanting ritual and social equality, of being excluded, and of lacking physical and topical representation are ignored, belittled, or weaponized as supposed indicators of lack of faith or "external" influence. Therefore, when Hammer highlights the discursive disconnect between legal and symbolic arguments about woman-led prayer, it is not only a discursive issue. It is intentional avoidance of considering the role of experience. Since experience has no role in the mythological, ahistorical, politically defined "tradition," there is no reason to address the very real psychological, sociological, and spiritual impact of exclusion and lack of representation.

And let us be clear. The impact is not positive. Exclusion and lack of representation result in two outcomes. The first is that the broader community is denied the benefit and enhancement that comes from having more diversity in authoritative and ritual leadership and in knowledge production and dissemination. The experiences and perspectives voiced by women can enhance the community. They can add something to what is already present. To be precise, they can add something to the spiritual development of women and all members of the community. The second outcome of exclusion and lack of representation is harm. Women—not all but many—experience psychological and spiritual harm. Harm can run the gamut from neglect to explicit dehumanization. The experience of harm is directly connected to phenomena such as unmosqueing, the development of third spaces, and demands for inclusive measures within existing communities and mosques. The recent founding of the Women's Mosque of America, for example, points to both harm and a new priority granted to women's experience. Interviews with the founders, Sana Muttalib and M. Hasna, cite disillusionment with nonegalitarian practices and facilities as one of the motivations for its establishment.[119] Moreover, they emphasize experience, stating that the Women's Mosque of America is designed to "provide an atmosphere in which Muslim women are surrounded by their peers and feel comfortable exploring more active leadership roles in a safe space."[120] All of these phenomena—which are valid and legitimate options—are symptoms of the crises of tradition that arise when the experience is denied and crammed into exclusionary models.

But what if we dared to ask questions from the perspective of experience? What if, on the question of woman-led prayer, we not only asked about legal precedent or consensus of past male scholars, not only claimed a singular "as it has always been," but also asked about the impact on women themselves? What if we asked how women's humanity and spirituality are affected by limitations and exclusions in this area? What if we asked what it meant for women to never see themselves represented in such practices and functions? More radically, what if the answers to these questions were taken to be vital concerns in interpretation, vital means of continuing to enact prophetic practice?

The great irony is that Muslims in the United States clearly understand the importance of representation, but we appear to overlook this knowledge when it comes to questions of gender and sex in relation to tradition. The American Muslim community—a community that experiences so much religious-based prejudice and so little representation—continues to internally perpetuate similar bias and lack of representation. Gender and sex are somehow immune from the standard critique of lack of representation. We bemoan notions of bias, systemic privilege, and lack of representation in relation to religious identity. We critique the fact that Muslims are rarely given the ability to speak for themselves or about themselves. We cheer when we even see Muslims in public spaces, roles, and positions of authority, whether as athletes, scientists, artists, or politicians. Representation matters. It is a hint of change, and it is the opening for more change. We know that representation matters in shaping the general views of Muslims in this country and also matters to the spiritual and emotional well-being of individual Muslims themselves. Invisibilization—through exclusion and lack of accurate representation—is a painful lesson, and it is lesson that is taught and learned through habitual, normalized acts. It is therefore a lesson only interrupted by attentiveness to actual experience and inclusion. Woman-led prayer is one mode of strategic and ethical interruption.

Like Ruether, Zareena Grewal also centers debates over tradition and crisis in her study of authority and knowledge acquisition within the American Muslim community.[121] Writing about student travelers who seek Islamic knowledge in other countries, she observes that the dominant tendency among these students is to define tradition in "simple, static terms," as an "object that can be found, excavated, and brought home."[122] Tradition, thus defined, "requires an unthinking conformity to the past."[123] Grewal argues that intra-Islamic debates, under this definition, can only be explained as exceptional, problematic, or as ruptures in the singular tradition. Student travelers, moreover, are motivated by a crisis of authority. This crisis arises from the perception that traditional knowledge is inaccessible in the contemporary US context or inadequate for responding to contemporary challenges. Traveling abroad to acquire authoritative, traditional knowledge is seen as a resolution to this crisis.

Grewal herself diverges from the dominant understanding of tradition among student travelers and defines tradition as a discursive phenomenon in which debates indicate the "health" of the tradition. Tradition is dynamic over time and space. It is also in perpetual relationship with both the past and the present. Grewal, though, nuances the relationship of tradition to the past: "Tradition is built on the past, and yet its relationship to the past is not natural but discursive, constituted by discontinuities as much as continuities."[124] Tradition is not simple continuation or direct transmission. Transmission of past tradition into present context is the job of the "custodians of tradition" who engage in a process of evaluation, selection, and synthesis. Grewal explains that the authority assigned to these custodians extends to their interpretations irrespective of whether those interpretations are actually the same as the original tradition. The synthesized interpretations will be presented as such, but they are not simple restatement. In this process, the main debate is over the criteria custodians use to synthesize tradition, that is, the way they mediate tradition and decide "which elements should be emphasized, highlighted, even added in order to ensure tradition's survival in the future."[125] Survival of the tradition requires it be relevant and meaningful for American Muslims. The conundrum, however, is that the very conception of tradition and crisis embraced by student travelers limits their ability to authoritatively participate in this more complex and necessary form of mediation.[126] The static reduction of tradition to a "fossilized body" relegates student travelers to the role of "mere carriers of tradition, maintaining tradition at best."[127] They are not taught the skills nor invested with the authority to synthesize and mediate tradition. They are preservers. The result, according to Grewal, is that debate within American Muslim communities is stifled and denied under the claim of scholarly consensus; issues that are relevant to and pressing in the American community are left without sufficient response or consideration. In line with Ruether, Grewal claims that the crisis remains until a new and responsive narrative arises. Crisis actually propels the creation of a new narrative.[128]

Grewal's ethnographic research underscores the limitations of dominant notions of tradition and the role of experience and experiential responsiveness. Her research also vividly illustrates the interconnections between the crisis of tradition based on nonresponsiveness to experience and the crisis of authority based on a static conception of tradition. These two crises feed off each other. The static conception of tradition mutes conversations about context and experience, while simultaneously defining authority and knowledge in an impotent manner. This, in turn, exacerbates the crisis of tradition, the failure of tradition to respond to and speak to contemporary experience. Attempts to draw attention to this failure are then squelched through invocations of fixed consensus and usurpation of interpretative agency. Islamic feminists—including proponents of women-led prayer—provoke this very reaction because they attempt to *interrupt* the cycle of crises. They claim leadership and refuse to be passive carriers of tradition alone. They claim the right to be mediators and synthesizers of tradition. This is part of the reason why woman-led prayer and egalitarian efforts are perceived as a threat. They are actually threats, not to a dynamic, responsive Islamic tradition but to the false notion of a static, fossilized tradition promoted by orthodoxy. Islamic feminists' refusal to be carriers and preservers alone is also the reason why our work holds so much potential and possibility. Our work is grounded in a blatant refusal to let the tradition die from unresponsiveness and reification. We refuse to be victimized by unresponsiveness and reification, and we refuse to participate in the further inscription of unresponsiveness and reification.

The notion of an uncontested, unchanging, singular tradition is not solely a conceptual or historical idea. It is also projected onto present-day Muslim communities. In the context of woman-led prayer, this manifests most readily in the dismissal of woman-led prayer because it supposedly incites *fitna*, here defined as communal dissension. Anything that challenges or disturbs communal unity is problematic. The concern for unity sounds beautiful and valuable, yet it is essential to probe the burdens and assumptions of that unity. Who bears the burden in such calls for unity? And what kind of unity is being invoked? It is women and allies who advocate for woman-led prayer and greater inclusion that bear the burden. The call for unity generally is not a call to hear and address concerns about female exclusion or to work toward an organic unity; it is often a reassertion of dominant, androcentric norms under the guise of unity. As a projection of the singular "tradition," the community must also be one. Reassertions of and prioritization of communal unity are calls to stop problematizing androcentrism in prayer leadership and in the mosque, to relinquish these concerns in light of a higher value. Those with power and privilege within communities make this call and define the higher value. But their call is also reinforced and internalized by women. Women can be very effective in policing each other and themselves back into expectations of the dominant norm and intra-Islamic stereotypes of a "good" Muslim woman. However, there is no essential value in unity itself. If unity becomes the helpmate of suppression, denial, and inequality, then it is devoid of value *and* replete with injustice.

West's analysis of white superiority is especially germane in this context. White superiority is ingrained through repeated patterns of ritual and social interaction. These patterns norm-alize white superiority; they make it seem natural and hence invisible. This results in the denial of racism within communities and especially within "universal" and unifying ritual forms. Denial, in turn, leads to a lack of analysis and grappling with racism. West herself extends this analysis to treatment of women in some black churches. Her analysis is therefore pertinent to male dominance and androcentrism in Muslim communities. Assertions of imposed unity, a static tradition, and unchanged/unchangeable ritual all function to naturalize androcentrism. Through the tangle of conceptual assertions and ritual reinforcements, androcentrism appears to be self-evident, appears to be just the way things are, have always been, and will always be. I must though reiterate that West's analysis also remains directly applicable to racism and ethnocentrism within Muslim communities. Racism and ethnocentrism are also often denied and naturalized. Moreover, in line with wadud's critique of the way romantic rhetoric about motherhood obscures systemic issues, racism is similarly masked by appeals to romantic views of Islam doing away with all racial distinctions. This ideal is not the real.

West links white superiority in ritual with other claims to superiority, in particular the presentation of the Christian community as special or unique. As many of the theologians I engage in this book argue, one form of superiority tends not to be too far away from another. In Muslim communities, claims to religious superiority are also implicated in the concept of a singular tradition and a unified, uniform community (*umma*). The assertion of the inherent supremacy of the Muslim *umma* over other religious communities works to normalize androcentrism and impose unity. If the *umma* is inherently superior—even the best community (*khayr umma*, Q 3:110)—then what is there is to address? What change or development could be needed? God's favored community cannot possibly be wrong or improved.

The issue here is threefold. First, claims to inherent religious superiority in and of themselves are tenuous based on the Qur'an and other foundational sources.[129] Such claims often appear authoritative and as common sense, but, as Hammer argues, this has a lot to do with their congruence with ingrained expectations of religious distinctions and distinctiveness. Second, the presentation of the Muslim *umma* as inherently superior to and distinct from other religious communities lays the groundwork for all challenges to dominant norms to be dismissed as external impositions on the Muslim *umma*. This move is readily apparent in the common description of Islamic feminist ideas as motivated by external concerns and commitments, not deep commitment to the living Islamic tradition. And finally, assertions of the inherent supremacy of the Muslim *umma* collapse the space between the ideal *umma* and existing, real Muslim communities and individuals.

Asma Afsaruddin highlights the exegetical genesis and clarifies the importance of this collapse in her analysis of Qur'anic descriptions of Muslims as a middle/moderate community (*umma wasat*) and the People of the Book as a balanced/moderate community (*umma muqtasida*).[130] Some early exegetes understood the similar communal designations to simply refer to moderation manifest in practices of justice. Such praiseworthy moderation could potentially be present among members of various religious traditions and was not automatically present among Muslims. However, by the late ninth century, *umma wasat* was interpreted as indicating "first and foremost the favored status of Muslims over other religious communities."[131] This claim depended on a variety of innovative exegetical strategies and tools, including abrogation (*naskh*) and supersession, since it had to explain how *umma wasat* could denote distinctive, communal superiority while a similar designation was applied to other religious communities. Ultimately, the result was widespread presentation of the Muslim community as the most excellent community, the drawing of "sharp confessional boundaries" between religious communities, and the disassociation of the concept of *umma* from concrete action.[132] Excellence was imagined as an static feature of the Muslim community. It was no longer solely related to performance of meritorious actions.

I have written extensively about the conflation of the ideal excellent community (*khayr umma*) with actual historical and contemporary Muslim communities.[133] It is not my intention to rehash the intricacies of those arguments here. However, what I will add is this conflation—that is, the collapse of the space between ideal and real *umma*—impedes manifestations of the prophetic example and transformative *taqwa*. The notions of a static tradition, unity above all else, and religious superiority coalesce to effectively—yet detrimentally—foreclose attempts to respond to experience, context, *and* tradition. The ideal *umma*—the *khayr umma*—is the aspirational ideal, but it is not the real nor it is found in the past. We have not achieved *khayr umma*, and therefore we cannot ever be complacent. We cannot uncritically embrace particular formulations of exegesis, law, and practice as if they were absolute and guaranteed expressions of the ideal community. These formulations are attempts to manifest that ideal. They are works in progress and in context.

Therefore, drawing on Williams' distinction between the Black Church and African American denominational churches, I contend that we must reassert a similar distinction within Muslim communities. While this distinction seems conceptual, it is of great pragmatic necessity. The distinction between ideal and real *umma* opens up a space in which difficult, yet critically loving and necessary conversations can occur. In short it opens up a space of transformation. In place of an emphasis on *conforming*, this space shifts the emphasis to *transforming*, transforming individuals, transforming the community, and transforming society. And this transformation is not the imposition of a static set of "forever" norms but the quest to increasingly and consistently manifest transformative *taqwa*. These transforming communities are communities that strive to embody—in all bodies—the prophetic example and are willing to engage in the demanding and tricky task of negotiating traditional and contemporary needs and diverse forms of inclusion. In the transformative *umma*, unity can still be a goal, but it will have to be a goal that is worked toward and that acknowledges privilege and embraces diversity. There are Muslim communities in the United States that represent aspects of this transformative idea. These are communities in which social justice programs flourish, challenging conversations about race occur, and inclusion is prioritized. Yet, it remains true that even in many mosques that actively foreground conscientization on a host of social issues, gender and sex—especially in relation to ritual practice—are consistently less discussed and examined. As I have already indicated, this distinctive treatment is a remnant of androcentrism and male privilege. Like other forms of superiority and privilege, it needs to be troubled.

Transformative communities moreover are not defined in opposition to or in fear of other communities. This requires reassessment of claims to superiority, including the comparative jabs present in some Islamic feminist theology. It also requires suspicion of hard and fast boundaries between religious traditions, especially because of the role these boundaries play in propping up claims to superiority and discrediting perspectives because they are supposedly "un-Islamic." At the same time, less emphasis should be placed on the external reception of intra-Muslim conversations. There is significant pressure and concern surrounding the way Muslim critiques of Islam and Muslim practices are used and manipulated by others. This is a real concern. It certainly happens, and there are certainly even Muslims who capitalize on this. My assertion, however, is that even though it will continue to happen—critiques will continue to be used as fodder for Islamophobic rants and policies—we must do the work anyhow. The critiques and conversations are a necessary part of transformative *taqwa*. Neither internal nor external hegemony should be permitted to impede this work.

If the space between ideal and real *umma* is acknowledged and reclaimed, then the idea of change itself is also transformed. The stinging and authoritarian rhetoric of *bid'a* (negative innovation) carries so much weight because of dominant conceptions of tradition and *umma*. Again, if they are singular and perfect, then change can be nothing but drifting further away from perfection. In the transformative space between real and ideal *umma*, change is more a form of ritualizing than holistic ritual substitution or rejection. It is responsiveness to context and experience, and a desire to continue the tradition of dynamism. In this view, woman-led prayer is not a negative innovation or abandonment of ritual. It is a concrete display of ritualizing that not only refuses to relinquish the ritual form but also insists on a balance of continuity and responsiveness precisely so that the ritual of *salat* continues to be central and powerful.

Reclamation of the transformative space also impacts strategies of change. There are diverse strategies related to female inclusion and woman-led prayer, ranging from Silver's call for woman-led prayer as civil disobedience to female programmatic participation to incremental inclusion efforts designed to ensure space and decision-making in mosques. While the relative merit and effectiveness of strategies is often debated, they are all part of the transformative process. They are not inconsistent with each other, nor do they arise out of totally distinct concerns. Some try to distinguish incremental inclusion efforts from the more "radical" civil (theological?) disobedience of woman-led prayer—or vice versa—but the strategies are all connected. They are all concerned with androcentrism, gendered assumptions, and resultant impacts on women and communities. Therefore, strategically, I do not think there is a singular path or order of steps toward inclusion. What I will say, though, is that incremental inclusion efforts must be excessively vigilant because they are highly susceptible to co-optation within the dominant androcentric norm. This is what Johnson warns against in her discussion of symbolic inclusion and change. Not all strategies destabilize the norm; some can be added on without doing so. Co-optation is visible in the way that major Muslim institutions in the United States responded to the 2005 prayer by beginning to have more "tame" inclusion conversations. Those conversations, though, did not reference woman-led prayer, and thus sought to reinscribe a hard and fast boundary between women-led prayer and other strategies of inclusive change. Moreover, inclusion measures were concessions granted by dominant institutions and centers of authority. I am not critiquing or minimizing incremental inclusion efforts but drawing attention to the effectiveness of dominant systems in retaining their privilege. I refuse to accept the androcentric division between various inclusion strategies. Both incremental and intentionally corrective strategies—that is, strategies that jolt the system by embodying the goal—are necessary for transformation toward deep egalitarianism.

Accusations of *bid'a* are often an intentional tool of privilege and orthodoxy, but there also exists a very real and beautiful concern about doing what is good and correct, both socially and ritually. This beautiful concern can be co-opted and manipulated under a static, singular, androcentric tradition. If we can reassert the transformative space between ideal and real *umma*, however, this beautiful concern can take root in new soil. It can propel visibilization, conscientization, and prioritization of the marginalized. Perhaps this is optimistic, but I experience this thriving concern within Muslim communities. I also experience it being trampled and confined by assertions of the impossibility of change, the irrelevance of certain concerns (including egalitarianism), and the absolute distinction between Islam and all else. Muslim communities can reclaim this transformative space. Moreover, they have to in order for the tradition to continue, for individual spiritual development, and for healthy and just communities.

8

Epilogue

LIVING WORDS, DIVERSE VOICES

THE FINAL CHAPTER, in many ways, weaves together the central themes of this book. Dominant systems of privilege are invested in upholding boundaries, whether based on gender, race, or religious identity. Experience is authoritative. Embodiment matters. Ritual is a manifestation *and* site of change. Communities must reclaim agency and embrace the challenge of responsiveness. Denial is a form of invisibilization and injustice. Conscientization is essential. The prophetic example and transformative *taqwa* call us to do more than imitate. Interreligious spaces and engagements are opportunities that enrich both in their similarities and distinctions.

My goal in this book has been to listen, to learn, and think with Muslim and Christian theologians and scholars, to hear stories I have not heard, to consider the questions unasked, and to imagine some small pieces of the yet to be imagined. In the process, I have become increasingly convinced of a few things. Muslim women scholars and Islamic feminists have made and continue to make deep contributions to the Muslim community. Islamic and Christian theologians have so very much to learn from each other. Comparative feminist theology is not an interesting add-on. It is a direct challenge to androcentric and patriarchal boundary inscription, a refusal to play by those rules. And it is also a commitment-impelled response to the call to continuously engage the Divine Word.

We are called to do so in relation to our experience, tradition, context, and our multiple, overlapping identities. We are called to care enough and love enough to inhabit this space without releasing productive tensions. The Divine Word comes to transform, not to confirm the status quo or force bodies and context to conform to a mythological ideal. It comes to problematize, engage, and catalyze action. The Word of God is provocative and transformative. We are to be provoked and transformed. It is in continuing to grapple with and be open to this transformation that we continue the pursuit of justice. It is in asking the hard questions and in having the hard discussions. It is in sitting with the creative anxiety that arises once we truly entertain the notion that change is and must be possible. These are challenging demands. They are not comfortable. But they are rich and productive. They are inspiring and inspired. They are the Word alive in the world; the Word still speaking to our contexts, our concerns, our sorrows, our struggles, and our aspirations.

Notes

CHAPTER I

1. Azizah Y. al-Hibri, "An Introduction to Muslim Women's Rights," in *Windows of Faith: Muslim Women Scholar-Activists in North America*, ed. Gisela Webb (Syracuse: Syracuse University Press, 2000), 51–71, here 68. See also Azizah al-Hibri, "Who Defines Women's Rights? A Third World Woman's Response," *Human Rights Brief* 2, no. 1 (1994): 9, 11.), https://www.wcl.american.edu/hrbrief/v2i1/alhibr21. htm; Jesse Londin, "The Life and Career of Muslim Women Lawyers for Human Rights: Dr. Azizah Al-Hibri, KARAMAH," *LawCrossing Interview*, http://www. lawcrossing.com/article/336/Dr-Azizah-al-Hibri-KARAMAH/.

2. al-Hibri, "An Introduction to Muslim Women's Rights," 67–68.

3. Fatima Seedat, "When Islam and Feminism Converge," *The Muslim World* 103 (July 2013): 404–420, here 406.

4. See Yvonne Yazbeck Haddad, Jane I. Smith, and Kathleen M. Moore, "Competing Discourses," in *Muslim Women in America: The Challenge of Islamic Identity Today* (New York: Oxford University Press, 2006), 143–164; Pew Research Center, "How Americans Feel about Religious Groups" (July 16, 2014), accessed on July 27, 2015, http://www.pewforum.org/2014/07/16/how-americans-feel-about-religious-groups/.

5. Lila Abu-Lughod, *Do Muslim Women Need Saving?* (Cambridge, MA: Harvard University Press, 2013), 26–29. See also Saba Mahmood, *Politics of Piety: The Islamic Revival and the Feminist Subject* (Princeton, NJ: Princeton University Press, 2005), 196–197.

6. Haddad, Smith, and Moore, *Muslim Women in America*, 22–24.

7. Gayatri Chakravorty Spivak, "Can the Subaltern Speak?," in *Marxism and the Interpretation of Culture*, ed. Cary Nelson and Lawrence Grossberg (Urbana: University of Illinois Press, 1988), 271–313, here 296–297. See also Abu-Lughod, *Do Muslim Women Need Saving?*, 33, 46–47.

8. Juliane Hammer, *American Muslim Women, Religious Authority, and Activism: More Than a Prayer* (Austin: University of Texas Press, 2012), 147–149. For a more extensive exploration of the various "Western" representations of Muslim women, see Mohja Kahf, *Western Representations of the Muslim Woman: From Termagant to Odalisque* (Austin: University of Texas Press, 1999). See also Haddad, Smith, and Moore, *Muslim Women in America*, 26–27, 32–33.

9. Leila Ahmed, *Women and Gender in Islam: Historical Roots of a Modern Debate* (New Haven, CT: Yale University Press, 1992), 155.

10. See Mahmood, *Politics of Piety*, 1–2; Katherine Bullock, *Rethinking Muslim Women and the Veil: Challenging Historical and Modern Stereotypes* (Herndon, VA: IIIT, 2002), 37–40; Jasmin Zine, "Creating a Critical Faith-Centered Space for Antiracist Feminism: Reflections of a Muslim Scholar-Activist," *Journal of Feminist Studies in Religion* 20, no. 2 (Fall 2004): 167–187, here 173.

11. Zine, "Creating a Critical Faith-Centered Space," 173.

12. Fazlur Rahman, *Islam and Modernity: Transformation of an Intellectual Tradition* (Chicago: University of Chicago Press, 1982).

13. amina wadud, *Qur'an and Woman: Rereading the Sacred Text from a Woman's Position* (New York: Oxford University Press, 1999), 1–2.

14. Ayesha Chaudhry, *Domestic Violence and the Islamic Tradition: Ethics, Law, and the Muslim Discourse on Gender* (Oxford: Oxford University Press, 2013).

15. For example, see al-Tabari's commentary on the Qur'an (Abu Ja'far Muhammad b. Jarir al-Tabari, *The Commentary on the Qur'an: Being an Abridged Translation of* Jami al-bayan an ta'wil ay al-Qur'an, ed. W. F. Madelung and A. Jones [New York: Oxford University Press, 1987]).

16. Hibba Abugideiri, "Revisiting the Islamic Past, Deconstructing Male Authority: The Project of Islamic Feminism," *Religion and Literature* 42, no. 1/2 (Spring/Summer 2010): 133–139, here 134.

17. Aysha Hidayatullah, "The Qur'anic Rib-ectomy: Scriptural Purity, Imperial Dangers, and Other Obstacles to the Interfaith Engagement of Feminist Qur'anic Interpretation," in *Women in Interreligious Dialogue*, ed. Catherine Cornille and Jillian Maxey, Interreligious Dialogue Series 5 (Eugene, OR: Cascade, 2013), 152–154.

18. Hidayatullah, "The Qur'anic Rib-ectomy," 154–155.

19. Hammer, *American Muslim Women*, 189–192; Zine, "Creating a Critical Faith-Centered Space," 169–170; Laura Zahra McDonald, "Islamic Feminism," *Feminist Theory* 9, no. 3 (2008): 347–354, here 353.

20. Valentine M. Moghadam, "Islamic Feminism and Its Discontents: Toward a Resolution of the Debate," *Signs* 27, no. 4 (Summer 2002): 1135–1171, here 1142; Margot Badran, "Between Secular and Islamic Feminism/s: Reflections on the Middle East and Beyond," *Journal of Middle East Women's Studies* 1, no. 1 (Winter 2005): 6–28, here 6. This article is reprinted in Margot Badran, *Feminism in Islam: Secular and Religious Convergences* (Oxford: Oneworld, 2009), 300–322.

See also Haideh Moghissi, *Feminism and Islamic Fundamentalism: The Limits of Postmodern Analysis* (London: Zed Books, 1999), 6; miriam cooke, *Women Claim Islam: Creating Islamic Feminism through Literature* (New York: Routledge, 2001), ix; Hidayatullah, *Feminist Edges*, 36–45; Seedat, "When Islam and Feminism Converge"; Fatima Seedat, "Islam, Feminism, and Islamic Feminism: Between Inadequacy and Inevitability," *Journal of Feminist Studies in Religion* 29, no. 2 (Fall 2013): 25–45.

21. Moghadam, "Islamic Feminism and Its Discontents," 1142; Moghissi, *Feminism and Islamic Fundamentalism*, 134, 140–142. See also McDonald, "Islamic Feminism," 348–349. Hammed Shahidian describes Islamic feminism as "inadequate" and as an "oxymoron." (Hammed Shahidian, "The Politics of the Veil: Reflections on Symbolism, Islam, and Feminism," *Thamyris: Mythmaking from Past to Present* 4, no. 2 [1997]: 325–337.) Shahrzad Mojab describes Islamic feminism as a "contradiction in terms" that "justifies unequal gender relationships." (Shahrzad Mojab, "Theorizing the Politics of 'Islamic Feminism,'" *Feminist Review* 69 [Winter 2001]: 124–146. See also Shahrzad Mojab, "Islamic Feminism: Alternative or Contradiction?," *Fireweed*, no. 47 [Winter 1995]: 18–25.)

22. Moghissi, *Feminism and Islamic Fundamentalism*, 140, 134, 148.

23. Moghissi, *Feminism and Islamic Fundamentalism*, 126.

24. Moghadam, "Islamic Feminism and Its Discontents," 1158.

25. Margot Badran, "Engaging Islamic Feminism," in *Islamic Feminism: Current Perspectives*, ed. Anitta Kynsilehto (Tampere, Finland: Tampere Peace Research Institute, 2008), 25–35, here 34. Mir-Hosseini provides two classifications for this perspective: Muslim Traditionalists and Islamic Fundamentalists. (See Ziba Mir-Hosseini, "Beyond 'Islam' and 'Feminism,'" *IDS Bulletin* 42, no. 1 [January 2011]: 67–77, here 71.)

26. See, Zara Faris, http://zarafaris.com/; Seedat, "When Islam and Feminism Converge," 405.

27. McDonald "Islamic Feminism," 352.

28. Ahmed, *Women and Gender*, 237; Seedat, "When Islam and Feminism Converge," 405; Seedat, "Islam, Feminism, and Islamic Feminism," 40.

29. See al-Hibri, "An Introduction to Muslim Women's Rights," 51–71.

30. Badran, *Feminism in Islam*, 242; cooke, *Women Claim Islam*, ix.

31. Badran, "Between Secular and Islamic Feminism/s," 6.

32. Badran, *Feminism in Islam*, 242.

33. Badran, *Feminism in Islam*, 245.

34. Badran, "Between Secular and Islamic Feminism/s," 10.

35. Riffat Hassan, "Feminist Theology: The Challenges for Muslim Women," in *Women and Islam: Critical Concepts in Sociology*, ed. Haideh Moghissi (London: Routledge, 2005), 195–208, here 199.

36. Badran, "Engaging Islamic Feminism," 31.

37. Badran, "Between Secular and Islamic Feminism/s," 15.

38. Asma Barlas, "Four Stages of Denial, or, My On-Again, Off-Again Affair with Feminism: Response to Margot Badran" (paper presented at Ithaca College, October 2006), 2. Available online at http://faculty.ithaca.edu/abarlas/. See also Asma Barlas, "Engaging Feminism: Provincializing Feminism as a Master Narrative," in *Islamic Feminism: Current Perspectives*, ed. Anitta Kynsilehto (Tampere, Finland: Tampere Peace Research Institute, 2008), 15–23.

39. Barlas, "Four Stages of Denial," 2.

40. Barlas, "Engaging Feminism," 22–23.

41. Badran, "Between Secular and Islamic Feminism/s," 13; Barlas, "Four Stages of Denial," 4.

42. Seedat, "When Islam and Feminism Converge," 404–420; Seedat, "Islam, Feminism, and Islamic Feminism," 25–45.

43. Seedat, "Islam, Feminism, and Islamic Feminism," 40.

44. Their major works include Riffat Hassan, "Feminism in Islam," in *Feminism and World Religions*, ed. Arvind Sharma and Katherine K. Young (Albany: State University of New York Press, 1999), 248–278; wadud, *Qur'an and Woman*; amina wadud, *Inside the Gender Jihad: Women's Reform in Islam* (Oxford: Oneworld, 2006); Asma Barlas, *"Believing Women" in Islam: Unreading Patriarchal Interpretations of the Qur'an* (Austin: University of Texas Press, 2002). Some helpful surveys of their writings include: Hidayatullah, *Feminist Edges*; Asma Barlas, "Amina Wadud's Hermeneutics of the Qur'an: Women Rereading Sacred Texts," in *Modern Muslim Intellectuals and the Qur'an*, ed. Suha Taji-Farouki (London: Oxford University Press, 2006), 97–124; Jerusha Tanner Lamptey, *Never Wholly Other: A Muslima Theology of Religious Pluralism* (New York: Oxford University Press, 2014), 81–96; Hammer, *American Muslim Women*, 56–76; Haddad, Smith, and Moore, *Muslim Women in America*, 154–160.

45. Barlas, *"Believing Women" in Islam*, 33. See also Aysha Hidayatullah, "Inspiration and Struggle: Muslim Feminist Theology and the Work of Elizabeth Schüssler Fiorenza," *Journal of Feminist Studies in Religion* 25, no. 1 (2009): 162–170, here 167.

46. wadud, *Qur'an and Woman*, 2.

47. wadud, *Qur'an and Woman*, 17–20, 23–25, 44–53; Barlas, *"Believing Women" in Islam*, 136; Hassan, "Feminism in Islam," 262.

48. Hassan, "Feminism in Islam," 249.

49. Ayesha S. Chaudhry, "Producing Gender-Egalitarian Islamic Law: A Case Study of Guardianship (*Wilayah*) in Prophetic Practice," in *Men in Charge? Rethinking Authority in Muslim Legal Tradition*, ed. Ziba Mir-Hosseini, Mulki Al-Sharmani, and Jana Rumminger (London: Oneworld, 2015), 89.

50. Chaudhry, "Producing Gender-Egalitarian Islamic Law," 89; Hidayatullah, *Feminist Edges*, 81–86.

51. wadud, *Qur'an and Woman*, 3–4, 30–31; wadud, *Inside the Gender Jihad*, 193–198.

52. Hidayatullah, *Feminist Edges*, 132.

53. Barlas, *"Believing Women" in Islam*, 64–66; Hassan, "Feminism in Islam," 248–250.

54. Riffat Hassan, "Muslim Women and Post-Patriarchal Islam," in *After Patriarchy: Feminist Transformations of the World Religions*, ed. Paula M. Cooey, William R. Eakin, and Jay B. McDaniel (Maryknoll, NY: Orbis, 1998, 43), 39–64.

55. Hassan, "Feminism in Islam," 254.

56. Hidayatullah, "The Qur'anic Rib-ectomy," 150–151.

57. al-Hibri, "An Introduction to Muslim Women's Rights," 53.

58. al-Hibri, "An Introduction to Muslim Women's Rights," 54–55.

59. Hidayatullah, *Feminist Edges*, 147.

60. Hidayatullah, *Feminist Edges*, 176.

61. wadud, *Inside the Gender Jihad*, 198–203.

62. amina wadud, "The Ethics of *Tawhid* over the Ethics of *Qiwamah*," in *Men in Charge? Rethinking Authority in Muslim Legal Tradition*, ed. Ziba Mir-Hosseini, Mulki Al-Sharmani, and Jana Rumminger (London: Oneworld, 2015), 256–274.

63. Chaudhry, "Producing Gender-Egalitarian Islamic Law," 89.

64. Chaudhry, "Producing Gender-Egalitarian Islamic Law," 90–91.

65. Kecia Ali, "Progressive Muslims and Islamic Jurisprudence: The Necessity for Critical Engagement with Marriage and Divorce Law," in *Progressive Muslims: on Justice, Gender and Pluralism*, ed. Omid Safi (Oxford: Oneworld, 2003), 163–189, here 164–167. See also Kecia Ali, *Sexual Ethics and Islam: Feminist Reflections on Qur'an, Hadith, and Jurisprudence* (London: Oneworld, 2016).

66. Ali, "Progressive Muslims and Islamic Jurisprudence," 164.

67. Sa'diyya Shaikh, "Islamic Law, Sufism and Gender: Rethinking the Terms of the Debate," in *Men in Charge? Rethinking Authority in Muslim Legal Tradition*, ed. Ziba Mir Hosseini, Mulki Al-Sharmani, and Jana Rumminger (London: Oneworld, 2015), 106–131, here 107. See also Sa'diyya Shaikh, *Sufi Narratives of Intimacy: Ibn Arabi, Gender and Sexuality* (Chapel Hill: University of North Carolina Press, 2012).

68. Shaikh, "Islamic Law, Sufism and Gender," 107.

69. Shaikh, "Islamic Law, Sufism and Gender," 128.

70. Hidayatullah, *Feminist Edges*, 175–176; Ali, "Progressive Muslims and Islamic Jurisprudence," 182.

71. Abugideiri, "Revisiting the Islamic Past," 137–138.

72. Abugideiri, "Revisiting the Islamic Past," 139.

73. See, for example, Riffat Hassan, "Engaging in Interreligious Dialogue: Recollections and Reflections of a Muslim Woman," *Journal of Ecumenical Studies* 49, no. 1 (Winter 2014): 134–139.

74. Hidayatullah, "The Qur'anic Rib-ectomy," 150–167, 150–151.

75. Hidayatullah, "The Qur'anic Rib-ectomy," 160, 164.

76. Hidayatullah, "The Qur'anic Rib-ectomy," 150–167, 150–151. See also wadud, *Inside the Gender Jihad*, 122.

77. Hidayatullah, "Inspiration and Struggle," 170.

78. Hidayatullah, "The Qur'anic Rib-ectomy," 157–158.

79. Zayn Kassam, "Constructive Interreligious Dialogue Concerning Muslim Women," in *Women in Interreligious Dialogue*, ed. Catherine Cornille and Jillian Maxey, Interreligious Dialogue Series 5 (Eugene, OR: Cascade, 2013), 127–149.

80. Kassam, "Constructive Interreligious Dialogue," 149.

81. Aysha Hidayatullah, "Feminist Interpretation of the Qur'an in a Comparative Feminist Setting," *Journal of Feminist Studies in Religion* 30, no. 2 (Fall 2014): 115–129, here 129.

CHAPTER 2

1. For example, Ednan Aslan, Marcia Hermansen, and Elif Medeni, eds., *Muslima Theology: The Voices of Muslim Women Theologians* (Frankfurt am Main: Peter Lang, 2013). The editors use "*Muslima* theology," yet acknowledge it is not used or used in this sense by all Muslim women scholars, activists, or theologians.

2. Celene Ayat Lizzio, "Gendering Ritual: A Muslima's Reading of the Laws of Purity and Ritual Preclusion," in *Muslima Theology: The Voices of Muslim Women Theologians*, ed. Ednan Aslan, Marcia Hermansen, and Elif Medeni (Frankfurt am Main: Peter Lang, 2013), 167–179, here 178.

3. wadud, *Inside the Gender Jihad*, 24–37, 39–42, 158–162; Barlas, *"Believing Women" in Islam*, 13–15.

4. Hassan, "Feminism in Islam," 253, 257–261.

5. Shaikh, "Islamic Law, Sufism and Gender," 106–107, 128–129.

6. Ali, *Sexual Ethics and Islam*, 14–22.

7. Asma Lamrabet, "What Does the Qur'an Say about The Interfaith Marriage?" (January 2013), http://www.asma-lamrabet.com/articles/what-does-the-qur-an-say-about-the-interfaith-marriage/.

8. Jerusha Lamptey, *Interfaith Marriage: A Muslima Response*, McGinley Lecture Series (New York: Fordham University Press, 2014), 36–43.

9. I write about religious diversity in Lamptey, *Never Wholly Other*.

10. See Delores Williams, *Sisters in the Wilderness: The Challenge of Womanist God-Talk* (Maryknoll: Orbis, 1993); Ada María Isasi-Díaz, *Mujerista Theology: A Theology for the 20th Century* (Maryknoll: Orbis, 1996); Chung Hyun Kyung, *Struggle to Be the Sun Again: Introducing Asian Women's Theology* (Maryknoll: Orbis, 1990); Mercy Amba Oduyoye, *Introducing African Women's Theology* (Sheffield: Sheffield Academic, 2001).

11. See also Aysha Hidayatullah, "Inspiration and Struggle."

12. Lamptey, *Never Wholly Other*.

13. Lamptey, *Never Wholly Other*, 92–95. See also wadud, *Qur'an and Woman*, 96; amina wadud, "Towards a Qur'anic Hermeneutics of Social Justice: Race, Class, and Gender," *Journal of Law and Religion* 12, no. 1 (1195–1996): 37–50; Riffat Hassan, "The Qur'anic Perspective on Religious Pluralism," in *Peace-Building by, between, and beyond Muslims and Evangelical Christians*, ed. Mohammed Abu-Nimer and David

Augsburger (Lanham, MD: Lexington Books, 2009), 91–101; Barlas, *"Believing Women" in Islam*, 146; Asma Barlas, "Reviving Islamic Universalism: East/s, West/s, and Coexistence" (paper presented at the Conference on Contemporary Islamic Synthesis, Alexandria, Egypt, October 2003), 7; Asma Barlas, "Hearing the Word, as a Muslim: Thirteen Passages of the Qur'an and Religious Difference" (paper presented at Cornell University Vespers, November 2007), 6.

14. See also wadud, *Qur'an and Woman*, 96; wadud, "Towards a Qur'anic Hermeneutics of Social Justice."

15. Francis X. Clooney, S.J., *Comparative Theology: Deep Learning across Religious Borders* (Malden, MA: Wiley Blackwell, 2010), 10.

16. A. Bagus Laksana, "Comparative Theology: Between Identity and Alterity," in *The New Comparative Theology: Interreligious Insights from the Next Generation*, ed. Francis X. Clooney, S.J. (London: T & T Clark, 2010), 1–20.

17. Catherine Cornille, "The Confessional Nature of Comparative Theology," *Studies in Interreligious Dialogue* 24, no. 1 (2014): 9–15, here 9–11.

18. Clooney, *Comparative Theology*, 14–16; James Fredericks, *Faith among Faiths: Christian Theology and Non-Christian Religions* (Mahwah, NJ: Paulist, 1999), 45, 165–166; James Fredericks, *Buddhists and Christians: Through Comparative Theology to Solidarity* (Maryknoll, NY: Orbis, 2004), xii–xiii.

19. Fredericks, *Buddhists and Christians*, xii; Fredericks, *Faith among Faiths*, 164.

20. Fredericks, *Buddhists and Christians*, 109–110.

21. Clooney, *Comparative Theology*, 13.

22. Fredericks, *Faith among Faiths*, 163.

23. Michelle Voss Roberts, *Tastes of the Divine: Hindu and Christian Theologies of Emotion* (New York: Fordham University Press, 2014); Jeannine Hill Fletcher, "What Counts as 'Catholic'? What Constitutes 'Comparative'?," and "Response to Daria Schnipkoweit," *Studies in Interreligious Dialogue* 24, no. 1 (2014): 78–85, 91–93.

24. Zayn Kassam, "Response to Daniel Madigan," in *Catholicism and Interreligious Dialogue*, ed. James L. Heft, S.M. (New York: Oxford University Press, 2012), 75–77, here 75; Clooney, *New Comparative Theology*, 199; Clooney, *Comparative Theology*, 16–19.

25. Clooney, *Comparative Theology*, 7; Fredericks, *Faith among Faiths*, 169.

26. Fredericks, *Faith among Faiths*, 175–176.

27. Clooney, *Comparative Theology*, 16; Voss Roberts, *Tastes of the Divine*, xxii; Reid B. Locklin and Hugh Nicholson, "The Return of Comparative Theology," *Journal of the American Academy of Religion* 78, no. 2 (June 2010): 477–514, here 499.

28. Fredericks, *Faith among Faiths*, 178; Peter Phan, "From Soteriology to Comparative Theology and Back: A Response to S. Mark Heim," in *Understanding Religious Pluralism: Perspectives from Religious Studies and Theology*, ed. Peter Phan and Jonathan Ray (Eugene, OR: Pickwick, 2014), 260–264, here 262; John J. Thatamanil, *The Immanent Divine* (Minneapolis, MN: Fortress, 2006), 23–24; Tracy Sayuki Tiemeier, "Comparative Theology as a Theology of Liberation," in *The New*

Comparative Theology: Interreligious Insights from the Next Generation, ed. Francis X. Clooney, S.J. (London: T & T Clark, 2010), 129–150, here 139.

29. Michelle Voss Roberts, *Dualities: A Theology of Difference* (Louisville, KY: Westminster John Knox, 2010), 18.

30. Voss Roberts, *Tastes of the Divine*, xxii; Francis X. Clooney, S.J., "Afterword: Some Reflections in Response to Teaching Comparative Theology in the Millennial Classroom," in *Comparative Theology in the Millennial Classroom*, ed. Mara Brecht and Reid B. Locklin (New York: Routledge, 2016), 219–234, here 227.

31. Mohammed Arkoun, *The Unthought in Contemporary Islamic Thought* (London: Saqi Books, 2002).

32. Locklin and Nicholson, "The Return of Comparative Theology," 493.

33. Daniel Joslyn-Siemiatkoski, "Comparative Theology and the Status of Judaism: Hegemony and Reversals," in *The New Comparative Theology: Interreligious Insights from the Next Generation*, ed. Francis X. Clooney, S.J. (London: T & T Clark, 2010), 89–108, here 96–97, 108; Lamptey, *Never Wholly Other*, 71–73.

34. James L. Fredericks, "Off the Map: The Catholic Church and Its Dialogue with Buddhists," in *Catholicism and Interreligious Dialogue*, ed. James L. Heft, S.M. (New York: Oxford University Press, 2012), 127–144, here 128.

35. Fredericks, "Off the Map," 141, 143.

36. Kristin Beise Kiblinger, "Relating Theology of Religions and Comparative Theology," in *The New Comparative Theology: Interreligious Insights from the Next Generation*, ed. Francis X. Clooney, S.J. (London: T & T Clark, 2010), 21–42; Jeffery D. Long, "(Tentatively) Putting the Pieces Together: Comparative Theology in the Tradition of Sri Ramakrishna," in *The New Comparative Theology: Interreligious Insights from the Next Generation*, ed. Francis X. Clooney, S.J. (London: T & T Clark, 2010), 151–170, here 152.

37. See *Nostra Aetate* 2, available online at http://www.vatican.va/archive (accessed May 2016).

38. See *Dominus Iesus*, available online at http://www.vatican.va/archive (accessed May 2016).

39. Francis X. Clooney, S.J., *Divine Mother, Blessed Mother: Hindu Goddesses and the Virgin Mary* (New York: Oxford University Press, 2005).

40. Michelle Voss Roberts, "Gendering Comparative Theology," in *The New Comparative Theology: Interreligious Insights from the Next Generation*, ed. Francis X. Clooney, S.J. (London: T & T Clark, 2010), 109–128, here 114–115; Voss Roberts, *Dualities*, 4–5.

41. Voss Roberts, *Dualities*, 12; Voss Roberts, "Gendering Comparative Theology," 116.

42. Voss Roberts, "Gendering Comparative Theology," 127.

43. Voss Roberts, "Gendering Comparative Theology," 118–124.

44. Cornille, "Confessional Nature," 13–15.

45. Fredericks, "Off the Map," 143.

46. Voss Roberts, "Gendering Comparative Theology," 123–124.

47. Tiemeier, "Comparative Theology," 133, 140; Hugh Nicholson, "The New Comparative Theology and the Problem of Theological Hegemonism," in *The New Comparative Theology: Interreligious Insights from the Next Generation*, ed. Francis X. Clooney, S.J. (London: T & T Clark, 2010), 43–62.

48. Tiemeier, "Comparative Theology," 148–149.

49. Jeannine Hill Fletcher, "Gift to the Prophet from a King: The Politics of Women in Interreligious Dialogue," in *Women and Interreligious Dialogue*, ed. Catherine Cornille and Jillian Maxley, Interreligious Dialogue Series 5 (Eugene, OR: Cascade, 2013), 27–48, here 48.

50. Seyyed Hossein Nasr, *Ideals and Realities of Islam* (Chicago: ABC International Group, 2000). See also Joseph Lumbard, "Discernment, Dialogue, and the Word of God," in *Criteria of Discernment in Interreligious Dialogue*, ed. Catherine Cornille, Interreligious Dialogue Series 1 (Eugene, OR: Cascade, 2009), 143–152; Daniel Madigan, "Muslim Christian Dialogue in Difficult Times," in *Catholicism and Interreligious Dialogue*, ed. James L. Heft, S.M. (New York: Oxford University Press, 2012), 57–74, here 58; Daniel Madigan, "Jesus and Muhammad: The Sufficiency of Prophecy," in *Bearing the Word: Prophecy in Biblical and Qur'anic Perspective*, ed. Michael Ipgrave (London: Church House Publishing, 2005), 90–99, here 95; Annemarie Schimmel, *And Muhammad Is His Messenger: The Veneration of the Prophet in Islamic Piety* (Chapel Hill: University of North Carolina Press, 1985), 24.

51. Nasr, *Ideals and Realities*, 31.

52. Lumbard, "Discernment, Dialogue," 144.

53. Lumbard, "Discernment, Dialogue," 144.

54. Schimmel, *And Muhammad Is His Messenger*, 24.

55. Daniel A. Madigan, "Mutual Theological Hospitality: Doing Theology in the Presence of the 'Other,'" in *Muslim and Christian Understanding: Theory and Application of "A Common Word,"* ed. Waleed El-Ansary and David K. Linnan (New York: Palgrave Macmillan, 2010), 57–68, here 5, 7; Madigan, "Jesus and Muhammad," 93, 95.

56. Madigan, "Jesus and Muhammad," 93, 96; Madigan, "Mutual Theological Hospitality," 7; Madigan, "Muslim-Christian Dialogue," 72.

57. Nasr, *Ideals and Realities*, 30.

58. Nasr, *Ideals and Realities*, 36.

59. Daniel A. Madigan, "Particularity, Universality, and Finality: Insights from the Gospel of John," in *Communicating the Word: Revelation, Translation, and Interpretation in Christianity and Islam*, ed. David Marshall (Washington, DC: Georgetown University Press, 2011), 14–32, here 19. See also Daniel Madigan, S.J., "People of the Word: Reading John with a Muslim," *Review and Expositor* 104 (Winter 2007): 81–95, here 81; Madigan, "Mutual Theological Hospitality," 9. Reza Shah-Kazemi also draws a connection between the Logos, as depicted in the Gospel of John, and the Qur'an. (Reza Shah-Kazemi, "Light upon Light? The Qur'an and the Gospel of John," in *Interreligious Hermeneutics*, ed. Catherine

Cornille and Christopher Conway, Interreligious Dialogue Series 2 [Eugene, OR: Cascade, 2010], 116–148, here 123–125.)

60. Madigan, "Particularity, Universality, and Finality," 19; Madigan, "Muslim-Christian Dialogue," 58.

61. Nasr, *Ideals and Realities*, 32; Madigan, "Muslim-Christian Dialogue," 58; Madigan, "Jesus and Muhammad," 95; Daniel A. Madigan, "Mary and Muhammad: Bearers of the Word," *Australasian Catholic Record* 80 (2003): 417–427.

62. Madigan, "Muslim-Christian Dialogue," 65.

63. Rosemary Radford Ruether, *Sexism and God-Talk: Toward a Feminist Theology* (Boston: Beacon Press, 1993), 125–126.

64. Madigan, "Mutual Theological Hospitality," 9.

65. For example, Oduyoye, *Introducing African Women's Theology*, 51–65.

66. Clooney, *New Comparative Theology*, 199.

CHAPTER 3

1. For example, Hidayatullah, *Feminist Edges*; Shadaab Rahemtulla, *Qur'an of the Oppressed: Liberation Theology and Gender Justice in Islam* (New York: Oxford University Press, 2017).

2. wadud, *Qur'an and Woman*; Barlas, *"Believing Women" in Islam*; Hassan, "Feminism in Islam."

3. Asma Barlas, "Secular and Feminist Critiques of the Qur'an: Anti-Hermeneutics as Liberation?" *Journal of Feminist Studies in Religion* 32, no. 2 (December 2016): 111–121, here 112.

4. Barlas, "Secular and Feminist Critiques," 112, 114, 118.

5. Barlas, *"Believing Women" in Islam*, 13–18, 33. See also Hidayatullah, "Inspiration and Struggle," 167.

6. Asma Barlas, "A Response," *Journal of Feminist Studies in Religion* 32, no. 2 (December 2016): 148–151, here 150.

7. Ziba Mir-Hosseini, Mulki Al-Sharmani, and Jana Rumminger, eds., *Men in Charge? Rethinking Authority in Muslim Legal Tradition* (London: Oneworld, 2015).

8. See Ayesha Chaudhry, *Domestic Violence and the Islamic Tradition: Ethics, Law, and the Muslim Discourse on Gender* (Oxford: Oxford University Press, 2013).

9. wadud, *Qur'an and Woman*, 16–23. Qur'an 4:1: "People, be mindful (manifest *taqwa*) of your Sustainer, who created you from a single soul (*nafs*), and from it created its pair (*zawj*), and from the pair of them spread countless men and women far and wide; be conscious of God (manifest *taqwa*) in whose name you make requests of one another."

10. Ali, "Progressive Muslims and Islamic Jurisprudence," 164–167; Kecia Ali, "On Critique and Careful Reading," *Journal of Feminist Studies in Religion* 32, no. 2 (December 2016): 121–126, here 122.

11. Ali, "On Critique," 124.

12. See Hidayatullah, *Feminist Edges*.

13. Aysha Hidayatullah, "Claims to the Sacred," *Journal of Feminist Studies in Religion* 32, no. 2 (December 2016): 134–138, here 135–136. See also Hidayatullah, *Feminist Edges*, 160–165.

14. Hidayatullah, *Feminist Edges*, 153.

15. Hidayatullah, *Feminist Edges*, 147–151.

16. Hidayatullah, *Feminist Edges*, 153.

17. Not all gender-focused scholarship on the Qur'an, especially with a historical focus, shares this position. See for example Karen Bauer, "In Defense of Historical-Critical Analysis of the Qur'an," *Journal of Feminist Studies in Religion* 32, no. 2 (December 2016): 126–130.

18. Barlas, "Secular and Feminist Critiques," 117–119.

19. Barlas, "A Response," 151.

20. amina wadud, "Can One Critique Cancel All Previous Efforts?," *Journal of Feminist Studies in Religion* 32, no. 2 (December 2016):130–134, here 131.

21. wadud, "Can One Critique," 131.

22. wadud, "Can One Critique," 133.

23. Hidayatullah, *Feminist Edges*, 153.

24. Hidayatullah, *Feminist Edges*, 193.

25. Bauer, "In Defense of Historical-Critical Analysis of the Qur'an," 126, 128.

26. wadud, "Can One Critique, 132.

27. Barlas, "Secular and Feminist Critiques," 118.

28. Barlas, "Secular and Feminist Critiques," 114.

29. Hidayatullah, *Feminist Edges*, 145.

30. Hidayatullah, "Claims," 135.

31. Hidayatullah, "Claims," 137.

32. Hidayatullah, *Feminist Edges*, 193–194. See also Hidayatullah, "Claims," 136.

33. Hidayatullah, *Feminist Edges*, 144–145. See also Nasr Abu Zayd, *Reformation of Islamic Thought: A Critical Historical Analysis* (Amsterdam: Amsterdam University Press, 2006), 95–99; Raja Rhouni, *Secular and Islamic Feminist Critiques in the Work of Fatima Mernissi* (Leiden: Brill, 2010), 34–36, 252–254, 257–261.

34. Hidayatullah, *Feminist Edges*, 195.

35. Hidayatullah, *Feminist Edges*, 172–177.

36. Fatima Seedat, "Beyond the Text: Between Islam and Feminism," *Journal of Feminist Studies in Religion* 32, no. 2 (December 2016): 138–142, here 138.

37. Seedat, "Beyond the Text," 140.

38. Seedat, "Beyond the Text," 140.

39. Sa'diyya Shaikh, "A Tafsir of Praxis: Gender, Marital Violence, and Resistance in a South African Muslim Community," in *Violence against Women in Contemporary World Religions: Roots and Cures*, ed. Daniel C. Maguire and Sa'diyya Shaikh (Cleveland: The Pilgrim Press, 2007), 66–89.

40. Seedat, "Beyond the Text," 141.

41. See Barlas, "Secular and Feminist Critiques," 111–121.

42. Seedat, "Beyond the Text," 142.

43. Seedat, "Beyond the Text," 139.

44. wadud, "Can One Critique," 132.

45. wadud, "Can One Critique," 132.

46. wadud, "Can One Critique," 133.

47. Hidayatullah, *Feminist Edges*, 176.

48. wadud, *Inside the Gender Jihad*, 212–213.

49. wadud, *Inside the Gender Jihad*, 213.

50. wadud, *Inside the Gender Jihad*, 214–215.

51. wadud, *Inside the Gender Jihad*, 197.

52. See, Mark 8.27–30 and Matthew 16:13–20. For a brief overview of central feminist debates, see "Christology," in Marcella Maria Althaus-Reid and Lisa Isherwood, *Controversies in Feminist Theology* (London: SCM, 2007), 81–105.

53. See Ruether, *Sexism and God-Talk*; Rosemary Radford Ruether, *Gaia and God: An Ecofeminist Theology of Earth Healing* (San Francisco: HarperSanFrancisco, 1992); Rosemary Radford Ruether, *Visionary Women: Three Medieval Mystics* (Minneapolis, MN: Fortress, 2002); Rosemary Radford Ruether, *Goddesses and the Divine Feminine: A Western Religious History* (Berkeley: University of California Press, 2005); Rosemary Radford Ruether, *Women and Redemption: A Theological History* (Minneapolis, MN: Fortress, 1998, 2012).

54. Se Kwok Pui-lan, *Postcolonial Imagination and Feminist Theology* (Louisville, KY: Westminster John Knox, 2005); Kwok Pui-lan, *Introducing Asian Feminist Theology* (Cleveland: Pilgrim, 2000); Kwok Pui-lan, *Globalization, Gender, and Peacebuilding: The Future of Interfaith Dialogue* (New York: Paulist, 2012); Kwok Pui-lan, *Discovering the Bible in the Non-Biblical World* (Maryknoll, NY: Orbis, 1995).

55. Jacquelyn Grant, *White Women's Christ and Black Women's Jesus: Feminist Christology and Womanist Response* (Atlanta: Scholars Press, 1989). See also Jacquelyn Grant, *Perspectives on Womanist Theology* (Atlanta: ITC Press, 1995); Jacquelyn Grant and Randall C. Bailey, eds., *The Recovery of Black Presence: An Interdisciplinary Exploration; Essays in Honor of Dr. Charles B. Copher* (Nashville: Abingdon, 1995).

56. See Ada María Isasi-Díaz, *En la Lucha/In the Struggle: Elaborating a Mujerista Theology* (Minneapolis, MN: Fortress, 2003); Ada María Isasi-Díaz, *La Lucha Continues: Mujerista Theology* (Maryknoll, NY: Orbis, 2004); Isasi-Díaz, *Mujerista Theology*.

57. Ruether, *Sexism and God-Talk*, 116.

58. Ruether, *Sexism and God-Talk*, 117.

59. Ruether, *Sexism and God-Talk*, 117.

60. Ruether, *Sexism and God-Talk*, 120.

61. Ruether, *Sexism and God-Talk*, 121.

62. Ruether, *Sexism and God-Talk*, 121–122.

63. Ruether, *Sexism and God-Talk*, 122.

64. Ruether, *Sexism and God-Talk*, 123.

65. Ruether, *Sexism and God-Talk*, 125.

66. Ruether, *Sexism and God-Talk*, 125.

67. Ruether, *Sexism and God-Talk*, 126.

68. Ruether, *Sexism and God-Talk*, 126.

69. Ruether, *Sexism and God-Talk*, 126.

70. Ruether, *Sexism and God-Talk*, 128.

71. Ruether, *Sexism and God-Talk*, 130.

72. Ruether, *Sexism and God-Talk*, 132.

73. Ruether, *Sexism and God-Talk*, 134.

74. Ruether, *Sexism and God-Talk*, 134.

75. Ruether, *Sexism and God-Talk*, 136.

76. Ruether, *Sexism and God-Talk*, 137.

77. Ruether, *Sexism and God-Talk*, 137.

78. Ruether, *Sexism and God-Talk*, 138.

79. Kwok Pui-lan, *Postcolonial Imagination*, 169. See also Kwok Pui-lan, "Ecology and Christology," *Feminist Theology* 5, no. 15 (May 1997): 113–125.

80. Kwok, *Postcolonial Imagination*, 170.

81. Kwok, *Postcolonial Imagination*, 171.

82. Kwok, *Postcolonial Imagination*, 172.

83. Kwok, *Postcolonial Imagination*, 174.

84. Kwok, *Postcolonial Imagination*, 174–182.

85. Kwok, *Postcolonial Imagination*, 182.

86. Kwok, *Postcolonial Imagination*, 183–184.

87. Kwok, *Postcolonial Imagination*, 184.

88. Kwok, *Postcolonial Imagination*, 184.

89. Jacquelyn Grant, *White Women's Christ and Black Women's Jesus* (Atlanta: Scholars Press, 1989), 1–3.

90. Grant, *White Women's Christ*, 63, 67, 78.

91. Grant, *White Women's Christ*, 67–68, 73.

92. Grant, *White Women's Christ*, 75.

93. Grant, *White Women's Christ*, 82.

94. Grant, *White Women's Christ*, 82.

95. Grant, *White Women's Christ*, 91, 115, 151.

96. Grant, *White Women's Christ*, 109–110.

97. Grant, *White Women's Christ*, 120, 126.

98. Grant, *White Women's Christ*, 139, 143.

99. Grant, *White Women's Christ*, 144–145.

100. Grant, *White Women's Christ*, 146.

101. Grant, *White Women's Christ*, 171–172.

102. Grant, *White Women's Christ*, 179–180.

103. Grant, *White Women's Christ*, 185.

104. Grant, *White Women's Christ*, 3.

105. Grant, *White Women's Christ*, 198–199.

106. Grant, *White Women's Christ*, 204–205.

107. Grant, *White Women's Christ*, 209.

108. Grant, *White Women's Christ*, 6.

109. Grant, *White Women's Christ*, 210.

110. Grant, *White Women's Christ*, 216–217.

111. Grant, *White Women's Christ*, 217.

112. Grant, *White Women's Christ*, 217.

113. Isasi-Díaz, *La Lucha Continues*, 241. (While I do not engage their perspectives in this chapter, some other Latina feminist theologians, including María Pilar Aquino, critique Isasi-Diaz's formulation of mujerista theology. See, for example, María Pilar Aquino, "Latina Feminist Theology: Central Features," in *A Reader in Latina Feminist Theology: Religion and Justice*, ed. María Pilar Aquino, Daisy L. Machado, and Jeanette Rodríguez (Austin: University of Texas Press, 2002), 133–160.

114. Isasi-Díaz, *La Lucha Continues*, 254.

115. Isasi-Díaz, *La Lucha Continues*, 242.

116. Isasi-Díaz, *La Lucha Continues*, 242–243.

117. Isasi-Díaz, *La Lucha Continues*, 242–243.

118. Isasi-Díaz, *La Lucha Continues*, 242.

119. Isasi-Díaz, *La Lucha Continues*, 243–244.

120. Isasi-Díaz, *La Lucha Continues*, 247–248.

121. Isasi-Díaz, *La Lucha Continues*, 248.

122. Isasi-Díaz, *La Lucha Continues*, 251.

123. Isasi-Díaz, *La Lucha Continues*, 252–253.

124. Isasi-Díaz, *La Lucha Continues*, 247, 252–253.

125. Isasi-Díaz, *La Lucha Continues*, 253.

126. Isasi-Díaz, *La Lucha Continues*, 257.

127. Isasi-Díaz, *La Lucha Continues*, 253.

128. Isasi-Díaz, *La Lucha Continues*, 254.

129. Isasi-Díaz, *La Lucha Continues*, 254.

130. Isasi-Díaz, *La Lucha Continues*, 254.

131. Isasi-Díaz, *La Lucha Continues*, 263.

132. Isasi-Díaz, *La Lucha Continues*, 259.

133. Isasi-Díaz, *La Lucha Continues*, 259.

134. Isasi-Díaz, *La Lucha Continues*, 260.

135. Isasi-Díaz, *La Lucha Continues*, 260.

136. Laury Silvers, "'In the Book We Have Left Out Nothing': The Ethical Problem of the Existence of Verse 4:34 in the Qur'an," *Comparative Islamic Studies* 2, no.2 (2006): 171–180, here 171.

137. Shaikh, "Islamic Law, Sufism, and Gender, 111.

138. While I do not ultimately agree with all their conclusions, Rhouni and Hidayatullah also examine whether the Qur'an is a set of norms. See Rhouni, *Secular and Islamic Feminist Critiques*, 253–254; Hidayatullah, *Feminist Edges*, 172–177.

139. For example, see wadud, *Qur'an and Woman*, 2–3; Barlas, *"Believing Women,"* 7–10.

140. Chaudhry, *Domestic Violence*, 40, 53–55, 97–99.

141. Chaudhry, *Domestic Violence*, 80–94.

142. Chaudhry, *Domestic Violence*. 135–136, 140, 196–199, 220–221.

143. Ali, *Sexual Ethics and Islam*, xxxii–xxxiv, 1–27. See also Ali, "Progressive Muslims and Islamic Jurisprudence," 163–189.

144. Sa'diyya Shaikh also discusses the importance of going beyond precedent. See Shaikh, "Islamic Law, Sufism and Gender," 128.

145. wadud, *Qur'an and Woman*, 5–7; Barlas, *"Believing Women,"* 6, 17, 63, 76.

146. wadud, *Qur'an and Woman*, 2.

147. Shaikh also discusses experience in Sa'diyya Shaikh, "Feminism, Epistemology and Experience: Critically (En)gendering the Study of Islam," *Journal for Islamic Studies* 33 (2013): 30, 35, 44.

148. wadud, *Inside the Gender Jihad*, 200.

149. Abou El Fadl describes this as a "faith-based objection." See Khaled Abou El Fadl, *Speaking in God's Name: Islamic Law, Authority, and Women* (Oxford: Oneworld, 2001), 209–218.

150. Seedat, "Beyond the Text," 142.

151. See Kelly Brown Douglas, *The Black Christ* (Maryknoll: Orbis, 1994); JoAnne Marie Terrell, *Power in the Blood?: The Cross in the African American Experience* (Maryknoll: Orbis, 1998); Eboni Marshall Turman, *Toward a Womanist Ethic of Incarnation: Black Bodies, the Black Church, and the Council of Chalcedon* (New York: Palgrave McMillian, 2013).

152. wadud, *Inside the Gender Jihad*, 192–193, 197, 205, 212–214.

153. Qur'an 30:28: "God gives you an example from your own lives. Do you let those whom your right hand possesses be equal partners in the wealth which We have given you? Do you fear them as you fear each other? Thus, do We detail Our signs (*ayat*) for those who reason."

154. Qur'an 30:28: "But those who do wrong follow their own desires without knowledge. Who can guide those God leaves to stray, who have no one to help them?"

155. Isasi-Díaz, La Lucha *Continues*, 254.

156. Grant, *White Women's Christ*, 6.

157. Farid Esack, *Qur'an, Liberation and Pluralism: An Islamic Perspective of Interreligious Solidarity against Oppression* (Oxford: Oneworld, 1997), 98–103. See also Farid Esack, "Islam and Social Justice: Beyond Simplistic Apologia," in *What Men Owe to Women: Men's Voices from World Religions*, ed. John C. Raines and Daniel C. Macguire (Albany: State University of New York Press, 2001), 187–210, here 187.

158. For example, Qur'an 2:177.
159. Qur'an 2:177: "True goodness does not consist in turning your face towards East or West. The truly good are those who believe in God and the Last Day, in the angels, the Scripture, and the prophets; who give away some of their wealth, however much they cherish it, to their relatives, to orphans, the needy, travelers and beggars, and to liberate those in bondage; those who establish and maintain the prayer and pay the prescribed alms; who keep pledges whenever they make them; who are steadfast in misfortune, adversity, and times of danger. These are the ones who are true, and it is they who are conscious of God (*muttaqun*)."
160. wadud, *Inside the Gender Jihad*, 215.
161. Qur'an 4:34: "Men are in authority (*qawwamun*) over women because God has preferred some over others and because they spend of their wealth. Righteous women are obedient and guard in secret what God would have them guard. Concerning those women from whom you fear disobedience/rebellion (*nushuuz*), admonish them, abandon them in bed, and hit them (*dribuhunna*, from *daraba*). If they obey you, do not seek a way against them. God is Most High, Great."
162. Chaudhry, *Domestic Violence*, 196–221.
163. wadud, *Inside the Gender Jihad*, 200–204.

CHAPTER 4

1. Muhammad Muhsin Khan, trans., *The Translation of the Meanings of Sahih al-Bukhari*, vol. 7 (Riyadh: Darussalam, 1997), Hadith 5186, 80.
2. See Fatima Mernissi, *The Veil and the Male Elite: A Feminist Interpretation of Women's Rights in Islam* (New York: Basic Books, 1991), 64–76; Abou El Fadl, *Speaking in God's Name*, 215–217, 224–231.
3. This description appears most prominently in the first chapter of the Qur'an, Surah al-fatiha.
4. Hidayet Şefkatli Tuksal, "Misogynist Reports in the Hadith Literature," in *Muslima Theology: The Voices of Muslim Women Theologians*, ed. Ednan Aslan, Marcia Hermansen, and Elif Medeni (Frankfurt Am Main: Peter Lang, 2013), 133–154, here 134.
5. Tuksal, "Misogynist Reports," 134–135, 136–151.
6. For example, see Mohammad Akram Nadwi, *Al-Muhaddithat: The Women Scholars in Islam* (Oxford: Interface Publications, 2013).
7. Khan, *The Translation of the Meanings of Sahih al-Bukhari*, vol. 7, Hadith 5783–5969, 373–447. See also L. Clarke, "Hijab According to the Hadith: Text and Interpretation," in *The Muslim Veil in North America: Issues and Debates*, ed. Sajida Sultana Alvi, Homa Hoodfar, and Sheila McDonough (Toronto: Women's Press, 2003), 214–286.
8. Chaudhry, "Producing Gender-Egalitarian Islamic Law," 89–90; Kecia Ali, "The Disobedient Prophet in Muslim Thought," *Journal of Religious Ethics* 39, no. 3 (September 2011): 391–398, here 391.

9. Barlas, *"Believing Women" in Islam*, 46.

10. Chaudhry, "Producing Gender-Egalitarian Islamic Law," 90.

11. Kecia Ali, "'A Beautiful Example': The Prophet Muhammad as a Model for Muslim Husbands," *Islamic Studies* 43, no. 2 (2004): 273–291, here 274–275. See also Chaudhry, "Producing Gender-Egalitarian Islamic Law," 94; Ayesha S. Chaudhry, "'I Wanted One Thing and God Wanted Another . . .': The Dilemma of the Prophetic Example and the Qur'anic Injunction on Wife-Beating," *Journal of Religious Ethics* 39, no. 3 (September 2011): 416–439.

12. See Barlas, *"Believing Women" in Islam*, 67.

13. Chaudhry, "Producing Gender-Egalitarian Islamic Law," 89; Ali, "The Disobedient Prophet," 392.

14. Hassan, "Feminism in Islam," 249.

15. Barlas, *"Believing Women" in Islam*, 37, 45, 63.

16. Ali, "'A Beautiful Example,'" 276. See also Barlas, *"Believing Women" in Islam*, 64–66; Hassan, "Feminism in Islam," 248–250.

17. Hassan, "Muslim Women and Post-Patriarchal Islam," 39–64.

18. Mernissi, *The Veil and the Male Elite*, 44–48, 53–60, 72, 78–80.

19. Hatice Arpaguş, "The Position of Woman in the Creation: A Qur'anic Perspective," in *Muslima Theology: The Voices of Muslim Women Theologians*, ed. Ednan Aslan, Marcia Hermansen, and Elif Medeni (Frankfurt Am Main: Peter Lang, 2013), 115–132, here 125.

20. Arpaguş, "The Position of Woman in the Creation," 125–127.

21. Arpaguş, "The Position of Woman in the Creation," 127.

22. Hassan, "Feminism in Islam," 254. See also Hidayatullah, "The Qur'anic Ribectomy," 161–164.

23. Chaudhry, "Producing Gender-Egalitarian Islamic Law," 89; Hidayatullah, *Feminist Edges*, 81–86; Sa'diyya Shaikh, "Knowledge, Women and Gender in the Hadith: A Feminist Interpretation," *Islam and Christian-Muslim Relations* 15, no. 1 (January 2004): 99–108, here 107; Ali, *Sexual Ethics and Islam*, 175.

24. Clarke, "Hijab According to the Hadith," 216.

25. Clarke, "Hijab According to the Hadith," 258.

26. Ali, "'A Beautiful Example,'" 274. See also Ali, *Sexual Ethics and Islam*, 173–192.

27. Ali, "'A Beautiful Example,'" 286.

28. Mernissi, *The Veil and the Male Elite*, 44–48; Chaudhry, "'I Wanted One Thing,'" 417.

29. Ali, "'A Beautiful Example,'" 288; Clarke, "Hijab According to the Hadith," 216.

30. Clarke, "Hijab According to the Hadith," 262.

31. Clarke, "Hijab According to the Hadith," 262–265.

32. Clarke, "Hijab According to the Hadith," 285.

33. Clarke, "Hijab According to the Hadith," 216–246.

34. Clarke, "Hijab According to the Hadith," 263.

35. Shaikh, "Knowledge, Women and Gender," 99–108.

36. Clarke, "Hijab According to the Hadith," 265.

37. Ali, "'A Beautiful Example,'" 286.
38. Ali, "'A Beautiful Example,'" 274–283.
39. Ali, "'A Beautiful Example,'" 290.
40. Ali, "The Disobedient Prophet," 393.
41. Ali, "The Disobedient Prophet," 391–398.
42. Chaudhry, "'I Wanted One Thing,'" 421.
43. Chaudhry, "'I Wanted One Thing,'" 437.
44. Chaudhry, "'I Wanted One Thing,'" 437.
45. Chaudhry, "Producing Gender-Egalitarian Islamic Law," 90–91.
46. Chaudhry, "Producing Gender-Egalitarian Islamic Law," 92.
47. Shaikh, "Knowledge, Women and Gender," 105.
48. Shaikh, "Knowledge, Women and Gender," 105–107.
49. Mernissi, *The Veil and the Male Elite*, 72–78; Chaudhry, "Producing Gender-Egalitarian Islamic Law," 101; Tuksal, "Misogynist Reports," 133.
50. Chaudhry, "Producing Gender-Egalitarian Islamic Law," 104; Shaikh, "Knowledge, Women and Gender," 107.
51. Clarke, "Hijab According to the Hadith," 262.
52. Clarke, "Hijab According to the Hadith," footnote #145, 285.
53. Clarke, "Hijab According to the Hadith," footnote #145, 285.
54. Shaikh, "Knowledge, Women and Gender," 100.
55. Hidayatullah, "Inspiration and Struggle," 163.
56. Hidayatullah, "Inspiration and Struggle," 167.
57. Elizabeth Schüssler Fiorenza, *Bread Not Stone: The Challenge of Feminist Biblical Interpretation* (Boston: Beacon Press, 1984, 1995); Elizabeth Schüssler Fiorenza, *But She Said: Feminist Practices of Biblical Interpretation* (Boston: Beacon Press, 1984, 1995). Other important works include: Elizabeth Schüssler Fiorenza, *Changing Horizons: Explorations in Feminist Interpretation* (Minneapolis, MN: Fortress, 2014); Elizabeth Schüssler Fiorenza, *Wisdom Ways: Introducing Feminist Biblical Interpretation* (Maryknoll, NY: Orbis, 2001); Elizabeth Schüssler Fiorenza, *Empowering Memory and Movement: Thinking and Working across Borders* (Minneapolis, MN: Fortress, 2014).
58. Musa W. Dube, *Postcolonial Feminist Interpretation of the Bible* (St. Louis, MO: Chalice, 2000); Musa Dube, *Other Ways of Reading: African Women and the Bible* (Atlanta: Society of Biblical Literature, 2001); Musa Dube, *The HIV and AIDS Bible: Some Selected Essays* (Scranton, PA: University of Scranton Press, 2008).
59. Phyllis Trible, *God and the Rhetoric of Sexuality* (Philadelphia: Fortress, 1984); Phyllis Trible, *Texts of Terror: Literary-Feminist Readings of Biblical Narratives* (Philadelphia: Fortress, 1978).
60. Schüssler Fiorenza, *Bread Not Stone*, 1.
61. Schüssler Fiorenza, *Bread Not Stone*, xiv, 7. She also distinguishes her specific usage of this phrase from other usages on pages 173–174. See also Schüssler Fiorenza, *Empowering Memory and Movement*, 372–373.

62. Schüssler Fiorenza, *Bread Not Stone*, 42, 158.

63. Schüssler Fiorenza, *Bread Not Stone*, 9.

64. Schüssler Fiorenza, *Bread Not Stone*, 10.

65. Schüssler Fiorenza, *Bread Not Stone*, 25.

66. Schüssler Fiorenza, *Bread Not Stone*, 28. See also 11.

67. Schüssler Fiorenza, *Bread Not Stone*, 11. See also Schüssler Fiorenza, *Empowering Memory and Movement*, 528–530.

68. Schüssler Fiorenza, *Bread Not Stone*, 12–13.

69. Schüssler Fiorenza, *Bread Not Stone*, 32, 138.

70. Schüssler Fiorenza, *Bread Not Stone*, 33.

71. Schüssler Fiorenza, *Bread Not Stone*, 36–38.

72. Schüssler Fiorenza, *Bread Not Stone*, 163, 168.

73. Schüssler Fiorenza, *But She Said*, 52–55. See also Schüssler Fiorenza, *Wisdom Ways*, 165–204; Schüssler Fiorenza, *Bread Not Stone*, 15. In the latter text, she refers to the fourth strategy as the "hermeneutics of creative actualization."

74. Schüssler Fiorenza, *But She Said*, 52.

75. Schüssler Fiorenza, *But She Said*, 53.

76. Schüssler Fiorenza, *But She Said*, 76.

77. Schüssler Fiorenza, *But She Said*, 76.

78. Schüssler Fiorenza, *But She Said*, 53; Schüssler Fiorenza, *Bread Not Stone*, 15–18. While I do not discuss it in this chapter, her engagement with the story of Martha, Mary, and Jesus in the Gospel of Luke (Luke 10:38–42) provides a concise and concrete illustration of her application of these four strategies. (Schüssler Fiorenza, *But She Said*, 55–75.)

79. Schüssler Fiorenza, *But She Said*, 53.

80. Schüssler Fiorenza, *But She Said*, 53–54. See also Schüssler Fiorenza, *Bread Not Stone*, 19–20.

81. Schüssler Fiorenza, *But She Said*, 54.

82. Schüssler Fiorenza, *Bread Not Stone*, 19.

83. Schüssler Fiorenza, *But She Said*, 54. See also Schüssler Fiorenza, *Bread Not Stone*, 15–18.

84. Schüssler Fiorenza, *But She Said*, 54. See also Schüssler Fiorenza, *Bread Not Stone*, 140.

85. Schüssler Fiorenza, *Bread Not Stone*, 18.

86. Schüssler Fiorenza, *But She Said*, 54. See also Schüssler Fiorenza, *Bread Not Stone*, 20–22.

87. Schüssler Fiorenza, *But She Said*, 55.

88. Schüssler Fiorenza, *But She Said*, 54–55.

89. Schüssler Fiorenza, *But She Said*, 73.

90. Schüssler Fiorenza, *Bread Not Stone*, 21.

91. Dube, *Postcolonial Feminist Interpretation*, 7.

92. Dube, *Postcolonial Feminist Interpretation*, 7; Musa Dube, "Toward a Post-Colonial Feminist Interpretation of the Bible," in *Hope Abundant: Third World and Indigenous Women's Theology*, ed. Kwok Pui-lan (Maryknoll, NY: Orbis, 2010), 89–102, here 92. (originally published 1997 in *Semeia*)

93. Dube, "Toward a Post-Colonial Feminist," 91. See also Dube, *Postcolonial Feminist Interpretation*, 15–16.

94. Dube, "Toward a Post-Colonial Feminist," 92.

95. Dube, *Postcolonial Feminist Interpretation*, 7. See also Musa Dube, "Feminist Theologies of a World Scripture(s) in the Globalization Era," in *The Oxford Handbook of Feminist Theology*, ed. Mary McClintock Fulkerson and Sheila Briggs (New York: Oxford University Press, 2013), 382–401.

96. Dube, "Toward a Post-Colonial Feminist," 93–94; Dube, *Postcolonial Feminist Interpretation*, 16–17.

97. Dube, "Toward a Post-Colonial Feminist," 94.

98. Dube, "Toward a Post-Colonial Feminist," 94.

99. Dube, *Postcolonial Feminist Interpretation*, 15–20.

100. Dube, *Postcolonial Feminist Interpretation*, 18.

101. Dube, *Postcolonial Feminist Interpretation*, 20–21, 73–77.

102. Dube, "Toward a Post-Colonial Feminist," 95; Dube, *Postcolonial Feminist Interpretation*, 23–25, 117–118.

103. Dube, *Postcolonial Feminist Interpretation*, 26–39. It is not my intention to arbitrate the debates between Schüssler Fiorenza and Dube. For more perspectives on their mutual critiques and depictions, see Kwok Pui-lan, "Elisabeth Schüssler Fiorenza and Postcolonial Studies," *Journal of Feminist Studies in Religion* 25, no. 1 (2009): 191–207.

104. Dube, *Postcolonial Feminist Interpretation*, 36–37.

105. Dube, *Postcolonial Feminist Interpretation*, 42–43. See also Dube, *Other Ways of Reading*, 8.

106. Dube, *Postcolonial Feminist Interpretation*, 53–57.

107. Dube, *Postcolonial Feminist Interpretation*, 53.

108. Dube, *Postcolonial Feminist Interpretation*, 57.

109. Dube, *Postcolonial Feminist Interpretation*, 108–109.

110. Dube, *Other Ways of Reading*, 1.

111. Dube, *Other Ways of Reading*, 3–4, 14.

112. Dube, *Postcolonial Feminist Interpretation*, 122–123.

113. Dube, *Other Ways of Reading*, 8–9.

114. Dube, *Other Ways of Reading*, 9.

115. Dube, *Postcolonial Feminist Interpretation*, 115–117, 39–41. See also Dube, "Toward a Post-Colonial Feminist," 98.

116. Dube, *Postcolonial Feminist Interpretation*, 24.

117. Dube, "Toward a Post-Colonial Feminist," 97.

118. Dube, "Toward a Post-Colonial Feminist," 99.

119. Dube, *Postcolonial Feminist Interpretation*, 122–123.

120. Phyllis Trible, "Eve and Adam: Genesis 2–3 Reread," in *Womanspirit Rising: A Feminist Reader in Religion*, ed. Carol P. Christ and Judith Plaskow (New York: HaperCollins, 1992), 74–83.

121. Phyllis Trible, "Eve and Miriam: From the Margins to the Center," in *Feminist Approaches to the Bible*, ed. Hershel Shanks (Washington: Biblical Archaeology Society, 1996), 5–24, here 9–10.

122. Trible, "Eve and Adam," 74.

123. See Trible, *Texts of Terror*.

124. Trible, "Eve and Adam," 75; Trible, "Eve and Miriam," 11–12.

125. Trible, "Eve and Adam," 76.

126. Trible, "Eve and Adam," 76; Trible, "Eve and Miriam," 13–14.

127. Trible, "Eve and Adam," 77.

128. Trible, "Eve and Adam," 77.

129. Trible, "Eve and Adam," 78.

130. Trible, "Eve and Adam," 78.

131. Trible, "Eve and Adam," 79.

132. Trible, "Eve and Adam," 79.

133. Trible, "Eve and Adam," 79.

134. Trible, "Eve and Adam," 80.

135. Trible, "Eve and Adam," 80.

136. Trible, "Eve and Adam," 81.

137. Hidayatullah, "The Qur'anic Rib-ectomy," 164; Chaudhry, "Producing Gender-Egalitarian Islamic Law," 88, 95.

138. Clarke, "Hijab According to the Hadith," 252.

139. Chaudhry, " 'I Wanted One Thing,' " 418. See also Jonathan Brown, "Even If It's Not True It's True: Using Unreliable Hadiths in Sunni Islam," *Journal of Religious Ethics* 39, no. 3 (September 2011): 1–52.

140. See, Schüssler Fiorenza, *But She Said*, 53.

141. Tuksal, "Misogynist Reports," 137.

142. Clarke, "Hijab According to the Hadith," 262.

143. Clarke, "Hijab According to the Hadith," 215, 270.

144. Mernissi, *The Veil and the Male Elite*, 10.

145. Mernissi, *The Veil and the Male Elite*, 9, 10, 195.

146. Mohja Kahf, " 'The Water of Hajar' and Other Poems: A Performance of Poetry and Prose," *The Muslim World* 91 (Spring 2001): 31–44, here 31.

147. Kahf, " 'The Water of Hajar,' " 38.

148. Chaudhry, "Producing Gender-Egalitarian Islamic Law," 92.

149. Aisha Geissinger, *Gender and Muslim Constructions of Exegetical Authority: A Rereading of the Classical Genre of Qur'an Commentary* (Leiden: Brill, 2015), 211, 247. See also Aisha Geissinger, "No, a Woman Did Not 'Edit the Qur'ān': Towards a Methodologically Coherent Approach to a Tradition Portraying a Woman and

Written Quranic Materials," *Journal of the American Academy of Religion* 85, no. 2 (January 2017): 416–445.

150. Georgina L. Jardim also discusses various female figures as rhetorical constructions. See Georgina L. Jardim, *Rediscovering the Female Voice in Islamic Scripture: Women and Silence* (Surrey: Ashgate, 2014), 35–64.

151. Geissinger, *Gender and Muslim Constructions*, 207–208.

152. Hidayatullah, "The Qur'anic Rib-ectomy," 150–151.

153. Hidayatullah, "The Qur'anic Rib-ectomy," 167.

154. See Lamptey, *Never Wholly Other*.

155. Hidayatullah, "The Qur'anic Rib-ectomy," 163.

156. Hidayatullah, "The Qur'anic Rib-ectomy," 154. See also Barbara Freyer Stowasser, *Women in the Qur'an, Traditions, and Interpretation* (New York: Oxford University Press, 1994), 22–23.

157. For example, Ruether, "Anthropology: Humanity as Male and Female," in *Sexism and God-Talk*, 93–115; Mary McClintock Fulkerson, "Contesting the Gendered Subject: A Feminist Account of the *Imago Dei*," in *Horizons in Feminist Theology: Identity, Tradition, and Norms*, ed. Rebecca Chopp and Sheila Greeve Davaney (Minneapolis, MN: Fortress, 1997), 99–115. Barlas mentions feminist diagnoses of the issues with the Genesis 2 account. (Barlas, *"Believing Women" in Islam*, 138–139.)

158. Hidayatullah, "The Qur'anic Rib-ectomy," 166–167.

159. Chaudhry, " 'I Wanted One Thing,' " 424.

160. Lamptey, *Never Wholly Other*, 21–24.

161. Nimat Hafez Barazangi, "The Absence of Muslim Women in Shaping Islamic Thought: Foundations of Muslims' Peaceful and Just Co-Existence," *Journal of Law and Religion* 24, no. 2 (2008–2009): 403–432, here 412.

162. Hill Fletcher, "Gift to the Prophet from a King," 28.

163. See Aysha Hidayatullah, "Mariyya the Copt: Gender, Sex, and Heritage in the Legacy of Muhammad's umm walad," *Islam and Christian-Muslim Relations* 23 (2010): 221–243.

164. Kecia Ali, *The Lives of Muhammad* (Cambridge, MA: Harvard University Press, 2014). See also Ruth Roded, "Muslim Women Reclaim the Life-Story of the Prophet: 'A'isha 'Abd al-Rahman, Assia Djebar, and Nadia Yassine," *The Muslim World* 103 (2013): 334–346.

165. Khan, *The Translation of the Meanings of Sahih al-Bukhari*, Hadith 5149, 65.

166. Chaudhry, "Producing Gender Egalitarian Islamic Law," 104; Shaikh, "Knowledge, Women and Gender," 107.

CHAPTER 5

1. Ali, " 'A Beautiful Example,' " 273–291.

2. Schimmel, *And Muhammad Is His Messenger*.

3. Schimmel, *And Muhammad Is His Messenger*, 25. See also Stowasser, *Women in the Qur'an*, 15–20.

4. Schimmel, *And Muhammad Is His Messenger*, 26.

5. Schimmel, *And Muhammad Is His Messenger*, 31.

6. Schimmel, *And Muhammad Is His Messenger*, 36, 40.

7. Schimmel, *And Muhammad Is His Messenger*, 55.

8. Schimmel, *And Muhammad Is His Messenger*, 238.

9. Schimmel, *And Muhammad Is His Messenger*, 60; Stowasser, *Women in the Qur'an*, 77.

10. Schimmel, *And Muhammad Is His Messenger*, 60.

11. See also Ali, "The Disobedient Prophet," 392; Ali, *Sexual Ethics and Islam*, 177–183.

12. See Lamptey, *Never Wholly Other*, 154–181.

13. Schimmel, *And Muhammad Is His Messenger*, 71.

14. Schimmel, *And Muhammad Is His Messenger*, 83–92.

15. Shaikh, "Islamic Law, Sufism, and Gender," 119. See also Schimmel, *And Muhammad Is His Messenger*, 134.

16. Schimmel, *And Muhammad Is His Messenger*, 134.

17. Barlas, *"Believing Women" in Islam*, 109.

18. Barlas, *"Believing Women" in Islam*, 112, 119.

19. Barlas, *"Believing Women" in Islam*, 120–121.

20. Barlas, *"Believing Women" in Islam*, 122.

21. Barlas, *"Believing Women" in Islam*, 122.

22. Barlas, *"Believing Women" in Islam*, 123.

23. Barlas, *"Believing Women" in Islam*, 128.

24. Ali, "The Disobedient Prophet," 391; Ali, " 'A Beautiful Example,' " 274.

25. Ali, *Sexual Ethics and Islam*, 175.

26. Ali, *Sexual Ethics and Islam*, 184–185.

27. Ali, *Sexual Ethics and Islam*, 185.

28. Ali, " 'A Beautiful Example,' " 274.

29. Chaudhry, "Producing Gender-Egalitarian Islamic Law," 89.

30. Chaudhry, "Producing Gender-Egalitarian Islamic Law," 90.

31. Chaudhry, "Producing Gender-Egalitarian Islamic Law," 104.

32. Stowasser, *Women in the Qur'an*, 85–87.

33. Barlas, *"Believing Women" in Islam*, 124.

34. Stowasser, *Women in the Qur'an*, 97–98; Barbara Freyer Stowasser, "The Mothers of the Believers in the Hadith," *The Muslim World* 82, no. 1–2 (January–April 1992): 1–36, here 4–7.

35. Stowasser, "The Mothers of the Believers," 6.

36. Shaikh, "Islamic Law, Sufism, and Gender," 122; Sa'diyya Shaikh, "In Search of 'Al-Insān': Sufism, Islamic Law, and Gender," *Journal of the American Academy of Religion* 77, no. 4 (December 2009): 781–822, here 802–806.

37. Shaikh, "Islamic Law, Sufism, and Gender," 122; Shaikh, "In Search of 'Al-Insān,' " 806.

38. Shaikh, "Islamic Law, Sufism, and Gender," 125–126.

39. Stowasser, *Women in the Qur'an*, 20.

40. Stowasser, *Women in the Qur'an*, 77; Jardim, *Rediscovering the Female Voice*, 37.

41. Shaikh, "Islamic Law, Sufism, and Gender," 126.

42. Schimmel, *And Muhammad Is His Messenger*, 24.

43. Schimmel, *And Muhammad Is His Messenger*, 72.

44. For a brief overview of central feminist debates, see "The Virgin Mary: Many Images, Many Interests," in Marcella Maria Althaus-Reid and Lisa Isherwood, *Controversies in Feminist Theology* (London: SCM, 2007), 63–80.

45. Marcella Althaus-Reid, *Indecent Theology: Theological Perversions in Sex, Gender and Politics* (London: Routledge, 2000), 57.

46. Elina Vuola, *Limits of Liberation: Praxis as Method of Latin American Liberation Theology and Feminist Theology* (Helsinki: Suomalainen Tiedeakatemia, 1997).

47. Elisabeth Schüssler Fiorenza, *Transforming Vision: Explorations in Feminist Theology* (Minneapolis, MN: Fortress, 2011), 197.

48. Schüssler Fiorenza, *Transforming Vision*, 198. See also Elisabeth Schüssler Fiorenza, *Jesus: Miriam's Child, Sophia's Prophet; Critical Issues in Feminist Christology*, Second Edition (London: Bloomsbury, 2015), 179–184.

49. Schüssler Fiorenza, *Transforming Vision*, 201.

50. Schüssler Fiorenza, *Transforming Vision*, 210–213.

51. Schüssler Fiorenza, *Jesus: Miriam's Child*, 184–186; Schüssler Fiorenza, *Transforming Vision*, 202–203.

52. Schüssler Fiorenza, *Transforming Vision*, 203.

53. Schüssler Fiorenza, *Transforming Vision*, 203–204; Schüssler Fiorenza, *Jesus: Miriam's Child*, 187–190.

54. Schüssler Fiorenza, *Transforming Vision*, 203.

55. Schüssler Fiorenza, *Transforming Vision*, 203.

56. Schüssler Fiorenza, *Transforming Vision*, 205.

57. Schüssler Fiorenza, *Jesus: Miriam's Child*, 190.

58. Schüssler Fiorenza, *Jesus: Miriam's Child*, 191. See also Tina Beattie, *God's Mother, Eve's Advocate: A Marian Narrative of Women's Salvation* (London: Continuum, 2002).

59. Schüssler Fiorenza, *Jesus: Miriam's Child*, 192.

60. Schüssler Fiorenza, *Jesus: Miriam's Child*, 192.

61. Schüssler Fiorenza, *Jesus: Miriam's Child*, 195.

62. Schüssler Fiorenza, *Transforming Vision*, 207.

63. Schüssler Fiorenza, *Transforming Vision*, 207.

64. See also Schüssler Fiorenza, *Jesus: Miriam's Child*, 200–205.

65. Schüssler Fiorenza, *Transforming Vision*, 209.

66. Elina Vuola, "Seriously Harmful for Your Health? Religion, Feminism and Sexuality in Latin America," in *Liberation Theology and Sexuality*, 2nd ed., ed. Marcella Althaus-Reid (London: SCM, 2006, 2009), 137–162, here 139.

67. Vuola, "Seriously Harmful," 143; Elina Vuola, "La *Morenita* on Skis: Women's Popular Marian Piety and Feminist Research on Religion," in *The Oxford Handbook of Feminist Theology*, ed. Mary McClintock Fulkerson and Sheila Briggs (Oxford: Oxford University Press, 2012), 494–524, here 497.

68. Vuola, "Seriously Harmful," 143.

69. Vuola, *Limits of Liberation*, 174.

70. Vuola, "Seriously Harmful," 141–142; Vuola, *Limits of Liberation*, 161, 176–177.

71. Vuola, *Limits of Liberation*, 178.

72. Vuola, "Seriously Harmful," 145.

73. Vuola, "Seriously Harmful," 145. Vuola, here, engages with the work of Evelyn Stevens on *marianismo* and *machismo*. See, Evelyn P. Stevens, *Marianismo: The Other Face of Machismo in Latin America* (Pittsburgh: University of Pittsburgh Press, 1973).

74. Vuola, *Limits of Liberation*, 163; Vuola, "La *Morenita* on Skis," 499–500.

75. Vuola, "Seriously Harmful," 148.

76. Vuola, "Seriously Harmful," 148, 154.

77. Vuola, "La *Morenita* on Skis," 494, 503.

78. Vuola, "Seriously Harmful," 152.

79. Vuola, "Seriously Harmful," 150.

80. Vuola, "La *Morenita* on Skis," 503.

81. Vuola, "Seriously Harmful," 152–154.

82. Vuola, "La *Morenita* on Skis," 497, 516.

83. Vuola, "Seriously Harmful," 150.

84. Vuola, "La *Morenita* on Skis," 516–517.

85. Marcella Althaus-Reid, "When God Is a Rich White Woman Who Does Not Walk: The Hermeneutical Circle of Mariology and the Construction of Femininity in Latin America," *Theology and Sexuality* 1, no. 1 (1994): 55–72, here 55–56, 67; Althaus-Reid, *Indecent Theology*, 40, 46.

86. Marcella Maria Althaus-Reid and Lisa Isherwood, eds., *Controversies in Feminist Theology* (London: SCM, 2007), 73–75.

87. Althaus-Reid, "When God Is a Rich White Woman," 55.

88. Althaus-Reid, "When God Is a Rich White Woman," 56.

89. Althaus-Reid, "When God Is a Rich White Woman," 58, 66.

90. Althaus-Reid, "When God Is a Rich White Woman," 70.

91. Althaus-Reid, *Indecent Theology*, 34.

92. Althaus-Reid, *Indecent Theology*, 49.

93. Althaus-Reid, *Indecent Theology*, 39, 72.

94. Althaus-Reid, *Indecent Theology*, 35–36, 45.

95. Althaus-Reid, *Indecent Theology*, 40–43, 50, 72. See Ivone Gebara and Maria Clara Bingemer, *Mary: Mother of God, Mother of the Poor*, trans. Phillip Berryman (Eugene, OR: Wipf & Stock, 2004).

96. Althaus-Reid, *Indecent Theology*, 77–78.

97. Althaus-Reid, *Indecent Theology*, 44.

98. Althaus-Reid, *Indecent Theology*, 50–52, 70–71.

99. Althaus-Reid, *Indecent Theology*, 48.

100. Althaus-Reid, *Indecent Theology*, 57, 53–54.

101. Althaus-Reid, *Indecent Theology*, 49.

102. Althaus-Reid, *Indecent* Theology, 60–63.

103. Althaus-Reid, *Indecent Theology*, 36.

104. Althaus-Reid, *Indecent Theology*, 51–52.

105. Althaus-Reid, *Indecent Theology*, 36. See also Marcella Althaus-Reid, "Doing a Theology from Disappeared Bodies: Theology, Sexuality, and the Excluded Bodies of the Discourses of Latin American Liberation Theology," in *The Oxford Handbook of Feminist Theology*, ed. Mary McClintock Fulkerson and Sheila Briggs (Oxford: Oxford University Press, 2012), 441–455, here 445–449.

106. Althaus-Reid, *Indecent Theology*, 40.

107. Althaus-Reid, "When God Is a Rich White Woman," 70.

108. Althaus-Reid, "When God is a Rich White Woman," 71.

109. Althaus-Reid, "When God is a Rich White Woman," 63–64. See also Althaus-Reid and Isherwood, *Controversies in Feminist Theology*, 78–80. Other scholars, including Tina Beattie, also discuss Mary in relation to queer theology. See, Tina Beattie, "Queen of Heaven," in *Queer Theology: Rethinking the Western Body*, ed. Gerard Loughlin (Malden, MA: Blackwell, 2007), 293–304; Edwin Greelee, "Qu(e)er(y)ing Mary: Popular Mariology as Visual Liberation Theology," *Decolonial Horizons* no. 2 (2016): 75–104.

110. Althaus-Reid, "When God Is a Rich White Woman," 70.

111. Althaus-Reid, "When God is a Rich White Woman," 71.

112. Althaus-Reid, "When God Is a Rich White Woman," 79.

113. Althaus-Reid, "When God Is a Rich White Woman," 84.

114. Nasr, *Ideals and Realities*, 32; Madigan, "Muslim-Christian Dialogue," 58; Madigan, "Jesus and Muhammad," 95; Madigan, "Mary and Muhammad," 417–427.

115. For example, see Beverly Roberts Gaventa and Cynthia L. Rigby, eds., *Blessed One: Protestant Perspectives on Mary* (Louisville, KY: Westminster John Knox, 2002); Nora O. Lozano-Díaz, "Ignored Virgin or Unaware Women: A Mexican–American Protestant Reflection on The Virgin of Guadalupe," in *A Reader in Latina Feminist Theology: Religion and Justice*, ed. María Pilar Aquino, Daisy L. Machado, and Jeanette Rodríguez (Austin: University of Texas Press, 2002), 204–216.

116. Stowasser, *Women in the Qur'an*, 20.

117. See Qur'an 19:16–58. See also Stowasser, *Women in the Qur'an*, 77; Jardim, *Rediscovering the Female Voice*, 61–62. Kecia Ali also discusses how the Qur'anic text functions to exclude women from the role of messenger. (Kecia Ali, "Destabilizing Gender, Reproducing Maternity: Mary in the Qur'an," unpublished manuscript, 2017, 6–9).

118. Shaikh, "Islamic Law, Sufism, and Gender," 126–127.

119. Stowasser, *Women in the Qur'an*, 77–81; Jardim, *Rediscovering the Female Voice*, 61–63.

120. Jardim, *Rediscovering the Female Voice*, 37, 63. See also Shaikh, "Islamic Law, Sufism, and Gender," 126.

121. Shaikh, "In Search of 'Al-Insān,'" 795.

122. Shaikh, "In Search of 'Al-Insān,'" 797.

123. Shaikh, "In Search of 'Al-Insān,'" 797–798.

124. Shaikh, "Islamic Law, Sufism, and Gender," 107.

125. See, Lamptey, *Never Wholly Other*.

126. Nasr, *Ideals and Realities*, 32. See also Madigan, "Muslim-Christian Dialogue," 58; Madigan, "Jesus and Muhammad," 95; Madigan, "Mary and Muhammad," 417–427.

127. Althaus-Reid, *Indecent Theology*, 40, 49.

128. Khan, *The Translation of the Meanings of Sahih al-Bukhari*, Vol. 4, Book 54, No. 460. See also Chaudhry, *Domestic Violence*, 41–48; Abou El Fadl, *Speaking in God's Name*, 214.

129. Khan, *The Translation of the Meanings of Sahih al-Bukhari*, Vol. 1, Book 6, Number 301. See also Chaudhry, *Domestic Violence*, 44–46; Tuksal, "Misogynist Reports," 134–135, 136–151.

130. Stowasser, *Women in the Qur'an*, 85–87; Stowasser, "The Mothers of the Believers," 6.

131. Stowasser, "The Mothers of the Believers," 4.

132. Stowasser, "The Mothers of the Believers," 19–23.

133. Stowasser, "The Mothers of the Believers," 23.

134. Stowasser, "The Mothers of the Believers," 26, 34–35.

135. Jardim, *Rediscovering the Female Voice*, 44–46, 49, 53–57.

136. Jardim, *Rediscovering the Female Voice*, 60, 50.

137. Jardim here refers to Farid Esack. (Jardim, *Rediscovering the Female Voice*, 38.)

138. Chaudhry, "Producing Gender-Egalitarian Islamic Law," 90–92.

139. Chaudhry, "'I Wanted One Thing,'" 421.

140. Chaudhry, "Producing Gender-Egalitarian Islamic Law," 92.

141. Ali, "Destabilizing Gender," 1.

142. Ali, "Destabilizing Gender," 2.

143. Ali, "Destabilizing Gender," 3.

144. Althaus-Reid, *Indecent Theology*, 64.

145. Ali, "Destabilizing Gender," 23.

CHAPTER 6

1. Ali, "Progressive Muslims and Islamic Jurisprudence," 164–167; Shaikh, "Islamic Law, Sufism, and Gender," 106–112, 128; Shaikh, *Sufi Narratives of Intimacy*, 222–228;

Shaikh, "Knowledge, Women and Gender," 107; Chaudhry, *Domestic Violence*, 11–14, 196–198. (Chaudhry discusses competing cosmologies, patriarchal and egalitarian).

2. Shaikh, "Islamic Law, Sufism, and Gender," 112.
3. Shaikh, "Islamic Law, Sufism, and Gender," 111–112.
4. Shaikh, "Islamic Law, Sufism, and Gender," 129.
5. wadud, *Inside the Gender Jihad*, 28.
6. wadud, "The Ethics of *Tawhid*," 265. See also 257.
7. wadud, *Inside the Gender Jihad*, 28.
8. wadud, "The Ethics of *Tawhid*," 267.
9. wadud, *Qur'an and Woman*, 26.
10. See also wadud, *Qur'an and Woman*, 29.
11. wadud, *Inside the Gender Jihad*, 24–32; wadud, "The Ethics of *Tawhid*," 257, 271–273.
12. wadud, *Inside the Gender Jihad*, 30–31; wadud, "The Ethics of *Tawhid*," 271.
13. wadud, "The Ethics of *Tawhid*," 271.
14. wadud, *Qur'an and Woman*, 15; wadud, *Inside the Gender Jihad*, 32; Barlas, *"Believing Women" in Islam*, 129; Hassan, "Feminism in Islam," 262.
15. Shaikh, "Islamic Law, Sufism, and Gender," 119. See also Shaikh, *Sufi Narratives of Intimacy*, 75–84.
16. Shaikh, "Islamic Law, Sufism, and Gender," 120; Shaikh, *Sufi Narratives of Intimacy*, 79, 203. See also Shaikh, "In Search of 'Al-Insān.'"
17. Shaikh, "Islamic Law, Sufism, and Gender," 121.
18. wadud, *Qur'an and Woman*, 19.
19. wadud, *Qur'an and Woman*, 20.
20. wadud, *Qur'an and Woman*, 21.
21. wadud, *Qur'an and Woman*, 21.
22. Barlas, *"Believing Women" in Islam*, 133, 136.
23. wadud, *Qur'an and Woman*, 22, 26.
24. Hidayatullah, *Feminist Edges*, 154–156.
25. wadud, "The Ethics of *Tawhid*," 271.
26. wadud, *Qur'an and Woman*, 23.
27. wadud, *Qur'an and Woman*, 23.
28. wadud, *Qur'an and Woman*, 25.
29. Hidayatullah, "The Qur'anic Rib-ectomy," 150–151.
30. Hassan, "Feminism in Islam," 253.
31. Hassan, "Feminism in Islam," 254.
32. Hassan, "Feminism in Islam," 254.
33. Hassan, "Feminism in Islam," 254–255.
34. Hassan, "Feminism in Islam," 257. See also Barlas, *"Believing Women" in Islam*, 136.
35. Hassan, "Feminism in Islam," 260. See also Riffat Hassan, "Woman and Man's 'Fall': A Qur'anic Theological Perspective," in *Muslima Theology: The Voices of Muslim Women Theologians*, ed. Ednan Aslan, Marcia Hermansen, and Elif Medeni (Frankfurt Am Main: Peter Lang, 2013), 101–113.

36. Hassan, "Feminism in Islam," 268.

37. Barlas, *"Believing Women" in Islam*, 138–139.

38. Hassan, "Feminism in Islam," 262.

39. Barlas, *"Believing Women" in Islam*, 129.

40. See also Lamptey, *Never Wholly Other*, 244–246; Barlas, *"Believing Women" in Islam*, 142.

41. Shaikh, "Islamic Law, Sufism, and Gender," 114.

42. Shaikh, "Islamic Law, Sufism, and Gender," 108, 117–118. See also Shaikh, *Sufi Narratives of Intimacy*, 221–222.

43. wadud, "The Ethics of *Tawhid*," 269. See also wadud, *Inside the Gender Jihad*, 32–37.

44. wadud, *Inside the Gender Jihad*, 33–37; wadud, "The Ethics of *Tawhid*," 269, 273. See also Nina Hoel and Sa'diyya Shaikh, "Sexing Islamic Theology: Theorising Women's Experience and Gender through *'abd-Allah* and *khalifah*," *Journal for Islamic Studies* 33 (2013): 127–150, here 131.

45. wadud, *Inside the Gender Jihad*, 23.

46. wadud, *Inside the Gender Jihad*, 24.

47. Barlas, *"Believing Women" in Islam*, 140.

48. See, Hoel and Shaikh, "Sexing Islamic Theology," 133–134.

49. Lamptey, *Never Wholly Other*, 146. See also 142–154.

50. Lamptey, *Never Wholly Other*, 237–238.

51. Barlas, *"Believing Women" in Islam*, 142.

52. Barlas, *"Believing Women" in Islam*, 142.

53. Barlas, *"Believing Women" in Islam*, 145.

54. See Lamptey, *Never Wholly Other*.

55. Barlas, *"Believing Women" in Islam*, 148. See also wadud, *Inside the Gender Jihad*, 25–27.

56. Barlas, *"Believing Women" in Islam*, 140.

57. Hoel and Shaikh, "Sexing Islamic Theology," 128–135.

58. Hoel and Shaikh, "Sexing Islamic Theology," 135.

59. Hoel and Shaikh, "Sexing Islamic Theology," 128.

60. See, for example, Ruether, *Sexism and God-Talk*, 93–117, 159–192; Emilie M. Townes, *Womanist Ethics and the Cultural Production of Evil* (New York: Palgrave Macmillan, 2006).

61. M. Shawn Copeland, *Enfleshing Freedom: Body, Race, Being* (Minneapolis, MN: Fortress, 2010).

62. Jeannine Hill Fletcher, *Motherhood as Metaphor: Engendering Interreligious Dialogue* (New York: Fordham University Press, 2012); Jeannine Hill Fletcher, *Monopoly on Salvation? A Feminist Approach to Religious Pluralism* (New York: Continuum, 2005).

63. Delores S. Williams, *Sisters in the Wilderness: The Challenge of Womanist God-Talk* (Maryknoll, NY: Orbis, 1993).

64. Copeland, *Enfleshing Freedom*, 8.

65. Copeland, *Enfleshing Freedom*, 7.
66. Copeland, *Enfleshing Freedom*, 2.
67. Copeland, *Enfleshing Freedom*, 3.
68. Copeland, *Enfleshing Freedom*, 9–15.
69. Copeland, *Enfleshing Freedom*, 15.
70. Copeland, *Enfleshing Freedom*, 29–38.
71. Copeland, *Enfleshing Freedom*, 38.
72. Copeland, *Enfleshing Freedom*, 38.
73. Copeland, *Enfleshing Freedom*, 52.
74. Copeland, *Enfleshing Freedom*, 62. Although I focus on Copeland's theological anthropology, she also examines Christology in relation to sexuality. See 62–84.
75. Copeland, *Enfleshing Freedom*, 83.
76. Copeland, *Enfleshing Freedom*, 9.
77. Copeland, *Enfleshing Freedom*, 23–24.
78. Copeland, *Enfleshing Freedom*, 25, 24.
79. Copeland, *Enfleshing Freedom*, 85–88.
80. Copeland, *Enfleshing Freedom*, 92.
81. Copeland, *Enfleshing Freedom*, 92.
82. Copeland, *Enfleshing Freedom*, 89.
83. Copeland, *Enfleshing Freedom*, 2, 93, 95.
84. Copeland, *Enfleshing Freedom*, 100.
85. Hill Fletcher, *Motherhood as Metaphor*.
86. Hill Fletcher, *Motherhood as Metaphor*, 5.
87. Hill Fletcher, *Motherhood as Metaphor*, 4.
88. Hill Fletcher, *Motherhood as Metaphor*, 6.
89. Hill Fletcher, *Motherhood as Metaphor*, 40.
90. Hill Fletcher, *Motherhood as Metaphor*, 40.
91. Hill Fletcher, *Motherhood as Metaphor*, 45.
92. Hill Fletcher, *Motherhood as Metaphor*, 50.
93. Hill Fletcher, *Motherhood as Metaphor*, 53.
94. Hill Fletcher, *Motherhood as Metaphor*, 56–57.
95. Hill Fletcher, *Motherhood as Metaphor*, 54–55.
96. Hill Fletcher, *Motherhood as Metaphor*, 208.
97. Hill Fletcher, *Motherhood as Metaphor*, 73.
98. Hill Fletcher, *Motherhood as Metaphor*, 110.
99. Hill Fletcher, *Motherhood as Metaphor*, 112.
100. Hill Fletcher, *Motherhood as Metaphor*, 121.
101. Hill Fletcher, *Motherhood as Metaphor*, 131.
102. Hill Fletcher, *Motherhood as Metaphor*, 128–129.
103. Hill Fletcher, *Motherhood as Metaphor*, 168.
104. Hill Fletcher, *Motherhood as Metaphor*, 170–175.
105. Hill Fletcher, *Motherhood as Metaphor*, 180.

106. Hill Fletcher, *Motherhood as Metaphor*, 184.

107. Hill Fletcher, *Motherhood as Metaphor*, 195–196, 201.

108. Williams, *Sisters in the Wilderness*, xi–xiii.

109. Williams, *Sisters in the Wilderness*, xiv.

110. Williams, *Sisters in the Wilderness*, 144–177.

111. Williams, *Sisters in the Wilderness*, 2. See also Delores Williams, "Hagar in African American Biblical Appropriation," in *Hagar, Sarah, and Their Children: Jewish, Christian, and Muslim Perspectives*, ed. Phyllis Trible and Letty M. Russell (Louisville, KY: Westminster John Knox, 2006), 177–184, here 171.

112. Williams, *Sisters in the Wilderness*, 2.

113. Williams, *Sisters in the Wilderness*, 2–5.

114. Williams, *Sisters in the Wilderness*, 14–22.

115. Williams, *Sisters in the Wilderness*, 21.

116. Williams, *Sisters in the Wilderness*, 26.

117. Williams, *Sisters in the Wilderness*, 32.

118. Williams, *Sisters in the Wilderness*, 3.

119. Williams, "Hagar," 172–173.

120. Williams, *Sisters in the Wilderness*, 40, 61, 88.

121. Williams, *Sisters in the Wilderness*, 108.

122. Williams, *Sisters in the Wilderness*, 118.

123. Williams, "Hagar," 122.

124. Williams, "Hagar," 125, 129, 136.

125. Williams, "Hagar," 172.

126. Williams, "Hagar," 174.

127. Williams, "Hagar," 178.

128. Williams, "Hagar," 174–178.

129. Williams, "Hagar," 181–182.

130. See Lamptey, *Never Wholly Other*, 194–197, 212–217, 228–232.

131. Lamptey, *Never Wholly Other*, 141–154.

132. wadud, "The Ethics of *Tawhid*," 258. See also Debra Mubashshir Majeed, "Womanism Encounters Islam: A Muslim Scholar Considers the Efficacy of a Method Rooted in the Academy and the Church," in *Deeper Shades of Purple: Womanism in Religion and Society*, ed. Stacey M. Floyd-Thomas (New York: New York University Press, 2006), 38–53. Sherman Jackson also explores classical Islamic theology in relation to the "problem of black suffering." See Sherman A. Jackson, *Islam and The Problem of Black Suffering* (New York: Oxford University Press, 2009).

133. wadud, "The Ethics of *Tawhid*," 259.

134. wadud, "The Ethics of *Tawhid*," 259.

135. wadud, *Inside the Gender Jihad*, 123, 125.

136. Italics added. wadud, *Inside the Gender Jihad*, 126.

137. wadud, *Inside the Gender Jihad*, 129–143, 152–153.

138. wadud, *Inside the Gender Jihad*, 143.

139. wadud, *Inside the Gender Jihad*, 143.

140. wadud, *Inside the Gender Jihad*, 148.

141. wadud, *Inside the Gender Jihad*, 143.

142. wadud, *Inside the Gender Jihad*, 144. See also 152–153.

143. wadud, *Inside the Gender Jihad*, 155–157.

144. Hibba Abugideiri, "Hagar: A Historical Model for 'Gender Jihad,'" in *Daughters of Abraham: Feminist Thought in Judaism, Christianity, and Islam*, ed. John Esposito and Yvonne Haddad (Gainesville: University Press of Florida, 2001), 81–107, here 82, 84–85.

145. Abugideiri, "Hagar," 82–83.

146. Copeland, *Enfleshing Freedom*, 100.

147. Esack, *Qur'an, Liberation and Pluralism*, 98–103.

148. Esack, *Qur'an, Liberation and Pluralism*, 98.

149. Esack, *Qur'an, Liberation and Pluralism*, 87.

CHAPTER 7

1. Some helpful resources on feminist liturgy include: Marjorie Procter-Smith and Janet Walton, eds., *Women at Worship: Interpretations of North American Diversity* (Louisville, KY: Westminster John Knox, 1993); Janet Walton, *Feminist Liturgy: A Matter of Justice* (Collegeville, MN: Liturgical, 2000); "Part IV: Feminist Liturgical and Artistic Frontiers," in *New Feminist Christianity: Many Voices, Many Views*, ed. Mary E. Hunt and Diann L. Neu (Woodstock, VT: Skylight Paths Publishing, 2010), 167–232; Marjorie Procter-Smith, *In Her Own Rite: Constructing Feminist Liturgical Tradition* (Nashville: Abingdon, 1990); Teresa Berger, *Dissident Daughters: Feminist Liturgies in Global Context* (Louisville, KY: Westminster John Knox, 2001).

2. Hammer, *American Muslim Women*.

3. For example, Hammer, *American Muslim Women*.

4. Ahmed Elewa and Laury Silvers, "'I Am One of the People': A Survey and Analysis of Legal Arguments on Women-Led Prayer in Islam," *Journal of Law and Religion* 26, no. 1 (2010–2011): 141–171, here 153–158; Shaikh, "Islamic Law, Sufism, and Gender," 127–128.

5. wadud, *Inside the Gender Jihad*, 168. See also 185–186.

6. Nina Hoel, "Sexualising the Sacred, Sacralising Sexuality: An Analysis of Public Responses to Muslim Women's Religious Leadership in the Context of a Cape Town Mosque," *Journal for the Study of Religion* 26, no. 2 (2013): 25–42, here 35–36.

7. Hammer, *American Muslim Women*, 56–71.

8. Hammer, *American Muslim Women*, 56.

9. Hammer, *American Muslim Women*, 140.

10. Hoel, "Sexualising the Sacred," 36.

11. Laury Silvers, "Islamic Jurisprudence, 'Civil' Disobedience, and Woman-Led Prayer," in *The Columbia Sourcebook of Muslims in the United States*, ed. Edward E. Curtis IV (New York: Columbia, 2008): 246–252, here 247. See also Meena Sharify-Funk and Munira Kassam Haddad, "Where Do Women 'Stand' in Islam? Negotiating Contemporary Muslim Prayer Leadership in North America," *Feminist Review* 102, no. 1 (2012): 41–61, here 45, 59.

12. Ingrid Mattson, "Can a Woman Be an Imam? Debating Form and Function in Muslim Women's Leadership," in *The Columbia Sourcebook of Muslims in the United States*, ed. Edward E. Curtis IV (New York: Columbia, 2008): 252–263, here 253.

13. Hammer, *American Muslim Women*, 3, 15. See also Silvers "Islamic Jurisprudence," 252.

14. See Juliane Hammer, "Invisible Giants: On Women, Mosques, and Radical Activism by Juliane Hammer," *Feminism and Religion Online* (October 15, 2015), accessed July 2017, https://feminismandreligion.com/2015/10/15/invisible-giants-on-women-mosques-and-radical-activism-by-juliane-hammer/.

15. Elewa and Silvers, " 'I *Am* One of the People,' " 142.

16. Sharify-Funk and Haddad, "Where Do Women 'Stand' in Islam?," 59. See also 42, 46.

17. Tutin Aryanti, "A Claim to Space: Debating Female Religious Leadership in a Muhammadiyah Mosque in Indonesia," *The Muslim World* 103 (July 2013): 375–388, here 383. See also Marion Holmes Katz, *Prayer in Islamic Thought and Practice* (New York: Cambridge University Press, 2013), 139.

18. Elewa and Silvers, " 'I *Am* One of the People,' " 141.

19. Aryanti, "A Claim to Space," 384.

20. wadud, *Inside the Gender Jihad*, 175.

21. Aryanti, "A Claim to Space," 387.

22. Mattson, "Can a Woman Be an Imam?," 253–254.

23. Hoel, "Sexualising the Sacred," 37.

24. Mattson, "Can a Woman Be an Imam?," 254, 263. See also Abugideiri, "Hagar," 88–90; Hibba Abugideiri, "The Renewed Woman of American Islam: Shifting Lens to the 'Gender Jihad'?," *The Muslim World* 91, no. 1/2 (Spring 2001): 1–18.

25. wadud, *Inside the Gender Jihad*, 183; Silvers, "Islamic Jurisprudence," 248.

26. Silvers, "Islamic Jurisprudence," 248.

27. Etin Anwar, "Sexing the Prayer: The Politics of Ritual and Feminist Activism in Indonesia," in *Muslima Theology: The Voices of Muslim Women Theologians*, ed. Ednan Aslan, Marcia Hermansen, and Elif Medeni (Frankfurt Am Main: Peter Lang, 2013), 197–216, here 198; Elewa and Silvers, " 'I *Am* One of the People,' " 141.

28. Anwar "Sexing the Prayer," 198.

29. Hoel, "Sexualising the Sacred," 25.

30. Hoel, "Sexualising the Sacred," 30.

31. Hoel, "Sexualising the Sacred," 29.

32. Aryanti, "A Claim to Space," 385.

33. Aryanti, "A Claim to Space," 385.

34. See Anwar "Sexing the Prayer," 206–210.

35. Elewa and Silvers, " 'I *Am* One of the People,' " 149.

36. Hoel, "Sexualising the Sacred," 32.

37. Hoel, "Sexualising the Sacred," 32–33.

38. Hoel, "Sexualising the Sacred," 32–35. See also Elewa and Silvers, " 'I *Am* One of the People,' " 149.

39. Hoel, "Sexualising the Sacred," 25.

40. Hoel, "Sexualising the Sacred," 37. See also Aryanti, "A Claim to Space," 387.

41. wadud, *Inside the Gender Jihad*, 172, 177–178.

42. wadud, *Inside the Gender Jihad*, 181. See also Hammer, *American Muslim Women*, 75.

43. wadud, *Inside the Gender Jihad*, 180–183.

44. wadud, *Inside the Gender Jihad*, 172. See also 183.

45. wadud, *Inside the Gender Jihad*, 180.

46. Hammer, *American Muslim Women*, 21.

47. wadud, *Inside the Gender Jihad*, 182.

48. Hammer, *American Muslim Women*, 36–37.

49. Anwar, "Sexing the Prayer," 212–214.

50. Elewa and Silvers, " 'I *Am* One of the People,' " 141–171; Mattson, "Can a Woman Be an Imam?," 255; Anwar "Sexing the Prayer," 204; Silvers, "Islamic Jurisprudence," 249; Katz, *Prayer in Islamic Thought*, 189.

51. See Anwar, "Sexing the Prayer," 208; Celene Ayat Lizzio, "Gendering Ritual: A Muslima's Reading of the Laws of Purity and Ritual Preclusion," in *Muslima Theology: The Voices of Muslim Women Theologians*, ed. Ednan Aslan, Marcia Hermansen, and Elif Medeni (Frankfurt Am Main: Peter Lang, 2013), 174; Aryanti, "A Claim to Space," 379.

52. Silvers, "Islamic Jurisprudence," 249.

53. Silvers, "Islamic Jurisprudence," 249.

54. Hammer, *American Muslim Women*, 100–103; Elewa and Silvers, " 'I *Am* One of the People,' " 163–166.

55. Hammer, *American Muslim Women*, 119.

56. Aryanti, "A Claim to Space," 382.

57. wadud, *Inside the Gender Jihad*, 186.

58. wadud, *Inside the Gender Jihad*, 176, 186.

59. Silvers, "Islamic Jurisprudence," 247; Elewa and Silvers, " 'I *Am* One of the People,' " 150.

60. Silvers, "Islamic Jurisprudence," 250.

61. Elizabeth A. Johnson, *Ask the Beasts: Darwin and the God of Love* (London: Bloomsbury, 2014); Elizabeth A. Johnson, *Truly Our Sister: A Theology of Mary in the Communion of Saints* (New York: Continuum, 2003); Elizabeth

A. Johnson, *She Who Is: The Mystery of God in Feminist Theological Discourse* (New York: Crossroads, 1992).

62. Traci C. West, *Disruptive Christian Ethics: When Racism and Women's Lives Matter* (Louisville, KY: Westminster John Knox, 2006); Traci C. West, *Wounds of the Spirit: Black Women, Violence, and Resistance Ethics* (New York: New York University Press, 1999).

63. Williams, *Sisters in the Wilderness*, 205.

64. Williams, *Sisters in the Wilderness*, 206.

65. Williams, *Sisters in the Wilderness*, 206.

66. Williams, *Sisters in the Wilderness*, 214.

67. Williams, *Sisters in the Wilderness*, 219.

68. Williams, *Sisters in the Wilderness*, 215.

69. Williams, *Sisters in the Wilderness*, 218–219.

70. Johnson, *She Who Is*, 18.

71. Johnson, *She Who Is*, 33–35.

72. Johnson, *She Who Is*, 36.

73. Johnson, *She Who Is*, 36.

74. Johnson, *She Who Is*, 39.

75. Johnson, *She Who Is*, 42–57.

76. Johnson, *She Who Is*, 44–45.

77. Johnson, *She Who Is*, 45.

78. Johnson, *She Who Is*, 47.

79. Johnson, *She Who Is*, 47.

80. Johnson, *She Who Is*, 49.

81. Johnson, *She Who Is*, 241–245, 54–55.

82. Johnson, *She Who Is*, 56–57.

83. Ruether, *Sexism and God-Talk*, 12–18.

84. Ruether, *Sexism and God-Talk*, 12.

85. Ruether, *Sexism and God-Talk*, 12.

86. Ruether, *Sexism and God-Talk*, 12.

87. Ruether, *Sexism and God-Talk*, 13.

88. Ruether, *Sexism and God-Talk*, 13.

89. Ruether, *Sexism and God-Talk*, 14.

90. Ruether, *Sexism and God-Talk*, 15.

91. Ruether, *Sexism and God-Talk*, 15–16.

92. Ruether, *Sexism and God-Talk*, 16–18. I have written elsewhere in more detail about the crises of tradition. See Lamptey, *Never Wholly Other*, 99–103.

93. West, *Disruptive Christian Ethics*, 112.

94. West, *Disruptive Christian Ethics*, 112.

95. West, *Disruptive Christian Ethics*, 114.

96. West, *Disruptive Christian Ethics*, 116.

97. West, *Disruptive Christian Ethics*, 117.

98. West, *Disruptive Christian Ethics*, 118.

99. West, *Disruptive Christian Ethics*, 122.

100. West, *Disruptive Christian Ethics*, 123.

101. West, *Disruptive Christian Ethics*, 124.

102. West, *Disruptive Christian Ethics*, 125.

103. West, *Disruptive Christian Ethics*, 117.

104. West, *Disruptive Christian Ethics*, 128.

105. West, *Disruptive Christian Ethics*, 129.

106. West, *Disruptive Christian Ethics*, 132.

107. West, *Disruptive Christian Ethics*, 132.

108. West, *Disruptive Christian Ethics*, 133.

109. West, *Disruptive Christian Ethics*, 134–135.

110. West, *Disruptive Christian Ethics*, 138.

111. See Lamptey, *Never Wholly Other*, xiii–xiv; Laleh Bakhtiar, trans., *The Sublime Qur'an* (Chicago: IslamicWorld, 2007).

112. One organization working extensively on racism within Muslim communities in the United States is Muslim Anti-Racism Collaborative (MuslimARC). For more information see http://www.muslimarc.org/.

113. Katz, *Prayer in Islamic Thought*, 9.

114. Katz, *Prayer in Islamic Thought*, 139, 148, 203–208; Marion Holmes Katz, *Women in the Mosque: A History of Legal Thought and Social Practice* (New York: Columbia University Press, 2014), 263–265.

115. Katz, *Prayer in Islamic Thought*, 185–186. See also Katz, *Women in the Mosque*, 259–265, 275–277.

116. Katz, *Prayer in Islamic Thought*, 196–202.

117. Katz, *Prayer in Islamic Thought*, 199.

118. Katz, *Prayer in Islamic Thought*, 202.

119. For example, Avianne Tan, "Why Muslim Woman Started 1st All-Female Mosque in the US," *ABC News*, February 4, 2015.

120. Women's Mosque of America website, accessed July 25, 2015, http://womensmosque.com/faq/.

121. Zareena Grewal, *Islam Is a Foreign Country: American Muslims and the Global Crisis of Authority* (New York: New York University Press, 2014).

122. Grewal, *Islam Is a Foreign Country*, 36.

123. Grewal, *Islam Is a Foreign Country*, 36.

124. Grewal, *Islam Is a Foreign Country*, 259.

125. Grewal, *Islam Is a Foreign Country*, 261.

126. Grewal, *Islam Is a Foreign Country*, 264–268.

127. Grewal, *Islam Is a Foreign Country*, 266.

128. Grewal, *Islam Is a Foreign Country*, 286–288.

129. See Lamptey, *Never Wholly Other*.

130. Asma Afsaruddin, "The Hermeneutics of Inter-Faith Relations: Retrieving Moderation and Pluralism as Universal Principles in Qur'anic Exegesis," *Journal of Religious Ethics*, 37, no. 2 (June 2009): 331–354.

131. Afsaruddin, "The Hermeneutics of Inter-Faith Relations," 333.

132. Afsaruddin, "The Hermeneutics of Inter-Faith Relations," 347.

133. Lamptey, *Never Wholly Other*, 171–179. See also 140–171.

Bibliography

Abou El Fadl, Khaled. *Speaking in God's Name: Islamic Law, Authority, and Women*. Oxford: Oneworld, 2001.

Abu Zayd, Nasr. *Reformation of Islamic Thought: A Critical Historical Analysis*. Amsterdam: Amsterdam University Press, 2006.

Abugideiri, Hibba. "Hagar: A Historical Model for 'Gender Jihad.'" In *Daughters of Abraham: Feminist Thought in Judaism, Christianity, and Islam*, edited by John Esposito and Yvonne Haddad, 81–107. Gainesville: University Press of Florida, 2001.

——. "The Renewed Woman of American Islam: Shifting Lens to the 'Gender *Jihad*'?" *The Muslim World* 91, no. 1/2 (Spring 2001): 1–18.

——. "Revisiting the Islamic Past, Deconstructing Male Authority: The Project of Islamic Feminism." *Religion and Literature* 42, no. 1/2 (Spring/Summer 2010): 133–139.

Afsaruddin, Asma. "Discerning a Qur'anic Mandate for Mutually Transformative Dialogue." In *Criteria of Discernment in Interreligious Dialogue*, edited by Catherine Cornille, 101–121. Interreligious Dialogue Series 1. Eugene, OR: Cascade, 2009.

——, ed. *Hermeneutics and Honor in Islamic/ate Societies*. Harvard Middle East Monograph Series. Cambridge, MA: Harvard University Press, 1999.

——. "The Hermeneutics of Inter-Faith Relations: Retrieving Moderation and Pluralism as Universal Principles in Qur'anic Exegesis." *Journal of Religious Ethics* 37, no. 2 (June 2009): 331–354.

Ahmed, Leila. *Women and Gender in Islam*. New Haven, CT: Yale University Press, 1992.

Ali, Kecia. "'A Beautiful Example': The Prophet Muhammad as a Model for Muslim Husbands." *Islamic Studies* 43, no. 2 (2004): 273–291.

——. "Destabilizing Gender, Reproducing Maternity: Mary in the Qur'an." Unpublished manuscript, 2017.

——. "The Disobedient Prophet in Muslim Thought." *Journal of Religious Ethics* 39, no. 3 (September 2011): 391–398.

———. *The Lives of Muhammad.* Cambridge, MA: Harvard University Press, 2014.

———. "On Critique and Careful Reading." *Journal of Feminist Studies in Religion* 32, no. 2 (December 2016): 121–126.

———. "Progressive Muslims and Islamic Jurisprudence: The Necessity for Critical Engagement with Marriage and Divorce Law." In *Progressive Muslims: On Justice, Gender and Pluralism*, edited by Omid Safi, 163–189. Oxford: Oneworld, 2003.

———. *Sexual Ethics and Islam: Feminist Reflections on Qur'an, Hadith and Jurisprudence.* Oxford: Oneworld, 2006.

Althaus-Reid, Marcella Maria. "Doing a Theology from Disappeared Bodies: Theology, Sexuality, and the Excluded Bodies of the Discourses of Latin American Liberation Theology." In *The Oxford Handbook of Feminist Theology*, edited by Mary McClintock Fulkerson and Sheila Briggs, 441–455. Oxford: Oxford University Press, 2012.

———. *Indecent Theology: Theological Perversions in Sex, Gender and Politics.* London: Routledge, 2000.

———. "When God Is a Rich White Woman Who Does Not Walk: The Hermeneutical Circle of Mariology and the Construction of Femininity in Latin America." *Theology and Sexuality* 1, no. 1 (1994): 55–72.

Althaus-Reid, Marcella Maria, and Lisa Isherwood. *Controversies in Feminist Theology.* London: SCM, 2007.

Anwar, Etin. "Sexing the Prayer: The Politics of Ritual and Feminist Activism in Indonesia." In *Muslima Theology: The Voices of Muslim Women Theologians*, edited by Ednan Aslan, Marcia Hermansen, and Elif Medeni, 197–216. Frankfurt Am Main: Peter Lang, 2013.

Aponte, Edwin David, and Miguel A. De La Tore, eds. *Handbook of Latina/o Theologies.* St. Louis, MS: Chalice, 2006.

Aquino, María Pilar. "Latina Feminist Theology: Central Features." In *A Reader in Latina Feminist Theology: Religion and Justice*, edited by María Pilar Aquino, Daisy L. Machado, and Jeanette Rodríguez, 133–160. Austin: University of Texas Press, 2002.

———. *Our Cry for Life: Feminist Theology from Latin America.* Maryknoll, NY: Orbis, 1993.

Aquino, María Pilar, Daisy L. Machado, and Jeanette Rodríguez, eds. *A Reader in Latina Feminist Theology.* Austin: University of Texas Press, 2002.

Arkoun, Mohammed. *The Unthought in Contemporary Islamic Thought.* London: Saqi Books, 2002.

Arpaguş, Hatice. "The Position of Woman in the Creation: A Qur'anic Perspective." In *Muslima Theology: The Voices of Muslim Women Theologians*, edited by Ednan Aslan, Marcia Hermansen, and Elif Medeni, 115–132. Frankfurt Am Main: Peter Lang, 2013.

Aryanti, Tutin. "A Claim to Space: Debating Female Religious Leadership in a Muhammadiyah Mosque in Indonesia." *The Muslim World* 103 (July 2013): 375–388.

Aslan, Ednan, Marcia Hermansen, and Elif Medeni, eds. *Muslima Theology: The Voices of Muslim Women Theologians*. Frankfurt am Main: Peter Lang, 2013.

Badran, Margot. "Between Secular and Islamic Feminism/s: Reflections on the Middle East and Beyond." *Journal of Middle East Women's Studies* 1, no. 1 (Winter 2005): 6–28.

———. "Engaging Islamic Feminism." In *Islamic Feminism: Current Perspectives*, edited by Anitta Kynsilehto, 25–35. Tampere, Finland: Tampere Peace Research Institute, 2008.

———. *Feminism in Islam: Secular and Religious Convergences*. Oxford: Oneworld, 2009.

Bakhtiar, Laleh, trans. *The Sublime Qur'an*. Chicago: IslamicWorld, 2007.

Barlas, Asma. "Amina Wadud's Hermeneutics of the Qur'an: Women Rereading Sacred Texts." In *Modern Muslim Intellectuals and the Qur'an*, edited by Suha Taji-Farouki, 97–124. London: Oxford University Press, 2006.

———. *"Believing Women" in Islam: Unreading Patriarchal Interpretations of the Qur'an*. Austin: University of Texas Press, 2002.

———. "Engaging Feminism: Provincializing Feminism as a Master Narrative." In *Islamic Feminism: Current Perspectives*, edited by Anitta Kynsilehto, 15–23. Tampere, Finland: Tampere Peace Research Institute, 2008.

———. "Four Stages of Denial, or, My On-Again, Off-Again Affair with Feminism: Response to Margot Badran." Paper presented at Ithaca College, October 2006.

———. "Hearing the Word, as a Muslim: Thirteen Passages of the Qur'an and Religious Difference." Paper presented at Cornell University Vespers, November 2007.

———. "A Response." *Journal of Feminist Studies in Religion* 32, no. 2 (December 2016): 148–151.

———. "Reviving Islamic Universalism: East/s, West/s, and Coexistence." Paper presented at the Conference on Contemporary Islamic Synthesis, Alexandria, Egypt, October 2003.

———. "Secular and Feminist Critiques of the Qur'an: Anti-Hermeneutics as Liberation?" *Journal of Feminist Studies in Religion* 32, no. 2 (December 2016): 111–121.

Barazangi, Nimat Hafez. "The Absence of Muslim Women in Shaping Islamic Thought: Foundations of Muslims' Peaceful and Just Co-Existence." *Journal of Law and Religion* 24, no. 2 (2008–2009): 403–432.

Bauer, Karen. "In Defense of Historical-Critical Analysis of the Qur'an." *Journal of Feminist Studies in Religion* 32, no. 2 (December 2016): 126–130.

Beattie, Tina. *God's Mother, Eve's Advocate: A Marian Narrative of Women's Salvation*. London: Continuum, 2002.

———. "Queen of Heaven." In *Queer Theology: Rethinking the Western Body*, edited by Gerard Loughlin, 293–304. Malden, MA: Blackwell, 2007.

Berger, Teresa. *Dissident Daughters: Feminist Liturgies in Global Context*. Louisville, KY: Westminster John Knox, 2001.

Brown, Jonathan. "Even If It's Not True It's True: Using Unreliable Hadiths in Sunni Islam." *Journal of Religious Ethics* 39, no. 3 (September 2011): 1–52.

Brown, William P., ed. *Engaging Biblical Authority: Perspectives on the Bible as Scripture.* Louisville, KY: Westminster John Knox, 2007.

Brown Douglas, Kelly. *The Black Christ.* Maryknoll, NY: Orbis, 1994.

Brecht, Mara, and Reid B. Locklin, eds. *Comparative Theology in the Millennial Classroom: Hybrid Identities, Negotiated Boundaries.* New York: Routledge, 2016.

Bullock, Katherine. *Rethinking Muslim Women and the Veil: Challenging Historical and Modern Stereotypes.* Herndon, VA: IIIT, 2002.

Chakravorty Spivak, Gayatri. "Can the Subaltern Speak?" In *Marxism and the Interpretation of Culture,* edited by Cary Nelson and Lawrence Grossberg, 271–313. Urbana: University of Illinois Press, 1988.

Chaudhry, Ayesha S. *Domestic Violence and the Islamic Tradition: Ethics, Law, and the Muslim Discourse on Gender.* Oxford: Oxford University Press, 2013.

———. "'I Wanted One Thing and God Wanted Another . . . ': The Dilemma of the Prophetic Example and the Qur'anic Injunction on Wife-Beating." *Journal of Religious Ethics* 39, no. 3 (September 2011): 416–439.

———. "Producing Gender-Egalitarian Islamic Law: A Case Study of Guardianship (*Wilayah*) in Prophetic Practice." In *Men in Charge? Rethinking Authority in Muslim Legal Tradition,* edited by Ziba Mir Hosseini, Mulki Al-Sharmani, and Jana Rumminger, 88–105. London: Oneworld, 2015.

Chia, Edmund Kee-Fook. "Is Interfaith Theology Possible?" *Studies in Interreligious Dialogue* 18, no. 1 (2008): 112–117.

Clarke, L. "Hijab According to the Hadith: Text and Interpretation." In *The Muslim Veil in North America: Issues and Debates,* edited by Sajida Sultana Alvi, Homa Hoodfar, and Sheila McDonough, 214–286. Toronto: Women's Press, 2003.

Clooney, Francis X., S.J. "Afterword: Some Reflections in Response to Teaching Comparative Theology in the Millennial Classroom." In *Comparative Theology in the Millennial Classroom,* edited by Mara Brecht and Reid B. Locklin, 219–234. New York: Routledge, 2016.

———. *Comparative Theology: Deep Learning across Religious Borders.* Malden, MA: Wiley Blackwell, 2010.

———. *Divine Mother, Blessed Mother: Hindu Goddesses and the Virgin Mary.* New York: Oxford University Press, 2005.

———, ed. *The New Comparative Theology: Interreligious Insights from the Next Generation.* London: T & T Clark, 2010.

cooke, miriam. "Multiple Critique: Islamic Feminist Rhetorical Strategies." In *Postcolonialism, Feminism and Religious Discourse,* edited by Laura E. Donaldson and Kwok Pui-lan, 142–160. New York: Routledge, 2002.

———. *Women Claim Islam: Creating Islamic Feminism through Literature.* New York: Routledge, 2001.

Copeland, M. Shawn. *Enfleshing Freedom: Body, Race, Being.* Minneapolis, MN: Fortress, 2010.

Cornille, Catherine. "The Confessional Nature of Comparative Theology." *Studies in Interreligious Dialogue* 24, no. 1 (2014): 9–15.

——, ed. *Criteria of Discernment in Interreligious Dialogue.* Interreligious Dialogue Series 1. Eugene, OR: Cascade, 2009.

——. *The Im-Possibility of Interreligious Dialogue.* New York: Herder and Herder, 2008.

Cornille, Catherine, and Christopher Conway, eds. *Interreligious Hermeneutics.* Interreligious Dialogue Series 2. Eugene, OR: Cascade, 2010.

Cornille, Catherine, and Jillian Maxley, eds. *Women and Interreligious Dialogue.* Interreligious Dialogue Series 5. Eugene, OR: Cascade, 2013.

Dube, Musa W. "Feminist Theologies of a World Scripture(s) in the Globalization Era." In *The Oxford Handbook of Feminist Theology*, edited by Mary McClintock Fulkerson and Sheila Briggs, 382–401. New York: Oxford University Press, 2013.

——. *The HIV and AIDS Bible: Some Selected Essays.* Scranton, PA: University of Scranton Press, 2008.

——. *Other Ways of Reading: African Women and the Bible.* Atlanta: Society of Biblical Literature, 2001.

——. *Postcolonial Feminist Interpretation of the Bible.* St. Louis, MO: Chalice, 2000.

——. "Toward a Post-Colonial Feminist Interpretation of the Bible." In *Hope Abundant: Third World and Indigenous Women's Theology*, edited by Kwok Pui-lan, 89–102. Maryknoll, NY: Orbis, 2010.

Dube, Musa W., Andrew M. Mbuvi, and Dora R. Mbuwayesango, eds. *Postcolonial Perspectives in African Biblical Interpretations.* Atlanta: Society of Biblical Literature, 2012.

Duderija, Adis. "Toward a Scriptural Hermeneutics of Islamic Feminism." *Journal of Feminist Studies in Religion* 31, no. 2 (Fall 2015): 45–64.

Elewa, Ahmed and Laury Silvers. "'I *Am* One of the People': A Survey and Analysis of Legal Arguments on Women-Led Prayer in Islam." *Journal of Law and Religion* 26, no. 1 (2010–2011): 141–171.

Esack, Farid. "Islam and Social Justice: Beyond Simplistic Apologia." In *What Men Owe to Women: Men's Voices from World Religions*, edited by John C. Raines and Daniel C. Macguire, 187–210. Albany: State University of New York Press, 2001.

——. *Qur'an, Liberation and Pluralism: An Islamic Perspective of Interreligious Solidarity against Oppression.* Oxford: Oneworld, 1997.

Fredericks, James. *Buddhists and Christians: Through Comparative Theology to Solidarity.* Maryknoll, NY: Orbis, 2004.

——. *Faith among Faiths: Christian Theology and Non-Christian Religions.* Mahwah, NJ: Paulist, 1999.

——. "Off the Map: The Catholic Church and Its Dialogue with Buddhists." In *Catholicism and Interreligious Dialogue*, edited by James L. Heft, S.M., 127–144. New York: Oxford University Press, 2012.

Fredericks, James, and Tracy Sayuki Tiemeier, eds. *Interreligious Friendship after Nostra Aetate*. New York: Palgrave Macmillan, 2015.

Fulkerson, Mary McClintock. *Changing the Subject: Women's Discourses and Feminist Theology*. Minneapolis, MN: Fortress, 1994.

———. "Contesting the Gendered Subject: A Feminist Account of the Imago Dei." In *Horizons in Feminist Theology: Identity, Tradition, and Norms*, edited by Rebecca Chopp and Sheila Greeve Davaney, 99–115. Minneapolis, MN: Fortress, 1997.

Fulkerson, Mary McClintock, and Marcia W. Mount Shoop. *A Body Broken, A Body Betrayed: Race, Memory, and Eucharist in White-Dominant Churches*. Eugene, OR: Cascade, 2015.

Gaventa, Beverly Roberts, and Cynthia L. Rigby, eds. *Blessed One: Protestant Perspectives on Mary*. Louisville, KY: Westminster John Knox, 2002.

Gebara, Ivone, and Maria Clara Bingemer. *Mary: Mother of God, Mother of the Poor*. Translated by Phillip Berryman. Eugene, OR: Wipf & Stock, 2004.

Geissinger, Aisha. *Gender and Muslim Constructions of Exegetical Authority: A Rereading of the Classical Genre of Qur'an Commentary*. Leiden: Brill, 2015.

———. "No, a Woman Did Not 'Edit the Qur'ān': Towards a Methodologically Coherent Approach to a Tradition Portraying a Woman and Written Quranic Materials." *Journal of the American Academy of Religion* 85, no. 2 (January 2017): 416–445.

Grant, Jacquelyn. *Perspectives on Womanist Theology*. Atlanta: ITC Press, 1995.

———. *White Women's Christ and Black Women's Jesus: Feminist Christology and Womanist Response*. Atlanta: Scholars Press, 1989.

Grant, Jacquelyn, and Randall C. Bailey, eds. *The Recovery of Black Presence: An Interdisciplinary Exploration; Essays in Honor of Dr. Charles B. Copher*. Nashville: Abingdon, 1995.

Greelee, Edwin. "Qu(e)er(y)ing Mary: Popular Mariology as Visual Liberation Theology." *Decolonial Horizons*, no. 2 (2016): 75–104.

Grewal, Zareena. *Islam Is a Foreign Country: American Muslims and the Global Crisis of Authority*. New York: New York University Press, 2014.

Grung, Anne Hege. *Gender Justice in Muslim-Christian Readings: Christian and Muslim Women in Norway Making Meaning of Texts from the Bible, the Koran, and the Hadith*. Leiden: Brill, 2016.

Haddad, Yvonne Yazbeck, Jane I. Smith, and Kathleen M. Moore. *Muslim Women in America: The Challenge of Islamic Identity Today*. New York: Oxford University Press, 2006.

Hammer, Juliane. *American Muslim Women, Religious Authority, and Activism: More Than a Prayer*. Austin: University of Texas Press, 2012.

———. "Invisible Giants: On Women, Mosques, and Radical Activism by Juliane Hammer." *Feminism and Religion Online* (October 15, 2015). Accessed July 2017. https://feminismandreligion.com/2015/10/15/invisible-giants-on-women-mosques-and-radical-activism-by-juliane-hammer/.

Harris, Melanie, and Kate Ott, eds. *Faith, Feminism and Scholarship: The Next Generation*. New York: Palgrave Macmillan, 2011.

Hassan, Riffat. "Engaging in Interreligious Dialogue: Recollections and Reflections of a Muslim Woman." *Journal of Ecumenical Studies* 49, issue 1 (Winter 2014): 134–139.

———. "Feminism in Islam." In *Feminism and World Religions*, edited by Arvind Sharma and Katherine K. Young, 248–278. Albany: State University of New York, 1999.

———. "Feminist Theology: The Challenges for Muslim Women." In *Women and Islam: Critical Concepts in Sociology*, edited by Haideh Moghissi, 195–208. London: Routledge, 2005.

———. "Muslim Women and Post-Patriarchal Islam." In *After Patriarchy: Feminist Transformations of the World Religions*, edited by Paula M. Cooey, William R. Eakin, and Jay B. McDaniel, 39–64. Maryknoll, NY: Orbis, 1998.

———. "The Qur'anic Perspective on Religious Pluralism." In *Peace-Building by, between, and beyond Muslims and Evangelical Christians*, edited by Mohammed Abu-Nimer and David Augsburger, 91–101. Lanham, MD: Lexington Books, 2009.

———. "Woman and Man's 'Fall': A Qur'anic Theological Perspective." In *Muslima Theology: The Voices of Muslim Women Theologians*, edited by Ednan Aslan, Marcia Hermansen, and Elif Medeni, 101–113. Frankfurt Am Main: Peter Lang, 2013.

Heft, James L., S.M., ed. *Catholicism and Interreligious Dialogue*. New York: Oxford University Press, 2012.

al-Hibri, Azizah Y. "An Introduction to Muslim Women's Rights." In *Windows of Faith: Muslim Women Scholar-Activists in North America*, edited by Gisela Webb, 51–71. Syracuse: Syracuse University Press, 2000.

———. "Who Defines Women's Rights? A Third World Woman's Response." *Human Rights Brief* 2, no. 1 (1994): 9, 11.

Hidayatullah, Aysha. "Claims to the Sacred." *Journal of Feminist Studies in Religion* 32, no. 2 (December 2016): 134–138.

———. *Feminist Edges of the Qur'an*. New York: Oxford University Press, 2014.

———. "Feminist Interpretation of the Qur'an in a Comparative Feminist Setting." *Journal of Feminist Studies in Religion* 30, no. 2 (Fall 2014): 115–129.

———. "Inspiration and Struggle: Muslim Feminist Theology and the Work of Elisabeth Schüssler Fiorenza." *Journal of Feminist Studies in Religion* 25, no. 1 (Spring 2009): 162–170.

———. "Mariyya the Copt: Gender, Sex, and Heritage in the Legacy of Muhammad's *umm walad*." *Islam and Christian-Muslim Relations* 23 (2010): 221–243.

———. "The Qur'anic Rib-ectomy: Scriptural Purity, Imperial Dangers, and Other Obstacles to the Interfaith Engagement of Feminist Qur'anic Interpretation." In *Women in Interreligious Dialogue*, edited by Catherine Cornille and Jillian Maxey, 150–167. Interreligious Dialogue Series 5. Eugene, OR: Cascade, 2013.

Hill Fletcher, Jeannine. "Gift to The Prophet from a King: The Politics of Women in Interreligious Dialogue." In *Women and Interreligious Dialogue*, edited by Catherine Cornille and Jillian Maxley, 27–48. Interreligious Dialogue Series 5. Eugene, OR: Cascade, 2013.

————. *Monopoly on Salvation? A Feminist Approach to Religious Pluralism*. New York: Continuum, 2005.

————. *Motherhood as Metaphor: Engendering Interreligious Dialogue*. New York: Fordham University Press, 2013.

————. "What Counts as 'Catholic'? What Constitutes 'Comparative'?" and "Response to Daria Schnipkoweit." *Studies in Interreligious Dialogue* 24, no. 1 (2014): 78–85, 91–93.

Hoel, Nina, "Sexualising the Sacred, Sacralising Sexuality: An Analysis of Public Responses to Muslim Women's Religious Leadership in the Context of a Cape Town Mosque." *Journal for the Study of Religion* 26, no. 2 (2013): 25–42.

Hoel, Nina, and Sa'diyya Shaikh. "Sexing Islamic Theology: Theorising Women's Experience and Gender through *'abd-Allah* and *khalifah*." *Journal for Islamic Studies* 33 (2013): 127–150.

Hunt, Mary E., and Diann L. Neu, eds. *New Feminist Christianity: Many Voices, Many Views*. Woodstock, VT: Skylight Paths Publishing, 2010.

Isasi-Díaz, Ada María. *En la Lucha/In the Struggle: Elaborating a Mujerista Theology*. Minneapolis, MN: Fortress, 2003.

————. *La Lucha Continues: Mujerista Theology*. Maryknoll, NY: Orbis, 2004.

————. *Mujerista Theology: A Theology for the 20th Century*. Maryknoll: Orbis, 1996.

Isasi-Díaz, Ada María, and Eduardo Mendieta, eds. *Decolonizing Epistemologies: Latina/o Theology and Philosophy*. New York: Fordham University Press, 2012.

Isherwood, Lisa. *Liberating Christ: Exploring the Christologies of Contemporary Liberation Movements*. Cleveland: The Pilgrim Press, 1999.

Jackson, Sherman A. *Islam and The Problem of Black Suffering*. New York: Oxford University Press, 2009.

Jardim, Georgina. *Recovering the Female Voice in Islamic Scripture: Women and Silence*. Surrey, England: Ashgate, 2014.

Johnson, Elizabeth A. *Ask the Beasts: Darwin and the God of Love*. London: Bloomsbury, 2014.

————. *She Who Is: The Mystery of God in Feminist Theological Discourse*. New York: Crossroads, 1992.

————. *Truly Our Sister: A Theology of Mary in the Communion of Saints*. New York: Continuum International, 2003.

Joslyn-Siemiatkoski, Daniel. "Comparative Theology and the Status of Judaism: Hegemony and Reversals." In *The New Comparative Theology: Interreligious Insights from the Next Generation*, edited by Francis X. Clooney, S.J., 89–108. London: T & T Clark, 2010.

Junior, Nyasha. *An Introduction to Womanist Biblical Interpretation.* Louisville, KY: Westminster John Knox, 2015.

Kahf, Mohja. "'The Water of Hajar' and Other Poems: A Performance of Poetry and Prose." *The Muslim World* 91 (Spring 2001): 31–44.

———. *Western Representations of the Muslim Woman: From Termagant to Odalisque.* Austin: University of Texas Press, 1999.

Kassam, Zayn. "Constructive Interreligious Dialogue Concerning Muslim Women." In *Women in Interreligious Dialogue*, edited by Catherine Cornille and Jillian Maxey, 127–149. Interreligious Dialogue Series 5. Eugene, OR: Cascade, 2013.

———. "Response to Daniel Madigan." In *Catholicism and Interreligious Dialogue*, edited by James L. Heft, S.M., 75–77. New York: Oxford University Press, 2012.

Katz, Marion Holmes. *Prayer in Islamic Thought and Practice.* New York: Cambridge University Press, 2013.

———. *Women in the Mosque: A History of Legal Thought and Social Practice.* New York: Columbia University Press, 2014.

Khan, Muhammad Muhsin, trans. *The Translation of the Meanings of Sahih al-Bukhari.* Riyadh: Darussalam, 1997.

Kiblinger, Kristin Beise. "Relating Theology of Religions and Comparative Theology." In *The New Comparative Theology: Interreligious Insights from the Next Generation*, edited by Francis X. Clooney, S.J., 21–42. London: T & T Clark, 2010.

Kim-Kort, Mihee. *Making Paper Cranes: Toward an Asian American Feminist Theology.* St. Louis, MS: Chalice, 2012.

Kwok Pui-lan. *Discovering the Bible in the Non-Biblical World.* Maryknoll, NY: Orbis, 1995.

———. "Ecology and Christology." *Feminist Theology* 5, no. 15 (May 1997): 113–125.

———. "Elisabeth Schüssler Fiorenza and Postcolonial Studies." *Journal of Feminist Studies in Religion* 25, no. 1 (2009): 191–207.

———. *Globalization, Gender, and Peacebuilding: The Future of Interfaith Dialogue.* New York: Paulist, 2012.

———. *Introducing Asian Feminist Theology.* Cleveland: Pilgrim, 2000.

———. *Postcolonial Imagination and Feminist Theology.* Louisville, KY: Westminster John Knox, 2005.

———. *Struggle to Be the Sun Again: Introducing Asian Women's Theology.* Maryknoll: Orbis, 1990.

Laksana, A. Bagus. "Comparative Theology: Between Identity and Alterity." In *The New Comparative Theology: Interreligious Insights from the Next Generation*, edited by Francis X. Clooney, S.J., 1–20. London: T & T Clark, 2010.

Lamptey, Jerusha. *Interfaith Marriage: A Muslima Response.* McGinley Lecture Series. New York: Fordham University Press, 2014.

———. *Never Wholly Other: A Muslima Theology of Religious Pluralism.* New York: Oxford University Press, 2014.

Lamrabet, Asma. "What Does the Qur'an Say about The Interfaith Marriage?" January 2013. http://www.asma-lamrabet.com/articles/what-does-the-qur-an-say-about-the-interfaith-marriage/.

Lizzio, Celene Ayat. "Gendering Ritual: A Muslima's Reading of the Laws of Purity and Ritual Preclusion." In *Muslima Theology: The Voices of Muslim Women Theologians*, edited by Ednan Aslan, Marcia Hermansen, and Elif Medeni, 167–180. Frankfurt am Main: Peter Lang, 2013.

Locklin, Reid B., and Hugh Nicholson. "The Return of Comparative Theology." *Journal of the American Academy of Religion* 78, no. 2 (June 2010): 477–514.

Londin, Jesse. "The Life and Career of Muslim Women Lawyers for Human Right: Dr. Azizah Al-Hibri, KARAMAH." *LawCrossing Interview*. https://www.lawcrossing.com/article/336/Dr-Azizah-al-Hibri-KARAMAH/.

Long, Jeffery D. "(Tentatively) Putting the pieces Together: Comparative Theology in the Tradition of Sri Ramakrishna." In *The New Comparative Theology: Interreligious Insights from the Next Generation*, edited by Francis X. Clooney, S.J., 151–170. London: T & T Clark, 2010.

Lozano-Díaz, Nora O. "Ignored Virgin or Unaware Women: A Mexican–American Protestant Reflection on the Virgin of Guadalupe." In *A Reader in Latina Feminist Theology: Religion and Justice*, edited by María Pilar Aquino, Daisy L. Machado, and Jeanette Rodríguez, 204–216. Austin: University of Texas Press, 2002.

Lumbard, Joseph. "Discernment, Dialogue, and the Word of God." In *Criteria of Discernment in Interreligious Dialogue*, edited by Catherine Cornille, 143–152. Interreligious Dialogue Series 1. Eugene, OR: Cascade, 2009.

Madigan, Daniel, S.J. "Jesus and Muhammad: The Sufficiency of Prophecy." In *Bearing the Word: Prophecy in Biblical and Qur'anic Perspective*, edited by Michael Ipgrave, 90–99. London: Church House Publishing, 2005.

——. "Mary and Muhammad: Bearers of the Word." *Australasian Catholic Record* 80 (2003): 417–427.

——. "Muslims and Christians: Where Do We Stand? 2003 Jesuit Seminar Series." *Eureka Street* 13, no. 7 (September 2003): 26–32.

——. "Muslim-Christian Dialogue in Difficult Times" and "Responses." In *Catholicism and Interreligious Dialogue*, edited by James Heft, 57–87. New York: Oxford University Press, 2012.

——. "Mutual Theological Hospitality: Doing Theology in the Presence of the 'Other.'" *In Muslim and Christian Understanding: Theory and Application of "A Common Word,"* edited by Waleed El-Ansary and David K. Linnan, 57–68. New York: Palgrave Macmillan, 2010.

——. "Particularity, Universality, and Finality: Insights from the Gospel of John." In *Communicating the Word: Revelation, Translation, and Interpretation in Christianity and Islam*, edited by David Marshall, 14–32. Washington, DC: Georgetown University Press, 2011.

————. "People of the Word: Reading John with a Muslim." *Review and Expositor* 104 (Winter 2007): 81–95.

Mahmood, Saba. *Politics of Piety: The Islamic Revival and the Feminist Subject.* Princeton, NJ: Princeton University Press, 2005.

Majeed, Debra Mubashshir. "Womanism Encounters Islam: A Muslim Scholar Considers the Efficacy of a Method Rooted in the Academy and the Church." In *Deeper Shades of Purple: Womanism in Religion and Society*, edited by Stacey M. Floyd-Thomas, 38–53. New York: New York University Press, 2006.

Marshall, Gul Aldikacti. "A Question of Compatibility: Feminism and Islam in Turkey." *Critique: Critical Middle Eastern Studies* 17, no. 3 (2008): 223–238.

Mattson, Ingrid. "Can a Woman Be an Imam? Debating Form and Function in Muslim Women's Leadership." In *The Columbia Sourcebook of Muslims in the United States*, edited by Edward E. Curtis IV, 252–263. New York: Columbia University Press, 2008.

McDonald, Laura Zahra. "Islamic Feminism." *Feminist Theory* 9, no. 3 (2008): 347–354.

McFague, Sallie. *Metaphorical Theology: Models of God in Religious Language.* Philadelphia: Fortress, 1982.

————. *Models of God: Theology for an Ecological, Nuclear Age.* Philadelphia: Fortress, 1987.

Mernissi, Fatima. *The Veil and the Male Elite: A Feminist Interpretation of Women's Rights in Islam.* New York: Basic Books, 1991.

Mir-Hosseini, Ziba. "Beyond 'Islam' and 'Feminism.'" *IDS Bulletin* 42, no. 1 (January 2011): 67–77.

Mir-Hosseini, Ziba, Mulki Al-Sharmani, and Jana Rumminger, eds. *Men in Charge? Rethinking Authority in Muslim Legal Tradition.* London: Oneworld, 2015.

Mojab, Shahrzad. "Islamic Feminism: Alternative or Contradiction?" *Fireweed*, no. 47 (Winter 1995): 18–25.

————. "Theorizing the Politics of 'Islamic Feminism.'" *Feminist Review* 69 (Winter 2001): 124–146.

Moghadam, Valentine M. "Islamic Feminism and Its Discontents: Toward a Resolution of the Debate." *Signs* 27, no. 4 (Summer 2002): 1135–1171.

Moghissi, Haideh. *Feminism and Islamic Fundamentalism: The Limits of Postmodern Analysis.* London: Zed Books, 1999.

Nadwi, Mohammad Akram. *Al-Muhaddithat: The Women Scholars in Islam.* Oxford: Interface Publications, 2013.

Nasr, Seyyed Hossein. *Ideals and Realities of Islam.* Chicago: ABC International Group, 2000.

Nicholson, Hugh. "A Correlational Model of Comparative Theology." *Journal of Religion* 85, no. 2 (2005): 191–213.

————. "The New Comparative Theology and the Problem of Theological Hegemonism." In *The New Comparative Theology: Interreligious Insights from the Next Generation*, edited by Francis X. Clooney, S.J., 43–62. London: T & T Clark, 2010.

———. "The Reunification of Theology and Comparison in the New Comparative Theology." *Journal of the American Academy of Religion* 77, no. 3 (September 2009): 609–646.

Oduyoye, Mercy Amba. *Introducing African Women's Theology.* Sheffield: Sheffield Academic, 2001.

Parsons, Susan Frank, ed. *The Cambridge Companion to Feminist Theology.* New York: Cambridge University Press, 2002.

Pew Research Center. "How Americans Feel about Religious Groups." July 16, 2014. http://www.pewforum.org/2014/07/16/how-americans-feel-about-religious-groups/.

Phan, Peter. "From Soteriology to Comparative Theology and Back: A Response to S. Mark Heim." In *Understanding Religious Pluralism: Perspectives from Religious Studies and Theology*, edited by Peter Phan and Jonathan Ray, 260–264. Eugene, OR: Pickwick, 2014.

Rahman, Fazlur. *Islam and Modernity: Transformation of an Intellectual Tradition.* Chicago: University of Chicago Press, 1982.

Procter-Smith, Marjorie. *In Her Own Rite: Constructing Feminist Liturgical Tradition.* Nashville: Abingdon, 1990.

Procter-Smith, Marjorie, and Janet Walton, eds. *Women at Worship: Interpretations of North American Diversity.* Louisville, KY: Westminster John Knox, 1993.

Rahemtulla, Shadaab. *Qur'an of the Oppressed: Liberation Theology and Gender Justice in Islam.* New York: Oxford University Press, 2017.

Rahman, Fazlur. *Major Themes of the Qur'an.* Edited by Ebrahim Moosa. Chicago: University of Chicago Press, 2009.

———. *Revival and Reform in Islam: A Study of Islamic Fundamentalisms.* Edited by Ebrahim Moosa. Oxford: Oneworld, 2000.

Rhouni, Raja. *Secular and Islamic Feminist Critiques in the Work of Fatima Mernissi.* Leiden: Brill, 2010.

Rinaldo, Rachel. *Mobilizing Piety: Islam and Feminism in Indonesia.* New York: Oxford University Press, 2013.

Roded, Ruth. "Muslim Women Reclaim the Life-Story of the Prophet: 'A'isha 'Abd al-Rahman, Assia Djebar, and Nadia Yassine." *The Muslim World* 103 (2013): 334–346.

Ruether, Rosemary Radford. *Gaia and God: An Ecofeminist Theology of Earth Healing.* San Francisco: HarperSanFrancisco, 1992.

———. *Goddesses and the Divine Feminine: A Western Religious History.* Berkeley: University of California Press, 2005.

———. *Mary: The Feminine Face of the Church.* London: SCM Press, 1979.

———. *Sexism and God-Talk: Toward a Feminist Theology.* Boston: Beacon, 1983, 1993.

———. *Visionary Women: Three Medieval Mystics.* Minneapolis, MN: Fortress, 2002.

———. *Women and Redemption: A Theological History.* Minneapolis, MN: Fortress, 1998, 2012.

Schimmel, Annemarie. *And Muhammad Is His Messenger: The Veneration of the Prophet in Islamic Piety*. Chapel Hill: University of North Carolina Press, 1985.

Schüssler Fiorenza, Elisabeth. *Bread Not Stone: The Challenge of Feminist Biblical Interpretation*. Boston: Beacon Press, 1984, 1995.

———. *But She Said: Feminist Practices of Biblical Interpretation*. Boston: Beacon Press, 1984, 1995.

———. *Changing Horizons: Explorations in Feminist Interpretation*. Minneapolis, MN: Fortress, 2014.

———. *Empowering Memory and Movement: Thinking and Working across Borders*. Minneapolis, MN: Fortress, 2014.

———. *In Memory of Her: A Feminist Theological Reconstruction of Christian Origins*. New York: Crossroads, 1994.

———. *Jesus: Miriam's Child, Sophia's Prophet: Critical Issues in Feminist Christology*. 2nd ed. London: Bloomsbury, 2015.

———. *Transforming Vision: Explorations in Feminist Theology*. Minneapolis, MN: Fortress, 2011.

———. *Wisdom Ways: Introducing Feminist Biblical Interpretation*. Maryknoll, NY: Orbis, 2001.

Seedat, Fatima. "Beyond the Text: Between Islam and Feminism." *Journal of Feminist Studies in Religion* 32, no. 2 (December 2016): 138–142.

———. "Islam, Feminism, and Islamic Feminism: Between Inadequacy and Inevitability." *Journal of Feminist Studies in Religion* 29, no. 2 (Fall 2013): 25–45.

———. "When Islam and Feminism Converge." *The Muslim World* 103 (July 2013): 404–420.

Segovia, Fernando F., and Mary Ann Tolbert, eds. *Reading from This Place: Volume 1. Social Location and Biblical Interpretation in the United States*. Minneapolis, MN: Fortress, 1995.

Shah-Kazemi, Reza. "Light upon Light? The Qur'an and the Gospel of John." In *Interreligious Hermeneutics*, edited by Catherine Cornille and Christopher Conway, 116–148. Interreligious Dialogue Series 2. Eugene, OR: Cascade, 2010.

Shahidian, Hammed. "The Politics of the Veil: Reflections on Symbolism, Islam, and Feminism." *Thamyris: Mythmaking from Past to Present* 4, no. 2 (1997): 325–337.

Shaikh, Sa'diyya. "Feminism, Epistemology and Experience: Critically (En)gendering the Study of Islam." *Journal for Islamic Studies* 33 (2013): 14–47.

———. "In Search of 'Al-Insān': Sufism, Islamic Law, and Gender." *Journal of the American Academy of Religion* 77, no. 4 (December 2009): 781–822.

———. "Islamic Law, Sufism and Gender: Rethinking the Terms of the Debate." In *Men in Charge? Rethinking Authority in Muslim Legal Tradition*, edited by Ziba Mir Hosseini, Mulki Al-Sharmani, and Jana Rumminger, 106–131. London: Oneworld, 2015.

———. "Knowledge, Women and Gender in the Hadith: A Feminist Interpretation." *Islam and Christian-Muslim Relations* 15, no. 1 (January 2004): 99–108.

———. *Sufi Narratives of Intimacy: Ibn Arabi, Gender and Sexuality.* Chapel Hill: University of North Carolina Press, 2012.

———. "A Tafsir of Praxis: Gender, Marital Violence, and Resistance in a South African Muslim Community." In *Violence against Women in Contemporary World Religions: Roots and Cures*, edited by Daniel C. Maguire and Sa'diyya Shaikh, 66–89. Cleveland: The Pilgrim Press, 2007.

Sharify-Funk, Meena, and Munira Kassam Haddad. "Where Do Women 'Stand' in Islam? Negotiating Contemporary Muslim Prayer Leadership in North America." *Feminist Review* 102, no. 1 (2012): 41–61.

Silvers, Laury. "'In the Book We Have Left Out Nothing': The Ethical Problem of the Existence of Verse 4:34 in the Qur'an." *Comparative Islamic Studies* 2, no. 2 (2006): 171–180.

———. "Islamic Jurisprudence, 'Civil' Disobedience, and Woman-Led Prayer." In *The Columbia Sourcebook of Muslims in the United States*, edited by Edward E. Curtis IV, 246–252. New York: Columbia University Press, 2008.

Soskice, Janet Martin, and Diana Lipton, eds. *Feminism and Theology: Oxford Readings in Feminism.* New York: Oxford University Press, 2003.

———, eds. *Oxford Readings in Feminism: Feminism and Theology.* Oxford: Oxford University Press, 2003.

Speight, R. Marston. "Hadith." In *The Oxford Encyclopedia of the Islamic World*, edited by John L. Esposito, vol. 2. New York: Oxford University Press, 1995. http://www.oxfordislamicstudies.com/article/opr/t236/e0286.

Stevens, Evelyn P. *Marianismo: The Other Face of Machismo in Latin America.* Pittsburgh: University of Pittsburgh Press, 1973.

Stowasser, Barbara Freyer. "The Mothers of the Believers in the Hadith." *The Muslim World* 82, no. 1–2 (January–April 1992): 1–36.

———. *Women in the Qur'an, Traditions, and Interpretation.* New York: Oxford University Press, 1994.

al-Tabari, Abu Ja'far Muhammad b. Jarir. *The Commentary on the Qur'an: Being an Abridged Translation of Jami al-bayan an ta'wil ay al-Qur'an.* Edited by W. F. Madelung and A. Jones. New York: Oxford University Press, 1987.

Tan, Avianne. "Why Muslim Woman Started 1st All-Female Mosque in the US." *ABC News*, February 4, 2015.

Taylor, Lisa K., and Jasmin Zine, eds. *Muslim, Women, Transnational Feminism and the Ethics of Pedagogy: Contested Imaginaries in Post-9/11 Cultural Practice.* New York: Routledge, Taylor & Francis, 2014.

Teel, Karen. *Racism and the Image of God.* New York: Palgrave Macmillan, 2010.

Terrell, JoAnne Marie. *Power in the Blood? The Cross in the African American Experience.* Maryknoll: Orbis, 1998.

Thatamanil, John J. *The Immanent Divine.* Minneapolis, MN: Fortress, 2006.

Tiemeier, Tracy Sayuki. "Comparative Theology as a Theology of Liberation." In *The New Comparative Theology: Interreligious Insights from the Next Generation*, edited by Francis X. Clooney, S.J., 129–150. London: T & T Clark, 2010.

——. "Interreligious Reading in the Context of Dialogue: When Interreligious Reading 'Fails.'" *Modern Theology* 29, no. 4 (October 2013): 138–153.

Townes, Emilie M. *Womanist Ethics and the Cultural Production of Evil*. New York: Palgrave Macmillan, 2006.

Trible, Phyllis. "Eve and Adam: Genesis 2–3 Reread." In *Womanspirit Rising: A Feminist Reader in Religion*, edited by Carol P. Christ and Judith Plaskow, 74–83. San Francisco: HarperSanFrancisco, 1992.

——. "Eve and Miriam: From the Margins to the Center." In *Feminist Approaches to the Bible*, edited by Hershel Shanks, 5–24. Washington: Biblical Archaeology Society, 1996.

——. *God and the Rhetoric of Sexuality*. Philadelphia: Fortress, 1984.

——. *Texts of Terror: Literary-Feminist Readings of Biblical Narratives*. Philadelphia: Fortress, 1978.

Tuksal, Hidayet Şefkatli. "Misogynist Reports in the Hadith Literature." In *Muslima Theology: The Voices of Muslim Women Theologians*, edited by Ednan Aslan, Marcia Hermansen, and Elif Medeni, 133–154. Frankfurt Am Main: Peter Lang, 2013.

Turman, Eboni Marshall. *Toward a Womanist Ethic of Incarnation: Black Bodies, the Black Church, and the Council of Chalcedon*. New York: Palgrave Macmillan, 2013.

Vuola, Elina. "La *Morenita* on Skis: Women's Popular Marian Piety and Feminist Research on Religion." In *The Oxford Handbook of Feminist Theology*, edited by Mary McClintock Fulkerson and Sheila Briggs, 494–524. Oxford: Oxford University Press, 2012.

——. *Limits of Liberation: Praxis as Method of Latin American Liberation Theology and Feminist Theology*. Helsinki: Suomalainen Tiedeakatemia, 1997.

——. "Seriously Harmful for Your Health? Religion, Feminism and Sexuality in Latin America." In *Liberation Theology and Sexuality*, 2nd ed., edited by Marcella Althaus-Reid, 137–162. London: SCM, 2006, 2009.

Voss Roberts, Michelle. *Dualities: A Theology of Difference*. Louisville, KY: Westminster John Knox, 2010.

——. "Gendering Comparative Theology." In *The New Comparative Theology: Interreligious Insights from the Next Generation*, edited by Francis X. Clooney, S.J., 109–128. London: T & T Clark, 2010.

——. *Tastes of the Divine: Hindu and Christian Theologies of Emotion*. New York: Fordham University Press, 2014.

wadud, amina. "Can One Critique Cancel All Previous Efforts?" *Journal of Feminist Studies in Religion* 32, no. 2 (December 2016): 130–134.

——. "Engaging *Tawhid* in Islam and Feminisms." *International Feminist Journal of Politics* 10, no. 4 (December 2008): 435–438.

———. "The Ethics of *Tawhid* over the Ethics of *Qiwamah*." In *Men in Charge? Rethinking Authority in Muslim Legal Tradition*, edited by Ziba Mir Hosseini, Mulki Al-Sharmani, and Jana Rumminger, 256–274. London: Oneworld, 2015.

———. *Inside the Gender Jihad: Women's Reform in Islam*. Oxford: Oneworld, 2006.

———. *Qur'an and Woman: Rereading the Sacred Text from a Woman's Position*. New York: Oxford University Press, 1999.

———. "Towards a Qur'anic Hermeneutics of Social Justice: Race, Class, and Gender." *Journal of Law and Religion* 12, no. 1 (1995–1996): 37–50.

Walton, Janet. *Feminist Liturgy: A Matter of Justice*. Collegeville, MN: Liturgical, 2000.

Webb, Gisela, ed. *Windows of Faith: Muslim Women Scholar-Activists in North America*. Syracuse: Syracuse University Press, 2000.

West, Traci C. *Disruptive Christian Ethics: When Racism and Women's Lives Matter*. Louisville, KY: Westminster John Knox, 2006.

———. *Wounds of the Spirit: Black Women, Violence, and Resistance Ethics*. New York University Press, 1999.

Williams, Delores S. "Hagar in African American Biblical Appropriation." In *Hagar, Sarah, and Their Children: Jewish, Christian, and Muslim Perspectives*, edited by Phyllis Trible and Letty M. Russell, 177–184. Louisville, KY: Westminster John Knox, 2006.

———. *Sisters in the Wilderness: The Challenge of Womanist God-Talk*. Maryknoll: Orbis, 1993.

Zine, Jasmin. "Creating a Critical Faith-Centered Space for Antiracist Feminism: Reflections of a Muslim Scholar-Activist." *Journal of Feminist Studies in Religion* 20, no. 2 (Fall 2004): 167–187.

Index